Lecture Notes in Computer Science 10006

Commenced Publication in 1973
Founding and Former Series Editors:
Gerhard Goos, Juris Hartmanis, and Jan van Leeuwen

Editorial Board

More information about this series at http://www.springer.com/series/7410

Ion Bica · Reza Reyhanitabar (Eds.)

Innovative Security Solutions for Information Technology and Communications

9th International Conference, SECITC 2016
Bucharest, Romania, June 9–10, 2016
Revised Selected Papers

 Springer

Editors
Ion Bica
Military Technical Academy
Bucharest
Romania

Reza Reyhanitabar
NEC Laboratories Europe
Heidelberg
Germany

ISSN 0302-9743   ISSN 1611-3349   (electronic)
Lecture Notes in Computer Science
ISBN 978-3-319-47237-9   ISBN 978-3-319-47238-6   (eBook)
DOI 10.1007/978-3-319-47238-6

Library of Congress Control Number: 2016953301

LNCS Sublibrary: SL4 – Security and Cryptology

This Springer imprint is published by Springer Nature
The registered company is Springer International Publishing AG
The registered company address is: Gewerbestrasse 11, 6330 Cham, Switzerland

Preface

This volume contains the papers presented at SECITC 2016: The 9th International Conference on Security for Information Technology and Communications (www.secitc.eu), held during June 9–10, 2016, in Bucharest.

SECITC 2016 received 35 submissions from 14 different countries. Each submission was reviewed by at least three Program Committee members. Moreover, 13 external reviewers gave comments on their areas of expertise. The committee decided to accept 16 papers, and the program also featured four invited talks.

For nine years SECITC has been bringing together computer security researchers, cryptographers, industry representatives, and graduate students. The conference focuses on research on any aspect of security and cryptography. The papers present advances in the theory, design, implementation, analysis, verification, or evaluation of secure systems and algorithms. One of the conference's primary goals is to bring together researchers belonging to different communities and provide a forum that facilitates the informal exchanges necessary for the emergence of new scientific collaborations.

Many people contributed to the success of SECITC 2016. First, we would like to thank the authors for submitting their work to SECITC 2016. We deeply thank the Program Committee members as well as the external reviewers for their volunteer work of reading and discussing the submissions. We would like to thank our distinguished invited speakers for accepting our invitation and for their papers. We thank the Organizing Committee and Technical Support Team for their dedication in organizing and running the conference. We would like to thank the members of the SECITC International Advisory Board. Finally, we would like to express our thanks to Springer for continuing to support the SECITC conference.

The conference was organized by the Military Technical Academy, Bucharest University of Economic Studies and Advanced Technologies Institute, Romania.

August 2016   Ion Bica
                                                                  Reza Reyhanitabar

Organization

Program Committee

Elena Andreeva	KU Leuven, Belgium
Ludovic Apvrille	Telecom ParisTech, France
Gildas Avoine	INSA Rennes, France
Ion Bica (Chair)	Military Technical Academy, Romania
Catalin Boja	Bucharest University of Economic Studies, Romania
Christophe Clavier	Université de Limoges, France
Paolo D'Arco	University of Salerno, Italy
Roberto De Prisco	University of Salerno, Italy
Eric Freyssinet	Ministry of Interior/Cyberthreats Delegation, France
Helena Handschuh	Rambus – Cryptography Research, USA
Shoichi Hirose	University of Fukui, Japan
Xinyi Huang	Fujian Normal University, China
Miroslaw Kutylowski	Wroclaw University of Technology, Poland
Bart Mennink	KU Leuven, Belgium
Kazuhiko Minematsu	NEC Corporation, Japan
Yi Mu	University of Wollongong, Australia
David Naccache	Ecole Normale Superieure, France
Udaya Parampalli	The University of Melbourne, Australia
Victor Patriciu	Military Technical Academy, Romania
Josef Pieprzyk	Queensland University of Technology, Australia
Reza Reyhanitabar (Chair)	NEC Laboratories Europe, Germany
Pierangela Samarati	Università degli Studi di Milano, Italy
Damien Sauveron	University of Limoges, France
Emil Simion	Advanced Technologies Institute and University Politehnica of Bucharest, Romania
Agusti Solanas	Smart Health Research Group, Rovira i Virgili University, Spain
Rainer Steinwandt	Florida Atlantic University, USA
Cristian Toma	Bucharest University of Economic Studies, Romania
Denis Trcek	University of Ljubljana, Slovenia
Michael Tunstall	Rambus – Cryptography Research, USA
Qianhong Wu	Beihang University, China
Kan Yasuda	NTT Corporation, Japan
Lei Zhang	East China Normal University, China

Additional Reviewers

Batista, Edgar

Best, Scott

Blazy, Olivier

Casino, Fran

Catuogno, Luigi

De Mulder, Elke

Hamburg, Mike

Li, Jiangtao

Lugou, Florian

Marson, Mark

Wu, Xin-Wen

Zhang, Yuexin

Zheng, James

Contents

Security Technologies for ITC

Invited Talks

Circular Security Reconsidered

F. Betül Durak[1] and Serge Vaudenay[2(✉)]

[1] State University of New Jersey, Rutgers, New Brunswick, USA
`fbdurak@cs.rutgers.edu`
[2] Ecole Polytechnique Fédérale de Lausanne (EPFL), Lausanne, Switzerland
`serge.vaudenay@epfl.ch`

Abstract. The notion of circular security of pseudorandom functions (PRF) was introduced in Distance Bounding Protocols. So far, only a construction based on a random oracle model was proposed. Circular security stands between two new notions which we call Key Dependent Feedback (KDF) security and Leak security. So far, only a construction based on a random oracle was proposed. We give an algebraic construction based on a q-DDH assumpsion. We first prove that a small-domain Verifiable Random Functions (VRF) from Dodis-Yampolskiy is a circular secure PRF. We then use the extension to large-domain VRF by augmented cascading by Boneh et al. This gives the first construction in the standard model.

1 Introduction

Pseudorandom functions (PRFs) were first introduced by Goldreich, Goldwasser, and Micali [10]. They play a fundamental role in cryptography with many applications. They are used for encryption, authentication, signatures, and many more cryptographic tools.

Briefly, a secure PRF is a deterministic function using a random secret key which is not distinguishable from a truly random function when used as a black box. They can be realized by random oracles. However, it is important to build cryptosystems in the standard model, i.e. without using random oracle heuristics since secure systems in the random oracle model can sometimes be trivially insecure under the instantiation of the oracle [8].

Moreover, as shown in [4], we cannot solely rely on the normal secure PRF assumption for Distance Bounding (DB) protocols, since the secret is often used as a key of PRF and is also externally used outside the PRF. In DB protocols, the circular secure PRF guarantees the normal security of PRF, even when we encrypt some functions of the key. So far, only one construction based on random oracle has been given and constructing a circular secure PRF without random oracle was left as an open problem. We present an algebraic construction of circular secure PRF in Sect. 4 without using random oracles. The security is based on a stronger variant of the q-DDH assumption using a fixed generator g. The construction demonstrates that a circular secure PRF can exist without random oracles. However, making instances for DB protocols is still open.

© Springer International Publishing AG 2016
I. Bica and R. Reyhanitabar (Eds.): SECITC 2016, LNCS 10006, pp. 3–19, 2016.
DOI: 10.1007/978-3-319-47238-6_1

2   Preliminaries

2.1   Pseudorandom Functions

Definition 1. *Consider a security parameter k and a parameter n. Let f_s be a function from $\{0,1\}^* \rightarrow \{0,1\}^n$, where $s \leftarrow \{0,1\}^k$ is chosen uniformly at random. Consider a function family $\mathcal{F}$ of all functions from $\{0,1\}^*$ to $\{0,1\}^n$ and a function F chosen from that family uniformly at random. For an adversary $\mathcal{A}$ limited to complexity T, we define the following Game:*

PRF Security Game with Bit b:

- *The challenger picks a secret s and $F \in \mathcal{F}$ at random.*
- *$\mathcal{A}$ queries its oracle and gets either $f_s(x)$ (if $b = 1$) or $F(x)$ (if $b = 0$).*
- *$\mathcal{A}$ returns a bit b'.*

The advantage is $Adv^{PRF}_{f_s}(\mathcal{A}) = \left| Pr[\mathcal{A}^{O_{f_s}} = 1] - Pr[\mathcal{A}^{O_F} = 1] \right|$. We say that the function f_s is a (ϵ, T)-secure PRF if for any distinguisher $\mathcal{A}$ limited to a complexity T, the advantage of $\mathcal{A}$ in the PRF Game is bounded by ϵ.

The PRF Game is depicted on Fig. 1. We have $Adv^{PRF}_{f_s}(\mathcal{A}) = \Pr[b' = 1 | b = 0] - \Pr[b' = 1 | b = 1]$.

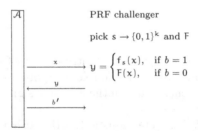

Fig. 1. PRF Game

2.2   Circular Secure Pseudorandom Functions

Definition 2. *Given a security parameter k, and some parameters m, n, consider $s \in \{0,1\}^k$, a family $\mathcal{L}$ of functions $L : \{0,1\}^k \rightarrow \mathbb{G}^m$, the set $\mathcal{F}$ of all functions $F : \{0,1\}^* \rightarrow \mathbb{G}^n$, where $\mathbb{G}$ is an additive group, and a function F chosen from that family. We define an oracle $O_{s,F}(x, L, A, B) = A \cdot L(s) + B \cdot F(x)$ using the dot product over $\mathbb{G}$. We assume that L is taken from $\mathcal{L}$ and $x \in \{0,1\}^*$, $A \in \mathbb{G}^m$, $B \in \mathbb{G}^n$. Let $(f_s)_{s \in \{0,1\}^k}$ be a family of functions in $\mathcal{F}$. For an adversary $\mathcal{A}$ limited to complexity T, we define the following Game:*

Circular-PRF Security Game with Bit b:

- *The challenger picks a secret s and $F \in \mathcal{F}$ at random.*
- *$\mathcal{A}$ queries its oracle and gets either $A \cdot L(s) + B \cdot f_s(x)$ (if $b = 1$) or $A \cdot L(s) + B \cdot F(x)$ (if $b = 0$).*
- *$\mathcal{A}$ returns a bit b'.*

The advantage is $Adv_{f_s}^{circular}(\mathcal{A}) = \left| Pr[\mathcal{A}^{O_{s,f_s}} = 1] - Pr[\mathcal{A}^{O_{s,F}} = 1] \right|$.

We say that the family f_s is an (ϵ, T)-circular-PRF with respect to $\mathcal{L}$ if for any distinguisher limited to a complexity T, the advantage of distinguishing O_{s,f_s} from $O_{s,F}$ is bounded by ϵ.

We require 2 conditions:

- *for any pair of queries (x, L, A, B) and (x', L', A', B'), if $x = x'$, then $L = L'$;*

- *for any $x \in \{0,1\}^*$, if (x, L, A_i, B_i), $i = 1, ..., \ell$ is a list of queries using this value x, then*

$$\forall \lambda_1, ..., \lambda_\ell \in \mathbb{G}, \quad \textstyle\sum_{i=1}^{\ell} \lambda_i B_i = 0 \;\Rightarrow\; \sum_{i=1}^{\ell} \lambda_i A_i = 0$$

We depict the circular-PRF Game in Fig. 2.

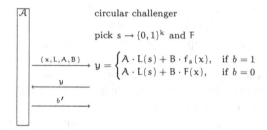

Fig. 2. Circular-PRF Game

Note that the last condition implies that $B = 0 \Rightarrow A = 0$ for each query.

Definition 2 is equivalent to the circular security definition in [5,6], if we take for $\mathcal{L}$ the set of all linear functions. On the other hand, if $\mathcal{L}$ is a set of all functions with "polynomially bounded representation", the definition is equivalent to the circular security defined in [7]. In [7], the function L could indeed be some non-linear function. We define that $L_\mu(s) = map(\mu \cdot s)$ using the dot product over $\mathbb{Z}_2^k$, where μ is a chosen vector and map is a given mapping from $\mathbb{Z}_2$ to $\mathbb{G}$. In the construction from [7], however, we only need the set $\mathcal{L}$ of the L_μ functions for all μ vectors and map is fixed.

For simplicity, we later on assume that $\mathcal{L}$ has a single element L.

For $n = 1$, we can always reduce to $B = 1$ and no x repetition, and obtain $O_{s,F}(x, L, A) = A \cdot L(s) + F(x)$.

We note that there exists no circular security if the adversary can set L to f_s(without knowing the secret s). Indeed, we let $(f_s)_{s \in \{0,1\}^k}$ be a pseudorandom family. We define an adversary $\mathcal{A}$ who queries the oracle with a tuple of $(x, L(s), A, B)$, where $x = 1$, $L(s) = f_s(1)$, and $B = -A$. The O_{s,f_s} oracle returns $A \cdot f_s(1) - A \cdot f_s(1) = 0$ if it is real oracle. Therefore, $\mathcal{A}$ outputs 1 in circular security Game, if the oracle responds with zero, and it outputs 0 otherwise. Clearly, the oracle replies the query with zero if it is the real oracle, then $\mathcal{A}$ outputs 1 with probability 1. On the other hand, if it is the ideal oracle, the response from the oracle is non-zero and $\mathcal{A}$ outputs 1 with probability bounded by $\frac{1}{p}$. Therefore, $Adv_{f_s}^{circular}(\mathcal{A}) \geq 1 - \frac{1}{p}$ where p is the cardinality of $\mathbb{G}$.

3 Derived PRF Notions

3.1 Secure Key-Dependent Feedback PRF

Consider a security parameter k, and the parameters n and m. Let $\mathbb{G}$ be a group. Given a secret $s \leftarrow_{\$} \{0,1\}^k$, and an arbitrary function $L : \{0,1\}^k \to \mathbb{G}^m$ producing column vectors with elements in $\mathbb{G}$, we let F be a function chosen from the function family $\mathcal{F} : \{0,1\}^* \to \mathbb{G}^n$ uniformly at random. Let $(f_s)_{s \in \{0,1\}^k}$ be a family of functions from $\{0,1\}^* \to \mathbb{G}^n$. We define an oracle $O_{s,\cdot}$ such that for a matrix $M \in \mathbb{Z}^{n \times m}$ and an input $x \in \{0,1\}^*$, $O_{s,F}(x, M) = ML(s) + F(x)$ and $O_{s,f_s}(x, M) = ML(s) + f_s(x)$ using the matrix product defined from $\mathbb{Z}^{n \times m} \times \mathbb{G}^m$ to a column vector in $\mathbb{G}^n$, where each element in $\mathbb{G}^n$ is output of matrix product multiplication of each row of $M \in \mathbb{Z}^m$ with $\mathbb{G}^m$. The above is when $\mathbb{G}$ has additive notations. With multiplicative ones, we write $O_{s,f_s} = L(s)^M f_s(x)$

The condition for using O_{s,f_s} or $O_{s,F}$ is that for any pair of queries (x, M) and (x', M'), if $x = x'$, then $M = M'$. Equivalently, since f_s and F are deterministic functions, we can require that x never repeats in queries. Then, we can define an oracle $O_F(x, M) = F(x)$ which does not use M. Clearly, if x does not repeat in queries, $O_{s,F}$ is indistinguishable from O_F. This motivates the definition below.

Definition 3. *Given a security parameter k, let f_s be a function from $\{0,1\}^* \to \mathbb{G}$. Let $L : \{0,1\}^k \to \mathbb{G}^m$ be a function. For an adversary $\mathcal{A}$ limited to complexity T, we define the following Game:*

KDF-PRF Security Game with Bit b:

- *The challenger picks a secret s and $F \in \mathcal{F}$ at random.*
- *$\mathcal{A}$ queries its oracle and gets either $ML(s) + f_s(x)$ (if $b = 1$) or $ML(s) + F(x)$ (if $b = 0$).*
- *$\mathcal{A}$ returns a bit b'.*

The advantage is $Adv_{f_s}^{KDF}(\mathcal{A}) = |Pr(b' = 1|b = 0) - Pr(b' = 1|b = 1)|$.

We say that the family $(f_s)_{s \in \{0,1\}^k}$ is a (ϵ, T) Key-dependent Feedback secure (KDF-secure) PRF with respect to L if for any distinguisher limited to a complexity T, the advantage of $\mathcal{A}$ in the KDF-PRF Game is bounded by ϵ.

The corresponding KDF-PRF Game is depicted in Fig. 3.

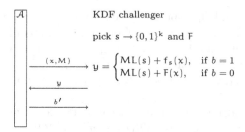

Fig. 3. KDF-PRF Game

Lemma 1. *(Circular security implies KDF security) Let f_s be any PRF to $\mathbb{G}^m$ where $\mathbb{G}$ is a group. For any KDF adversary $\mathcal{A}$ for f_s of complexity T, there exists a circular adversary $\mathcal{B}$ for f_s of complexity $T + \mathcal{O}(nmQ)$, where Q is the number of queries made by $\mathcal{A}$ such that:*

$$Adv_{f_s}^{KDF}(\mathcal{A}) = Adv_{f_s}^{circular}(\mathcal{B})$$

Proof. Given an adversary $\mathcal{A}$ playing against KDF-secure oracle, we build another adversary $\mathcal{B}$ that plays against circular-secure oracle. Let (x_i, M_i) be a query made by an adversary $\mathcal{A}$ against its KDF-secure oracle. We define the adversary $\mathcal{B}$ simulating $\mathcal{A}$ by taking its queries, and transforming each (x_i, M_i) into $(x_i, L, A_{i,j}, B_{i,j})$ queries. For each (x_i, M_i), the adversary $\mathcal{B}$ sets $A_{i,j}$ as the jth row of M_i, where $1 \leq j \leq n$, and set $B_{i,j}$ to the jth row of the $n \times n$ identity matrix. Notice that, since the linear combinations of $B_{i,j}$s do not vanish (they are the rows of identity matrix), we do not have any problem with the condition that for the queries $(x_i, L, A_{i,j}, B_{i,j})$, the linear combinations of $A_{i,j}$ vanishes with same x_i whenever the linear combination of $B_{i,j}$s vanishes in $\mathcal{B}$'s queries. $\mathcal{B}$ uses these queries to query its circular secure oracle and responds them with the replies it gets from its oracle. When $\mathcal{A}$ is done with its queries, it returns its output. Then, $\mathcal{B}$ uses the same output to return its oracle as its output. Hence, the advantage of $\mathcal{A}$ is equal to the advantage of $\mathcal{B}$. If the simulation of $\mathcal{A}$ wins, so is $\mathcal{B}$. Therefore, any PRF which is (ϵ, Q)-circular secure is also KDF-secure.□

Lemma 2. *(KDF security implies non-adaptive circular security) Let f_s be any PRF. Let $\mathbb{G}$ be a group in KDF-security Game. For any circular adversary $\mathcal{B}$ of complexity T making non-adaptive queries on the same x, there exists a KDF adversary $\mathcal{A}$ of complexity $T + \mathcal{O}((n^2 + m^2 + n^3)Q)$ such that:*

$$Adv_{f_s}^{circular}(\mathcal{B}) = Adv_{f_s}^{KDF-secure}(\mathcal{A})$$

Proof. Given a non-adaptive adversary $\mathcal{B}$ playing with a circular-secure oracle, we build another adversary $\mathcal{A}$ that plays with the KDF-secure oracle. We take all Q non-adaptive queries as (A_i, B_i) for each x, where $1 \leq i \leq Q$, $A_i \in \mathbb{Z}^m$ and $B_i \in \mathbb{Z}^n$ made by circular adversary $\mathcal{B}$, we transform the queries (A_i, B_i) made by circular adversary $\mathcal{B}$ into a pair of matrix (A, B) of size $Q \times m$ and $Q \times n$ respectively. We define the matrices $A = (A_1 \cdots A_Q)^T$ and $B = (B_1 \cdots B_Q)^T$

formed by rows of A_i and B_i respectively. We know that for any row λ, $\lambda \cdot B = 0$ implies $\lambda \cdot A = 0$. So, if we take a vector X of n undeterminates, any combination $\lambda \cdot BX$ vanishing implies $\lambda \cdot A = 0$. So, the equation $BM = A$ has a solution M in $\mathbb{Z}^{n \times m}$. We make the KDF query (x, M) to get $y = M \times L(s) + f(x)$. Then, by $BM \cdot L(s) + B \times f(x) = A \times L(s) + B \times f(x)$ so we obtain the answer of the circular oracle.

Hence, if $\mathcal{B}$ wins against its circular security oracle, $\mathcal{A}$ wins with the same advantage and with complexity $T + \mathcal{O}((n^2 + m^2 + n^3)Q)$. $\qquad\square$

Let f_s be any PRF. When we define the adversaries as non-adaptive adversaries, the previous two lemmas imply that f_s is non-adaptive circular-secure if and only if it is non-adaptive KDF-secure.

For $n = 1$, since x never repeats, we can see that the circular security and KDF security are equivalent.

We start our attempt to construct a KDF-secure PRF with 2 negative examples. In the first example, we define $f_s(x) = x^s$, which is shown to be not secure PRF based on Definition 1. Similarly, in the second negative example, we define $f_s(x) = g^x h^s$, and show that it is an insecure PRF under Definition 1.

Example 1. Let $f_s(x)$ be a function from $\mathbb{Z} \to Z_p^*$ for a prime number p defined as $f_s(x) = x^s$. $f_s(x)$ is not a secure PRF.

Let us make a single query with $x = 1$ to normal-secure PRF oracle. If we interact with the real oracle, the oracle returns $O_{s, f_s}(x) = x^s$. Clearly, the result we will get is 1, if the oracle is real, and we get a random integer if the oracle is random. It allows us to distinguish between O_{s, f_s} and $O_{s, F}$

Example 2. Let $f_s(x)$ be a function from $\mathbb{Z}$ to G for a group G, where $g, h \in G$ are arbitrary, defined as $f_s(x) = g^x h^s$. $f_s(x)$ is not a secure PRF.

Let us make two queries as $2x, x$ to normal-secure PRF oracle. If we interact with the real oracle, the oracle returns $O_{s, f_s}(2x) = g^{2x} h^s$ and $O_{s, f_s}(x) = g^x h^s$ respectively. Clearly, when we divide the results, we get g^x, which does not depend on the secret s, if the oracle is real, and we get a random string if the oracle is random. It allows us to distinguish between O_{s, f_s} and $O_{s, F}$.

3.2 *Leak*-PRF Security

Definition 4. *Given a security parameter k, let f_s be a function from $\{0, 1\}^* \to \mathbb{G}$. Let $L : \{0, 1\}^k \to \mathbb{G}^m$ be a function respectively let $L_g : \{0, 1\}^k \to \mathbb{G}^m$ be a function for all g in a given set. For an adversary $\mathcal{A}$ limited to complexity T, we define the Leak-PRF game (respectively the rnd-Leak-PRF Game) as follows:*

Leak-PRF (Respectively rnd-Leak-PRF) Security Game with Bit b:

- *The challenger picks a secret s, $F \in \mathcal{F}$ (and g in a given set) at random.*
- *The challenger computes $L(s)$ (respectively $L_g(s)$ corresponding to random g) and gives it (and g) to $\mathcal{A}$.*

- $\mathcal{A}$ queries its oracle and gets either $y_1 = f_s(x)$ (if $b = 1$) or $y_0 = F(x)$ (if $b = 0$).
- If $\mathcal{A}$ repeats a query x, the game aborts.
- $\mathcal{A}$ returns a bit b'.

The advantage is $Adv_{f_s}^{Leak}(\mathcal{A})(= Adv_{f_s}^{rnd-Leak}(\mathcal{A})) = |Pr(b' = 1|b = 0) - Pr(b' = 1|b = 1)|$.

The function f_s is a (ϵ, T)-secure Leak-PRF (respectively rnd-Leak-PRF) with respect to L if for any adversary $\mathcal{A}$ limited to the complexity T, the advantage of $\mathcal{A}$ in the Leak-PRF Game is bounded by ϵ.

The Leak-PRF (respectively rnd-Leak-PRF) Game is depicted in Fig. 4 (respectively in Fig. 5).

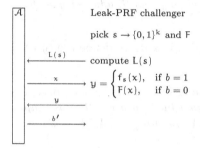

Fig. 4. Leak-PRF Game   **Fig. 5.** rnd-Leak-PRF Game

Theorem 1. (Leak-PRF Implies KDF-Security) Let f_s from $\{0,1\}^* \rightarrow \mathbb{G}$ be any PRF. We define $Leak(s) = L(s)$ in Leak-PRF Game. For any (ϵ, T)-secure KDF adversary for L, there exists a Leak adversary $\mathcal{B}$ complexity $T + \mathcal{O}(Q)$, where Q is the number of queries made by $\mathcal{A}$ s.t.

$$Adv_{f_s}^{KDF}(\mathcal{A}) = Adv_{f_s}^{Leak}(\mathcal{B})$$

Proof. Given an adversary $\mathcal{A}$ playing against KDF-secure oracle with $L(s)$, we build another adversary $\mathcal{B}$ that plays against $Leak$-PRF Game where $Leak(s) = L(s)$. In this Game $\mathcal{B}$ obtains $L(s)$ from its challenger as an output to its $Leak$ function. $\mathcal{B}$ simulates $\mathcal{A}$'s queries (M_i, x_i) for $i = 1..Q$ as following: $\mathcal{B}$ queries its oracle with x_i and receives either $y = f_s(x_i)$ or $y \leftarrow_\$ \mathbb{G}$. $\mathcal{B}$ adds y with $ML(s)$ using the leak of the secret to send $ML(s) + y$ to $\mathcal{A}$. $\mathcal{A}$ outputs a bit and $\mathcal{B}$ outputs its $Leak$-challenger with the same bit as $\mathcal{A}$. Hence if $\mathcal{A}$ wins against its oracle, $\mathcal{B}$ wins with the same advantage and with the complexity $T + Q$. □

4   Algebraic Construction

4.1   The Dodis-Yampolskiy Construction

The **q- decisional Diffie-Hellman** problem is defined in [3] as follows:
Let $\mathbb{G}$ be a group of prime order p. For $a \leftarrow_{\$} \mathbb{Z}_p$ and $g \in \mathbb{G}$ picked uniformly
at random, given a q-tuple $(g, g^a, g^{a^2}, \cdots g^{a^{q-1}})$, the q-DDH assumption states
that $g^{\frac{1}{a}}$ is indistinguishable from a random element in $\mathbb{G}$. More precisely, for any
adversary $\mathcal{A}$, the advantage of distinguishing $g^{\frac{1}{a}}$ from a random element in $\mathbb{G}$ is
bounded by ϵ.

Definition 5. *For $q > 1$, given a group $\mathbb{G}$ of prime order p, we define*
$Adv_q^{DDH}[\mathcal{A}, \mathbb{G}] = Pr[\mathcal{A}(g, g^a, \cdots, g^{a^{q-1}}, g^{\frac{1}{a}}) = 1] - Pr[\mathcal{A}(g, g^a, \cdots, g^{a^{q-1}}, h) = 1] \leq \epsilon$ *where the probability is over random choice of g, h, and a. We say that
the (T, q, ϵ)-DDH assumption holds in $\mathbb{G}$, if for all poly-time T adversary $\mathcal{A}$, the
$Adv_q^{DDH}[\mathcal{A}, \mathbb{G}]$ advantage is at least ϵ.*

When we let g be a generator of the group $\mathbb{G}$ and fix it, we define the (g, q)-
DDH assumption as follows:

Definition 6. *For $q > 1$, we define $Adv_{g,q}^{DDH}$ similarly for g fixed and a probability over the random choice of h and a. We say that the (t, g, q, ϵ)-DDH assumption holds in $\mathbb{G}$, if for all poly-time T adversary $\mathcal{A}$, the $Adv_{g,q}^{DDH}[\mathcal{A}, \mathbb{G}]$ advantage
is at least ϵ.*

The q-DDH assumption is defined with a random generator while we fix
the generator g in the (g, q)-DDH assumption. Clearly, any poly-time q-DDH
adversary $\mathcal{A}$ has the same advantage of some poly time (g, q)-DDH adversary by
using some randomization tricks. We state that (g, q)-DDH assumption implies
q-DDH assumption. However, the other direction does not seem to hold.

Surprisingly, we have the implication for both directions for the
computational-DH (CDH) problem.

Theorem 2. *(Leak-PRFness of the Dodis-Yampolskiy Function [9]) Let k be
a security parameter and $\mathbb{G}$ be a group of prime order p generated by some
g. Assume that $(T + Qq.poly(k), g, q, \epsilon)$-DDH assumption holds in $\mathbb{G}$. Then,
$f_{s,h}(x) = h^{\frac{1}{x+s}}$ where $h \in \mathbb{G}$, $s \in \mathbb{Z}_p$ and x is in a domain D defined as a
subset of $\mathbb{Z}_p$ of size Q where $Q \leq q$, is an $(\epsilon Q + \frac{Q^2}{p}, T)$-secure Leak-PRF for
$L_g(s, h) = (g, g^s, ..., g^{s^{q-1}}, h, h^s, ..., h^{s^{q-Q}})$ over D. More precisely,*

$$Adv_{f_{s,h}}^{Leak}(\mathcal{A}) \leq \sum_{i=0}^{Q-1} Adv_{g,q}^{DDH}(\mathcal{B}_i, \mathbb{G}) + \frac{Q^2}{p}$$

for some distinguisher $\mathcal{B}_i$, where $i = 0, ..., Q - 1$.
*We have the same statements with q-DDH and rnd-Leak-PRF security but
L_g defined on a random g. And, the proof follows as same.*

Proof. Suppose there exists an adversary $\mathcal{A}$ that plays *Leak*-PRF security Game to distinguish between $f_{s,h}(x) = h^{\frac{1}{x+s}}$ and a random element in $\mathbb{G}$. Let $D = \{x_1, ..., x_Q\}$. We design a sequence of games $Game_i$ for $i = 0, ..., Q$ between a challenger and the *Leak*-PRF adversary $\mathcal{A}$. We define the probability p_i to output 1 of $\mathcal{A}$ in $Game_i$, where $Game_i$ is defined as:

- The challenger picks a secret (s, h) at random and reveals $Leak(s, h) = (g, g^s, ..., g^{s^{q-1}}, h, h^s, ..., h^{s^{q-Q}})$ to $\mathcal{A}$.
- The challenger also picks a random function F to answer the queries x_j from $\mathcal{A}$ with:
  - if $j \le i$, the challenger answers by $F(x_j)$.
  - if $j > i$, the challenger answers by $f_{s,h}(x_j)$.

Note that the way to answer depends on the value x_j of the query and not on the sequence number of the query in time.

It is clear that $Game_0$ is the *Leak*-PRF Game with real function $f_{s,h}$ and $Game_Q$ is the *Leak*-PRF Game with random function F. Hence, the advantage of $\mathcal{A}$ to distinguish between $f_{s,h}(x) = h^{\frac{1}{x+s}}$ and a random element in $\mathbb{G}$ is $|p_0 - p_Q|$. We like to show that $|p_0 - p_Q|$ is negligible. Given the sequence of games, we build an adversary called $\mathcal{B}_i$ such that $|p_i - p_{i+1}| = Adv_{g,q}^{DDH}(\mathcal{B}_i, \mathbb{G}) + \frac{Q}{p}$ for $0 \le i \le Q - 1$. Then, we achieve that $|p_0 - p_Q| = \sum_i Adv_{g,q}^{DDH}(\mathcal{B}_i, \mathbb{G}) + \frac{Q^2}{p}$. Thus, we only need to prove that $Game_i$ is indistinguishable from $Game_{i+1}$.

We build our adversary $\mathcal{B}_i$ that uses $\mathcal{A}$ to break the (t, q, ϵ)-DDH assumption in group $\mathbb{G}$. In other words, when an adversary $\mathcal{B}_i$ is given a challenge tuple $(g, g^a, ..., g^{a^{q-1}}, \Gamma) \in \mathbb{G}^{q+1}$, where Γ is either $g^{\frac{1}{a}}$ or a random element in $\mathbb{G}$, $\mathcal{B}$ can distinguish Γ by using $\mathcal{A}$.

We start with $\mathcal{B}_i$ given its challenge tuple to simulate the queries made by $\mathcal{A}$ to its oracle. The adversary $\mathcal{B}_i$ simulates $\mathcal{A}$ by taking its challenge query and responding it using its own challenge tuple $(g, g^a, ..., g^{a^{q-1}}, \Gamma)$ as follows:

$\mathcal{B}_i$ sets $s = a - x_i$ to generate a private key for adversary $\mathcal{A}$ and selects a random $r \in \mathbb{Z}_p^*$. It does not know what s is because a is not known. Using Binomial Theorem, $\mathcal{B}_i$ computes $(g, g^s, g^{s^2}, ..., g^{s^{q-1}})$ from $(g, g^a, ..., g^{a^{q-1}})$. Define the function $f(z) = r \times \Pi_{y \in D - \{x_i\}}(z + y) = \sum_{j=0}^{Q-1} c_j z^j$, where $y \ne x_i$. Since $\mathcal{B}$ knows g^{s^j}, where $1 \le j \le q - 1$ and $Q \le q$, it computes $h = g^{f(s)}$ as follows:

$$g^{f(s)} = g^{\sum_{j=0}^{q-1}(c_j s^j)} = \Pi_{j=0}^{q-1}(g^{s^j})^{c_j}$$

$\mathcal{B}_i$ can further compute $h^s, ...h^{s^{q-Q}}$ similarly.

In the (g, q)-DDH challenge, we pick $a \in \mathbb{Z}_p$ uniformly at random. We know that g is a generator and that $r \ne 0$ is random. If $f(s) \ne 0$, or equivalently, $a \ne x_i - x_j$ for all $j \ne i$, we have that (s, h) is uniformly distributed among pairs such that $h \ne 1$ and $s \ne -x_j$ for all $j \ne i$. So, (s, h) follows a distribution which is indistinguishable from the one in $Game_i$ to $Game_{i+1}$. More precisely, the failure probability that a is some $x_j - x_i$ is $\frac{Q-1}{p}$. The failure probability that $h = 1$ is $\frac{1}{p}$. So, the cumulated failure probability between the (g, q)-DDH game, $Game_i$ and $Game_{i+1}$ is bounded by $\frac{Q}{p}$.

Then, $\mathcal{B}_i$ gives the tuple $Leak(s,h) = (g, g^s, ..., g^{s^{q-1}}, h, h^s, ..., h^{s^{q-Q}})$ to $\mathcal{A}$. Let (x_j) be a query made by $\mathcal{A}$ to its $Leak$-secure PRF oracle, where $1 \leq j \leq Q$. Wherever $\mathcal{A}$ queries the challenger $\mathcal{B}_i$ with x_j

- if $j < i$, $\mathcal{B}_i$ simulates the answer to $\mathcal{A}$ with $F(x_j)$ by lazy sampling.
- if $j > i$, $\mathcal{B}_i$ simulates the answer to $\mathcal{A}$ with $f_{s,h}(x_j)$ as follows:
  Let $f_j(s)$ be a function defined as:

$$f_j(s) = \frac{f(s)}{s+x_j} = \sum_{j=0}^{q-2} d_j s^j$$

where it is polynomial of degree $q - 2$. Notice that $f_{s,h}(x_j) = h^{\frac{1}{s+x_j}} = g^{f_j(s)}$ is computable by $\mathcal{B}_i$ from the tuple $(g, g^s, g^{s^2}, ..., g^{s^{q-1}})$.

- if $j = i$, $\mathcal{B}_i$ answers as following:
  Let $f_i(s)$ be another function defined as:

$$f_i(s) = \frac{f(s)}{s+x_i} = \sum_{i=0}^{q-2} \gamma_i s^i + \frac{\gamma}{a}$$

Notice that $f(s)$ is not divisible by $(s + x_i)$, so $\gamma \neq 0$. $\mathcal{B}_i$ replies the challenge query (x_i) by computing $y = (\Gamma)^\gamma g^{\sum_{i=0}^{q-2} \gamma_i s^i}$.

If $\Gamma = g^{\frac{1}{a}} = g^{\frac{1}{s+x_i}}$, then y is $g^{f_i(s)} = f_{s,h}(x_i)$. If Γ is random, since $\gamma \neq 0$, y is random as well.

Clearly, if Γ in $\mathcal{B}_i$'s challenge tuple is $g^{\frac{1}{a}}$, then we are in $Game_{i+1}$. Otherwise, we are in $Game_i$. Hence, $|p_i - p_{i+1}| \leq Adv_{g,q}^{DDH}(\mathcal{B}_i, \mathbb{G}) + \frac{Q}{p}$.

Therefore, we have $|p_0 - p_Q| \leq Q\varepsilon + \frac{Q^2}{p}$.

The running time of the reduction is upper bounded by simulating oracle queries by $\mathcal{B}_i$. Per query, $\mathcal{B}_i$ performs $3q - 2$ multiplications and exponentiations which take $(3q - 2).poly(k)$. Since $\mathcal{A}$ can make at most Q queries, the running time of $\mathcal{A}$ is bounded by $Qq.poly(k) = t$. Hence, $f_{s,g}(x)$ is a $(\epsilon q, Qq.poly(k))$-secure $Leak$-PRF. □

4.2   Extension to KDF-Security and Circular Security

We have just shown that a function $f_{s,h}(x) = h^{\frac{1}{s+x}}$ defined from $[\mathbb{Z} \times \mathbb{G}] \times D$ to $\mathbb{G}$, where D is a subset of $\mathbb{Z}_p$ of size q, is a $Leak$-secure pseudorandom function for a small domain size q under (g, q)-DDH assumption.

Theorem 3. *(KDF Security of the Dodis-Yampolskiy Function) Let k be a security parameter and $\mathbb{G}$ be a group of prime order p generated by some g. Assume that $(T + q^2.poly(k), g, q, \epsilon)$-DDH assumption holds in $\mathbb{G}$. We define $L(s,h) = (g^s, h)$. Then, $f_{s,h}(x) = h^{\frac{1}{x+s}}$ where $h \in \mathbb{G}$, $s \in \mathbb{Z}_p$ and x is in a domain D defined as a subset of $\mathbb{Z}_p$ of size q, is a $(q\epsilon + \frac{q^2}{p}, T)$-secure KDF-secure PRF for $L(s,h)$ when the real oracle defined as $O_{s,h,f}(x, M) = L(s,h)^M f(x) = g^{\alpha s} h^\beta f_{s,h}(x)$ for $M = (\alpha, \beta)$.*

The proof follows from Theorems 1 and 2.

For the parameter $n = 1$, KDF-security is equivalent to circular security. So, $f_{s,h}$ is both KDF-secure and circular-secure for L under the (g, q)-DDH assumption.

4.3   Parallel Leak Security

Definition 7. *Consider a security parameter k, a set K, an integer t, a group $\mathbb{G}$ and a secure PRF $f_{s,h} : [\mathbb{Z} \times \mathbb{G}] \times D \to \mathbb{G}$, where the domain $D \subset \mathbb{Z}_p$ is of size q and the secret consists of $s \in \mathbb{Z}$ and $h \in K$. We let $L(s, h_i)$ be a leak function for $1 \leq i \leq t$. We define t related keys as $(s, h_1), ..., (s, h_t)$, where $h_i \in K$. We define $Leak(s, h_1, ..., h_t) = (L(s, h_1), ..., L(s, h_t))$ and $f^t_{s,h_1,...,h_t}(x, i) = f_{s,h_i}(x)$.*

We say that the function $f_{s,h}$ is a t-parallel Leak secure for L if the function $f^t_{s,h_1,...,h_t}$ is Leak-secure for Leak.

We state that if the function $f_{s,h}$ defined in Theorem 3 is a *Leak*-secure PRF and (g, q)-DDH assumption holds in $\mathbb{G}$, then $f^t_{s,h_1,...,h_t}$ is a t-parallel *Leak* secure PRF for all q polynomial with the following Lemma.

Lemma 3. *(Parallel Leak Security of the Dodis-Yampolskiy Function) We let $f_{s,h}(x) = h^{\frac{1}{x+s}}$ be a function in $\mathbb{G}$ generated by some g, in which the (g, q)-DDH assumption holds. The input x is defined as an element of a domain D of size Q, where $Q \leq q$. For every t-parallel Leak secure adversary $\mathcal{A}$ for $L_g(s, h_i) = (g, g^s, ..., g^{s^{q-1}}, h_i, h_i^s, ..., h_i^{s^{q-Q}})$, there exists a Leak adversary $\mathcal{B}_0$ for L_g and (g, q)-DDH adversary $\mathcal{B}_1$ such that*

$$Adv^{Leak}_{f^t_{s,h_1,...,h_t}}(\mathcal{A}) \leq Adv^{Leak}_{f_{s,h}}(\mathcal{B}_0) + t.Adv^{DDH}_{g,q}(\mathcal{B}_1, \mathbb{G})$$

We can state a same Lemma with q-DDH assumption and rnd-Leak-PRF security but L_g depends on a random g. The proof follows as same.

Proof. The proof uses a sequence of three Games between a challenger and a parallel *Leak* secure PRF adversary $\mathcal{A}$ that attacks $f^t_{s,h_1,...,h_t}$. For $i = 0, 1, 2, 3$, we define the probability to win for $\mathcal{A}$ as p_i at the end of Game i.

Game 0. (Fig. 6) The challenger picks a random key as $(s, h_1, ..., h_t)$. The t-parallel *Leak* adversary $\mathcal{A}$ receives $L_g(s, h_i)$ for $1 \leq i \leq t$ and queries its challenger with (x, i). The challenger behaves as a real oracle for $f^t_{s,h_1,...,h_t}$, meaning that it replies the query with $h_i^{\frac{1}{x+s}}$.

Game 1. (Fig. 7) The challenger picks a random function $u : D \to \mathbb{G}$, random exponents $r_1, ..., r_t$ in $\mathbb{Z}_p$, and s, h. It sets $h_i = h^{r_i}$. An adversary $\mathcal{A}$ receives $L_g(s, h_i)$ for $1 \leq i \leq t$ and queries its challenger with (x, i). The challenger replies the query with $u(x)^{r_i}$.

We show that Game 0 and Game 1 are indistinguishable if $f_{s,h}$ is a *Leak* secure PRF. We construct a *Leak*-secure adversary $\mathcal{B}_0$ whose running time is same as $\mathcal{A}$ and such that

$$|p_1 - p_0| = Adv^{Leak}_{f_{s,h}}(\mathcal{B}_0) \tag{1}$$

The *Leak* adversary $\mathcal{B}_0$ interacts with its *Leak* oracle and simulates the $f^t_{s,h_1,...,h_t}$ challenger for $\mathcal{A}$. More precisely, $\mathcal{B}_0$ receives its $L_g(s, h) = (g, g^s, ..., g^{s^{q-1}}, h, h^s, ..., h^{s^{q-Q}})$ from its challenger and chooses random $r_1, ..., r_t \in \mathbb{Z}_p$. Then, $\mathcal{B}_0$ computes $Leak(s, h_i) = (g, g^s, ..., g^{s^{q-1}}, h_i, h_i^s, ..., h_i^{s^{q-Q}})$, where

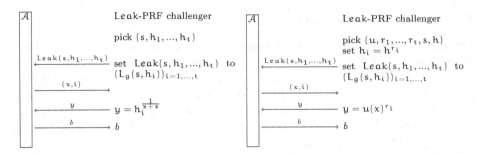

Fig. 6. *Game* 0.   **Fig. 7.** *Game* 1.

$h_i = h^{r_i}$ for $1 \leq i \leq t$. Whenever $\mathcal{A}$ issues a query with (x,i), $\mathcal{B}_0$ queries its *Leak* oracle with (x) to obtain its response y and $\mathcal{B}_0$ responds $\mathcal{A}$ with y^{r_i}. Finally, $\mathcal{B}_0$ outputs same as $\mathcal{A}$'s output.

When *Leak* oracle responds $\mathcal{B}_0$'s query, $y = h^{\frac{1}{x+s}}$ with random key (s,h), then $\mathcal{B}_0$ response to $\mathcal{A}$ is $y^{r_i} = h_i^{\frac{1}{x+s}}$, where we define $h_i = h^{r_i}$. Hence, in this case, $\mathcal{B}_0$ simulates Game 0. See Fig. 8.

When *Leak* oracle responds $\mathcal{B}_0$'s query with a random function $y = u(x)$, then $\mathcal{B}_0$ response to $\mathcal{A}$ is $y^{r_i} = u(x)^{r_i}$. Hence, in this case, $\mathcal{B}_0$ simulates Game 1. See Fig. 9.

Thus, we prove the Eq. (1).

Game 2. The challenger picks a random function $\omega : D \times [t] \rightarrow \mathbb{G}$ and some $h_1, ..., h_t$. The adversary $\mathcal{A}$ receives $L_g(s, h_i)$ for $1 \leq i \leq t$ and queries its challenger with (x,i). The challenger replies the query with $\omega(x,i)$.

The proof for indistinguishability of Game 1 and Game 2 follows from [2, Lemma 1], where we have $|p_1 - p_2| \leq t.Adv_{g,q}^{DDH}(\mathcal{B}_1, \mathbb{G})$ with a (g,q)-DDH adversary $\mathcal{B}_1$.

The advantage of $Adv_{f_t^t,h_1,...,h_t}^{KDF}(\mathcal{A})$ which is equal to $|p_0 - p_2|$ is bounded by $Adv_{f_{s,h}}^{KDF}(\mathcal{B}_0) + t.Adv_{g,q}^{DDH}(\mathcal{B}_1, \mathbb{G})$ as it is claimed. This completes the proof. $\square$

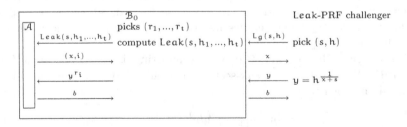

Fig. 8. *Leak*-PRF Game (real)

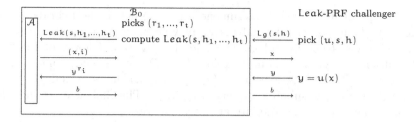

Fig. 9. *Leak*-PRF Game (ideal)

4.4 The Boneh-Montgomery-Raghunathan Augmentation

In [1], a classical cascade function constructs a PRF with a large domain from a PRF with a small domain by cascading. Given that, in [3], an algebraic PRF structure is constructed based on the extended results of this classical cascade function. However, as stated in [3], the classical cascade construction requires the output of the underlying PRF to be at least as long as its secret key. Boneh et al. eliminates the requirement by injecting a supplemental secret. Therefore, we will use Boneh-Montgomery-Raghunathan's augmented cascade result.

The augmented cascade pseudorandom function, defined in [3], gives a secure PRF with domain D^n from a secure PRF with domain D, where $D \subset \mathbb{Z}_p$ of size q. More precisely, let $f_{s,h} : [\mathbb{Z} \times \mathbb{G}] \times D \to \mathbb{G}$ be a secure PRF. The augmented cascade PRF of $f_{s,h}$, denoted as $f^{*n}_{s_1,\dots,s_n,h} : [\mathbb{Z}^n \times \mathbb{G}] \times D^n \to \mathbb{G}$ is defined on input key $(s_1,\dots,s_n,h) \in [\mathbb{Z}^n \times \mathbb{G}]$ and value $(x_1,\dots,x_n) \in D^n$ as:

$h_0 = h$

$for\ i = 1,\dots,n$ do

$\quad h_i \leftarrow f_{s_i,h_{i-1}}(x_i)$

output h_n.

If we plug $f_{s,h}(x) = h^{\frac{1}{s+x}}$ in an augmented cascade, we obtain a secure pseudorandom function $f^{*n}_{s_1,\dots,s_n,h}(x_1,\dots,x_n) = h^{\frac{1}{(s_1+x_1)\dots(s_n+x_n)}}$ in exponential domain size q^n.

Theorem 4. *Let $\mathbb{G}$ be a group of prime order p generated by some g. Assume that (t,g,q,ϵ)-DDH assumption holds in $\mathbb{G}$. Let $L_g(s_1,\dots,s_n,h) = (g^{s_1},\dots,g^{s_n},h)$. We define $f^{*n}_{s_1,\dots,s_n,h}$ as in Boneh-Montgomery-Raghunathan augmentation over D^n where D is size of q. The augmented cascade $f^{*n}_{s_1,\dots,s_n,h} = h^{\frac{1}{(s_1+x_1)\dots(s_n+x_n)}}$ is a Leak-secure PRF. More precisely,*

$$Adv^{Leak}_{f^{*n}_{s_1,\dots,s_n,h}}(\mathcal{A}) = \sum_{i=1}^{n} Adv^{Leak}_{f^t_{s,h_1,\dots,h_t}}(\mathcal{B}_i)$$

for some t-parallel Leak adversary $\mathcal{B}_i$.

Proof. The proof uses a hybrid argument where we define the hybrids as following: Let $\mathcal{A}$ be a *Leak*-PRF adversary playing against augmented cascade function. We construct hybrid game H_i for $0 \le i \le n$ (shown in Fig. 10). The challenger picks a random function $F : D^i \mapsto \mathbb{G}$ and random keys $(s_1, ..., s_n, h) \in \mathbb{Z}^n \times \mathbb{G}$. $\mathcal{A}$ gets its $L_g(s_1, s_2, ..., s_n, h)$ function and plays the regular PRF Game: he submits a query $(x_1, ..., x_n)$. The challenger applies the function F to obtain h_i and then iteratively computes h_n:

$h_i = F(x_1, ..., x_i)$
for $j = i+1, ..., n$ do
$\quad h_j \leftarrow f_{s_j, h_{j-1}}(x_j)$
output h_n.

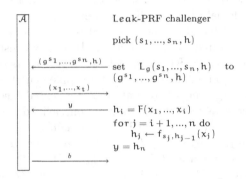

Fig. 10. H_i Game against cascade function.

The challenger returns h_n to $\mathcal{A}$. Let p_i be the probability that $\mathcal{A}$ returns 1 in H_i. It is clear that in H_0, the adversary $\mathcal{A}$ interacts with f^{*n} while in H_n, it interacts with a random function $F : D^n \mapsto \mathbb{G}$. Therefore, the *Leak*-PRF advantage of $\mathcal{A}$ is $Adv_{f^{*n}}^{Leak}(\mathcal{A}) = |p_n - p_0| = \sum_i (p_i - p_{i-1})$.

We construct a t-parallel *Leak* adversary $\mathcal{B}_i$ such that $Adv_{f_{s,h_1,...,h_t}^{Leak}}^{Leak}(\mathcal{B}_i) = |p_{i+1} - p_i|$ (in Fig. 11, we show the construction where the *Leak*-PRF challenger replied with real function). The adversary $\mathcal{B}_i$ simulates the challengers in H_i or H_{i+1}. To do that, $\mathcal{B}_i$ needs to simulate a random function $F : D^i \mapsto \mathbb{G}$. For this purpose, $\mathcal{B}_i$ defines an injection $Index : D^{i-1} \mapsto \{1, ..., t\}$.

Now, $\mathcal{B}_i$ receives $Leak(s, h_1, ..., h_t) = (g, g^s, ..., g^{s^{q-1}}, h_k^s, ..., h_k^{s^{q-Q}})$ for each $1 \le k \le t$ from its t-parallel *Leak* secure challenger. Then, $\mathcal{B}_i$ picks $(h, s_1, ..., s_{i-1}, s_{i+1}, ..., s_n)$ at random and sets $s_i = s$ ($\mathcal{B}_i$ does not know what s is). Given the $Leak(s, h_1, ..., h_t) = (g, g^s, ..., g^{s^{q-1}}, h_k, ..., h_k^{s^{q-Q}})$ for each $1 \le k \le t$, $\mathcal{B}$ can compute $L_g(s_1, ..., s_n, h)$ from his selection. $\mathcal{B}_i$ simulates $\mathcal{A}$ by sending him $L_g(s_1, ..., s_n, h)$.

When $\mathcal{A}$ queries $(x_1, ..., x_n)$, $\mathcal{B}_i$ computes $\ell = Index(x_1, ..., x_{i-1})$. If ℓ is not defined, it takes the next available index in $\{1, ..., t\}$ to define it. $\mathcal{B}_i$ queries its

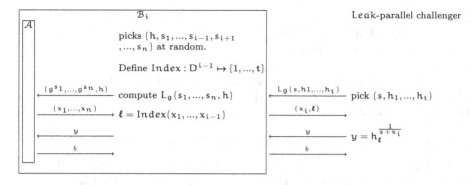

Fig. 11. *Leak*-PRF Game (real)

t-parallel Leak challenger with (x_i, ℓ) and obtains a $\overline{h}_i \in \mathbb{G}$. Note that $\overline{h}_i$ is either random or is equal to $y = f_{s,h_\ell} = h_\ell^{\frac{1}{s+x_i}}$ for some random key (s, h_ℓ). $\mathcal{B}_i$ finishes the cascade as:

$$\overline{h}_i = y$$
$$for\ j = i+1, ..., n\ \text{do}$$
$$\overline{h}_i \leftarrow f_{s_i, \overline{h}_{i-1}}(x_i)$$

output $\overline{h}_n$.

Finally $\mathcal{B}_i$ returns $\overline{h}_n$ $\mathcal{A}$. Eventually $\mathcal{A}$ outputs a bit $b \in \{0,1\}$. $\mathcal{B}_i$ outputs the same b to its challenger.

The Index function together with the random selection of the h_ℓ simulates well a random function on $(x_1, ..., x_{i-1})$. So, p_{i-1} is the probability that $\mathcal{B}_i$ returns $b = 1$ in the game with the real function.

When $\mathcal{B}_i$'s challenger responds with an ideal function, the random selection of the function Index together with the random selection of the h_ℓ makes $(x_1, ..., x_i) \rightarrow \overline{h}_i$ simulates well a random function. So, p_{i-1} is the probability that $\mathcal{B}_i$ returns $b = 1$ in the game with the ideal function.

Hence, $|p_n - p_0| = \sum_i Adv_{f_{s,h_1,...,h_t}^t}^{Leak}(\mathcal{B}_i)$, which is what we claim. Hence, due to Leak-parallel security, we obtain the result.   □

4.5   Related Key Secure PRF

Let us define the following game using a bit b for an adversary $\mathcal{A}$ playing against a challenger:

- Pick K in $\mathcal{K}$ at random.
- Let $\mathcal{A}$ make queries to $GEN(\phi, x)$ with $\phi \in \Phi$
- $\mathcal{A}$ outputs b'

$\underline{proc\ GEN(\phi, x)}$

$K' \leftarrow \phi(K)$;
If $K' = \bot$ then return $\bot$;

If $T[K'] = \bot$ then
   if $b = 1$ then $T[K'] \leftarrow F(K, x)$;
   if $b = 0$ then $T[K'] \leftarrow \{0,1\}^r$;
Return $T[K']$

For all ppt adversary $\mathcal{A}$, a pseudorandom function F is a RKA secure PRF with respect to a function family Φ if $Adv_{\mathcal{A},\Phi} = |Pr(b' = 1|b = 1) - Pr(b' = 1|b = 0)|$ is bounded by ϵ.

Example 3. $f_{s,h}(x) = h^{\frac{1}{x+s}}$ is not RKA secure PRF for $\phi(s,h) = (s + \Delta, h)$.

Let the adversary make two queries to GEN with $((s,h), x)$ and $((s,h), x - \Delta)$. If we are in real world $(b = 1)$, then the outputs are $h^{\frac{1}{x+s}}$ for both queries. Clearly, these two outputs are same if we are in real world. We get two random strings if we are in ideal world $(b = 0)$. It allows us to correctly guess bit b.

5   Conclusion

We define a new security notion called Key Dependent Feedback(KDF) security inspired from circular security of pseudorandom functions introduced in Distance Bounding Protocols. We give an algebraic structure of PRF under KDF security. We prove that a small-domain Verifiable Random Functions(VRF) from Dodis-Yampolskiy is a circular secure PRF which easily extends to efficiently large-domain VRF by augmented cascading by Boneh et al.

We have constructed a circular-secure PRF function with no random oracle and under (g, q)-DDH assumption. Unfortunately, we proved circular security from *Leak* security. For this reason, this construction is not well suited to distance bounding. Indeed, the construction of DB protocols using circular-secure PRF rely on the fact that leaking L would leak the entire secret, so, cannot be *Leak*-secure. Hence, the problem of making a circular-secure PRF which is not *Leak*-secure is still an open problem.

Acknowledgments. The first author was supported in part by NSF grant CNS-1453132.

We thank Dr. Reza Reyhanitabar for helpful discussions and valuable comments.

References

1. Bellare, M., Canetti, R., Krawczyk, H.: Pseudorandom functions revisited: the cascade construction and its concrete security. In: Proceedings of the 37th Annual Symposium on Foundations of Computer Science, pp. 514–523, October 1996
2. Boneh, D., Halevi, S., Hamburg, M., Ostrovsky, R.: Circular-secure encryption from decision Diffie-Hellman. In: Wagner, D. (ed.) CRYPTO 2008. LNCS, vol. 5157, pp. 108–125. Springer, Heidelberg (2008)
3. Boneh, D., Montgomery, H.W., Raghunathan, A.: Algebraic pseudorandom functions with improved efficiency from the augmented cascade. In: Proceedings of the 17th ACM Conference on Computer and Communications Security, CCS 2010, pp. 131–140. ACM (2010)

4. Boureanu, I., Mitrokotsa, A., Vaudenay, S.: On the pseudorandom function assumption in (secure) distance-bounding protocols. In: Hevia, A., Neven, G. (eds.) LatinCrypt 2012. LNCS, vol. 7533, pp. 100–120. Springer, Heidelberg (2012)

5. Boureanu, I., Mitrokotsa, A., Vaudenay, S.: Practical and provably secure distance-bounding. In: Desmedt, Y. (ed.) ISC 2013. LNCS, vol. 7807, pp. 248–258. Springer, Heidelberg (2015). doi:10.1007/978-3-319-27659-5_18

6. Boureanu, I., Mitrokotsa, A., Vaudenay, S.: Practical and provably secure distance-bounding. J. Comput. Secur. **23**(2), 229–257 (2015)

7. Boureanu, I., Vaudenay, S.: Optimal proximity proofs. In: Lin, D., Yung, M., Zhou, J. (eds.) Inscrypt 2014. LNCS, vol. 8957, pp. 170–190. Springer, Heidelberg (2015). doi:10.1007/978-3-319-16745-9_10

8. Canetti, R., Goldreich, O., Halevi, S.: The random oracle methodology, revisited. J. ACM (JACM) **51**, 557–594 (2004)

9. Dodis, Y., Yampolskiy, A.: A verifiable random function with short proofs and keys. In: Vaudenay, S. (ed.) PKC 2005. LNCS, vol. 3386, pp. 416–431. Springer, Heidelberg (2005). doi:10.1007/978-3-540-30580-4_28

10. Goldreich, O., Goldwasser, S., Micali, S.S.: How to construct random functions. J. ACM (JACM) **33**, 792–807 (1986)

Visual Cryptography

Models, Issues, Applications and New Directions

Paolo D'Arco$^{(\boxtimes)}$ and Roberto De Prisco

Dipartimento di Informatica, University of Salerno,
Via Giovanni Paolo II, 132, 84084 Fisciano, SA, Italy
{pdarco,robdep}@unisa.it

Abstract. Since its introduction, visual cryptography has received considerable attention within the cryptographic community. In this paper we give a quick look at the salient moments of its history, focusing on the main models, on open issues, on its applications and on some prospectives.

Keywords: Visual cryptography · Models · Applications · Secure computation

1 Introduction

Visual Cryptography, in its simplest form, enables the sharing, in an unconditionally private way, of a black-and-white secret image among a set of parties.

In a sharing phase, each party receives a transparency containing a printed image, which looks like a collection of black and white random pixels. The transparency does not leak any information about the secret image. In a reconstruction phase, when a properly chosen subset of transparencies are superposed and perfectly aligned, the secret image is reconstructed.

The peculiarity of the technique is that the *human visual system* performs the reconstruction process: no machinery, computing mathematical operations, is required. Hence, it can be used by *everyone*: once the transparencies have been generated and privately distributed, cryptographic tools or skills are not needed to reconstruct the secret image.

Introduced by Naor and Shamir [44] in 1994 in the cryptographic community, due to its aesthetic attractiveness and to the elegant mathematical combinatorial structures underlying the design of the schemes, it has been the subject of active and extensive investigations. Currently, it is a sound research field with a large body of literature.

1.1 Superposing Transparencies

Let us look at a simple example in order to understand which problems need to be solved to produce a secure sharing. The secret image can be seen as a

© Springer International Publishing AG 2016
I. Bica and R. Reyhanitabar (Eds.): SECITC 2016, LNCS 10006, pp. 20–39, 2016.
DOI: 10.1007/978-3-319-47238-6_2

matrix of black and white pixels[1]. Each transparency contains a random-looking collection of black pixels and white pixels. When two or more transparencies are superposed and perfectly aligned, in each position of the resulting image, there is a black pixel if in the corresponding position of the transparencies there is *at least* a black pixel. While, the pixel is equal to white if and only if in the corresponding position in *all* the transparencies the pixels are white. Fig. 1 summarizes the superposition law, while Fig. 2 reproduces the visual effect for two transparencies.

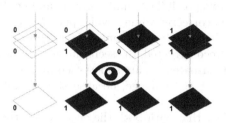

Fig. 1. Superposition law. The human eye performs the logical or operation.

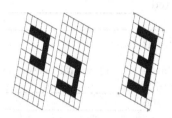

Fig. 2. Example of transparencies superposition.

Hence, for any privacy notion we could think about, it is clear that a *simple split* of the black pixels of the secret image among the pixels of the transparencies, in such a way that when superposed the secret image is reconstructed, *does not* work. It surely enables the reconstruction of the secret image but, at the same time, each transparency gives to his holder *partial information* about the secret image: each black pixel in the transparency corresponds to a black pixel in the reconstructed image.

Therefore, to avoid information leakage by each transparency, we need some non trivial sharing form. Fortunately, *two nice approaches* yield suitable solutions. To get the flavor, let us consider the basic case, in which a secret image is split in two transparencies. The first approach, by Naor and Shamir [44], encodes each pixel of the original image with a *collection* of black and white *subpixels* in each transparency, in such a way that each collection on each transparency could correspond to both a white pixel and a black pixel in reconstructed form.

---

[1] White pixels are actually transparent pixels, but we refer to them as to white pixels.

Only through the superposition the *nature* of the pixel is determined. With this encoding, a reconstructed white pixel of the original image has *always* some black subpixels, but it is still *visually distinguishable* from a black pixel because a black pixel has *more* black subpixels than a white one.

The second approach, due to Kafri and Keren [32], encodes a black pixel with a randomly chosen complementary pair of pixels on the two transparencies, i.e., black on the first and white on the second or vice versa, while it encodes a white pixel with two equal pixels on each transparency, i.e., either with a white pixel on both transparencies or with a black pixel on both transparencies, choosing, for each pixel, one of the two possibilities uniformly at random. Hence, a black pixel is always reconstructed correctly, while a white pixel is reconstructed *half of the times correctly* and *half of the times erroneously*. Even though half of the white pixels are erroneously reconstructed, the secret image, as a whole, is still *visually intelligible* when the transparencies are superposed but on a darker background compared to the original secret image, because half of the white pixels of the secret image have been turned to black.

Intuitively, it is clear that with both the encodings a transparency by itself does not provide any information, in an unconditionally secure way, on the corresponding secret image. Therefore, as we show in the following sections, in a *deterministic* way or in a *probabilistic* way, the secret image can be securely shared and visually recovered.

1.2   Organization of the Paper

We overview part of the large field of visual cryptography. More precisely, in Sect. 2 we describe Naor and Shamir's model and Kafri and Keren's model. We briefly discuss also Yang's model and its generalization due to Cimato et al. In Sect. 3 we provide a common framework for the formalization of the notion of visual cryptography scheme. Then, in Sect. 4, we discuss the main issues in the design: contrast, pixel expansion, randomness reduction. We survey some important results and point out open problems. Later on, is Sect. 5, we give a quick look at alternative models for visual cryptography: we consider models for grey and color images, for meaningful transparencies, for multiple secrets, as well as models using alternative properties for the physical superposition, and models robust against cheating. Then, in Sect. 6, we describe some classical applications proposed in the literature. This section offers to the reader some hints about potential uses of the techniques in real life. Finally, in Sect. 7, we focus on a new approach, which uses visual cryptography for general secure computation. Conclusions and final remarks are given in Sect. 8, which closes the paper.

2   Models for Visual Cryptography

In this section we introduce the models which implement the two ideas described before: the *deterministic* model, as we refer to the Naor and Shamir's model, and the *random grid* model, as we refer to the Kafri and Keren's model.

Deterministic Model. The deterministic model was introduced by Naor and Shamir [44]. In this model, each pixel of the secret image is expanded into a number $m \geq 2$ of subpixels in each transparency. Hence, the transparencies and the reconstructed secret image are larger than the original secret image. Consequently, the parameter m is referred to as the *pixel expansion*. Moreover, two thresholds ℓ and h, $0 \leq \ell < h \leq m$, together define the contrast, i.e., the visual quality, with which the secret image is reconstructed. More precisely, when the transparencies are superposed and aligned and the secret image is reconstructed, it is guaranteed that:

– if the secret pixel is *white*, then among the reconstructed m subpixels that correspond to the secret pixel, there are *at most* ℓ black subpixels
– if the secret pixel is *black*, then among the reconstructed m subpixels, there are *at least* h black subpixels.

Basically, the threshold ℓ quantifies the *maximal level of darkness* allowed in a collection of m subpixels which reconstructs a white pixel, while the threshold h quantifies the *minimal level of darkness* required in a collection of m subpixels which reconstructs a black pixel. Fig. 3 shows an example.

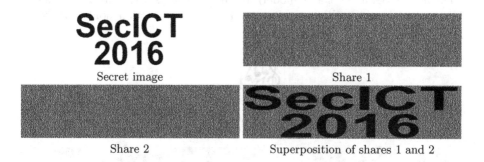

Secret image   Share 1

Share 2   Superposition of shares 1 and 2

Fig. 3. Example in the deterministic model.

Random Grid Model. The random grid model was introduced by Kafri and Keren [32]. Historically, this is the first model for visual cryptography, found independently and before the deterministic model [44]. Nevertheless, it received attention only after the deterministic model had been discovered and presented at the cryptographic community, when a large number of researchers started investigating the subject[2]. The model introduced by Kafri and Keren is called *random grid* because it uses random black and white images as building blocks for sharing secret images. In this model there is *no pixel expansion*, i.e., the parameter m is equal to 1. Therefore, the shares and the reconstructed image have the *same*

---

[2] Kafri and Keren proposed three constructions for sharing a secret image between two parties. Naor and Shamir, on the other hand, gave a general model, formalizing the properties that visual cryptography schemes need to satisfy, and constructions and bounds for threshold schemes. They also coined the term *Visual Cryptography*.

sizes of the original image. As we have explained before, the reconstruction is a probabilistic process since errors may occur: some white pixels are reconstructed as black pixels[3] but the original image is still visually intelligible. Fig. 4 shows an example.

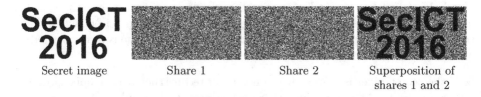

| Secret image | Share 1 | Share 2 | Superposition of shares 1 and 2 |

Fig. 4. Example in the random grid model.

Probabilistic Model. The probabilistic model was introduced by Yang [50] and generalized by Cimato et al. [13]. Each pixel of the secret image can be represented with a number $m \geq 1$ of pixels in each transparency. There still exist thresholds ℓ and h, $0 \leq \ell < h \leq m$, which together define the contrast.

For $m > 1$ (Cimato et al.'s model), it can be seen as a variant of the deterministic model, where the warranty about the reconstruction holds *only with*

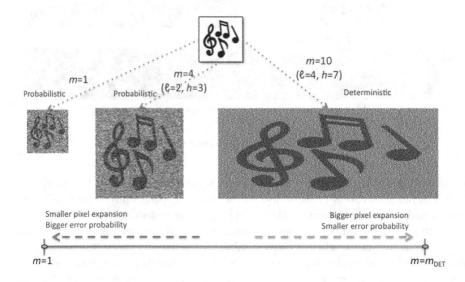

Fig. 5. Models

---

[3] In the other two constructions proposed by Kafri and Keren there are errors of both types, i.e., white pixels are reconstructed as black and black pixels are reconstructed as white. However, reconstruction is still possible as long as the errors are "not too many".

high probability. Precisely, occasionally the reconstruction can be wrong, allowing a reconstructed white pixel to have more than ℓ black subpixels, and a reconstructed black pixel to have less than h black subpixels.

Models Equivalence. In [23] it has been proved that all of the above models are strongly tied together. More specifically, for $m = 1$ (Yang's model), the probabilistic model is the same as the random grid model, while for m big enough the probabilistic model becomes deterministic. Hence, all the models described can be thought of as parameterized on the pixel expansion m, and on one extreme $(m = 1)$ we have the random grid/probabilistic model, while on the other extreme $(m$ big enough) we have the deterministic model. In between the two extremes we have the generalized probabilistic model; the intermediate probabilistic models trade the pixel expansion with the error probability, as depicted in Fig. 5.

3 Visual Cryptography Schemes

Independently of the choice, the models can be described by using a common framework. Let us introduce it.

3.1 Collections of Matrices

Let I be a secret image that needs to be visually shared among a set $\mathcal{P} = \{1, 2, \ldots, n\}$ of n parties. A trusted party, called the *dealer*, in order to share I, generates n images, printed on transparencies, called *shares*, and distributes them to the parties, giving in a private way one share to each party. Some subsets of parties, called *qualified*, are able to reconstruct the secret by pooling together and superposing their shares. All other subsets of parties, called *forbidden*, do not infer any information about the secret image neither by superposing their shares nor by any other computation on them.

A *visual cryptography scheme* (*VCS*, for short) is a method for encoding the secret image I into the n shares. The encoding process associates, to each pixel of the secret image I, a collection[4] of m subpixels that collectively represent a pixel of the secret image, in each of the n shares.

A *distribution matrix* M is an $n \times m$ matrix which represents the encoding of a single pixel by means of n shares. More precisely, row i of M represents the collection of subpixels printed on share i, which is used to encode a secret pixel of I. We use 0 to denote a white subpixel and 1 to denote a black subpixel. With this notation, the matrices are binary matrices and the superposition of subpixels corresponds to the logical or operation (see Fig. 1). However, since the symbols ◦ and • are self-explanatory, where convenient, we also use ◦ and • to denote, respectively, white and black.

---

[4] We stress that for deterministic visual cryptography it must be $m \geq 2$, i.e., the pixel *expansion* is unavoidable. The probabilistic and the random grid visual cryptography models instead allow $m = 1$.

A visual cryptography scheme is specified by *two collections* of distribution matrices, denoted with $\mathcal{C}_\circ = \{M_\circ^1, M_\circ^2, \ldots, M_\circ^{r_0}\}$ and $\mathcal{C}_\bullet = \{M_\bullet^1, M_\bullet^2, \ldots, M_\bullet^{r_1}\}$. To share a secret pixel of I, the dealer operates as follows: if the secret pixel is white, then he randomly chooses a distribution matrix from $\mathcal{C}_\circ$, and gives row i to party i; while, if the secret pixel is black, he randomly chooses a distribution matrix from $\mathcal{C}_\bullet$ and gives row i to party i. The sharing process is repeated for *every* pixel of the secret image.

An *access structure* $\mathcal{A} = (\mathcal{Q}, \mathcal{F})$ is a specification of the qualified subsets of parties $\mathcal{Q}$ and of the forbidden subsets of parties $\mathcal{F}$. Notice that if $Q \in \mathcal{Q}$, then any superset Q' of Q must belong to $\mathcal{Q}$. Another natural requirement is that any subset P of parties is either qualified or forbidden[5]. In most cases the access structure is a *threshold* access structure: $\mathcal{Q}$ consists of all the subsets of at least k parties, while $\mathcal{F}$ consists of all the subsets with at most $k - 1$ parties, with $2 \leq k \leq n$. Such structures are referred to as (k, n)-*threshold* access structures.

Given a distribution matrix M and a set of parties P, we denote with M_P the submatrix of M consisting only of the rows corresponding to parties in P. Moreover, we denote with $\text{Sup}(M)$ the superposition of the shares represented by the rows of M. Notice that $\text{Sup}(M)$ is a binary vector where the ith element is equal to the **or** of the ith column of M. Hence, $\text{Sup}(M_Q)$ is the pixel reconstructed by the parties of a qualified set Q. Given a vector v, we denote with $w(v)$ the Hamming weight of v, the number of 1s (i.e., the number of black subpixels) in v.

Definition 1. *A* $(\mathcal{Q}, \mathcal{F})$ *deterministic visual cryptography scheme* $\mathcal{S}$ *consists of two collections* $\mathcal{C}_\circ$ *and* $\mathcal{C}_\bullet$ *of* $n \times m$ *distribution matrices such that there exists two integers* ℓ *and* h, *such that* $0 \leq \ell < h \leq n$, *for which the following conditions are satisfied.*

1. **Reconstructability.** *For any qualified set* Q *it holds that: for any* $M \in \mathcal{C}_\circ$, *we have that* $w(\text{Sup}(M_Q)) \leq \ell$ *while, for any* $M \in \mathcal{C}_\bullet$, *we have that* $w(\text{Sup}(M_Q)) \geq h$.
2. **Security.** *For any forbidden set* F, *it holds that the two collections* $\mathcal{C}_\circ[F] = \{M_F | M \in \mathcal{C}_\circ\}$ *and* $\mathcal{C}_\bullet[F] = \{M_F | M \in \mathcal{C}_\bullet\}$ *are indistinguishable in the sense that they contain the same matrices with the same frequencies.*

The first condition guarantees that reconstructed white and black pixels are visually distinguishable. The second essentially says that a pixel reconstructed by a forbidden subset of parties can correspond to a white pixel or to a black pixel with exactly the same probability. We refer to ℓ and h as to the *contrast thresholds*.

Notice that, in many schemes, the collection $\mathcal{C}_\circ$ (resp. $\mathcal{C}_\bullet$) consists of all the matrices that can be obtained by permuting all the columns of a matrix B° (resp. $B^\bullet$). Therefore, the matrices B° and $B^\bullet$ are called the *base matrices*.

---

[5] In a more general form, it is possible to consider access structures where there are some subsets that are neither qualified nor forbidden; in such a case we simply don't care about what those subsets of parties can do with the shares.

When a scheme is described with base matrices the reconstructability and the security conditions can be simplified to the following:

1. **Reconstructability.** For any qualified set Q, we have that $w(\text{Sup}(B_Q^\circ)) \leq \ell$ and that $w(\text{Sup}(B_Q^\bullet)) \geq h$.
2. **Security.** For any forbidden set F, the two matrices B_F° and $B_F^\bullet$ are the same up to a permutation of the columns.

For the random grid model the contrast is defined by means of the *average light transmission*, which is the amount of light that can pass through a part of an image[6] Instead of considering a single pixel, the definition considers the whole image. More precisely, given a subset G of pixels of an image I, the average light transmission $\lambda(G)$ of G is

$$\lambda(G) = \frac{\#\text{white-pixels(G)}}{\#\text{pixels(G)}},$$

the number of white pixels in G, divided by the total number of pixels in G. Let $\mathcal{W}_I$ and $\mathcal{B}_I$ be, respectively, the entire white and black regions of I, and let $\mathcal{W}_I(R)$ and $\mathcal{B}_I(R)$ be the corresponding white and black regions of R, the reconstructed version of I. Denoting with $\lambda_\circ(R) = \lambda(\mathcal{W}_I(R))$ and $\lambda_\bullet(R) = \lambda(\mathcal{B}_I(R))$ the following definition holds.

Definition 2. *A $(\mathcal{Q}, \mathcal{F})$ random grid visual cryptography scheme S consists of two collections $\mathcal{C}_\circ$ and $\mathcal{C}_\bullet$ of $n \times 1$ distribution matrices such that, denoting with R the reconstructed version of I, the following two conditions are satisfied:*

1. **Reconstructability.** *There exists two thresholds, $\lambda_\circ$ and $\lambda_\bullet$, with $\lambda_\circ > \lambda_\bullet$, such that, for any qualified set Q, it holds that $\lambda_\circ(R) \geq \lambda_\circ$ and $\lambda_\bullet \geq \lambda_\bullet(R)$.*
2. **Security.** *For any forbidden set F, it holds that $\lambda_\circ(R) = \lambda_\bullet(R)$.*

The first condition guarantees that reconstructed white and black areas are visually distinguishable. The second essentially says that in the image reconstructed by a forbidden subset of parties the white and black areas are perfectly indistinguishable.

3.2   Examples of Schemes

To get some confidence with the framework, let us consider some simple examples. Assume that the set S of secret images contains all black-and-white square images I of $n \times n$ pixels. Let use denote with $Shr(\cdot)$ the algorithm used in the sharing phase by the dealer, and with $Rec(\cdot)$ the algorithm used in the reconstruction phase by a set of qualified parties. We consider collections consisting of exactly two distribution matrices, that is, $\mathcal{C}_\circ = \{\mathcal{C}_{\circ,0}, \mathcal{C}_{\circ,1}\}$, and $\mathcal{C}_\bullet = \{\mathcal{C}_{\bullet,0}, \mathcal{C}_{\bullet,1}\}$. The $Shr(\cdot)$ and $Rec(\cdot)$ algorithms are:

---

[6] Recall that in the model, for sharing a secret image, a random black and white image (a random grid) is used as starting point.

(2, 2)-VCS
$Shr(I)$

For every $i, j = 1, \ldots, n,$
   Choose uniformly at random $r_{i,j} \in \{0,1\}$
   Use row k of $\mathcal{C}_{I(i,j),r_{i,j}}$ to set $sh_k(i,j)$, for $k = 1, 2.$
 Output (sh_1, sh_2)

$Rec(sh_1, sh_2)$ Return $I = \mathrm{Sup}(sh_1, sh_2).$

The collections of distribution matrices, $\mathcal{C}_\circ = \{\mathcal{C}_{\circ,0}, \mathcal{C}_{\circ,1}\}$ and $\mathcal{C}_\bullet = \{\mathcal{C}_{\bullet,0}, \mathcal{C}_{\bullet,1}\}$, given by

$$\mathcal{C}_\circ = \left\{ \begin{bmatrix} \circ & \bullet \\ \circ & \bullet \end{bmatrix}, \begin{bmatrix} \bullet & \circ \\ \bullet & \circ \end{bmatrix} \right\} \qquad \mathcal{C}_\bullet = \left\{ \begin{bmatrix} \circ & \bullet \\ \bullet & \circ \end{bmatrix}, \begin{bmatrix} \bullet & \circ \\ \circ & \bullet \end{bmatrix} \right\}$$

realize a (2, 2)-VCS in the deterministic model. Indeed, both the Reconstructability and Security conditions hold.

- The contrast thresholds are $\ell = 1$ and $h = 2$. A white pixel is always reconstructed as a white subpixel and a black subpixel. A black pixel is always reconstructed as two black subpixels
- The restrictions of the collections $\mathcal{C}_\circ$ and $\mathcal{C}_\bullet$ to submatrices of one row contain the same submatrices with the same frequencies.

The scheme is a special case $(k = n = 2)$ of the (k,n)-VCS threshold scheme, given by Naor and Shamir in [44]. This scheme has been used to generate the example in Fig. 3.

Similarly, the following two collections of distribution matrices $\mathcal{C}_\circ = \{\mathcal{C}_{\circ,0}, \mathcal{C}_{\circ,1}\}$, and $\mathcal{C}_\bullet = \{\mathcal{C}_{\bullet,0}, \mathcal{C}_{\bullet,1}\}$, where

$$\mathcal{C}_\circ = \left\{ \begin{bmatrix} \circ \\ \circ \end{bmatrix}, \begin{bmatrix} \bullet \\ \bullet \end{bmatrix} \right\} \qquad \mathcal{C}_\bullet = \left\{ \begin{bmatrix} \circ \\ \bullet \end{bmatrix}, \begin{bmatrix} \bullet \\ \circ \end{bmatrix} \right\}$$

realize a (2, 2)-VCS in the random grid model (or the probabilistic model with $m = 1$). Indeed, both the Reconstructability and Security conditions hold.

- The two thresholds $\lambda_\circ$ and $\lambda_\bullet$ are $\lambda_\circ = \frac{1}{2}$ and $\lambda_\bullet = 0$. Indeed, $\lambda_\circ(R) = \frac{1}{2}$ while $\lambda_\bullet(R) = 0$.
- For each share sh it holds that $\lambda_\circ(sh) = \lambda_\bullet(sh) = \frac{1}{2}$.

The scheme is the first one of the three (2, 2)-VCS schemes, given by Kafri and Keren in [32]. This scheme has been used to generate the example in Fig. 4.

4   Issues

Constructions for (k,n)-VCS threshold schemes, for any integer k and n, such that $k \leq n$, and general access structures are known both for the deterministic model and the random grid (probabilistic) model, e.g., [2,10,11,23,44,57]. However, some issues are still open. Let us have a quick look at them.

4.1   Contrast

For deterministic schemes, three main measures of contrast have appeared in the literature: γ_{NS} (Naor and Shamir [44]), γ_{VV} (Verheul and van Tilborg [48]) and γ_{ES} (Eisen and Stinson [24]). The measure introduced by Naor and Shamir [44]) is defined by:

$$\gamma_{NS}(\mathcal{S}) = \frac{h - \ell}{m}. \tag{1}$$

Verheul and van Tilborg [48], on the other hand, defined:

$$\gamma_{VV}(\mathcal{S}) = \frac{h - \ell}{m(2m - h - \ell)}, \tag{2}$$

while, Eisen and Stinson [24], used:

$$\gamma_{ES}(\mathcal{S}) = \frac{h - \ell}{2m - h}. \tag{3}$$

Other notions have also been proposed by other authors, e.g., [18,40]. The constructions for threshold and general access structures in the deterministic model [2,44] have been evaluated according to γ_{NS}, e.g., [2,5,6,27,36,37,44]. However, Eisen and Stinson have provided convincing arguments in support of γ_{ES}, which currently seems to be the notion with the best match with the real world. Hence, we need to understand whether γ_{ES} is actually the optimal notion and, if this is the case, how to construct contrast-optimal schemes with respect to such a notion.

4.2   Pixel Expansion

In the deterministic model, pixel expansion and contrast are strictly related. Hence, some lower bounds which hold for γ_{NS} e.g., [4,44], might need to be revised with respect to the new notion γ_{ES}. Currently, we have lower bounds only for $(2, n)$-VCS threshold schemes with respect to γ_{ES} (see [24]).

4.3   Randomness Reduction

The issue of reducing the randomness the dealer needs to generate a scheme has been addressed in few papers, e.g., [20]. Recently, a new strategy for reducing randomness by encoding group of pixel has been outlined in [19]. There is room for findings and further investigations.

5   Alternative Models: Miscellaneous

Apart the three models briefly described before, many variants have been introduced and studied throughout the years. A detailed overview is out of the scope of this short abstract, but a few words about some of them are worthy, especially to give an idea of the breadth of the area: the interested reader can then use the references for deepening the aspects he is more curious about.

Visual Cryptography for Color Images. The three models concern with black-and-white images. Grey images and color images have also been considered. Grey images are treated by naturally extending the black-and-white image model: grey levels are represented with different quantities of black subpixels in the reconstructed pixels, obtained through superposition. Color images are not easy to deal with: indeed, some tricky questions arise from the complex behavior of color superposition. In the literature several models have been proposed but no agreement on a reference one has been achieved. In some of them, pixels of different colors cannot be superposed. Others exploit color superposition and the laws of color composition. The notion of contrast is not easy to define as well. However, in all of them, constructions have been proposed and the respective performances have been compared, e.g., [1,12,14,22,29,34,53].

Visual Cryptography with Meaningful Shares. Shares of a visual cryptography scheme are normally random looking images. Special sharing schemes have the capability of producing shares which are not random looking images but instead contain meaningful images; such schemes have been called *extended*[7]. In an extended visual cryptography scheme in each transparency is visible a different image; obviously, the images visible in the transparencies are unrelated to the secret image, and the security property still holds. The images on the transparencies provide a way to identify each transparency as belonging to a specific part. Extended visual cryptography schemes have been introduced in [3,44] and studied in other papers, e.g., [9,25,38].

Visual Cryptography for Multisecret. In a standard VCS parties share one secret image. It is possible to construct schemes for sharing more than one image, in such a way that each specific subset of qualified parties recovers a different image. In [42] a construction for the case when qualified subsets are pairs corresponding to adjacent nodes in a graph is provided; the scheme is also an "extended" scheme, in the sense explained in the previous paragraph. Several schemes for the special case of two parties have been proposed; in such schemes, the parties can recover more than one image by rotating the shares, so that different superpositions are produced. With square shaped shares only 4 possible rotations are possible; with circular shaped shares any rotation degree can be used (e.g., [26,45,55,56]). In some schemes the shares are translated instead of rotated; translation reduces the overall size of the reconstructed image, e.g., [26]. A suitable model and secure constructions for threshold and general access structures are interesting open problems.

Visual Cryptography with Alternative Approaches. The basic property of visual cryptography is that the reconstruction operation is performed by the human

---

[7] We remark that the adjective "extended" has been used also to denote other types of visual cryptography schemes with different additional properties; for example, in [33], "extended" schemes allow to share different secrets, one for each qualified subset.

eye. As remarked before, if we think of white as 0 and black as 1, the superposition operation corresponds to the logical or operation. Several researchers have considered visual cryptography schemes where the reconstruction operation is the xor operation. The use of the xor is justified by the fact that, for a special type of transparencies that exploit the light polarization, the superposition of the transparencies let the human eye perceives an xor as a result of the superposition. The idea and some schemes were proposed in [7]; several papers, e.g. [41,47], have provided schemes in this model. In [39] an interferometric encryption technique is used.

Visual Cryptography with Reversing. Some papers have considered the possibility of exploiting an extra operation in the reconstruction phase. This operation is called *reversing* and, as the name suggests, changes black pixels into white ones and vice versa. Some copy machines are able to reverse an image. The idea was introduced in [49] and other papers, e.g., [15,30,54] have considered this model.

Visual Cryptography Robust Against Cheating. In standard schemes, it is assumed that all parties are honest. Taking into consideration the possibility that some parties might be malicious, then precautions to avoid problems are needed. A cheater or a group of cooperating cheaters, by using fake shares could, for example, fool other parties by having them reconstruct a wrong secret. Several papers have considered this problem and proposed schemes that allow to detect cheaters, e.g., [21,28,31].

6   Applications

Visual cryptography has been proposed for several applications. Let us briefly look at some of them.

Educational Tool. Visual cryptography is quite a powerful tool for introducing to a general audience the basic ideas of *encryption* and *secure sharing* in an unconditional secure way. Throughout the years many presentations of the techniques and introductory articles have been written, e.g., starting from [46].

Identification and Authentication. Naor and Pinkas in [43] were the first ones to propose applications for visual identification and for visual authentication. The first, allow a human user to prove his identity to a verifier without using any computational device. The second, ensures that an adversary cannot convince a human recipient to accept any fake message. Concerning the latter, a real-life setting is the following: the user, when opening a new bank account, receives a set of transparencies, each with a unique identifier. Later on, when he makes an on-line transaction and asks the bank to credit a certain amount of money, for example, to an Internet seller, the bank to be sure of the source of the message sends to the user a transparency, which appears on the screen. The user, by superposing to it one of the transparencies previously received, precisely, the one with the same identifier which is shown on the transparency on the screen, is able to visually reconstruct as secret image an authorization code, which has to be typed on the keyboard and sent to the bank, in order to convince the bank that the money transfer request is an original one and comes from him (and it does not come from a malicious party). Compared to a similar and currently used method (give the user directly the series of codes needed to authenticate a transaction) this method has the advantage that codes are reconstructed only when the user needs to use them and thus cannot be stolen.

Access Control. Any public or private institution might give out visual shares of the password of a vault to two people who are supposed to be both present when the vault needs to be opened. A threshold scheme might also be used for generalizing the approach to more people, adding some flexibility. The same strategy can be applied to other similar access control problems in which human users are involved.

Electronic Voting: Chaum's Scheme. The most interesting application came from Chaum [8]. He designed a sophisticated voting scheme in which a voter gets a receipt satisfying two seemingly conflicting properties: the anonymous receipt allows her or anyone else on her behalf to check that the vote was counted in the final tally but, at the same time, it does not allow to use the receipt to prove what her vote was for. The receipt is one of two transparencies generated in the voting booth, when the vote choice is made (details in [8]).

Other applications have also been suggested to fight phishing, by merging together captchas and visual cryptography, and for watermarking and more generally for copyright protection of multimedia data. We refer the interested reader to Chapter 12 of [16], which overviews with more details some applications of visual cryptography.

7   New Directions

As pointed out in [17], the design of secure protocols which can be used *without the aid of a computer* and *without cryptographic knowledge* is an interesting and challenging research task. Indeed, protocols enjoying these features could be useful in a variety of settings where computers cannot be used or where people feel uncomfortable to interact with or trust a computer. Visual cryptography might play an important role in that respect.

Indeed, a novel method for performing secure two-party computations that merges together in a suitable way Yao's garbled circuit construction and visual cryptography has been proposed in [17]. It enables Alice and Bob to securely evaluate a function $f(\cdot, \cdot)$ of their inputs, x and y, through a *pure physical* process. Once Alice has prepared a set of properly constructed transparencies, Bob computes the function value $f(x, y)$ by applying a sequence of simple steps which require the use of a pair of scissors, superposing transparencies, and the human visual system. Let us briefly describe it.

7.1   Tool for Secure Computation

Yao's Construction. Yao's construction enables two parties, Alice and Bob, to privately evaluate a boolean function $f(\cdot, \cdot)$ on their inputs, x and y, in such a way that each party gets the result and, at the same time, *preserves* the privacy of its own input, apart from what can be inferred about it by the other party from its input and the function value $f(x, y)$, e.g., if the function $f(\cdot, \cdot)$ is the xor function, given x xor y and x there is no way to preserve the other input y.

The construction works as follows: the boolean function $f(\cdot, \cdot)$ is represented through a boolean circuit $C(\cdot, \cdot)$ for which, for each x, y, it holds that $C(x, y) = f(x, y)$. Yao's idea is to use the circuit as a *conceptual guide* for the computation which, instead of a sequence of and, or and not operations on strings of bits x and y, becomes a *sequence of decryptions* on sequences of ciphertexts. More precisely, one of the party, say Alice, given $C(\cdot, \cdot)$, computes a new object $\tilde{C}$, which is usually referred to as the *garbled circuit*, where:

- to each wire w of $C(\cdot, \cdot)$, are associated in $\tilde{C}$ two random keys, k_w^0 and k_w^1, which (secretly, the correspondence is not public) represent 0 and 1, and,
- to each gate $G(\cdot, \cdot)$ of $C(\cdot, \cdot)$, corresponds in $\tilde{C}$ a *gate table* $\tilde{G}$ with four rows, each of which is a *double encryption*, obtained by using two different keys $k_{w_1}^a$ and $k_{w_2}^b$, for $a, b \in \{0, 1\}$, of a message which is itself a random key $k_{w_3}^c$, for $c \in \{0, 1\}$. In details, each double encryption $E_{ab} = E_{k_{w_2}^b}(E_{k_{w_1}^a}(k_{w_3}^c))$ uses one of the four possible pairs of keys $(k_{w_1}^a, k_{w_2}^b)$, associated to the input wires (w_1, w_2) of gate $G(\cdot, \cdot)$, and the message which is encrypted is the random key $k_{w_3}^c$, associated to the wire w_3 of output of the gate $G(\cdot, \cdot)$ *if and only if* $G(a, b) = c$. The four double encryptions E_{00}, E_{01}, E_{10} and E_{11} are stored in the gate table rows in *random* order.

Once $\tilde{C}$ has been computed, Alice sends to Bob all the gate tables $\tilde{G}$ associated to the circuit gates $G(\cdot, \cdot)$, and *reveals* the random keys k_w^0 and k_w^1, associated to all the *output* wires w, and their correspondences with the values 0 and 1. Moreover, for the input wires of the circuit, she sends to Bob the random keys $k_{w_1}^{x_1}, k_{w_2}^{x_2}, \ldots, k_{w_n}^{x_n}$ corresponding to the bit-values of her own input $x = x_1 x_2 \ldots x_n$. To perform the computation represented by $\tilde{C}$, then Bob needs only the keys associated to the input wires corresponding to *his own* input. This issue can be solved by means of *executions* of 1-out-of-2 *oblivious transfer* protocols, through which Bob receives the random keys $k_{w_{n+1}}^{y_1}, k_{w_{n+2}}^{y_2}, \ldots, k_{w_{2n}}^{y_{2n}}$ corresponding to the bit-values of his own input $y = y_1 y_2 \ldots y_n$ and nothing else, while Alice from the transfer does not know which specific keys Bob has recovered.

Finally Bob, according to the topology of the original circuit $C(\cdot, \cdot)$, level after level, decrypts[8] *one and only one* entry from each gate table $\tilde{G}$ in $\tilde{C}$, until he computes *one and only one* random key associated to each output wire. The binary string which corresponds to the sequence of computed random keys, associated to the output wires, is the value $C(x, y)$. Bob sends the result of the computation to Alice.

Koleshnikov Approach. Kolesnikov [35] showed that a different approach to the function evaluation process in Yao's construction can be pursued. Roughly

---

[8] An encryption scheme allowing to verify whether a decryption is successful, providing a correctly decrypted value, or fails, providing garbage, is used.

speaking, instead of constructing the garbled circuit $\tilde{C}$ by using for each gate $G(\cdot,\cdot)$ a gate table $\tilde{G}$, containing a double encryption for each possible input pair of keys, it is possible to use *secret sharing schemes* designed to realize the functionalities implemented by the logical gates. Such schemes were referred to as *gate evaluation secret sharing schemes* (GESS, for short) [35]. Using a GESS, any time that two shares, say $sh_{w_1}^a$ and $sh_{w_2}^b$, associated to the input wires w_1 and w_2 of gate $G(\cdot,\cdot)$, are combined through the reconstruction function of the GESS, the secret s_{w_3}, associated to the output wire w_3 of gate $G(\cdot,\cdot)$ is recovered. It follows that an *explicit representation* $\tilde{G}$ of $G(\cdot,\cdot)$ is *not* needed any more, because all the information required to reconstruct the secret value associated to w_3, depending on the functionality of the target gate $G(\cdot,\cdot)$, is coded and, hence, *implicitly represented*, into the shares $sh_{w_1}^a$ and $sh_{w_2}^b$. Therefore, given the circuit $C(\cdot,\cdot)$, and by applying a bottom-up process, which starts from the circuit output wires and ends when the circuit input wires are reached, Alice can construct shares associated to the circuit input wires which encode *all the information* needed to evaluate $C(\cdot,\cdot)$ on every pair of inputs (x,y). Then, as in Yao's construction, Alice sends directly to Bob the shares corresponding to the bit-values of her own input x, while Bob, by means of *executions* of 1-out-of-2 *oblivious transfer* protocols, receives the shares corresponding to the bit-values of his own input y. Finally, Bob applies iteratively the GESS reconstruction functions, until the secrets associated to the output wires, which correspond to the value $C(x,y)$, are obtained.

A Visual Construction. In [17] it was shown how to build on Kolesnikov's idea in order to produce a circuit implementation by using visual cryptography, i.e., in such a way that the evaluation process ends up in a sequence of transparency superpositions. The first crucial step is to set up a *physical oblivious transfer*.

Let Alice's secrets be n-bit strings z_0 and z_1, let σ be Bob's bit-choice, and let $\perp$ denote no output. The 1-out-of-2-OT functionality is specified by $((z_0, z_1, \sigma) \to (\perp, z_\sigma))$. The construction proposed is partially inspired to the approach pursued in [8], when the voter comes out from the booth. Let us assume that the two secrets z_0 and z_1 are represented in form of transparencies, and Alice has two *indistinguishable envelopes* which *perfectly hide* the transparency inside. Alice and Bob proceed as follows:

1. Alice puts the two transparencies in the two envelopes, one in the first and one in the second, and closes both of them. She also adds to each envelope a paper post-it with number 0 and number 1, depending on the transparency which is inside. Then, she hands the two envelopes to Bob.
2. Bob turns his shoulders to Alice, checks that the envelopes are identical, takes the envelopes with the post-it corresponding to the secret he is interested in, removes the post-it from both envelopes, turns again in front of Alice, and inserts under Alice surveillance the remaining envelope in a paper-shredder which reduces the envelop and its content in dust.

In such a way, Bob gets one and only one transparency, while Alice does not know which one.

The second step is to produce a *visual equivalent* of a *GESS* scheme. In [17] it is showed how to do it, introducing the notion of *VGESS*, i.e., *visual gate evaluation secret sharing*.

With these tools, the visual protocol ends up in the same reduction of secure function evaluation to 1-out-of-2 OT given via Construction 1 in [35], but with *VGESSs* and physical OTs instead of *GESSs* and a digital OTs. It consists in a *Shares construction phase*, performed by Alice, and a *Computation phase*, performed by Alice and Bob.

To get an idea of how the protocol works, let us look at an example. The function f is equal to $f(x, y) = (x_1 \wedge y_1) \vee (x_2 \wedge y_2)$. The output values are represented through a totally white image (0) and a totally black image (1). Notice that, in the *Computation phase*, and specifically in the visual computation performed by Bob, any image with *at least* a white pixel corresponds to 0, while the *totally black* image corresponds to 1. In Fig. 6, Alice has completed the *Shares construction phase* and all the shares that are needed for the computation have been computed and have been associated to the input wires. For example, for the left input wire of G_1, the value 0 corresponds to share Sh_1^C, while the value 1 corresponds to the share Sh_1^D. The prepended bits, implemented by using a visual cryptography scheme too, says to which half of the right share the left share has to be superposed. For details, the reader is referred to [17].

Figure 7 shows an example of the *Computation phase*, with input values $x_1 = 0, x_2 = 1, y_1 = 1$ and $y_2 = 0$. Once Bob has received from Alice the shares associated to her input and, through two instances of the OT protocol, the shares associated to his input, then he can perform the computation. The reconstructed value as shown in the figure is correctly zero.

Notice that an investigation of a different approach to secure multiparty computation by using visual cryptography has been recently proposed in [19]. Indeed, in the general solutions for unconditionally secure multiparty computation, in order to compute new shares for the subsequent steps, parties process their input shares interactively or non-interactively. Along the same line, [19] looks at how transparencies can be efficiently manipulated in such a way that when the newly produced transparencies are superposed, the result of the function evaluation is obtained, while the input privacy is still preserved.

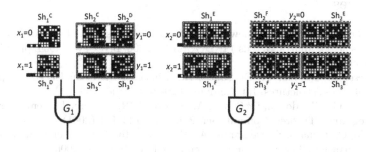

Fig. 6. Shares for evaluating function f

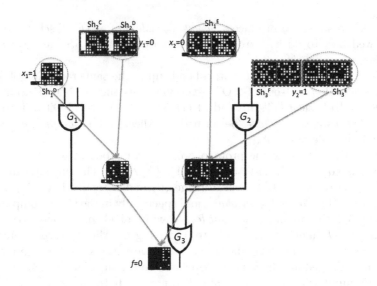

Fig. 7. Visual evaluation of f with input $((0,1),(1,0))$

8   Conclusions

We have proposed a brief excursus in the large field of visual cryptography. Starting from Naor and Shamir's and Kafri and Keren's models, we have described a common framework for visual cryptography schemes, and we have given a look at alternative models: for grey and color images, for meaningful transparencies, for multiple secrets, as well as models that exploit special properties for the superposition of transparencies and models robust against cheating. We have also described some classical applications and, finally, we have focused on a new approach, which uses visual cryptography for general secure computation. Along the way, we have pointed out issues and open problems, which could be objects of attention and further investigations in the next years. Years in which visual cryptography seems to be still a potentially useful technique.

References

1. Adhikari, A., Sikdar, S.: A new (2,n)-visual threshold scheme for color images. In: Johansson, T., Maitra, S. (eds.) INDOCRYPT 2003. LNCS, vol. 2904, pp. 148–161. Springer, Heidelberg (2003)
2. Ateniese, G., Blundo, C., De Santis, A., Stinson, D.R.: Visual cryptography for general access structures. Inf. Comput. **129**(2), 86–106 (1996)
3. Ateniese, G., Blundo, C., De Santis, A., Stinson, D.R.: Extended schemes for visual cryptography. Theoret. Comput. Sci. **250**(1–2), 143–161 (2001)
4. Blundo, C., Cimato, S., De Santis, A.: Visual cryptography schemes with optimal pixel expansion. Theoret. Comput. Sci. **369**(1–3), 169–182 (2006)
5. Blundo, C., D'Arco, P., De Santis, A., Stinson, D.R.: Contrast optimal threshold visual cryptography schemes. SIAM J. Discrete Math. **16**(2), 224–261 (2003)

6. Blundo, C., De Santis, A., Stinson, D.R.: On the contrast in visual cryptography schemes. J. Cryptol. **12**(4), 261–289 (1999)
7. Biham, E., Itzkovitz, A.: Visual cryptography with polarization. In: The Dagstuhl Seminar on Cryptography (1997) and Crypto 1998 RUMP Session (1998)
8. Chaum, D.: Secret-ballot receipts: true voter-verifiable elections. IEEE Secur. Priv. 38–47 (2004)
9. Chen, T.-H., Lee, Y.-S.: Yet another friendly progressive visual secret sharing scheme. In: 5th International Conference Intelligent Information Hiding and Multimedia Signal Processing, pp. 353–356 (2009)
10. Chen, T.-H., Tsao, K.-H.: Visual secret random grids sharing revisited. Pattern Recogn. **42**(9), 2203–2217 (2009)
11. Chen, T.-H., Tsao, K.-H.: Threshold visual secret sharing by random grids. J. Syst. Softw. **84**(7), 1197–1208 (2011)
12. Cimato, S., De Prisco, R., De Santis, A.: Optimal colored threshold visual cryptography schemes. Des. Codes Crypt. **35**, 311–335 (2005)
13. Cimato, S., De Prisco, R., De Santis, A.: Probabilistic visual cryptography schemes. Comput. J. **49**(1), 97–107 (2006)
14. Cimato, S., De Prisco, R., De Santis, A.: Colored visual cryptography without color darkening. Theoret. Comput. Sci. **374**(1–3), 261–276 (2007)
15. Cimato, S., De Santis, A., Ferrara, A.L., Masucci, B.: Ideal contrast visual cryptography schemes with reversing. Inf. Process. Lett. **93**(4), 199–206 (2005)
16. Cimato, S., Yang, C.-N.: Visual Cryptography and Secret Image Sharing. CRC Press, Boca Raton (2012). ISBN: 978-1-4398-3721-4
17. D'Arco, P., Prisco, R.: Secure two-party computation: a visual way. In: Padró, C. (ed.) ICITS 2013. LNCS, vol. 8317, pp. 18–38. Springer, Heidelberg (2014). doi:10. 1007/978-3-319-04268-8_2
18. D'Arco, P., De Prisco, R., De Santis, A.: Measure-independent characterization of contrast optimal visual cryptography schemes. J. Syst. Softw. **95**, 89–99 (2014)
19. D'Arco, P., De Prisco, R., Desmedt, Y.: Private visual share-homomorphic computation and randomness reduction in visual cryptography. In: ICITS 2016, 9–12 August 2016, Tacoma, Washington, USA (2016)
20. De Bonis, A., De Santis, A.: Randomness in secret sharing and visual cryptography schemes. Theoret. Comput. Sci. **314**(3), 351–374 (2004)
21. De Prisco, R., De Santis, A.: Cheating immune threshold visual secret sharing. Comput. J. **53**(9), 1485–1496 (2009)
22. De Prisco, R., De Santis, A.: Color visual cryptography schemes for black and white secret images. Theoret. Comput. Sci. **510**(28), 62–86 (2013)
23. De Prisco, R., De Santis, A.: On the relation of random grid and deterministic visual cryptography. IEEE Trans. Inf. Forensics Secur. **9**(4), 653–665 (2014)
24. Eisen, P.A., Stinson, D.R.: Threshold visual cryptography schemes with specified whiteness levels of reconstructed pixels. Des. Cods Crypt. **25**, 15–61 (2002)
25. Fang, W.P.: Friendly progressive visual secret sharing. Pattern Recogn. **41**(4), 1410–1414 (2008)
26. Feng, J.-B., Wu, H.-C., Tsai, C.-S., Chang, Y.-F., Chu, Y.-P.: Visual secret sharing for multiple secrets. Pattern Recogn. **41**(12), 3572–3581 (2008)
27. Hofmeister, T., Krause, M., Simon, H.U.: Contrast-optimal k out of n secret sharing schemes in visual cryptography. Theoret. Comput. Sci. **240**(2), 471–485 (2000)
28. Horng, G., Chen, T.-H., Tsai, D.-S.: Cheating in visual cryptography. Des. Codes Crypt. **38**(2), 219–236 (2006)
29. Hou, Y.-C.: Visual cryptography for color images. Pattern Recognit. **36**(7), 1619–1629 (2003)

30. Hu, C.-M., Tzeng, W.-G.: Compatible ideal contrast visual cryptography schemes with reversing. In: Zhou, J., Lopez, J., Deng, R.H., Bao, F. (eds.) ISC 2005. LNCS, vol. 3650, pp. 300–313. Springer, Heidelberg (2005). doi:10.1007/11556992_22
31. Hu, C., Tzeng, W.G.: Cheating prevention in visual cryptography. IEEE Trans. Image Process. **16**(1), 36–45 (2007)
32. Kafri, O., Keren, E.: Encryption of pictures and shapes by random grids. Opt. Lett. **12**(6), 377–379 (1987)
33. Klein, A., Wessler, M.: Extended visual cryptography schemes. Inf. Comput. **205**(5), 716–732 (2007)
34. Koga, H., Yamamoto, H.: Proposal of a lattice-based visual secret sharing scheme for color and gray-scale images. IEICE Trans. Fundam. Electron. Commun. Comput. Sci. **81–A**(6), 1262–1269 (1998)
35. Kolesnikov, V.: Gate evaluation secret sharing and secure one-round two-party computation. In: Roy, B. (ed.) ASIACRYPT 2005. LNCS, vol. 3788, pp. 136–155. Springer, Heidelberg (2005). doi:10.1007/11593447_8
36. Krause, M., Simon, H.U.: Determining the optimal contrast for secret sharing schemes in visual cryptography. Comb. Probab. Comput. **12**(3), 285–299 (2003)
37. Kuhlmann, C., Simon, H.U.: Construction of visual secret sharing schemes with almost optimal contrast. In: 11th ACM-SIAM Symposium on Discrete Algorithms, San Francisco, USA, pp. 262–272 (2000)
38. Lee, K.-H., Chiu, P.-L.: An extended visual cryptography algorithm for general access structures. IEEE Trans. Inf. Forensics Secur. **7**(1), 219–229 (2012)
39. Lee, S.-S., Na, J.-C., Sohn, S.-W., Park, C., Seo, D.-H., Kim, S.-J.: Visual cryptography based on interferometric encryption technique. ETRI J. **24**(5), 373–380 (2002)
40. Liu, F., Wua, C., Lin, X.: A new definition of the contrast of visual cryptography scheme. Inf. Process. Lett. **110**(7), 241–246 (2010)
41. Liu, F., Wu, C.K.: Optimal XOR based (2,n)-visual cryptography schemes. In: Shi, Y.-Q., Kim, H.J., Pérez-González, F., Yang, C.-N. (eds.) IWDW 2014. LNCS, vol. 9023, pp. 333–349. Springer, Heidelberg (2015)
42. Lu, S., Manchala, D., Ostrovsky, R.: Visual cryptography on graphs. J. Comb. Optim. **21**(1), 47–66 (2011)
43. Naor, M., Pinkas, B.: Visual authentication and identification. In: Kaliski, B.S. (ed.) CRYPTO 1997. LNCS, vol. 1294, pp. 322–336. Springer, Heidelberg (1997). doi:10.1007/BFb0052245
44. Naor, M., Shamir, A.: Visual cryptography. In: Santis, A. (ed.) EUROCRYPT 1994. LNCS, vol. 950, pp. 1–12. Springer, Heidelberg (1995). doi:10.1007/BFb0053419
45. Shyu, S.-J., Huang, S.-Y., Lee, Y.-K., Wang, R.-Z., Chen, K.: Sharing multiple secrets in visual cryptography. Pattern Recogn. **40**(12), 3633–3651 (2007)
46. Stinson, D.: Visual cryptography and threshold schemes. Dr. Dobbs J. (1998). http://www.drdobbs.com/visual-cryptography-threshold-schemes/184410530
47. Tulys, P., Hollman, H.D., van Lint, J.H., Tolhuizen, L.: XOR-based visual cryptography schemes. Des. Codes Crypt. **27**, 169–186 (2005)
48. Verheul, E.R., van Tilborg, H.C.A.: Constructions and properties of k out of n visual secret schemes. Des. Codes Crypt. **11**, 179–196 (1997)
49. Viet, D.Q., Kurosawa, K.: Almost ideal contrast visual cryptography with reversing. In: Okamoto, T. (ed.) CT-RSA 2004. LNCS, vol. 2964, pp. 353–365. Springer, Heidelberg (2004). doi:10.1007/978-3-540-24660-2_27
50. Yang, C.-N.: New visual secret sharing schemes using probabilistic method. Pattern Recogn. Lett. **25**(4), 481–494 (2004)

51. Yang, C.-N., Chen, T.-S.: Size-adjustable visual secret sharing schemes. IEICE Trans. Fundam. Electron. Commun. Comput. Sci. **E88–A**(9), 2471–2474 (2005)
52. Yang, C.-N., Chen, T.-S.: Aspect ratio invariant visual secret sharing schemes with minimum pixel expansion. Pattern Recogn. Lett. **26**(2), 193–206 (2005)
53. Yang, C.-N., Laih, C.-S.: New colored visual secret sharing schemes. Des. Codes Crypt. **20**, 325–335 (2000)
54. Yang, C.-N., Wang, C.-C., Chen, T.-S.: Visual cryptography schemes with reversing. Comput. J. **51**(6), 710–722 (2008)
55. Wu, H.C., Chang, C.C.: Sharing visual multi-secrets using circle shares. Comput. Stand. Interfaces **134**(28), 123–135 (2005)
56. Wu, C.-C., Chen, L.-H.: A study on visual cryptography. Master thesis, Institute of Computer and Information Science, National Chiao Tung University, Taiwan, R.O.C. (1998)
57. Wu, X., Sun, W.: Random grid-based visual secret sharing for general access structures with cheat-preventing ability. J. Syst. Softw. **85**(5), 1119–1134 (2012)

Paper Tigers: An Endless Fight

Mozhdeh Farhadi[1] and Jean-Louis Lanet[2(✉)]

[1] Tehran, Iran
[2] INRIA, LHS PEC, 263 Avenue Général Leclerc, 35042 Rennes, France
jean-louis.lanet@inria.fr

Abstract. Recently, researchers published several attacks on smart cards. Among these, software attacks are the most affordable, they do not require specific hardware (laser, EM probe, *etc.*). To prevent such attacks, smart card manufacturers embed dedicated software countermeasures to protect the sensitive system elements. They design countermeasure to mitigate an existing attack with global view of the security. An affordable countermeasure must have a high coverage with a low footprint. For that reasons the design of a mitigation technique is often a trade off between the memory usage and the efficiency of a countermeasure. We present here a survey bringing to the fore the countermeasures used to mitigate the attacks. We use the formalism of attack defense tree to have a synthetic and graphical view of the attack scenario.

Keywords: Java Card platform · Security · Attacks · Countermeasures · Attack tree

1 Introduction

In the 70's decade, the idea of Smart Card made a high level of security available to our everyday life [1]. This small device can keep securely sensitive data of the card holder, such as fingerprint or bank credit. Smart Card can be used in extremely diverse applications such as access control systems, digital signature, electronic purse and identity.

The Smart Cards can be divided into two main categories from their operating system point of view. One is the classic Smart Card operating system which prohibits load of new applications into the card after card issuance. On the other hand, there is another type of card operating system which is categorized as Open Platform. Java Card, Multos and Dot net Card are examples of Open Platforms. Open Platform cards which provide multi-application in a single card, allow loading new applications to the card even after card issuance. In the classic smart cards, code of the application which is part of the proprietary operating system is masked into the Read Only Memory (ROM) and thus loading new application code is prohibited. But in the Open Platform cards new applications can be loaded and installed into the Electrically Erasable Programmable ROM (EEPROM).

In 1997, Java Card with the main idea of Java which is "Write once, Run anywhere" was born. This Open Platform card provides application independence from the hardware. The Java Card manufacturer companies develop their

I. Bica and R. Reyhanitabar (Eds.): SECITC 2016, LNCS 10006, pp. 40–62, 2016.
DOI: 10.1007/978-3-319-47238-6_3

Java Card Runtime Environment (JCRE) for a Smart Card chip according to the Java Card specification published by Oracle [2]. On the other hand, the Java Card application providers develop their own applications using the Java Card Application Programming Interface (APIs) published as part of the specification. This standardized APIs provides a uniform interface to various Smart Card chips [5]. Thus, the Java Card applications can be installed on any Java Card platform only concerning the version competency of the Java Card specification. Java Card applications (applets) are loaded as Converted APplication (CAP) files into the card.

The Java Card platform provides security to the smart card world by its security features. But as it is an Open Platform card which provides loading new applications after issuance it increases the possibility to be target of attacks. Attackers can easily do experiments by loading test applets on the card and analyzing the results. Thus, the fight between attackers and Java Card platform designers starts. Whenever an attack is hindered by a countermeasure, another new attack is proposed by another attacker. The attackers use software, hardware or a combination of both to get access to the assets of the cards. In this paper we describe the software attacks and their countermeasures on the Java Card platform.

The logical attacks can be divided into three categories: attacks due to the specification, attacks with ill-typed code and attacks against bad implementation. Each kind of attack uses different hypotheses which are pointed out in this document.

The rest of the paper is organized as follows: first we give an overview of the security features of the Java Card platform. Second, we describe the attacks due to the specification. Third, we focus on attacks with Ill-typed code and fourth a description on the attacks against bad implementation will be presented. Finally, we conclude in the last section.

2 Security Features of the Java Card

Java Card uses a subset of the Java language and Java is considered as a secure language. This language pays attention to the security by blocking type mismatches, eliminating pointer use by the developers and control of array boundaries [3]. The following features of the Java Card platform play main roles in providing security:

Byte Code Verification: Byte Code Verification (BCV) ensures that the code is compliant with the Java Card specification rules. It verifies all the operations regarding the type system of the Java language.

Firewall mechanism: As Java Card is a multi-application card, the firewall takes care of applet isolation and controls the interaction between the applets [5]. In the Java Card, access to elements of other applets in different security contexts (packages) are not allowed. But the Java Card specification defined an interface which provides sharing services to the other applets. If an applet wants to share its services to other applets, it should define an interface which inherits from the shareable interface of the Java Card API.

Transaction mechanism: The Java Card specification defines the *transaction* mechanism to protect persistent data against events such as a power loss in the middle of a transaction operation. The Java Card applet developer can group some update operations into a transaction block. Thus, the atomicity of these updates is guaranteed. It means that in this block of code, all of these update operations are bounded together. Either all of the updates will be successfully done or none of these updates will be done.

In order to provide a synthetic view of each kind of attack, we present them using the graphical attack tree methodology. It has been introduced by Schneier [18] to analyze the different ways a system can be attacked. In this method, an undesirable event is defined and then the system is analyzed to represent the combination of basic events with AND and OR gates, that can lead to the undesirable event.

The root node of the tree represents the undesirable event. The nodes are refinements of this event, and leafs are the initial causes. It should be mentioned that an attack tree does not represent all possible cases of failure but a restricted set. A path from a leaf to the root represents an attack scenario. An event with a NON gate represents a countermeasure. If the countermeasure is not present, then the attack will succeed. One can remark that the closer to the root the countermeasure is, the better is the coverage of this countermeasure.

In analyzing a smart card, four undesirable events are accounted as system failure: code or data integrity and code or data confidentiality. The code integrity is the most important property among others. Because a failure in code integrity can lead to data and code confidentiality and also to data integrity. In this paper, the representation within the attack tree will focus on the code integrity as the root of each tree.

3   Attacks Due to the Specification

The Java Card specification [2], specifies the necessary behavior and environment that a Java Card implementation should provide. In the Java Card specification, there are some points related to the card behavior which were not clearly defined. These points were firstly showed by Erik Poll at Cardis 2004. In his paper [4], he shows that in some implementations of the Java Card specification, serious security wreckages can be found. These problems resulted from the ambiguity of the specification and the interpretation of the designers. In this section, we describe these ambiguities in more details.

3.1   Abusing the Transaction Mechanism

The *transaction* mechanism aims to provide atomicity to the operations on persistent data elements. In the Java Card API, a method is also defined to give the ability to cancel the transaction operations by the developer. If the applet encounters an internal problem, the JCSystem.abortTransaction can be called to abort the transaction. It should also be mentioned that the transaction mechanism only applies to persistent data and not to the transient data.

The transaction mechanism abuse, exploits the creation of an object inside a transaction and the mis-operation of the platform to completely clean up object references after the JCSystem.abortTransaction call. The clean up task of the platform was not clearly mentioned in the old Java Card specs (objects created during a transaction must be garbage collected) and it caused ambiguity in the implementation of the Java Card platforms (a reference to this object should remain, becoming a dangling pointer). The transaction mechanism abuse exploits this ambiguity.

They define two arrays: aPers and aLoc which refer to the same short array. When the transaction aborts, the aPers reference which refers to a persistent object is set to null. In some implementations, the Java Card platform does not also sets the reference of aLoc to null. After the transaction abortion, this reference can still be used but it is a dangling pointer. If the attacker defines a new byte array exactly after the JCSystem.abortTransaction, the memory manager allocates the previously canceled area. Thus it returns the reference of aPers to this recently created byte array (because the platform supposes that this reference is released). Thus, the attacker can get access to the new byte array as a short array.

In this example, the attacker can access to the newByteArray with accessing 10 cells of aLoc which is of type short, so it leads to get access to 20 bytes. As it can be seen, it is two times bigger than the allowed length for the byte array. By defining the byte array big enough, the amount of un-allowed data retrieval can be extended.

3.1.1   Countermeasures

To mitigate this attack, one effective countermeasure is to forbid load of applets that have used JCSystem.abortTransaction method in their source or binary code. This solution is often encountered on old cards.

Most of the recent Java Cards perform a rigid clean up of the objects inside a transaction after an JCSystem.abor-Transaction call. Thus, all the references of the objects used in a transaction should be equal to null after an abort event.

3.2   Abusing Shareable Interface Objects

The Java Card platform protects installed applets and packages from access by other applets in different security contexts by the firewall. In some cases, it is needed that applets in different security contexts communicate and use services of each other in the presence of the firewall. Thus, the Java Card specification has defined a sharing mechanism to share services of one applet to other applets belonging to different security contexts.

The mechanism which provides access to objects in different security contexts is called Shareable Interface Objects (SIO). To use this mechanism, one needs to create an interface by inheriting the `javacard.framework.Shareable` class of the Java Card. This interface defines which services are shared with other applets. The client applets refers to this interface and call shared methods of the server applet which implements this interface.

In [6], the authors use the sharing mechanism to create a type confusion and get access to non allowed memory areas. They create a server and client applet with a fine difference in the interfaces that they use. As the compilation and loading of the server and client applets are done in separate steps, the Java Card platform does not notice that the client and server applets are using different interfaces. When the applets are installed on the card, the client gets access to a data with a different type than the server applets get access to it. Thus, the server applet is accessing its own byte array as a short array, which is a type confusion. As explained in the previous section, this type confusion can lead to access to the array data twice the array data length.

3.2.1 Countermeasures

To mitigate the SIO abuse, the platform can count the number of bytes that each entity tries to get access to it. In the above type confusion, suppose that the server applet's array has a length equal to N bytes. In a non-secure implementation of the platform, accessing this byte array as a short array can lead to access $N*2$ bytes. This scenario is depicted in Figure 1.

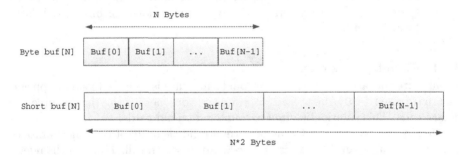

Fig. 1. Type confusion in accessing arrays

In a secure implementation of a Java Card platform, even if the attacker is able to get access to a byte array as a short array, he is only able to get access to the array with its defined length. The platform gives access to the arrays regarding the number of bytes and not regarding the number of elements of the array that occupies the memory.

As another countermeasure, the platform builds an internal table which stores definition of the methods in the interface, while loading the CAP into the card. On the other hand, it checks the methods that they call the interface methods regarding the definition of the methods in the Table. If there is a conflict, the platform will notice.

3.3   The Export File Fraudulence

The Java Card uses a two-step linking process [7]. The first step is done outside the card and the second step is performed inside the card.

In the off-card step, the Java Class files are converted to a CAP file. Each CAP file consists of at least eleven components. These components are: Header, Directory, Import, Applet, Class, Method, Static Field, Export, Constant Pool, Reference Location and Descriptor. There are also two optional components: Debug and Custom components.

In the process of conversion of a Java Class file into a CAP file, the necessary linkage information is stored in both off-card and on-card sides. In the off-card side, an export file carries this information which can be used for creating other CAP files afterward. The export files are publicly available files which are used to translate Java items into tokens in the off-card linking process.

The CAP file itself carries on-card linkage information in these three components: Constant Pool, Reference Location and Import components. The Constant Pool component contains the linking information between each tokens value and the corresponding reference in the method, class and/or package which needs to execute the byte code from the component. The Reference Location component specifies the offsets in the Method component where a token should be linked to a card internal reference [7]. The used packages by the applet is listed in the Import component of the CAP file. In the on-card linkage process, each token is converted to an internal reference.

In [7], Bouffard *et al.* use a manipulated export file to create a CAP file. In this fake CAP file, a malicious representation of an API method is provided. In their example they replace a malicious implementation of the buildKey API. This implementation stores a copy of the key it builds in a place of memory which can be retrieved by the attacker later. They insert the fake export file which contains malicious linking information into the export files' path and use it to create the CAP file. As the Java Card off-card linker uses a first match algorithm to find the export file for the linkage operation, it uses the fake export file. They also load the corresponding fake implementation of the buildKey API into the card. The attacker also loads the victim CAP file, which is the CAP file that has used the fake export file during creation. Thus, when the API is called inside the applet, the fake API will be called.

3.3.1   Countermeasures

To prevent this attack, the developer should protect the export files when provided by a third party. They must carefully check if the method name inside the export file can be confused with API method name.

3.4   Specification Ambiguity Attack Tree

The Fig. 2 depicts attack tree of the attacks due to specification ambiguity. The property that we expect to protect is the integrity of the code. And thus represents the root of the tree. A A_i label indicates an attack while a D_i represents a

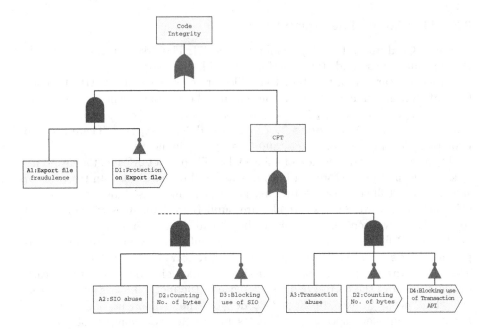

Fig. 2. Attack tree of the attacks due to the specification ambiguity

countermeasure. If one wants to setup a SIO abuse attack (A_2) it requires to neither count the number of elements (D_2) nor to block the use of shareable (D_3). The nodes in its hierarchy are OR gates, so the scenario is enough to succeed.

4   Attacks with Ill-Typed Code

Both Java and Java Byte Code languages are strongly typed languages. Type mismatches in the Java source code are detected at compile-time. To detect type mismatches at byte code level, a BCV, either off-card or on-card is required.

The byte code verification process is considered as a costly process, in terms of execution time and memory usage. Thus, currently most of the cards are not equipped with an on-card BCV. Recently, the Java Card specification 3 mandates the use of on-card BCV in the Java Card platforms for the connected edition. It is due to the fact that, in the off-line BCV approach, a verified CAP file can be manipulated by an attacker before loading it into the card. In [8], the authors developed a tool that can manipulate a cap file easily (for example after the CAP file is verified by an off-card BCV).

In the Global platform (GP) compliant Java Cards, off-card verified CAP files can be protected by Data Authentication Pattern (DAP) mechanism. In this mechanism, the CAP file is signed by a trusted authority and the resulted signature should be verified by the on-card representative of the signer before allowing the installation of the applet into the card. This mechanism needs to create Security Domain with DAP verification support and also inserting the required keys into the card. This scenario ensures integrity and authenticity of the CAP file.

The on-card BCV checks the CAP file when the applet is going to be loaded on the card. A manipulated CAP file can be detected by an on-card BCV. As the on-card BCV checks the CAP file in a static manner, some vulnerabilities that are related to the dynamic characteristic of the code, such as an overflow still remain undetected. To defeat such vulnerabilities, a defensive virtual machine can be used to check every operation before execution. But the performance issues of such a virtual machine should be taken into account leading to a trade off between performances and security.

In this section, we review attacks that are exploiting an ill-typed applet. The hypotheses are the ability to load applets on the card and the possibility to bypass the BCV mechanism.

4.1   The EMAN2

The Java Card Virtual Machine (JCVM) is a stack based machine. It creates frame in the stack for each method call and destroys it after method completion. Each frame comprised of two main parts: a data stack as a temporary place for the method's calculations and a locals area to store input parameters of the method and the method's local variables. To manage program flow, the Java Card virtual machine also keeps the return address of the caller method in an area with Last In, First Out (LIFO) structure like stack. The return address is considered as a system data and should be kept in a safe place far from access of attackers. There is a category of attacks which focus on changing the return address of the methods, called Control Flow Transfer (CFT) attacks.

In these attacks, the attacker is able to redirect program flow by changing the return address of a method to a desired address, usually to an easily editable area such as an array. The attacker changes program flow when the current method execution finishes and the control flow is resumed to the caller method. But if this address is modified by the attacker, the program flow will go to the desired address of the attacker and not to the caller's method. In some Java Cards, the return address of each method is stored in an area between locals and data stack. In such cards, if the attacker performs an overflow of the locals or an underflow from the stack, then he gets access to the return address of the method. The structure of the method's frame in such platforms is depicted in Fig. 3. This attack uses an ill-typed code to access the return address of the methods in a Java Card platform. The attacker modifies the return address of a method and redirects program flow to the address of a desired array. Then, he executes any malicious byte code by updating the array. It is supposed that the card is not equipped with an on-card BCV and the attacker has the card keys to load and install his own applet onto the card.

The EMAN2 attack introduced in [9] by Bouffard *et al.* at 2011. The authors characterize the frame by misuse of sload op-code and locate the return address

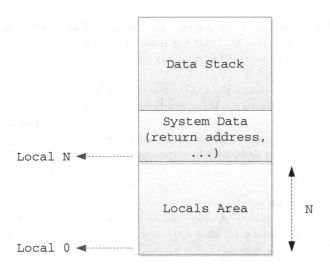

Fig. 3. A frame structure design in a Java Card platform

in the frame. As depicted in Fig. 3, if a method's frame has N locals, its local variables can be accessed using sload-0 to sload N-1 op-code. If the attacker uses sload N op-code and the platform does not throw any exception, it means that the platform does not detect overflow.

Listing 1.1. Method to retrieve address of an array

```
public short getMyAddressByte (byte[] tab) {
        short dummyValue = (byte)0x0A;
        tab[0] = (byte)0x12;
        return dummyValue;
}
```

In the cards that the system data is stored just above the locals area, the frame overflow may effectively lead to access to system data. In this case, the attacker gets access to the system data by increasing argument of sload op-code from N to whatever the length of these area is. After characterizing the system data area, and locating the return address in the system data, he updates the return address using sstore X, where X is the location of the return address in the frame. To complete this attack, the attacker needs to know the address of the array to redirect the program flow into it.

In the Listing 1.1, the targeted array is sent to the getMyAddressByte method. The corresponding op-code of the method getMyAddressByte is presented in the Listing 1.2.

Listing 1.2. Original code of getMyAddressByte method

```
Public short
   getMyAddressByte
        (byte[] tab){
03 //flags: 0 max_stack:3
21 //nargs: 2 max_locals:1
10 0A bspush 0x0A
31     sstore_2
19     aload_1
03     sconst_0
10 12 bspush 0x12
39     sastore
1E     sload_2
78     sreturn
}
```

Listing 1.3. Modified code of getMyAddressByte method

```
Public short
   getMyAddressByte
        (byte[] tab){
03 //flags: 0 max_stack:3
21 //nargs: 2 max_locals:1
10 0\,A bspush 0x0A
31     sstore_2
19     aload_1
78     sreturn
10 12 bspush 0x12
39     sastore
1E     sload_2
78     sreturn
}
```

The Listing 1.3 shows the manipulated version of the Listing 1.2. As it can be seen in the Listing 1.3, when the address of the array is pushed on top of the stack, the attacker returns this address by replacing the next op-codes with sreturn. Thus, the value on top of the stack, which is the address of the targeted array is returned by sreturn op-code.

4.1.1   Countermeasures

The EMAN2 attack, needs some conditions to succeed. The attacker must get access to the area above the locals, where the system data is stored. Thus, as a countermeasure a Java Card platform can check if an op-code is accessing an area out of the locals boundary. But these checks add an extra cost to each instruction while accessing locals. It has never observed.

Another countermeasure is to store system data in another area of RAM, in order to harden access of the attacker to this valuable data. The *Separate Stack* is to define another stack to store return addresses of the methods. This approach is discussed in more detail in Sect. 4.7 *Stack Underflow and Frame Overflow* and is often used.

The most implemented countermeasure is to check if a jump destination belongs to the minPC (minimum Program Counter) and maxPC (maximum Program Counter) value of the method. If the control flow has been transferred to a an array, this array is stored outside the bounds of the method and any execution of non linear code will be detected as illegal operation.

4.2   Subverting BC Linker Service to Characterize JC API

In [13], Hamadouche et al. introduced a method to characterize a Java Card platform in order to design rich shell code for that platform. To write a rich shell code, it is required to know the reference of the needed API methods and then directly calling the methods by their actual reference in the targeted platform.

Because most of the time the attacker hides his shell code inside an array, this code fragment is not subject to any linking process.

In the off-card linking step, while converting class files into a CAP file, the converter does not have any information about the reference of the methods or fields in the targeted card, so it uses tokens instead. At the loading step, the JCVM transforms these tokens in the Method component to their reference with the help of the Constant Pool component and the Reference Location component. Thus, as the reference of the objects, methods and other elements is not known for the attacker, he needs to firstly find these references in the targeted Java Card platform.

The authors in [13] create a set of malicious CAP files, whereas each of these CAP files contains a call to one of the JC API methods. They replace the instruction that precedes the token of the API method call in the Method component of the CAP file with a desired instruction. In the on-card linking step, this token will be translated to the reference of that specified API method in the card. Thus, if the attacker replaces the preceding instruction of that token to an instruction which prepares sending data out of the card, he can use this technique to find references of the methods in the targeted Java Card platform.

If the attacker wants to retrieve the address of the setOutgoingAndSend method of the Java Card API, he only needs to write an applet which uses this method and then replaces the invokevirtual instruction with the sspush instruction. This pushes the address of the setOutgoingAndSend method on the top of the operand stack. Then he can send it out of the card.

The authors used the on-card linker to retrieve reference of API methods in the targeted platform and send it out of the card. The corresponding CAP files are general and can be used to retrieve API references in other Java Cards without sufficient countermeasures.

4.2.1   Countermeasures

This attack is based on replacing an instruction that invokes a method with a desired instruction such as sspush. A countermeasure is to only resolve the token if the instruction requires a token (like invokevirtual, invokestatic, getstatic, setstatic, *etc.*) during the applet loading phase. Few cards implement such a policy.

4.3   The Stack Underflow Attack by Misuse of dup_x Instruction

In [10], Faugeron introduced a technique to get access to the data below the stack of the current executed method. She misuses the dup_x instruction to create an underflow and get access to elements stored below the current method. In some Java Cards, the system data such as context identifier are stored below the stack. Thus, in such cases the attacker can modify this data and gain privileged access to the card's resources.

The dup_x instruction takes two parameters which the first parameter indicates number of elements from the top of the stack that should be duplicated and inserted in the stack. The second parameter indicates the distance of the top of the stack that the duplicated elements should be inserted. The author misuses this operation by performing this instruction on a stack without enough data on it. In this case, the JCRE uses the system data below the current method as elements of the operand stack and the attacker gets access to them.

4.3.1 Countermeasures

This attack can be bypassed by a defensive JCVM which checks valid boundaries of the stack access for each operation that pops elements from the stack [10]. Few cards implement such a countermeasure.

4.4 The JSR/RET

The `jsr` and `ret` are two op-codes in the Java Card specification. The old Java compilers generated them while the `finally` statement was used after a `try-catch` statement [11]. Recent Java compilers do not generate the `jsr` and `ret` op-codes, but these two instructions must be supported by the JCVM only for backward compatibility.

The `jsr` and `ret` op-codes were used for executing subroutines [2]. The operand of the `jsr` instruction specifies the address of the subroutine that the program execution should be continued from there. Before jumping to the subroutine address, the JCVM pushes the return address (the address of the next instruction after the `jsr` instruction) into the stack. The compiler inserts an `astore` op-code as the first instruction of the subroutine to keep the return address in the locals area.

Using `ret` instruction, the return address from the local variables area is retrieved and pushed into the Java Program Counter (JPC) register. Thus, the program flow continues from the address of the next instruction of the `jsr` instruction.

The interesting point about this couple of instructions is that it provides easy access to the return address despite of where and how the return addresses are stored in the targeted Java Card platform. In [11], the authors misuse these couple of instructions to cause a CFT attack in the cards with no on-card BCV. The code in 1.4 shows how this attack is performed.

Listing 1.4. Byte code representation of `jsr/ret` abuse

```
short exploitJSRInstructionWithoutBCV () {
flags: 0 max_stack : 1 ;    nargs: 0 max_locals: 1
/*0053*/ L0: jsr L1
/*0056*/ sspush 0xCAFE
/*0059*/ sreturn
/*005a*/ sspush 0xBEEF
/*005D*/ sreturn
/*005E*/ L1: astore_1
/*005F*/ sinc 0x1, 0x4
/*0062*/ ret 0x1}
```

In the above code, after executing the code at line 0x53, the program flow jumps to the address 0x5E where the address of the next instruction (0x56) is stored in the local variable 1. But there is an instruction which manipulates the content of the local variable 1: sinc 0x1, 0x4. This line of code, adds 4 to the return address. Thus, when the subroutine execution finishes, the ret instruction pushes the manipulated return address (0x5A) into the JPC register. By executing the above code, the user will receive 0xBEEF instead of 0xCAFE at the output. Any other op-code which manipulates the content of the local variables can be used instead of sinc op-code to change the return address which is stored in the locals area.

This attack is based on performing arithmetic operations on the return address which is of reference type. Thus, if a Java Card platform is equipped with a typed stack, this attack can not be performed successfully, because in such Java Card platforms the operations on the stack are checked against their type. The authors of the article [11], proposed a method to successfully perform their attack on Java Cards with typed stack. They took advantage of putfield_<t>_this and getfield_<t>_this op-codes.

These two instructions manipulate instance data stored into the heap memory. The authors used putfield_a_this to store the return address into the heap area, and then used getfield_s_this op-code to retrieve and manipulate the return address as a short variable in a typed stack.

4.4.1   Countermeasures

The jsr/ret attack can be mitigated using a combination of a typed stack and inserting type checking in the heap memory. Inserting a type checker in the heap memory can stop misuse of the putfield_<t>_this and getfield_<t>_this op-codes to cause a type confusion and thus changing the return address as a short variable.

4.5   Stack Underflow by Abusing the Frame Creation Mechanism

In [17], the authors describe their attack method to get access to the (system) data below the operand stack. They use an ill-typed applet to cause a stack underflow. Each method in the Java Card has these following attributes which are determined at compile time: the size of the local variables ($nargs + max\_locals$) and the size of the operand stack (max_stack). The $nargs$ determines the number of arguments of a method whereas the max_locals determines maximum number of local variables for a method. These attributes are stored in the method_header_info structure of the corresponding method in the method component of the CAP file.

While the JCVM reaches to an invoke<> operation, it pops the arguments of the targeted method from the operand stack of the caller method and pushes them into the local variables area of the newly created frame for the targeted method of the invoke<> operation. The start of the newly created frame is equal to the value of the stack pointer (before invoking the method) minus the size of the local variables of the invoked method. Thus if an attacker illegally extends size of the local variables of a method, he will be able to get access to an illegal area as the area of the newly created frame.

The authors illegally extend the nargs value of the method and thus the frame allocation of the method is compromised. If the increase in the nargs be as much as it places the new frame below the start address of the stack, a stack underflow occurs. Thus the attacker will be able to get access to an undetermined memory area using aload op-code. This memory area might contain system data. The attacker might get system information by analyzing system data.

4.5.1 Countermeasures

This attack which uses ill-typed cap file can be blocked by the on-card BCV. Thus, presence of on-card BCV is the main countermeasure to this attack.

4.6 The ArrayCopyNonAtomic API Attack

The Java Card platform provides an API to copy the content of an array into another array. The Util.arrayCopyNonAtomic method has the following method signature: arrayCopyNonAtomic(byte[] src, short srcOff, byte[] dest, short destOff, short length)

In [12], the authors used this method to create a type confusion and get access to the meta-data of objects as data of array. The idea behind this attack is the fact that, while the type checking is the task of the BCV, if a card is not equipped with an on-card BCV, creating a type confusion might be possible.

In the Java Card's type system, an array is inherited from object. Arrays of different types (byte, short, etc.) are separated as branches of the type tree. In this attack, we created an ill-typed CAP file, where the source array were replaced by an object in separate branch than the byte type. The authors used reference of an instance of key class instead of the source array in Util.arrayCopyNonAtomic method and the card did not noticed this type confusion.

In the targeted platform, the card allowed to copy the content of the key object into the destination array. Thus, the authors were able to get access to a key object as an array and read its meta-data at the output. The code in Listing 1.5 is used to perform this attack.

Listing 1.5. Method used to retrieve key

```
public short CopyObject(byte[] dummyArray, DESKey deskey,
         APDU apdu){
Util.arrayCopyNonAtomic(dummyArray, (short)0, dummyArray,
         (short)0, (short)16);
apdu.setOutgoing();
apdu.setOutgoingLength((short)(16));
apdu.sendBytesLong(dummyArray,(short)0, (short)16);}
```

The code in Listing 1.6 shows the modification on the original code presented in the Listing 1.5. In the modified code, the source array is replaced by a key object.

Listing 1.6. Code snippet of `CopyObject` method

```
19 aload_1 -> 1A aload_2
03 sconst_0
19 aload_1
03 sconst_0
... ...
```

The reference of the *dummyArray* is replaced by the reference of the targeted key which is stored as Local variable 2. This type confusion attack can be repeated using other data types. The authors use `This` object to get more information about the platform's internals. They get access to the code of their applet in the EEPROM and also the reference of object's defined in their applet.

Moreover, they are able to write from an array directly into the memory by swapping the `src` and `dest` in the `arrayCopyNonAtomic` method. This gives them the capability to change their own code just using an API call.

4.6.1   Countermeasures

To mitigate this attack, it is needed to carefully check if the types of the data in the `arrayCopyNonAtomic` method is compliant with the type specified for each parameter. While performing this attack on the targeted platform, the authors noticed that the card raises an exception if the type of the `src` or `dest` array is `short`. Thus, it proves that the platform has implemented a type checker but it is not comprehensive. The platform designers have forgot that other types might be used for `src` and `dest` array.

This attack also uses arithmetic operations on the reference type. In the targeted Java Card platform, the authors had to increase the key reference by one to get access to the key value and its meta-data. Thus, if the platform be able to detect arithmatic operations on references, the `arrayCopyNonAtomic` attack can not be successfully exploited.

4.7   The Stack Underflow and Frame Overflow

As described earlier in Sect. 4.1, the JCVM is a stack based machine. In some Java Card platforms, the return address of a method with other useful information such as context of the method execution, number of local variables and *etc.* which we refer to them as system data, are stored below operand stack of each frame. An example of these type of stack implementation represented in Sect. 4.1. In some recent cards, two separate stacks are designed. One of them as the operand stack and the other one as the storage for the system data of each frame. We refer to this type of stack design as *Separate Stack*. In the *Separate Stack* design, the two stacks are growing as depicted in Fig. 4.

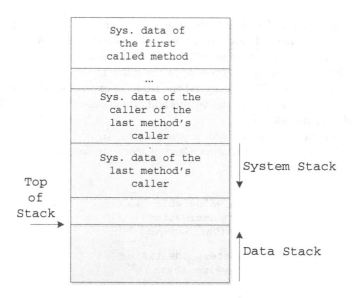

Fig. 4. *Separate Stack* scheme

In this section, we discuss a CFT attack in the cards that have implemented *Separate Stack*. This attack, which is described at [12], is based on creating a frame overflow and using underflow in the data stack to access and modify return addresses stored in the system stack. In this attack, the attacker uses an ill-typed applet to characterize system stack and then he changes the return address of a method in the system stack to direct program flow to his desired address.

The authors created a frame overflow by calling a recursive method 31 times in a Java Card which uses *Separate Stack*. Thus, They find how many calls of that recursive method creates a frame overflow. Then, they call the recursive method until one call before overflow occurrence (30 times). In the recursive method, they insert some specific byte codes which are only executed in the last call of the recursive method. These byte codes use sload X op-code to create an underflow in the stack. They also insert op-codes to send the value stored on the top of the stack to the terminal. Listing 1.7 shows this recursive method code.

Listing 1.7. The recursive method

```
private void exploreFrame(byte numberofCalls){
    if(numberofCalls==0) return;
    else
        if((numberofCalls==(byte)1)) {
                //an arbitrary code, we will change it
                //to a malicious code before loading
                //the CAP file into the card    }
        exploreFrame(--numberofCalls);
}
```

In the targeted Java Card platform, the authors created 256 CAP files which had used different operands for `sload` op-code, from 0 to 255. As the card did not raise any exception while executing these CAP files, they could experience frame overflow. Each `sload X` op-code in the different 256 CAP files returns a cell of the system stack. They analyzed the result of execution of these different CAP files. As they used a recursive method, they expected to find 30 equal values as the return address.

Analysis of the data of the system stack leaded to find the data pattern in the system data of the targeted Java Card platform as depicted in Fig. 5.

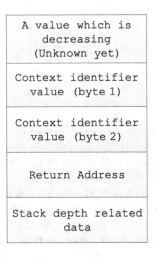

Fig. 5. General pattern for system stack

After characterizing system stack, the attacker are able to change the return addresses using `sstore` op-code. In the targeted Java Card platform, the authors could successfully change the program flow using this attack.

4.7.1 Countermeasures

This attack uses frame overflow and stack underflow. If one of these operations (frame overflow or stack overflow) is blocked, then the attack will not succeed. The following countermeasures mitigate this attack: A precise frame management be implemented to detect all violations of the boundaries, in such a way that the stack underflow can not generate a frame overflow [12].

The applet used in this attack is an ill-typed applet. If the card is equipped with an on-card BCV, the malicious op-codes is detected and the applet can not be installed on the card.

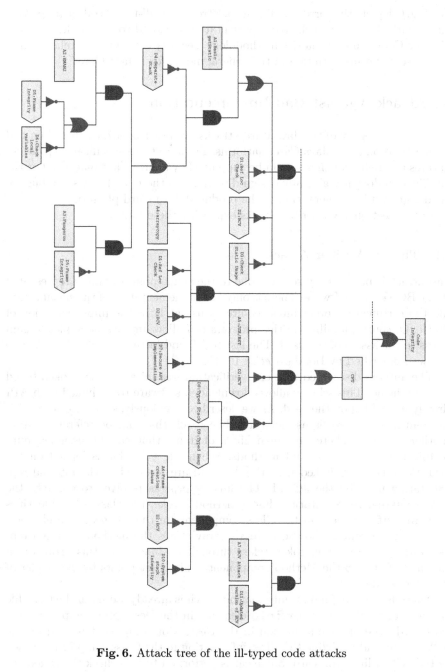

Fig. 6. Attack tree of the ill-typed code attacks

4.8   Ill-Typed Code Attack Tree

The Fig. 6 depicts the corresponding attack tree of the ill-typed code attacks. One can remark that the attack tree representation is closed to the model depicted with the Common Criteria [19] methodology: security concepts and relationship. It represents an instantiation of the general model for a Java Card.

5   Attack Against Bad Implementation

In the final category of the Java Card attacks, we describe attacks based on bad implementation of the Java Card platforms. The Java Card specification provides features and behavior that should be supported by a Java Card platform but the specification does not give any design direction. So there might be some bugs in the design and implementation of the produced Java Card platform.

In this section we describe attacks exploiting these bugs.

5.1   The BC Verifier Attack

This attack is particularly sensible due to the single point of failure represented by the BC Verifier software. There is only one implementation of the specification and the certification procedures require to use at least the implementation of Oracle. Of course, a failure in this program can allow any hostile applet to gain access to the assets of the card. The last bug found in this critical piece of code has been described by Bouffard *et al.* in [15,16].

The authors discovered that one verification was missing in the token-based linking scheme. This scheme allows downloaded software to be linked with API already embedded on the card. As we described previously, each externally visible item in a package is assigned a public token that can be referenced from another package. There are three kinds of items that can be assigned public tokens: classes, fields and methods. When the CAP file is loaded on the card, the tokens are linked with the API and are resolved to the internal representation used by the JCVM. The linking process resolves tokens into the JCVM internal representation. For a method invoke, the class token identifies a `class_info` element in the Class component. In the `class_info` element, the `public_virtual_method_table` array stores the methods internal representation. The method token refers through an index into this array to an absolute offset into the Method component. This offset points to the header of the refereed method.

This offset is a redundant information which is already stored in the CAP file in the `method_descriptor_info` elements in the Descriptor component. On most cards, the offset information in the Descriptor component is used by the BCV before loading, while the offset information in the Class component is used by the JCVM linker on card. Some cards perform a test to check the coherence between this redundant information. An ill-formed offset information in the Class component remains undetected by the BCV checks, but it is still used by some

JCVM linker on card. If the last entry of the public_virtual_method_table is removed then the on card linker will use the next bytes to form its offset. The Method component is the component loaded after the Class component and this is under the control of the attacker.

The authors have developed a proof of concept where they remove the last entry, design the header of the first method to be understandable either as a correct method header but also as an absolute offset allowing to jump in a dedicated fragment of code. This allowed them to execute any arbitrary shell code. The last version of the BCV corrects this flaw.

5.2 Stack Overflow and Changing the Security Context of a Method

In the Sect. 4.7, the authors used an ill-typed applet to get access to the system stack of a Java Card while the card has implemented *Separate Stack*. In [14], Dubreuil uses a well-typed applet to create frame overflow and get access to the system stack in a card equipped with *Separate Stack*. He uses the frame overflow to get access to all objects of the targeted Java Card platform and change the security context of a method to JCRE context. In his paper, he uses a verified Java Card applet which contains a method with some specified local variables and objects in it. He also calls other methods of his applet in order to fill the stack of the targeted Java Card platform. The targeted card, has implemented *Separate Stack*, thus its stacks are growing as depicted Fig. 4.

In his experiments on the targeted Java Card platform, he fills the stack until only two bytes of the data stack are available. Upper than these two bytes, the system data of the caller method is stored.

Then he calls a method which creates overflow in the data stack that causes to update system data of the previously called method (the caller of current method). This situation is depicted in Fig. 7. In the targeted Java Card platform,

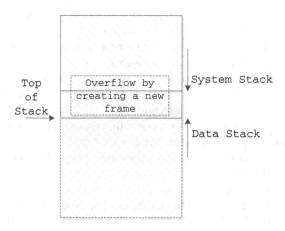

Fig. 7. Stack overflow in a card which uses *Separate Stack*

the platform does not notice that a frame overflow is occurred and the attacker misuses this vulnerability to change system data of the methods.

In the system data of each frame, the number of available local variables is also stored. Thus, he designs his last called method in a way to decrease number of local variables of the caller method to a desired number. For example if he changes the number of local variables of a method from 9 to 3, different data in the stack will be interpreted as the real data of that particular frame. Moreover, type of these data is also changed and type confusion can occur. This issue is showed in Fig. 8.

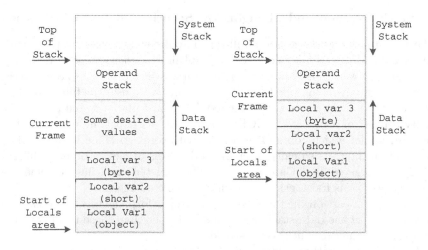

Fig. 8. Changing size of local variables in a frame

As it can be seen in Fig. 8, after changing the size of the local variables area, other bytes of the stack are interpreted as the original local variables. For example the bytes stored upper than the first local variable are interpreted as the first local variable. Suppose that for the first local variable which its type is reference, we can update it by a desired value with other types like short. Using this technique, the attacker can receive input data, for example as short type and update an area where a reference is stored. This can also happen to change the execution context of a method.

In this paper, the author could successfully change the context of a method to the JCRE context. The JCRE context is a privileged context, so the attacker can access to all objects despite of the existence of firewall mechanism.

The applet used for this attack is a completely verified applet and no modification after the conversion has been made on it. Only mismanagement in the stack pointer of this platform, leaded to change the security context of a method in the targeted Java Card. The author exploited this bug in the platform to dump all the objects of the targeted Java Card.

5.3   Bad Implementation Attack Tree

The Fig. 9 depicts attack tree of the bad implementation of the platform. Of course, this attack tree is only relevant to the published weaknesses and is probably larger.

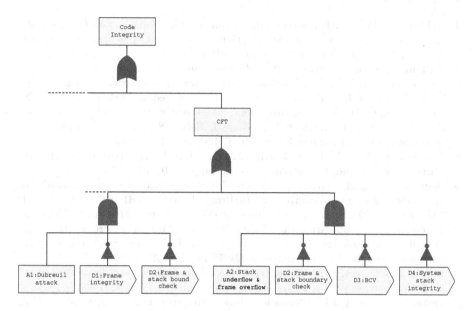

Fig. 9. Attack tree of the bad implementation attacks

6   Conclusion

In this paper, we pointed out the different categories of attacks against the most secure device: the smart card and in particular the Java Card. Researchers focused on hardware attacks while more simple attacks were still possible. Specification ambiguities, bugs in the implementations, characterization of platforms have led to pure software attacks against this platform. Most of the attacks can be mitigated either by correct implementations but also by implementing adequate countermeasures. We presented all this attack with the formalism of Attack Tree which provides a synthetic and graphical view of both the attack scenario but also the set of available countermeasures.

We verified that several implementations did not implement these countermeasures and thus are subject to attacks. Of course, the publicly available products are often old products and do not reflect the state of the art of current Java Card products. Nevertheless, some recent publications of Security Evaluation centers try to demonstrate that even recent products are subject to bad design.

References

1. Rankl, W., Effing, W.: Smart Card Handbook. Wiley, Hoboken (2004)
2. Oracle: Java Card Platform Specification. http://java.sun.com/javacard/specs. html
3. Sun Microsystems, Java Card Platform Security, Technical White Paper, October 2001
4. Hubbers, E., Poll, E.: Transactions and non-atomic API calls in Java Card: specification ambiguity and strange implementation behaviors. Department of Computer Science NIII-R0438, Radboud University Nijmegen (2004)
5. Witteman, M.: Java Card security. Inf. Secur. Bull. **8**, 291–298 (2003)
6. Mostowski, W., Poll, E.: Malicious code on Java Card smartcards: attacks and countermeasures. In: Grimaud, G., Standaert, F.-X. (eds.) CARDIS 2008. LNCS, vol. 5189, pp. 1–16. Springer, Heidelberg (2008). doi:10.1007/978-3-540-85893-5_1
7. Bouffard, G., Khefif, T., Lanet, J.-L., Kane, I., Salvia, S.C.: Accessing secure information using export file fraudulence. In: CRiSIS, pp. 1–5 (2013)
8. Noubissi, A., Séré, A., Iguchi-Cartigny, J., Lanet, J.-L., Bouffard, G., Boutet, J.: Cartes puce: attaques et contremesures. In: MajecSTIC 16.1112 (2009)
9. Bouffard, G., Iguchi-Cartigny, J., Lanet, J.-L.: Combined software and hardware attacks on the Java Card control flow. In: Prouff, E. (ed.) CARDIS 2011. LNCS, vol. 7079, pp. 283–296. Springer, Heidelberg (2011). doi:10.1007/978-3-642-27257-8_18
10. Faugeron, E.: Manipulating the frame information with an underflow attack. In: Francillon, A., Rohatgi, P. (eds.) CARDIS 2013. LNCS, vol. 8419, pp. 140–151. Springer, Heidelberg (2014). doi:10.1007/978-3-319-08302-5_10
11. Bouffard, G., Lanet, J.-L.: The ultimate control flow transfer in a Java based smart card. Comput. Secur. **50**(2015), 3346 (2015). doi:10.1016/j.cose.01.004
12. Farhadi, M. , Lanet, J.L.: Chronicle of Java Card death. J. Comput. Virol. Hacking Tech. 1–15 (2016). doi:10.1007/s11416-016-0276-0
13. Hamadouche, S., Bouffard, G., Lanet, J.-L., Dorsemaine, B., Nouhant, B., Magloire, A., Reygnaud, A.: Subverting byte code linker service to characterize Java Card API. In: Seventh Conference on Network and Information Systems Security (SAR-SSI), pp. 75–81 (2012)
14. Dubreuil J.: Java Card security, software and combined attacks. In: SSTIC (2016)
15. Lancia, J., Bouffard, G.: Java Card virtual machine compromising from a byte code verified applet. In: 14th CARDIS, Bochum, pp. 75–88 (2015)
16. Lancia, J., Bouffard, G.: Fuzzing and overflows in Java Card smart cards. In: SSTIC Conference, Rennes, France, June 2016
17. Laugier, B., Razafindralambo, T.: Misuse of frame creation to exploit stack underflow attacks on Java Card. In: Homma, N., Medwed, M. (eds.) CARDIS 2015. LNCS, vol. 9514, pp. 89–104. Springer, Heidelberg (2016). doi:10.1007/978-3-319-31271-2_6
18. Schneier, B.: Attack trees. Dr. Dobb J. **24**(12), 21–29 (1999)
19. Common Criteria, Common Criteria for Information Technology Security Evaluation, version 3.1, July 2009

Security of Identity-Based Encryption Schemes from Quadratic Residues

Ferucio Laurenţiu Ţiplea[⊠], Sorin Iftene, George Teşeleanu, and Anca-Maria Nica

Department of Computer Science,
"Alexandru Ioan Cuza" University of Iaşi, 700506 Iaşi, Romania
ferucio.tiplea@uaic.ro, {siftene,george.teseleanu,
anca.nica}@info.uaic.ro

Abstract. The aim of this paper is to provide an overview on the newest results regarding the security of identity-based encryption schemes from quadratic residuosity. It is shown that the only secure schemes are the Cocks and Boneh-Gentry-Hamburg schemes (except of anonymous variations of them).

1 Introduction

Identity-based cryptography (IBC) was proposed in 1984 by Shamir [19] who formulated its basic principles but he was unable to provide a solution to it, except for an identity-based signature (IBS) scheme. A standard scenario on using identity-based encryption (IBE) is as follows. Whenever Alice wants to send a message m to Bob, she encrypts m by using Bob's identity $ID(B)$. In order to decrypt the message received from Alice, Bob asks the Private-Key Generator PKG to deliver him the private key associated to $ID(B)$.

In 2000, Sakai, Ohgishi and Kasahara [17] have proposed an identity-based key agreement (IBKM) scheme, and one year later, Cocks [7] and Boneh and Franklin [5] have proposed the first IBE schemes. Cocks' solution is based on quadratic residues. It encrypts a message bit by bit and requires $2 \log n$ bits of cipher-text per bit of plain-text. The scheme is quite fast but its main disadvantage is the ciphertext expansion. The Boneh and Franklin's solution is based on bilinear maps. Moreover, Boneh and Franklin also proposed a formal security model for IBE, and proved that their scheme is secure under the Bilinear Diffie-Hellman (BDH) assumption.

The Cocks IBE scheme attracted the attention of many researchers. Of course, the main question raised by this scheme was about the space efficiency: how to extend it to encrypt arbitrarily large sequences of bits by reasonable large ciphertexts. A very elegant solution to this question was proposed by Boneh et al. [6]. Unfortunately, their solution suffers from a major deficiency: it makes use of a quartic deterministic time-complexity algorithm to compute solutions to some quadratic bi-variate congruences. Jhanwar and Barua tried to make a step further by proposing an efficient probabilistic algorithm [14] to replace the

© Springer International Publishing AG 2016
I. Bica and R. Reyhanitabar (Eds.): SECITC 2016, LNCS 10006, pp. 63–77, 2016.
DOI: 10.1007/978-3-319-47238-6_4

deterministic one. Unfortunately, their scheme, as well as some other variations, were recently shown insecure.

In this paper we review the newest security results on the IBE schemes based on quadratic residuosity assumption. We thus show that the only secure schemes are the Cocks and Boneh-Gentry-Hamburg schemes (due to space limitation we do not discuss on variations that provide anonymity). Our exposition starts with the Goldwasser-Micalli public-key encryption scheme as a warm-up, advances to the Cocks identity-based encryption scheme, and then to the Boneh-Gentry-Hamburg scheme. Finally, we focus on the insecurity of the Jhanwar-Barua scheme as well as variations of it.

2 Identity-Based Encryption

An IBE scheme consists of four probabilistic polynomial-time (PPT) algorithms: *Setup*, *Extract*, *Encrypt*, and *Decrypt*. The first one takes as input a security parameter and outputs the system public parameters together with a master key. The *Extract* algorithm takes as input an identity ID together with the public parameters and the master key and outputs a private key associated to ID. The *Encrypt* algorithm, starting with a message m, an identity ID, and the public parameters, encrypts m into some ciphertext c (the encryption key is ID or some binary string derived from ID). The last algorithm decrypts c into m by using the private key associated to ID.

A natural way to define security models for IBE is to extend the ones for public key encryption (PKE). Recall that for PKE, security models are obtained by combining *security goals* and *attack models*. Three fundamental security goals for PKE are:

1. *indistinguishability* (IND) [13], which means that, given a ciphertext of one of two plaintexts, the adversary is not able to distinguish which of the two messages was encrypted;
2. *semantic security* (SS) [13], which means that the adversary is not able to obtain any information about the plaintext from a given ciphertext;
3. *non-malleability* (NM) [8], which means that, given a ciphertext of a plaintext, the adversary is not able to construct another ciphertext whose plaintext is meaningfully related to the initial one.

The attack models for PKE, considered so far, are:

1. *chosen plaintext attack* (CPA) [13] – under this attack, the adversary can obtain ciphertexts of plaintexts of its choice (in the public key setting, giving the adversary the public key suffices to capture these attacks);
2. *non-adaptive chosen ciphertext attack* (CCA1) [15] – under this attack, the adversary obtains, in addition to the public key, access to a decryption oracle. This oracle can be queried only for the period of time preceding its being given the challenge ciphertext. The term "non-adaptive" refers to the fact that the decryption queries do not depend on the challenge ciphertext;

3. *adaptive chosen ciphertext attack* (CCA2) [16] – under this attack, the adversary gets, in addition to what it gets under the CCA1 attack, access to the decryption oracle after obtaining the challenge ciphertext. The only restriction is that the adversary may not query the oracle for the decryption of the challenge ciphertext. The term "adaptive" refers to the fact that the adversary may adapt its queries after obtaining the challenge ciphertext.

By combining security goals and attack models we obtain nine security models for PKE. For instance, indistinguishability against adaptive chosen ciphertext attack, abbreviated IND-CCA2, is the inability of an adversary to distinguish between two ciphertexts arising out of two equal length messages, although the adversary can adaptively access a decryption oracle. Relationships between these security notions for PKE have been deeply studied [3,4,11,13,20].

The security models for PKE can be adapted to IBE, but some care is needed because in this case a coalition of valid users (of an IBE scheme) can launch an attack against another user (of the same scheme) by pulling together their decryption keys. This aspect is modeled by ensuring the adversary with access to a key-extraction oracle. As for PKE, combining the security goals with the attack models we obtain nine security models for IBE. They are abbreviated by X-ID-Y, where X is a security goal and Y is an attack model. The relationships between these security models are pictorially represented in Fig. 1 [1]. As one can see, IND-ID-CCA2 is the strongest security model.

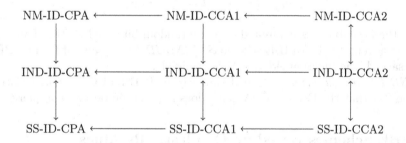

Fig. 1. Relationships between security models for IBE

Recall below the security models IND-IDCCA2 and IND-ID-CPA. For convenience, we will abbreviate IND-ID-CCA2 by IND-ID-CCA. These security models are best explained by means of a game played between the adversary $\mathcal{A}$ and a challenger.

<u>IND-ID-CCA Game</u>

Setup: The challenger takes a security parameter λ and runs $Setup(\lambda)$. It gives the adversary $\mathcal{A}$ the resulting system parameters PP, while keeping the master key msk to itself;

Phase 1: The adversary $\mathcal{A}$ issues a finite number of queries, where each query is of one of the following two forms:

Extraction_query(ID): The adversary queries the challenger for the private key corresponding to the identity ID. The challenger runs the *Extract* algorithm to generate the private key corresponding to ID and sends it to $\mathcal{A}$;

Decryption_query(ID, c): The adversary queries the challenger to decrypt the ciphertext c with the private key associated to ID. The challenger runs *Extract* to obtain the private key associated to ID and then runs *Decrypt* to decrypt c. Then, it sends the result to $\mathcal{A}$;

These queries may be asked adaptively, that is, each query may depends on the replies to the previous queries;

Challenge: Once the adversary decided that Phase 1 is over, it outputs two equal length plaintexts m_0 and m_1 and an identity ID^* which did not appear in any query in Phase 1 and on which it wishes to be challenged. The challenger picks a random bit $b \in \{0, 1\}$ and computes and sends $c^* = Encrypt(PP, ID^*, m_b)$ as a challenge to the adversary $\mathcal{A}$;

Phase 2: The adversary issues more queries just like in Phase 1, but with the following constraints: each *Extraction_query(ID)* must satisfy $ID \neq ID^*$, and each *Decryption_query(ID, c)* must satisfy $(ID, c) \neq (ID^*, c^*)$;

Guess: The adversary outputs a guess $b' \in \{0, 1\}$ and wins the game if $b = b'$.

The *advantage* of an adversary as in the IND-ID-CCA game in attacking an IBE scheme $\mathcal{S}$ is defined as a function on the security parameter λ

$$Adv_{\mathcal{A},\mathcal{S}}(\lambda) = |P(b = b') - 1/2|,$$

where the probability is computed over the random bits used by the challenger and the adversary $\mathcal{A}$. An IBE scheme $\mathcal{S}$ is *IND-ID-CCA secure* if for any PPT adversary $\mathcal{A}$, the function $Adv_{\mathcal{A},\mathcal{S}}(\lambda)$ is negligible.

IND-ID-CPA security is defined similarly to IND-ID-CCA security except for the fact that the IND-ID-CPA game does not contain decryption queries.

3   IBE Schemes Based on Quadratic Residues

The first IBE scheme not using pairings was proposed by Clifford Cocks in December 2001 [7], shortly after Dan Boneh and Matthew Franklin announced their IBE scheme in August 2001 [5][1]. The Cocks scheme is very elegant and *per se* revolutionary. It is based on the standard quadratic residuosity assumption modulo an RSA composite (in the random oracle model). In order to understand the Cocks' IBE scheme, as well as other IBE schemes based on the quadratic residuosity assumption, it is a good idea to start with the Goldwasser-Micali public key encryption (PKE) scheme [13]. But let us first recall a few concepts and notations on quadratic residues.

---

[1] It was revealed that Clifford Cocks, a mathematician in the United Kingdom's cryptography agency GCHQ, had years earlier devised his IBE scheme, but this was classified by the UK government.

The Jacobi symbol of an integer a modulo an integer n is denoted by $\left(\frac{a}{n}\right)$. J_n stands for the set of integers in $\mathbb{Z}_n^*$ whose Jacobi symbol is 1, QR_n denotes the set of quadratic residues in $\mathbb{Z}_n^*$, and $SQRT_n(a)$ is the set of square roots modulo n of a. $\mathbb{Z}_n[x]$ is the ring of polynomials over $\mathbb{Z}_n$. The QR advantage of an adversary $\mathcal{A}$ against an RSA generator $RSAgen(\lambda)$ is denoted by $QRAdv_{\mathcal{A},RSAgen}(\lambda)$ (λ is a security parameter). If this advantage is negligible for all adversaries $\mathcal{A}$, we say that the QR assumption holds for $RSAgen$. Given a pseudorandom function (PRF) F, $PRFAdv_{\mathcal{A},F}$ stands for the PRF advantage of $\mathcal{A}$ against F. F is secure if $PRFAdv_{\mathcal{A},F}$ is negligible for all $\mathcal{A}$.

3.1 The Goldwasser-Micali PKE Scheme

The main idea behind the Goldwasser-Micali PKE scheme is the following:

– each bit is viewed as one of the integers -1 or 1 (this can be simply done by encoding $b \in \{0,1\}$ by $(-1)^b$);
– sending the bit 1 is equivalent to sending a quadratic residue $c = r^2$ modulo a Blum integer $n = pq$, while sending the bit -1 is equivalent to sending $c = -r^2 \bmod n$;
– the decryption of c requires to decide whether c is a quadratic residue modulo n. This can efficiently be done if the factorization of n is known; otherwise, it is hard to distinguish between a quadratic residue and a quadratic non-residue (remark that the Jacobi symbol $\left(\frac{c}{n}\right)$ can efficiently be computed and it is always 1 due to the fact that n is a Blum integer).

Goldwasser-Micali PKE scheme [13]

$Setup(\lambda)$: Generate $(p,q) \leftarrow Blum\_gen(\lambda)$ and compute $n = pq$. Then, output the public key n, while the factorization (p,q) of n is the private key;

$Encrypt(m,n)$: To encrypt a bit $m \in \{-1,1\}$ by the public key n, choose at random $r \in \mathbb{Z}_n^*$ and output the ciphertext $c = r^2 \cdot m \bmod n$;

$Decrypt(c,(p,q))$: Return $m = 1$ if $c \in QR_n$, and -1, otherwise. This can efficiently be done by testing whether $\left(\frac{c}{p}\right) = 1$ and $\left(\frac{c}{q}\right) = 1$.

Theorem 1 [13]. *The Goldwasser-Micali PKE scheme is IND-CPA secure under the QR assumption for Blum_gen.*

3.2 The Cocks PKE and IBE Schemes

The decryption in the Goldwasser-Micali scheme needs the factorization of n. The scheme below proposed by Cocks [7] is based on a similar idea but the decryption does not depend on the factorization of n. Moreover, n can be an RSA modulus and not necessarily a Blum integer as in the Goldwasser-Micali scheme.

Cocks PKE scheme [7]

$Setup(\lambda)$: Generate $(p, q) \leftarrow Blum\_gen(\lambda)$ and compute $n = pq$. Choose uniformly at random a private key $r \in \mathbb{Z}_n^*$ and output the public key (n, a), where $a = r^2 \bmod n$;

$Encrypt(m, (n, a))$: To encrypt a bit $m \in \{-1, 1\}$ by the public key (n, a), choose at random $t \in \mathbb{Z}_n^*$ such that $\left(\frac{t}{n}\right) = m$ and output the ciphertext $c = t + at^{-1} \bmod n$;

$Decrypt(c, r)$: Output $\left(\frac{c+2r}{n}\right)$.

The generation of $t \in \mathbb{Z}_n^*$ with $\left(\frac{t}{n}\right) = m$ can be done by repetition because the probability of success for a random choice of t is $1/2$. The correctness of the Cocks public key encryption scheme simply follows from the congruence

$$c + 2r \equiv_n t(1 + 2rt^{-1} + (rt^{-1})^2) \equiv_n t(1 + rt^{-1})^2$$

which shows that $\left(\frac{c+2r}{n}\right) = \left(\frac{t}{n}\right) = m$.

Theorem 2 [7]. *The Cocks PKE scheme is IND-CPA secure under the QR assumption for Blum_gen.*

The Cocks public key encryption scheme can now easily be transformed into an IBE scheme. Let $h : \{0, 1\}^* \rightarrow J_n$ be a truly random function which maps identities into integers with the Jacoby symbol 1 modulo n. Now, the only subtlety is that we cannot detect whether the output of h is a quadratic residue modulo n or not (recall that the output of h is conceived as a public key). However, it can be easily seen that if $a = h(ID)$ is not a quadratic residue, then $-a$ is (recall that n is a Blum integer and, therefore, -1 is a quadratic non-residue). The solution is then to encrypt a bit $m \in \{-1, 1\}$ both by a and $-a$. The private key of the decryptor will be a square root of a, if $a \in QR_n$, or of $-a$, if $-a \in QR_n$.

One may also remark that $-a$ can be replace by any product $e \cdot a \bmod n$ between a public quadratic non-residue e and a. Moreover, in this case n is not required to be a Blum integer. Thus, we arrive at the following general version of the Cocks IBE scheme.

Cocks IBE scheme [7]

$Setup(\lambda)$: Generate $(p, q) \leftarrow RSAgen(\lambda)$ and compute $n = pq$. Generate uniformly at random $e \in J_n - QR_n$ and output the public parameters $PP = (n, e, h)$, where h is a hash function that maps identities to $J(n)$. The master key is the factorization of n, namely (p, q);

$Extract(p, q, ID)$: Let $a = h(ID)$. If $a \in QR(n)$, set the private key as a random square root r of a; otherwise set the private key as a random square root r of ea;

$Encrypt(PP, ID, m)$: Let $a = h(ID)$. To encrypt a bit $m \in \{-1, 1\}$, randomly choose $t_1, t_2 \in \mathbb{Z}_n^*$ such that $\left(\frac{t_1}{n}\right) = \left(\frac{t_2}{n}\right) = m$. Compute then $c_1 = t_1 + at_1^{-1} \bmod n$ and $c_2 = t_2 + eat_2^{-1} \bmod n$ and output the pair (c_1, c_2) as being the ciphertext associated to m;

$Decrypt((c_1, c_2), r)$: Set $c = c_1$ if $r^2 \equiv a \bmod n$, and $c = c_2$, otherwise. Then, $m = \left(\frac{c+2r}{n}\right)$.

The correctness of the Cocks IBE scheme follows in the same way as for the Cocks public key encryption scheme.

Theorem 3 [7,12]. *The Cocks IBE scheme is IND-CPA secure in the random oracle model under the QR assumption for RSAgen.*

The Cocks IBE scheme encrypts a message bit by bit, and each bit is encrypted by $2 \log n$ bits, where n is the RSA integer used by the scheme. Therefore, the Cocks IBE scheme can be considered very bandwidth consuming. As Cocks remarked in his paper [7], the scheme can be used in practice to encrypt short session keys in which case it becomes very attractive.

3.3 The Boneh-Gentry-Hamburg IBE Scheme

In the Cocks IBE scheme, t_1 and t_2 are generated such that $\left(\frac{t_1}{n}\right) = \left(\frac{t_2}{n}\right) = m$. Therefore, we may say that t_1 and t_2 encrypt m, and they are transmitted to the recipient in a hidden way: t_1 and t_2 are encapsulated into c_1 and c_2, respectively. One may think to another way of encrypting the bit m. Namely, generate at random $t_1, t_2 \in \mathbb{Z}_n^*$ and encrypt m by (c_1, d_1, c_2, d_2), where $c_1 = m \cdot \left(\frac{t_1}{n}\right)$, $c_2 = m \cdot \left(\frac{t_2}{n}\right)$, $d_1 = t_1 + at_1^{-1} \bmod n$, and $d_2 = t_2 + eat_2^{-1} \bmod n$, where $e \in J_n \setminus QR_n$ is public. The decryption can be simply performed by computing $c_1 \cdot \left(\frac{d_1+2r}{n}\right)$ or $c_2 \cdot \left(\frac{d_2+2r}{n}\right)$, depending on whether a or ua is a quadratic residue modulo n. The scheme obtained in this way is less efficient than the Cocks IBE scheme but, a positive answer to the following question would change things: is there any way to (efficiently) compute, from the public parameters, two pairs of polynomials (f, g) and $(\bar{f}, \bar{g})$ such that the following property holds

$$\left(\frac{g(s)f(r)}{n}\right) = \left(\frac{\bar{g}(s)\bar{f}r}{n}\right) = 1$$

for some s known only by the encryptor and some r known only by the decryptor? If this question would have a positive answer, than one could encrypt the bit m by $(c, \bar{c})$, where $c = m \cdot \left(\frac{g(s)}{n}\right)$ and $\bar{c} = m \cdot \left(\frac{\bar{g}(s)}{n}\right)$. The decryption would be obtained by multiplying c by $\left(\frac{f(r)}{n}\right)$ or $\bar{c}$ by $\left(\frac{\bar{f}(r)}{n}\right)$ (r would play the role of a private key).

The above idea was exploited by Boneh, Gentry, and Hamburg in [6].

Definition 1. *Let n be a positive integer, $a, S \in \mathbb{Z}_n^*$, and $f, g \in \mathbb{Z}_n[x]$. We say that (f, g) is a pair of (a, S)-associated polynomials if the following properties hold:*

1. *if $a, S \in QR_n$, then $f(r)g(s) \in QR_n$, for all $r \in SQRT_n(a)$ and $s \in SQRT_n(S)$;*

2. *if $a \in QR_n$, then $f(r)f(-r)S \in QR_n$, for all $r \in SQRT_n(a)$.*

Roughly speaking, the integer a will play the role of public key, while each $r \in SQRT_n(a)$ will be a private key. The square roots of S are used to randomize the encryption. Thus, the first condition in Definition 1, which is equivalent to $\left(\frac{g(s)}{n}\right) = \left(\frac{f(r)}{n}\right)$, guarantees the correctness of the decryption process: a bit m is encrypted by multiplying it by $\left(\frac{g(s)}{n}\right)$, and the result is decrypted by multiplying the ciphertext by $\left(\frac{f(r)}{n}\right)$. The second condition in Definition 1 is less intuitive: it is necessary to prove security.

The following IBE scheme, called *BasicIBE*, was proposed in [6].

BasicIBE scheme [6]

% In this scheme, $\mathcal{D}$ is an unspecified deterministic algorithm that on
% input (n, a, S) outputs a pair (f, g) of (a, S)-associated polynomials,
% where n is a positive integer and $a, S \in \mathbb{Z}_n^*$.

Setup(λ): Generate $(p, q) \leftarrow RSAgen(\lambda)$, compute $n = pq$, generate $e \in J_n \setminus QR_n$, and choose a hash function $h : \{0,1\}^* \times \{1, \ldots, \ell\} \rightarrow J_n$ for some integer $\ell \geq 1$. Output the public parameters $PP = (n, e, h)$; the master key $msk = (p, q, K)$ is the factorization of n together with a random key K of some pseudo-random function $F_K : \{0,1\}^* \times \{1, \ldots, \ell\} \rightarrow \{0, 1, 2, 3\}$ (F_K chooses one of the four square roots of $h(ID, i)$ or $eh(ID, i)$, depending on which of them is a quadratic residue);

Extract(msk, ID): For each $j \in \{1, \ldots, \ell\}$, let $a_j = h(ID, j)$ and $i_j = F_K(ID, j)$. If r_0, r_1, r_2, r_3 is a fixed total ordering of the square roots of a_j or ea_j (depending on which of them is a quadratic residue), then the private key is $r = (r_{i_1}, \ldots, r_{i_\ell})$;

Encrypt(PP, ID, m): Assume $m = m_1 \cdots m_\ell \in \{-1, 1\}^\ell$ is the ℓ-bit sequence to be encrypted. The encryption process is as follows:

– Generate at random $s \in \mathbb{Z}_n^*$ and set $S = s^2 \bmod n$;
– For $j := 1$ to ℓ do
  • Compute $a_j = h(ID, j)$;
  • Compute $(f_j, g_j) = \mathcal{D}(n, a_j, S)$ and $(\bar{f}_j, \bar{g}_j) = \mathcal{D}(n, ea_j, S)$;
  • Compute $c_j = m_j \cdot \left(\frac{g_j(s)}{n}\right)$ and $\bar{c}_j = m_j \cdot \left(\frac{\bar{g}_j(s)}{n}\right)$;

– Return $(c, \bar{c}, S)$, where $c = c_1 \cdots c_\ell$ and $\bar{c} = \bar{c}_1 \cdots \bar{c}_\ell$;

Decrypt$((c, \bar{c}, S), r)$: The decryption process is as follows:

– For $j := 1$ to ℓ do
  • Compute $a_j = h(ID, j)$;
  • If $a_j \in QR_n$ then $a'_j = a_j$ else $a'_j = ea_j$;
  • Compute $(f'_j, g'_j) = \mathcal{D}(n, a'_j, S)$;

- Compute $m_j = c_j \cdot \left(\frac{f'_j(r_{i_j})}{n} \right)$;
- Return $m = m_1 \cdots m_\ell$.

The following theorem clarifies the security of the $BasicIBE$ scheme.

Theorem 4 [6]. *For any efficient IND-ID-CPA adversary $\mathcal{A}$ attacking the $BasicIBE$ scheme, there exist two efficient algorithms $\mathcal{B}_1$ and $\mathcal{B}_2$, whose running time is about the same as that of $\mathcal{A}$, such that:*

$$IBEAdv_{\mathcal{A},BasicIBE}(\lambda) \leq 2 \cdot QRAdv_{\mathcal{B}_1,RSAgen}(\lambda) + PRFAdv_{\mathcal{B}_2,F}(\lambda),$$

provided that h is modeled as a random oracle, the QR assumption holds for RSAgen, and F is a secure pseudo-random function.

We emphasize that the $BasicIBE$ scheme is an abstract IBE scheme because no concrete algorithm $\mathcal{D}$ to compute (a, S)-associated polynomials is presented. In [6], the method proposed to construct such polynomials is based on the congruence $QC_n(a, S)$ given by

$$ax^2 + Sy^2 \equiv 1 \bmod n, \tag{1}$$

where $n = pq$ is an RSA modulus and $a, S \in \mathbb{Z}_n^*$. Any solution (x_0, y_0) to $QC_n(a, S)$ gives rise to two polynomials f and g

$$f(r) = x_0 r + 1 \bmod n$$
$$g(s) = 2(y_0 s + 1) \bmod n$$

that are (a, S)-associated (see [6] for details).

The $BasicIBE$ scheme is more space efficient than the Cocks IBE scheme: ℓ bits are encrypted by $2\ell + \log n$ bits. The time complexity of the $BasicIBE$ scheme depends on the time complexity of the algorithm $\mathcal{D}$. If this implements the method described above, then the encryptor must solve 2ℓ equations of the form $QC_n(a_i, S)$ and $QC_n(ea_i, S)$, for all $1 \leq i \leq \ell$. The decryptor needs to solve only ℓ of these equations.

An improvement at the decryptor side can be obtained starting from the remark that if (x_1, y_1) is a solution to $QC_n(a, S)$ and (x_2, y_2) is a solution to $QC_n(e, S)$, then (x_3, y_3) is a solution to $QC_n(ea, S)$, where $x_3 = \frac{x_1 x_2}{Sy_1 y_2 + 1} \bmod n$ and $y_3 = \frac{y_1 + y_2}{Sy_1 y_2 + 1} \bmod n$.

Therefore, the encryptor only needs to solve the equations $QC_n(a_i, S)$ for all $1 \leq i \leq \ell$, and the equation $QC_n(e, S)$. This means $\ell + 1$ equations instead of 2ℓ equations.

The algorithm proposed in [6] to find solutions to $QC_n(a, S)$ is quartic in the security parameter, making thus the $BasicIBE$ scheme more expensive than all standard IBE and public key encryption schemes.

3.4   Jhanwar-Barua's IBE Scheme and Other Variations

A significant step in computing solutions to $QC_n(a, S)$ was made by Barua and Jhanwar [2,14] who have established the following characterization result for the solutions in $\mathbb{Z}_n^2$ to the congruence $QC_n(a, S)$.

Theorem 5 [2,14]. *Let n be an RSA modulus and $a, S \in \mathbb{Z}_n^*$. The solutions to the congruence $QC_n(a, S)$ satisfy the following properties:*

1. *If $S \in QR_n$ then, for any $s \in SQRT_n(S)$ and any $t \in \mathbb{Z}_n^*$ with $(a+St^2, n) = 1$, the pair (x, y) of integers given by*

$$x = \frac{-2st}{a + St^2} \bmod n \, and \, y = \frac{a - St^2}{s(a + St^2)} \bmod n \qquad (2)$$

is a solution in $\mathbb{Z}_n^* \times \mathbb{Z}_n$ to the congruence $QC_n(a, S)$.
Moreover, any solution $(x, y) \in \mathbb{Z}_n^* \times \mathbb{Z}_n$ to the congruence $QC_n(a, S)$ is as above, for some $s \in SQRT_n(S)$ and $t \in \mathbb{Z}_n^*$ with $(a + St^2, n) = 1$.
2. *If $a \in QR_n$ then, for any $r \in SQRT_n(a)$ and any $t \in \mathbb{Z}_n^*$ with $(S+at^2, n) = 1$, the pair (x, y) of integers given by*

$$x = \frac{S - at^2}{r(S + at^2)} \bmod n \, and \, y = \frac{-2rt}{S + at^2} \bmod n \qquad (3)$$

is a solution in $\mathbb{Z}_n \times \mathbb{Z}_n^*$ to the congruence $QC_n(a, S)$.
Moreover, any solution $(x, y) \in \mathbb{Z}_n \times \mathbb{Z}_n^*$ to the congruence $QC_n(a, S)$ is as above, for some $r \in SQRT_n(a)$ and $t \in \mathbb{Z}_n^*$ with $(S + at^2, n) = 1$.

Theorem 5 leads to the following simple probabilistic algorithm $\mathcal{Q}(n, a, S)$ to compute solutions to the congruence $QC_n(a, S)$, when $S \in QR_n$ and a square root s of S is known (of course, the algorithm can be correspondingly rephrased for the case when $a \in QR_n$).

Scheme 1. $\mathcal{Q}(n, a, S)$

Input: n, a, S, and s as above
Output: a solution (x_0, y_0) to $QC_n(a, S)$
  1: randomly choose $t \in \mathbb{Z}_n^*$ such that $a + St^2 \in \mathbb{Z}_n^*$;
  2: output $x_0 = -2st(a + St^2)^{-1} \bmod n$ and $y_0 = (tx_0 + s^{-1}) \bmod n$.

We emphasize that the probabilistic algorithm $\mathcal{Q}$ described above can not directly be used as an instantiation for the deterministic algorithm $\mathcal{D}$ in the BasicIBE scheme because it does not guarantee a correct decryption. Jhanwar and Barua have used it via a way to combine solutions differently than the one in [6].

Lemma 1 [14]. *If $(x_1, y_1) \in \mathbb{Z}_n^2$ is a solution to the congruence $QC_n(a, S_1)$ and $(x_2, y_2) \in \mathbb{Z}_n^2$ is a solution to the congruence $QC_n(a, S_2)$, then $(x_{1,2}, y_{1,2}) \in \mathbb{Z}_n^2$ is a solution to the congruence $QC_n(a, S_1 S_2)$, where*

$$x_{1,2} = \frac{x_1 + x_2}{ax_1 x_2 + 1} \bmod n \quad and \quad y_{1,2} = \frac{y_1 y_2}{ax_1 x_2 + 1} \bmod n, \tag{4}$$

provided that $(ax_0 x_1 + 1, n) = 1$.

Moreover, $x_{1,2} \in \mathbb{Z}_n^*$ if and only if $(x_1 + x_2, n) = 1$.

Now we are able to describe the IBE scheme proposed by Jhanwar and Barua [14]. In this scheme, $\mathcal{Q}(n, a, S)$ is the probabilistic algorithm described above to find solutions to congruences $QC_n(a, S)$).

Jhanwar-Barua IBE (JB_IBE) scheme [14]

Setup(λ): Generate $(p, q) \leftarrow RSAgen(\lambda)$, compute $n = pq$, generate $e \in J_n \setminus QR_n$, and choose a hash function $h : \{0, 1\}^* \rightarrow J_n$. Output the public parameters $PP = (n, e, h)$; the master key $msk = (p, q, K)$ is the factorization of n together with a random key K of some pseudo-random function $F_K : \{0, 1\}^* \rightarrow \{0, 1, 2, 3\}$ (F_K chooses one of the four square roots of $h(ID)$ or $eh(ID)$);

Extract(msk, ID): The private key is $r = r_j$, where $j = F_K(ID)$ and r_0, r_1, r_2, r_3 is an ordering of the square roots modulo n of $h(ID)$ or $eh(ID)$, depending on which of them is a quadratic residue modulo n;

Encrypt(PP, ID, m): Assume $m = m_0 \cdots m_{\ell-1}$ is the ℓ-bit sequence to be encrypted. The encryption process is as follows:

- Compute $a = h(ID)$;
- Compute $k = \lceil \sqrt{\ell} \rceil$;
- For $i := 0$ to $k - 1$ do
  - Randomly choose $s_i \in \mathbb{Z}_n^*$ and compute $S_i = s_i^2 \bmod n$;
  - Compute $(x_i, y_i) \leftarrow \mathcal{Q}(n, a, S_i)$ and $(\bar{x}_i, \bar{y}_i) \leftarrow \mathcal{Q}(n, ea, S_i)$;
  - Compute $c_i = m_i \cdot \left(\frac{2s_i y_i + 2}{n}\right)$ and $\bar{c}_i = m_i \cdot \left(\frac{2s_i \bar{y}_i + 2}{n}\right)$;
- For $i := k$ to $\ell - 1$ do
  - Compute $1 \le \alpha \le k - 1$ and $0 \le \beta \le k - 1$ such that $i = \alpha \cdot k + \beta$;
  - Use Lemma 1 to compute y_i from (x_α, y_α) and (x_β, y_β), and $\bar{y}_i$ from $(\bar{x}_\alpha, \bar{y}_\alpha)$ and $(\bar{x}_\beta, \bar{y}_\beta)$;
  - Set $s_i = s_\alpha s_\beta \bmod n$;
  - Compute $c_i = m_i \cdot \left(\frac{2s_i y_i + 2}{n}\right)$ and $\bar{c}_i = m_i \cdot \left(\frac{2s_i \bar{y}_i + 2}{n}\right)$;
- Return $(c, \bar{c}, x, \bar{x})$, where $c = c_0 \cdots c_{\ell-1}$, $\bar{c} = \bar{c}_0 \cdots \bar{c}_{\ell-1}$, $x = (x_0, \ldots, x_{k-1})$, and $\bar{x} = (\bar{x}_0, \ldots, \bar{x}_{k-1})$;

Decrypt($(c, \bar{c}, x, \bar{x}), r$): The decryption process is as follows:

- Compute $a = h(ID)$;
- Compute $k = \lceil \sqrt{\ell} \rceil$;
- For $i := 0$ to $k - 1$ do

- If $a_i \in QR_n$ then $m_i = c_i \cdot \left(\frac{x_i r_j + 1}{n}\right)$ else $m_i = \bar{c}_i \cdot \left(\frac{\bar{x}_i r_j + 1}{n}\right)$;
- For $i := k$ to $\ell - 1$ do
  - Compute $1 \leq \alpha \leq k - 1$ and $0 \leq \beta \leq k - 1$ such that $i = \alpha \cdot k + \beta$;
  - Use Lemma 1 to compute either x_i from x_α and x_β, or $\bar{x}_i$ from $\bar{x}_\alpha$ and $\bar{x}_\beta$, depending on weather a or ea is a quadratic residue;
  - If $a_i \in QR_n$ then $m_i = c_i \cdot \left(\frac{x_i r_j + 1}{n}\right)$ else $m_i = \bar{c}_i \cdot \left(\frac{\bar{x}_i r_j + 1}{n}\right)$;
- Return $m = m_0 \cdots m_{\ell-1}$.

The soundness of JB_IBE scheme follows easily from how associated polynomials can be computed from solutions to congruences $QC_n(a, S)$ and from Lemma 1.

As one can see, in the JB_IBE scheme the encryptor needs to solve $2k$ congruences, where $k = \lceil \sqrt{\ell} \rceil$, while the decryptor solves none. The ciphertext length is $2\ell + 2k \log n$ bits for a plaintext of ℓ bits.

Regarding the security of the JB_IBE scheme, it was argued in [14] that the scheme is IND-ID-CPA secure. More precisely, it was shown the following.

Theorem 6 [14]. *For any efficient IND-ID-CPA adversary $\mathcal{A}$ against the JB_IBE scheme there exist efficient algorithms $\mathcal{B}_1$ and $\mathcal{B}_2$, whose running time is about the same as that of $\mathcal{A}$, such that*

$$IBEAdv_{\mathcal{A}, JB\_IBE}(\lambda) \leq PRFAdv_{\mathcal{B}_1, F}(\lambda) + 2 \cdot QRAdv_{\mathcal{B}_2, RSAgen}(\lambda) + \frac{1}{2^k},$$

provided that h is modeled as a random oracle, the QR assumption holds for RSAgen, and F is a secure pseudo-random function.

Unfortunately, the JB_IBE scheme is totally insecure. The first security flaw was remarked in [9] and it can simply described as follows. If $i = \alpha \cdot k + \beta$ and $j = \beta \cdot k + \alpha$, then $y_i = y_j$ (according to Lemma 1). Therefore, the bits m_i and m_j are encrypted by using the same Jacobi symbol. This allows an adversary to easily win the IND-ID-CPA security game (in the challenge phase, the adversary chooses two messages m^0 and m^1 such that m^0 has identical bits on the positions i and j, while m^1 has different bits on these positions). This security flaw can be overcame if we choose k larger than $\lceil \sqrt{\ell} \rceil$ and we combine (x_i, y_i) with (x_j, y_j) only for $i \leq j$ [9]. In fact, k should be the least integer satisfying $\frac{k(k+3)}{2} \geq \ell$.

Although we correct the JB_IBE scheme as above, the $JB\hat{\_}IBE$ scheme is still insecure because from $x_0, \ldots, x_{k-1}$ one can compute $\left(\frac{2s_i y_i + 2}{n}\right)$ for all i [18]. Indeed, let (x_1, y_1) be a solution to $QC_n(a, S_1)$ and (x_2, y_2) be a solution to $QC_n(a, S_2)$. By Lemma 1, $(x_{1,2}, y_{1,2})$ is a solution to $QC_n(a, S_1 S_2)$, where $x_{1,2}$ and $y_{1,2}$ are as in the lemma. Then, if $a \in QR_n$ and $r \in SQRT_n(a)$ we obtain

$$(x_1 r + 1)(x_2 r + 1) \equiv_n a x_1 x_2 + 1 + r(x_1 + x_2) \equiv_n (a x_1 x_2 + 1)(x_{1,2} r + 1)$$

which leads to

$$\left(\frac{x_{1,2} r + 1}{n}\right) = \left(\frac{x_1 r + 1}{n}\right)\left(\frac{x_2 r + 1}{n}\right)\left(\frac{a x_1 x_2 + 1}{n}\right) \tag{5}$$

Moreover, if $S_1, S_2 \in QR_n$, $s_1 \in SQRT_n(S_1)$, and $s_2 \in SQRT_n(S_2)$ we also have

$$\left(\frac{2s_1s_2y_{1,2}+2}{n}\right) = \left(\frac{2s_1y_1+2}{n}\right)\left(\frac{2s_2y_2+2}{n}\right)\left(\frac{ax_1x_2+1}{n}\right) \qquad (6)$$

no matter a is a quadratic residue or not (see [18] for more details).

Now, it is straightforward to show that the JB_IBE scheme is not IND-ID-CPA.

In [9], Elashry, Mu, and Susilo tried to improve the upper bound in Theorem 6 by dropping the factor $1/2^k$ by using Damgard's assumption. This assumption says that it is hard to predict the Jacobi symbol of the next integer of a polynomial length sequence of consecutive integers. More precisely, given a λ-bit RSA modulus n and an integer a, it is hard to predict $\left(\frac{a+poly(\lambda)+1}{n}\right)$ knowing

$$\left(\frac{a}{n}\right), \left(\frac{a+1}{n}\right), \ldots, \left(\frac{a+poly(\lambda)}{n}\right)$$

where $poly$ is a polynomial.

In [9], Damgard's assumption is used as follows. Let (x_1, y_1) be a solution to $QC_n(a, S_1)$ and (x_2, y_2) be a solution to $QC_n(a, S_2)$. By using Lemma 1, these two solutions can be combined into a solution $(x_{1,2}, y_{1,2})$ to $QC_n(a, S_1S_2)$. Then, the authors claimed that, by Damgard's assumption, the probability of getting the Jacobi symbol

$$\left(\frac{2s_1s_2y_3+2}{n}\right) \qquad (7)$$

from the sequence

$$\left(\frac{2s_1y_1+2}{n}\right), \left(\frac{2s_2y_2+2}{n}\right) \qquad (8)$$

is $1/2$ (s_1 and s_2 are square roots of S_1 and S_2, resp.). Apart from the fact that the authors in [9] consider Damgard's assumption as a proved result (which is not the case), Damgard's assumption cannot be applied to this case because in between $2s_1y_1 + 2$ and $2s_2y_2 + 2$ may exist an exponential (in the security parameter λ) number of integers. Moreover, (6) shows clearly that the Jacobi symbol (7) can easily be obtained from the Jacobi symbols in (8) (recall that a can be publicly computed and x_1 and x_2 are known either from the ciphertext or can be computed from the ciphertext).

Later [10], the same authors (Elashry, Mu, and Susilo) tried to reduce more the number of congruences to be solved in order to get associated polynomials, and proposed a JB_IBE-like scheme. As they have used Lemma 1 to combine solutions, the flaw described above [18] still remains.

4   Conclusions

Designing an IBE scheme from quadratic residuosity, more space efficient than the Cocks scheme, is an interesting and valuable objective. The solution proposed by Boneh, Gentry, and Hamburg comes with a very elegant idea: associated polynomials. Unfortunately, their solution uses a quartic time-complexity deterministic algorithm to compute such polynomials from congruences of the form $ax^2 + Sy^2 \equiv 1 \bmod n$. The characterization proposed by Jhanwar and Barua for the solutions to such congruences is a valuable mathematical achievement that leads to efficient probabilistic algorithms to compute solutions. Unfortunately again, this probabilistic algorithm cannot be used in conjunction with the Boneh-Gentry-Hamburg scheme. The way it can be used to obtain IBE schemes, proposed by Jhanwar and Barua, leads to insecure schemes. The insecurity is generated by the fact that the Jacobi symbol of a solution obtained by combining two solutions can be derived from public elements from the Jacobi symbols of the corresponding solutions.

Summing up, the only secure IBE schemes from quadratic residuosity are the Cocks and Boneh-Gentry-Hamburg ($BasicIBE$) schemes (due to space limitation, our exposition did not take into consideration the anonymous variants of these schemes).

References

1. Attrapadung, N., et al.: Relations among notions of security for identity based encryption schemes. In: Correa, J.R., Hevia, A., Kiwi, M. (eds.) LATIN 2006. LNCS, vol. 3887, pp. 130–141. Springer, Heidelberg (2006). doi:10.1007/11682462_16
2. Barua, R., Jhanwar, M.P.: On the number of solutions of the equation $Rx^2 + Sy^2 = 1(\bmod N)$. Indian J. Stat. **72–A**, 226–236 (2010)
3. Bellare, M., Desai, A., Pointcheval, D., Rogaway, P.: Relations among notions of security for public-key encryption schemes. In: Krawczyk, H. (ed.) CRYPTO 1998. LNCS, vol. 1462, pp. 26–45. Springer, Heidelberg (1998). doi:10.1007/BFb0055718
4. Bellare, M., Sahai, A.: Non-malleable encryption: equivalence between two notions, and an indistinguishability-based characterization. In: Wiener, M. (ed.) CRYPTO 1999. LNCS, vol. 1666, pp. 519–536. Springer, Heidelberg (1999)
5. Boneh, D., Franklin, M.: Identity-based encryption from the weil pairing. In: Kilian, J. (ed.) CRYPTO 2001. LNCS, vol. 2139, pp. 213–229. Springer, Heidelberg (2001). doi:10.1007/3-540-44647-8_13
6. Boneh, D., Gentry, C., Hamburg, M.: Space-efficient identity based encryption without pairings. In: Proceedings of 48th Annual IEEE Symposium on Foundations of Computer Science, FOCS 2007, pp. 647–657. IEEE Computer Society, Washington (2007)
7. Cocks, C.: An identity based encryption scheme based on quadratic residues. In: Honary, B. (ed.) Cryptography and Coding 2001. LNCS, vol. 2260, pp. 360–363. Springer, Heidelberg (2001)
8. Dolev, D., Dwork, C., Naor, M.: Non-malleable cryptography. In: Proceedings of 23rd Annual ACM Symposium on Theory of Computing, STOC 1991, pp. 542–552. ACM, New York (1991)

9. Elashry, I., Mu, Y., Susilo, W.: Jhanwar-Barua's Identity-Based Encryption Revisited. In: Au, M.H., Carminati, B., Jay Kuo, C.-C. (eds.) NSS 2014. LNCS, vol. 8792, pp. 271–284. Springer, Berlin (2014)

10. Elashry, I., Mu, Y., Susilo, W.: An efficient variant of Boneh-Gentry-Hamburg's identity-based encryption without pairing. In: Rhee, K.-H., Yi, J.H. (eds.) WISA 2014. LNCS, vol. 8909, pp. 257–268. Springer, Heidelberg (2015)

11. Goldreich, O., Lustig, Y., Naor, M.: On chosen ciphertext security of multiple encryptions. IACR Cryptology ePrint Archive 2002:89 (2002)

12. Goldwasser, S., Cocks' IBE scheme, bilinear maps. In: Advanced Cryptography. MIT Lecture Notes, vol. 6876 (2004)

13. Goldwasser, S., Micali, S.: Probabilistic encryption. J. Comput. Syst. Sci. **28**, 270–299 (1984)

14. Jhanwar, M.P., Barua, R.: A variant of Boneh-Gentry-Hamburg's pairing-free identity based encryption scheme. In: Yung, M., Liu, P., Lin, D. (eds.) Inscrypt 2008. LNCS, vol. 5487, pp. 314–331. Springer, Heidelberg (2009)

15. Naor, M., Yung, M.: Public-key cryptosystems provably secure against chosen ciphertext attacks. In: Proceedings of 22nd Annual ACM Symposium on Theory of Computing, STOC 1990, pp. 427–437. ACM, New York (1990)

16. Rackoff, C., Simon, D.R.: Non-interactive zero-knowledge proof of knowledge and chosen ciphertext attack. In: Feigenbaum, J. (ed.) CRYPTO 1991. LNCS, vol. 576, pp. 433–444. Springer, Heidelberg (1992). doi:10.1007/3-540-46766-1_35

17. Sakai, R., Ohgishi, K., Kasahara, M.: Cryptosystems based on pairings. In: Proceedings of Symposium on Cryptography and Information Security, Okinawa, Japan, January 2000. Springer, Berlin (2000)

18. Schipor, A.: On the security of Jhanwar-Barua identity-based encryption scheme. Personal communication (2016, submitted)

19. Shamir, A.: Identity-based cryptosystems and signature schemes. In: Blakley, G.R., Chaum, D. (eds.) CRYPTO 1984. LNCS, vol. 196, pp. 47–53. Springer, Heidelberg (1985). doi:10.1007/3-540-39568-7_5

20. Watanabe, Y., Shikata, J., Imai, H.: Equivalence between semantic security and indistinguishability against chosen ciphertext attacks. In: Desmedt, Y.G. (ed.) PKC 2003. LNCS, vol. 2567, pp. 71–84. Springer, Heidelberg (2002)

Cryptographic Algorithms and Protocols

Long-Term Secure One-Round Group Key Establishment from Multilinear Mappings

Kashi Neupane[(⊠)]

Department of Mathematics, University of North Georgia, Oakwood, GA, USA
knneupane@ung.edu

Abstract. A new concept of security, long-term security, was introduced by Bohli et al. in 2007 as a security guarantee of a protocol even some security assumptions become invalid after the completion of the protocol. Following the notion of long-term security of Bohli et al., we present a one-round long-term secure group key establishment protocol in the random oracle model. The resulting solution is built on a multilinear map and timestamps. The protocol also offers integrity and strong entity authentication. The proposed protocol remains secure if either a server, who shares a symmetric key with each user, is uncorrupted or a Graded Decisional Diffie Hellman problem is hard.

Keywords: Long-term security · Group key establishment · Multilinear maps · Timestamps

1 Introduction

Key establishment protocol is one of the central areas of modern cryptography. Once a common key is established, the key can be used for sending the large amount of data within the group members in presence of adversaries. Before public key cryptosytem was introduced, only symmetric key cryptosystems were in use. These days, it is a common practice to construct a cryptosystem by using either a symmetric key or a public key. There are advantages and drawbacks of both cryptosystems. The major advantage of a protocol based on a symmetric-key cryptosystem is that it is very efficient and easy to implement. The usual requirement for the security of a symmetric cipher is that the cost of breaking the scheme is close to exponential in the key length because its security is based on an assumption that no better attack than bruit force search is known. On the other hand, a protocol based on a public key cryptosystem is much more structured as compared to a symmetric cipher because of algorithmic advances in solving the underlying problem. The prediction of the cost of breaking the scheme is far more challenging for public-key cryptography. The major drawback of a protocol based on the former one is that a trusted server, a third party, knows the secret key, whereas the major drawback of a protocol based on the latter one is that the protocol is no more secure and useful in case the underlying harness assumption breaks in the future. A long-term secure protocol is constructed based on two

© Springer International Publishing AG 2016
I. Bica and R. Reyhanitabar (Eds.): SECITC 2016, LNCS 10006, pp. 81–91, 2016.
DOI: 10.1007/978-3-319-47238-6_5

hardness assumptions which are independent of each other. A combination of two independent hardness assumptions keeps the protocol secure, even if one of the hardness assumptions becomes invalid after the completion of the protocol.

Bohli et al. [3] introduced the concept of long-term security and proposed a long-term secure two-party key establishment protocol. Their protocol requires three rounds, and is based on Decisional Diffie-Hellman (DDH) assumption and an assumption which is close to real-or-random indistinguishability of a symmetric encryption scheme. Later Müller-Quade and Unruh [10] extended the notion of long-term security in Universally Composable framework. Based on Bohli et al. [3], Neupane and Steinwandt [12] proposed an authenticated long-term secure three-party key establishment protocol based on Bilinear Decisional Diffie-Hellman (BDDH) assumption and real-or-random indistinguishability. Moreover, Unruh [13] defined a variant of the Universal Composability framework, everlasting quantum-UC, and showed that the concept of long-term security can be implemented on secure communication and general multi-party computation using signature cards as trusted setup. Neupane [11] presented a more efficient, two-round protocol, based on BDDH assumption and real-or-random indistinguishability. In this paper, we propose an authenticated long-term secure group key establishment protocol based on an unauthenticated one-round protocol presented by Garg et al. [7] using timestamps proposed by Barbosa and Farshim [1]. We use Graded Decisional Diffie-Hellman (GDDH) assumption as an underlying hardness assumption for public key cryptosystem, whereas the notion of real-or-random indistinguishability has been used for the security of the underlying symmetric cipher.

2   Preliminaries

As cryptographic tools we use a symmetric encryption scheme and a signature scheme. As a mathematical tool we use Approximate Multilinear Mappings, proposed by Garg et al. [7], which they have named as Graded Encoding System. In this section, we review underlying cryptographic tools and the mathematical tool.

2.1   Digital Signature Scheme

A digital signature is a method to sign a message electronically by a user which can be verified by anybody later. A digital signature protects data from being altered, respectively enables the detection of modification. We quickly review the definition of a signature scheme—for more details we refer to Menezes et al. [9].

Definition 1 (Signature Scheme). *A signature scheme $S = (\mathcal{K}, \mathcal{S}, \mathcal{V})$ is a triple of polynomial-time algorithms:*

– *A probabilistic key generation algorithm $\mathcal{K}$ which takes the security parameter 1^k as its input, and returns a key pair (pk, sk)—a public verification key pk and matching secret signing key sk;*

– A probabilistic signing algorithm $\mathcal{S}$ which takes message $M \in \{0,1\}^*$ and secret signing key sk as its inputs, and returns a signature σ on M;
– A deterministic verification algorithm $\mathcal{V}$ which takes a public key pk, a message M, and a signature σ for M as its inputs, and returns 1 or 0, indicating whether σ is a valid signature for M under the public key pk.

For pairs (sk, pk) output by $\mathcal{K}$, we require that with overwhelming probability the following condition holds: $\mathcal{V}_{pk}(M, \mathcal{S}_{sk}(M)) = 1$, for all messages M.

Definition 2 (Existentially Unforgeable Signature Scheme Under Chosen Message Attacks (UF–CMA)). *A signature scheme $\mathcal{S}$ is said to be existentially unforgeable under chosen message attacks if for all probabilistic polynomial time adversaries $\mathcal{A}$ the following probability is negligible (in k):*

$$Pr[(pk, sk) \leftarrow \mathcal{K}; (M, \sigma) \leftarrow \mathcal{A}^{\mathcal{S}_{sk}(\cdot)} : \mathcal{V}_{pk}(M, \sigma) = 1 \wedge (M, \sigma) \neq (M_i, \sigma_i)],$$

where M_i denotes a message submitted by $\mathcal{A}$ to $\mathcal{S}_{sk}(\cdot)$.

2.2 Real-or-Random Indistinguishability

Based on one of Bellare et al. in [2], we present the concept of real-or-random indistinguishability and we refer to the latter paper for a more detailed discussion. First we review the definition of symmetric encryption scheme and then give the definition of real-or random indistinguishability.

Definition 3 (Symmetric Key Encryption Scheme). *A symmetric key encryption scheme $\mathcal{SE} = (\mathsf{Gen}, \mathsf{Enc}, \mathsf{Dec})$ is a triple of polynomial-time algorithms:*

– *A randomized key generation algorithm Gen on input of the security parameter 1^k returns a secret key $K \in \{0,1\}^*$;*
– *A randomized encryption algorithm Enc on input of a secret key K and a message $M \in \{0,1\}^*$ outputs a ciphertext $C \in \{0,1\}^*$;*
– *A deterministic decryption algorithm Dec which takes the key K and a ciphertext C as its inputs, and outputs either a message M or an error symbol $\perp$.*

The scheme is said to provide *correct decryption* if for any secret key K and any message M such that ciphertext $C \leftarrow \mathsf{Enc}_K(M)$, it is the case $\mathsf{Dec}_K(C) = M$.

To formalize the security notion needed later, we use a *real-or-random oracle* $\mathcal{E}_K(\mathcal{RR}(\cdot, b))$ with the following properties: on input $b \in \{0,1\}$ and a plaintext $M \in \{0,1\}^*$,

– returns an encryption $C \leftarrow \mathsf{Enc}_K(M)$ of M, if $b = 1$
– returns an encryption $C \leftarrow \mathsf{Enc}_K(r)$ of a uniformly at random chosen bitstring $r \leftarrow \{0,1\}^{|M|}$, if $b = 0$.

For a ppt algorithm $\mathcal{A}$ now consider the following experiment where $b \in \{0,1\}$ is fixed and unknown to $\mathcal{A}$: a secret key $K \leftarrow \mathsf{Gen}(1^k)$ is created, and $\mathcal{A}$ has unrestricted access to $\mathcal{E}_K(\mathcal{RR}(\cdot, b))$. Further, $\mathcal{A}$ has access to a decryption oracle $\mathcal{D}_K(\cdot)$ which executes $\mathsf{Dec}_K(\cdot)$, subject to the restriction that no messages must be queried to $\mathcal{D}_K(\cdot)$ that have been output by the real-or-random oracle. We measure $\mathcal{A}$'s advantage as the difference $\mathrm{Adv}_{\mathcal{A}}^{\mathrm{ror-cca}} =$

$$\mathrm{Adv}_{\mathcal{A}}^{\mathrm{ror-cca}}(k) := \Pr\left[1 \leftarrow \mathcal{A}^{\mathcal{E}_K(\mathcal{RR}(\cdot, 1)), \mathcal{D}_K(\cdot)}(1^k) \,\big|\, K \leftarrow \mathsf{Gen}(1^k)\right] - \\ \Pr\left[1 \leftarrow \mathcal{A}^{\mathcal{E}_K(\mathcal{RR}(\cdot, 0)), \mathcal{D}_K(\cdot)}(1^k) \,\big|\, K \leftarrow \mathsf{Gen}(1^k)\right]$$

Definition 4 (Real-or-Random Indistinguishability). *A symmetric encryption scheme $\mathcal{SE}$ is secure in the sense of real-or-random indistinguishability* (ROR-CCA), *if for all ppt algorithms $\mathcal{A}$, the advantage $\mathrm{Adv}_{\mathcal{A}}^{\mathrm{ror-cca}}$ is negligible (in k).*

2.3　Brief Overview of Encoding System

The Graded Encoding System is based on various level encoding of an element of a coset of a polynomial ring. After brief overview of the underlying mathematical tools, such as construction of a polynomial ring, and its coset, we introduce the notion of Graded Encoding System. We briefly review the multilinear map procedures, one of the fundamental tools of our key exchange protocol. Finally, we review the security assumption, Graded Decisional Diffie-Hellman (GDDH) assumption in which the protocol is based on. For more detailed information about GDDH, we refer to Garg et al. [7] and Coron et al. [6].

Consider a polynomial ring $R = \mathbb{Z}[x]/x^n + 1$ with an integer n which is large enough to ensure the security. One generates a secret short ring element $g \in R$ and generates a principal ideal $I = \langle g \rangle \subset R$. An integer parameter q and another random secret $z \in R/qR$ are also generated. With the use of such parameters, each coset $e + I$ of the quotient ring R/I is encoded in multiple levels. The level-i encoding of the element $e + I$ is an element of the form $[c/z^i]_q$, where c is an element from $e + I$. Such encodings can be added and multiplied, as long as the norm of the numerator remains shorter than q. More specifically, the product of κ encoding of level 1 gives the encoding of an element in the level κ. For such level-κ encodings, one can then define a zero-testing parameter, $p_{zt} = [hz^\kappa/g]_q$, for some small $h \in R$. This zero-testing parameter is used to determine whether a level-κ encoding c is zero or not by computing $[p_{zt} \cdot c/z^\kappa]_q = [hc/g]_q$. When c is small the product $[p_{zt} \cdot c/z^\kappa]_q$ is small, while c is large the product $[p_{zt} \cdot c/z^\kappa]_q$ is large. Hence, zero from non-zero can be distinguished. Moreover, using this zero-testing parameter, two encodings of the two different elements from two encodings of the same element can be distinguished by subtraction.

Garg et al. [7] defined their notion of an approximate multilinear map which they call graded encoding system. In this notion, there are levels of encodings. Ring elements $\alpha \in R$ are considered as plaintexts, $\alpha.g$ in the source group are considered as level-1 elements, and a product of i level encodings represents level-i encodings. So, level-κ corresponds to the target group from multilinear maps.

Now we review the definition of κ-graded encoding system and then GCDH assumption from Garg et al. [7].

Definition 5 (κ-Graded Encoding System). *A κ-Graded Encoding System for a ring R is a system of sets $\mathbb{S} = \{S_i^{(\alpha)} \subset \{0,1\}^* : \alpha \in R, 0 \leq i \leq \kappa\}$, with the following properties:*

- *For every fixed i, the sets $\{S_i^{(\alpha)} : \alpha \in R\}$ are disjoint.*
- *There are binary operations $+$ and $-$ (on $\{0,1\}^*$) such that for every $\alpha_1, \alpha_2 \in R$, every index $i \leq \kappa$, and every $u_1 \in S_i^{(\alpha_1)}$ and $u_2 \in S_i^{(\alpha_2)}$, it holds that $u_1 + u_2 \in S_i^{(\alpha_1+\alpha_2)}$ and $-u_1 \in S_i^{(-\alpha_1)}$, where $\alpha_1 + \alpha_2$ and $-\alpha_1$ are addition and negation in R.*
- *There is an associative binary association $\times$ on (on $\{0,1\}^*$) such that for every $\alpha_1, \alpha_2 \in R$, every i_1, i_2 with $i_1 + i_2 \leq \kappa$, and $u_1 \in S_{i_1}^{(\alpha_1)}$ and $u_2 \in S_{i_2}^{(\alpha_2)}$, it holds that $u_1 \times u_2 \in S_{i_1+i_2}^{(\alpha_1 \cdot \alpha_2)}$. Here $\alpha_1 \cdot \alpha_2$ is multiplication in R, and $i_1 + i_2$ is integer addition.*

2.4 Multilinear Map Procedures

Instance Generation. The randomized $\mathsf{InstGen}(1^\lambda, 1^\kappa)$ takes the security parameters λ and κ, as its inputs and returns $(\mathsf{params}, p_{zt})$, where params is a description of a κ-Graded Encoding System and p_{zt} is a zero-testing parameter.

Ring Sampler. The randomized $\mathsf{samp}(\mathsf{params})$ takes a nearly uniform element $\alpha \in_R R$ as its input, and returns a level-zero encoding $a \in S_0^{(\alpha)}$, Note that the encoding of a does not have to be uniform in $S_0^{(\alpha)}$.

Encoding. The $\mathsf{Enc}(\mathsf{params}, i, a)$ takes a level-zero encoding $a \in S_0^{(\alpha)}$ for some $\alpha \in R$ and index $i \leq \kappa$ as inputs and returns the level-i encoding $u \in S_i^{(\alpha)}$ for some α.

Re-Randomization. The randomized $\mathsf{reRand}(\mathsf{params}, i, u)$ rerandomizes encodings to the same level i, as long as the initial encoding u is under a given noise bound.

Addition and Negation. Given params and two encodings relative to the same level, $u_1 \in S_i^{(\alpha_1)}$ and $u_2 \in S_i^{(\alpha_2)}$, we have $\mathsf{add}(\mathsf{params}, u_1, u_2) \in S_i^{(\alpha_1+\alpha_2)}$ and $\mathsf{neg}(\mathsf{params}, u_1) \in S_i^{(-\alpha_1)}$, subject to bounds on the noise.

Multiplication. For $u_1 \in S_i^{(\alpha_1)}$ and $u_2 \in S_j^{(\alpha_2)}$, there is $\mathsf{mul}(\mathsf{params}, u_1, u_2) = u_1 \times u_2 \in S_{i+j}^{(\alpha_1 \cdot \alpha_2)}$.

Zero-Test. The procedure $\mathsf{Zero}(\mathsf{params}, p_{zt}, u)$ returns 1 if $u \in S_\kappa^{(0)}$ and 0 otherwise.

Extraction. This procedure extracts a "canonical" and "random" representation of ring elements from their level-κ encoding. More specifically, $\mathsf{ext}(\mathsf{params}, p_{zt}, u)$ outputs $s \in \{0,1\}^\lambda$ such that:

– For every $\alpha \in R$ and $u_1, u_2 \in S_\kappa^{(\alpha)}$, $\mathsf{ext}(\mathsf{params}, p_{zt}, u_1) = \mathsf{ext}(\mathsf{params}, p_{zt}, u_2)$,
– The distribution $\mathsf{ext}(\mathsf{params}, p_{zt}, u) : \alpha \in_R R, u \in S_\kappa^{(\alpha)}\}$ is nearly uniform over $\{0, 1\}^\lambda$.

2.5 Hardness Assumptions

Graded Decisional Diffie-Hellman Problem. Garg et al. [7] modeled their hardness assumptions based on the discrete logarithm and DDH assumptions in multilinear groups. Here we recall the concepts of graded DDH problem (GDDH problem) as defined by Garg et al. [7] and reviewed by Coron et al. [6] which they formalized as the following process:

– $(\mathsf{params}, p_{zt}) \leftarrow \mathsf{InstGen}(1^\lambda, 1^\kappa)$
– Choose $a_j \leftarrow \mathsf{samp}(\mathsf{params})$ for all $1 \leq j \leq \kappa + 1$, a_j is a randomly and uniformly generated element in R
– set $u_j \leftarrow \mathsf{reRand}(\mathsf{params}, 1, \mathsf{enc}(\mathsf{params}, 1, a_j))$ for all $1 \leq j \leq \kappa + 1$, u_j is an encoding at level 1
– Set $\tilde{u} = \mathsf{reRand}(\mathsf{params}, \kappa, \mathsf{enc}(\mathsf{params}, \kappa, \prod_{i=1}^{\kappa+1} a_i))$, $\tilde{u}$ is an encoding of the right product at level κ
– Set $\hat{u} = \mathsf{reRand}(\mathsf{params}, \kappa, \mathsf{enc}(\mathsf{params}, \kappa, r))$, $\hat{u}$ is an encoding of a random product, r at level κ

The GDDH distinguisher is given as input either $\tilde{u}$ (encoding of the right product) or $\hat{u}$ (encoding of a random product), along with the $\kappa+1$ level-one encodings u_j, and must decide which is the case.

Graded Decisional Diffie-Hellman GDDH Assumption. The Graded Decisional Diffie-Hellman Assumption is that the advantage of any efficient adversary is negligible in the security parameter against Graded Decisional Diffie-Hellman Problem.

3 Security Model

Our security model is based on the one used by Bohli et al. [4] and [8], which in turn builds on work by Bresson et al. [5]. Additionally, we extend the security model by using timestamps as proposed by Barbosa and Farshim [1] to capture the notion of timeliness. In this model, each user is given a local clock at the beginning. The security model we use for our analysis includes strong entity authentication as one of the security goals as in Bohli et al. [4].

Protocol Participants. We denote by $\mathcal{U} = \{U_0, \ldots, U_n\}$ a polynomial size set of *users*, which are modeled as ppt algorithms, and each $U \in \mathcal{U}$ can execute a polynomial number of protocol instances Π_U^s concurrently ($s \in \mathbb{N}$). User identities are assumed to be bitstrings of identical length k and to keep notation simple, throughout we will not distinguish between the bitstring identifying a user U and the algorithm U itself. To a protocol instance Π_U^s, the following seven variables are associated:

acc^s_U: a Boolean variable, which is set to TRUE if and only if the session key stored in sk^s_U has been accepted;

pid^s_U: stores the identities of those users in $\mathcal{U}$ with which a key is to be established, including U;

sk^s_U: is initialized with a distinguished NULL value and after a successful protocol execution stores the session key;

sid^s_U: stores a non-secret session identifier that can be used as public reference to the session key stored in sk^s_U;

state^s_U: stores state information;

term^s_U: a Boolean variable, which is set to TRUE if and only if the protocol execution has terminated;

used^s_U: indicates if this instance is involved in a protocol run.

Initialization. In this timestamps model, local clocks are introduced, we provide each party with a clock variable, which is initially set to zero. Before the actual protocol executions take place, a trusted initialization phase *without adversarial interference* is allowed. In this phase, a (verification key, signing key)-pair $(pk_U, sk^{\mathsf{sig}}_U)$ for an existentially unforgeable (EUF-CMA secure) signature scheme is generated for each $U \in \mathcal{U}$; sk^{sig}_U is given to U only, and pk_U is handed to all users in $\mathcal{U}$ and to the adversary. In addition, a secret key $k_U \leftarrow \mathsf{Gen}(1^k)$ for the underlying symmetric encryption scheme $(\mathsf{Gen}, \mathsf{Enc}, \mathsf{Dec})$ is generated for each user $U \in \mathcal{U}$; this key is given to each user U and the server S. Thus, after this initialization phase, the server shares a symmetric key k_U with each user $U \in \mathcal{U}$.

Adversarial Capabilities and Communication Network. The network is non-private, fully asynchronous and allows arbitrary point-to-point connections among users. The adversary $\mathcal{A}$ is modeled as ppt algorithm with full control over the communication network. More specifically, $\mathcal{A}$'s capabilities are captured by the following *oracles*:

$\mathsf{Send}(U, s, M)$: sends the message M to instance Π^s_U of user U and returns the protocol message output by that instance after receiving M. The Send oracle also enables $\mathcal{A}$ to initialize a protocol execution by sending a special message $M = \{U_{i_1}, \ldots, U_{i_r}\}$ to an unused instance $\prod^s_U$. After such a query, $\prod^s_U$ sets $\mathsf{pid}^s_U := \{U_{i_1}, \ldots, U_{i_r}\}$, $\mathsf{used}^s_U := \mathsf{TRUE}$, and processes the first step of the protocol.

$\mathsf{Reveal}(U, s)$: returns the session key sk^s_U if $\mathsf{acc}^s_U = \mathsf{TRUE}$ and a NULL value otherwise.

$\mathsf{Corrupt}(U)$: for a user $U \in \mathcal{U}$ this query returns U's long term signing key sk^{sig}_U.

$\mathsf{Tick}(U)$: increment the clock variable at user $U \in \mathcal{U}$ and its new value is returned.

In order to achieve any short of timeliness guarantee by capturing the notion of synchronization of clocks, we define the following:

Definition 6 (δ-Synchronization). *An adversary in the timed BCPQ model satisfies δ-synchronization if it never causes the clock variables of any two honest parties to differ by more than δ.*

Now we review the concept of entity authentication based on timestamps from [1]. Let $t_B(E)$ be the function returning the value of the local clock at B when the event E occurred. Let $\mathsf{acc}(\mathsf{A}, \mathsf{i})$ and $\mathsf{term}(\mathsf{B}, \mathsf{j})$ denote that the event $\prod_A^i$ accepted and the event that $\prod_B^j$ terminated respectively. Let $\prod_A^i$ and $\prod_B^j$ be two partnered oracles where the latter has terminated.

Definition 7 (β-Recent Entity Authentication ($\beta - \mathsf{REA}$)). *We say that a key exchange protocol provides β-recent initiator-to-responder authentication if it provides initiator-to-responder authentication, and furthermore for any honest responder oracle $\prod_B^j$ which has terminated with partner $\prod_A^i$, with A honest, we have $|t_B(\mathsf{term}(\mathsf{B}, \mathsf{j})) - t_A(\mathsf{acc}(\mathsf{A}, \mathsf{i}))| \le \beta$.*

In addition to the mentioned oracles, $\mathcal{A}$ has access to a Test oracle, which can be queried only once: the query $\mathsf{Test}(U, s)$ can be made with an instance $\prod_U^s$ that has accepted a session key. Then a bit $b \leftarrow \{0, 1\}$ is chosen uniformly at random; for $b = 0$, the session key stored in sk_U^s is returned, and for $b = 1$ a uniformly at random chosen element from the space of session keys is returned.

Definition 8 (Partnering). *Two instances $\prod_{U_i}^{s_i}$ and $\prod_{U_j}^{s_j}$ are partnered if $\mathsf{sid}_{U_i}^{s_i} = \mathsf{sid}_{U_j}^{s_j}$, $\mathsf{pid}_{U_i}^{s_i} = \mathsf{pid}_{U_j}^{s_j}$ and $\mathsf{acc}_{U_i}^{s_i} = \mathsf{acc}_{U_j}^{s_j} = \mathrm{TRUE}$.*

Based on this notion of partnering, we can specify what we mean by a *fresh* instance, i. e., an instance where the adversary should not know the session key:

Definition 9 (Freshness). *An instance $\prod_{U_i}^{s_i}$ is said to be fresh if the adversary queried neither $\mathsf{Corrupt}(U_j)$ for some $U_j \in \mathsf{pid}_{U_i}^{s_i}$ before a query of the form $\mathsf{Send}(U_k, s_k, *)$ with $U_k \in \mathsf{pid}_{U_i}^{s_i}$ has taken place, nor $\mathsf{Reveal}(U_j, s_j)$ for an instance $\prod_{U_j}^{s_j}$ that is partnered with $\prod_{U_i}^{s_i}$.*

It is worth noting that the above definition allows an adversary $\mathcal{A}$ to reveal *all* secret signing keys without violating freshness, provided $\mathcal{A}$ does not send any messages after having received the signing keys. As a consequence security in the sense of Definition 10 below implies forward secrecy: We write $\mathsf{Succ}_{\mathcal{A}}$ for the event $\mathcal{A}$ queries Test with a fresh instance and outputs a correct guess for the Test oracle's bit b. By

$$\mathrm{Adv}_{\mathcal{A}}^{\mathsf{ke}} = \mathrm{Adv}_{\mathcal{A}}^{\mathsf{ke}}(k) := \left| \Pr[\mathsf{Succ}] - \frac{1}{2} \right|$$

we denote the *advantage* of $\mathcal{A}$.

Definition 10 (Semantic Security). *A key establishment protocol is said to be (semantically) secure, if $\mathrm{Adv}_{\mathcal{A}}^{\mathsf{ke}} = \mathrm{Adv}_{\mathcal{A}}^{\mathsf{ke}}(k)$ is negligible for all ppt algorithms $\mathcal{A}$.*

In addition to the above standard security goal, we are also interested in *integrity* (which may be interpreted a form of "worst case correctness") and *strong entity authentication*:

Definition 11 (Integrity). *A key establishment protocol fulfills* integrity *if with overwhelming probability for all instances* $\prod_{U_i}^{s_i}$, $\prod_{U_j}^{s_j}$ *of uncorrupted users the following holds: if* $\mathrm{acc}_{U_i}^{s_i} = \mathrm{acc}_{U_j}^{s_j} =$TRUE *and* $\mathrm{sid}_{U_i}^{s_i} = \mathrm{sid}_{U_j}^{s_j}$, *then* $\mathrm{sk}_{U_i}^{s_i} = \mathrm{sk}_{U_j}^{s_j}$ *and* $\mathrm{pid}_{U_i}^{s_i} = \mathrm{pid}_{U_j}^{s_j}$.

Definition 12 (Strong Entity Authentication). *We say that* strong entity authentication *for an instance* $\prod_{U_i}^{s_i}$ *is provided if* $\mathrm{acc}_{U_i}^{s_i} =$TRUE *implies that for all uncorrupted* $U_j \in \mathrm{pid}_{U_i}^{s_i}$ *there exists with overwhelming probability an instance* $\prod_{U_j}^{s_j}$ *with* $\mathrm{sid}_{U_j}^{s_j} = \mathrm{sid}_{U_i}^{s_i}$ *and* $U_i \in \mathrm{pid}_{U_j}^{s_j}$.

4 The Proposed Group Key Establishment Protocol

4.1 Description of the Protocol

The proposed protocol is an authenticated long-term secure group key exchange protocol. The protocol completes in one round with the help of a trusted server S, and makes use of polynomial rings, timestamps, and random oracle $H : \{0,1\}^* \to \{0,1\}^k$. In this protocol, all parties are allowed to broadcast only one message simultaneously. By Enc we denote the encryption algorithm of a symmetric encryption scheme that is secure in the sense of ROR-CCA, and by

---

The Protocol:

Setup($1^\lambda, 1^N$) - Takes a security parameter $\lambda \in Z^+$ and the number of participants N as its inputs. It runs InstGen algorithm (params, P_{zt}) ← InstGen($1^\lambda, 1^{N-1}$) and outputs (params, P_{zt}) as the public parameter. Additionally, the server S selects $k^{\mathsf{srv}} \leftarrow \{0,1\}^k$ uniformly at random and for $i = 1, \ldots, n$ computes $c_i := \mathrm{Enc}_{k_{U_i}}(\mathrm{pid}, k^{\mathsf{srv}})$.

Publish(params, P_{zt}, i) - The server publishes (pid, $c_1, \ldots, c_n$). Each party U_i chooses a random level-zero encoding $d_i \leftarrow$ Samp(Params) as a secret key and publishes the corresponding level-one public-key $w_i \leftarrow$ Enc(params, $1, d_i$). Each party U_i checks the local time value t_i, signs the message $w_i \| t_i \| \mathrm{pid}$, constructs a message $m_i = w_i \| t_i \| \sigma_i(w_i \| t_i \| \mathrm{pid})$ by concatenation, and broadcasts it.

KeyGen(params, P_{zt}, d_i, $\{m_i\}_{i \neq j}$) - Upon receipt of m_i from each party, U_j accepts the message m_i from U_i if:
  - the signature σ_i is successfully verified
  - $t_i \in [t_j - \delta, t_j + \delta]$
  - list L does not contain the pair (m, t)
  - U_j updates the list L adding pair (m, t_j)
  If all the verifications are successful, then each party U_i multiplies its secret key d_i by the public keys of all its peers $v_j \leftarrow d_j \prod_{i \neq j} w_i$. Thus, each user gets a level $N - 1$ encoding of the product coset $\prod (d_i + I)$. Finally, each party uses the extraction routine to compute $K \leftarrow$ ext(params, P_{zt}, v_j) and sets the master key $mk = (K \| k^{\mathsf{srv}})$. Each user computes the session key and session id as $\mathrm{sk}_{U_i} := H(mk \| 0)$ and $\mathrm{sid}_{U_i} := H(mk \| 1)$ respectively.

Fig. 1. Secure group key establishment

σ we denote an existentially unforgeable signature scheme. Finally, each user computes a session key and a session id using the same master key. Here P_{zt} is a level $N - 1$ zero-test parameter as described in Sect. 2.3. In this construction, we insist that the order of the quotient ring R/I be a large prime. The proposed protocol for establishing a common session key among users $U_0, \ldots, U_N$ with $\kappa = N - 1$, is described in Fig. 1.

4.2 Security Analysis

The security of the protocol in Fig. 1 can be ensured secure provided that the Graded Decisional Diffie-Hellman assumption holds on a polynomial ring $\mathbb{Z}[x]/x^n + 1$, invoked symmetric scheme is secure, and the underlying signature scheme is existentially unforgeable. More specifically, we have the following:

Proposition 1. *Suppose the underlying symmetric encryption scheme is secure in the sense of* ROR-CCA, *the signature scheme used in the protocol is secure in the sense of* UF-CMA, *and the GDDH assumption holds. Then the protocol in Fig. 1 is semantically secure, fulfills integrity, and strong entity authentication holds to all involved instances in the timed BCPQ model provided that at least one of the following conditions holds:*

- *The server S is uncorrupted.*
- *The GDDH assumption for the underlying GDDH instance generator holds.*

The proposition is proved in two steps. First, we prove it where the BCDH assumption holds and thereafter we show the case where the server is uncorrupted. We prove the security of the protocol in both cases by using a short sequence of games. Because of the page limit we do not include a proof here.

Integrity. If the event Collision has not occurred, and all the instances of honest users agree on a common session identifier $H(mk\|1)$, then all the honest users will have the same "master key" mk—and therewith partner identifier. With the session key being computed as $H(mk\|0)$, we see that equality of session identifiers with overwhelming probability ensures identical session keys too.

Entity Authentication. Successful verification of the signatures and successful verification of validity of timestamps on the Round 1 messages, ensure the existence of a used instance for each intended communication partner and that the respective v_i values are identical. The latter implies equality of both the pid_i- and the sid_i-values.

5 Conclusion

In this paper, we proposed a long-term secure one-round authenticated group key establishment protocol in the random oracle model. The one round protocol can be seen as expensive in the sense that shared keys with a server, signature scheme, and two hardness assumptions are involved. One of the main features of the construction is that each user has to sign just a single message in comparison to other authenticated group key establishment protocols. The hardness assumptions used in the protocols are widely used. This protocol is very suitable where the communication cost is high and each user can send only one message during the construction. The proposed protocol is based on Graded Diffie-Hellman assumption, real-or-random indistinguishability, and makes use of timestamps. Additionally, the protocol ensures the entity authentication and integrity of the protocol.

References

1. Barbosa, M., Farshim, P.: Security analysis of standard authentication and key agreement protocols utilising timestamps. In: Preneel, B. (ed.) AFRICACRYPT 2009. LNCS, vol. 5580, pp. 235–253. Springer, Heidelberg (2009). doi:10.1007/978-3-642-02384-2_15
2. Bellare, M., Desai, A., Jokipii, E., Rogaway, P.: A concrete security treatment of symmetric encryption, September 2000. http://cseweb.ucsd.edu/~mihir/papers/sym-enc.html
3. Bohli, J.-M., Müller-Quade, J., Röhrich, S.: Long-term secure key establishment. In: Schmidt, A.U., Kreutzer, M., Accorsi, R. (eds.) Long-Term and Dynamical Aspects of Information Security: Emerging Trends in Information and Communication Security, pp. 87–95. Nova Science Publishers (2007)
4. Bohli, J.-M., Vasco, M.I.G., Steinwandt, R.: Secure group key establishment revisited. Int. J. Inf. Secur. 6(4), 243–254 (2007)
5. Bresson, E., Chevassut, O., Pointcheval, D., Quisquater, J.-J.: Provably authenticated group Diffie-Hellman key exchange. In: Proceedings of 8th ACM Conference on Computer and Communications Security, CCS 2001, pp. 255–264. ACM (2001)
6. Coron, J.-S., Lepoint, T., Tibouchi, M.: Practical multilinear maps over the integers. In: Canetti, R., Garay, J.A. (eds.) CRYPTO 2013. LNCS, vol. 8042, pp. 476–493. Springer, Heidelberg (2013). doi:10.1007/978-3-642-40041-4_26
7. Garg, S., Gentry, C., Halevi, S.: Candidate multilinear maps from ideal lattices. In: Johansson, T., Nguyen, P.Q. (eds.) EUROCRYPT 2013. LNCS, vol. 7881, pp. 1–17. Springer, Heidelberg (2013). doi:10.1007/978-3-642-38348-9_1
8. Katz, J., Yung, M.: Scalable protocols for authenticated group key exchange. In: Boneh, D. (ed.) CRYPTO 2003. LNCS, vol. 2729, pp. 110–125. Springer, Heidelberg (2003). doi:10.1007/978-3-540-45146-4_7
9. Menezes, A., Van Oorschot, P., Vanstone, S.: Handbook of Applied Cryptography. CRC Press, Boca Raton (1996)
10. Müller-Quade, J., Unruh, D.: Long-term security and universal composability. In: Vadhan, S.P. (ed.) TCC 2007. LNCS, vol. 4392, pp. 41–60. Springer, Heidelberg (2007). doi:10.1007/978-3-540-70936-7_3
11. Neupane, K.: Long-term secure two-round group key establishment from pairings. In: Kotulski, Z., Księżopolski, B., Mazur, K. (eds.) CSS 2014. CCIS, vol. 448, pp. 122–130. Springer, Heidelberg (2014)
12. Neupane, K., Steinwandt, R.: Server-assisted long-term secure 3-party key establishment. In: SECRYPT 2010 - Proceedings of International Conference on Security and Cryptography, Athens, Greece, 26–28 July 2010, pp. 372–378. SciTePress (2010)
13. Unruh, D.: Everlasting multi-party computation. In: Canetti, R., Garay, J.A. (eds.) CRYPTO 2013. LNCS, vol. 8043, pp. 380–397. Springer, Heidelberg (2013). doi:10.1007/978-3-642-40084-1_22

RSA Weak Public Keys Available on the Internet

Mihai Barbulescu[1]([✉]), Adrian Stratulat[1], Vlad Traista-Popescu[1],
and Emil Simion[2]

[1] Computer Science Department, Politehnica University of Bucharest,
Bucharest, Romania
mbarbulescu@stud.acs.upb.ro, {adrian.stratluat,vlad.traista}@cti.pub.ro
[2] Faculty of Applied Sciences, Department of Mathematical Models and Methods,
Politehnica University of Bucharest, Bucharest, Romania
esimion@fmi.unibuc.ro

Abstract. It is common knowledge that RSA can fail when used with weak random number generators. In this paper we present two algorithms that we used to find vulnerable public keys together with a simple procedure for recovering the private key from a broken public key. Our study focused on finding RSA keys with 512 and 1024 bit length, which are not considered safe, and finding a GCD is relatively fast. One database that we used in our study is made from 42 million public keys discovered when scanning TCP port 443 for raw X.509 certificates, between June 6, 2012 and August 4, 2013. Another database used in the study was made by crawling Github and retrieving the keys used by users to authenticate themselves when pushing to repositories they contribute to. We show that the percentage of broken keys with 512 bits is 3.7 %, while the percentage of broken keys with 1024 bits is 0.05 %. The smaller value is due to the fact that factorization of large numbers includes new prime numbers, unused in the small keys.

Keywords: RSA · Public keys · Weakness · Vulnerabilities · GCD · Euclid · Internet · Common factor

1 Introduction

Generating proper random numbers is essential in nowadays cryptography. Random number generation has been long studied from both practical and theoretical perspectives [15,17] and vulnerabilities were found due to bad implementation (e.g.: using `srand(time(NULL))` in C for seeding). Also another important fact of the RSA key is it's length. In history we can denote the following milestones of RSA factorization:

- In 2000, a 512-bit RSA number, having 155 digits, was factored using the Number Field Sieve factoring method, same method that was used in the previous record, from 1999, to factor a 140 digit RSA modulus [14].

© Springer International Publishing AG 2016
I. Bica and R. Reyhanitabar (Eds.): SECITC 2016, LNCS 10006, pp. 92–102, 2016.
DOI: 10.1007/978-3-319-47238-6_6

– Between 2006 and 2008, Linux distributions Debian and Ubuntu had a bug
  in which less than 220 possible keys for SSH, OpenVPN etc. were possible
  to generate. Instead of mixing in random data for the initial seed, the only
  "random" value that was used was the current process ID. On the Linux
  platform, the default maximum process ID is 32768, resulting in a very small
  number of seed values being used for all pseudo-random number generation
  operations (see [8]).
– On the 12th December 2009 a study reports factorization of 768-bit RSA
  and claims that factorization of 1024-bit RSA key is considered 1000 times
  harder [19].

Multiple approaches were done in order to find out how severe and how often
can a RSA vulnerability occur. For instance in [20] it was found only an order of
0.003 % of insecure public keys (which have a common factor) from data provided
by EFF SSL [5] in November 2001 containing 6185372 distinct X.509 certificates
having multiple RSA key lengths. The main goal of the project was testing the
validity of the assumption that different random choices are made each time keys
are generated.

Another approach [18] is a large-scale study of RSA and DSA keys, focusing
on keys which are used in TLS (HTTPS) and SSH in which 5.57 % TLS hosts
and 9.60 % SSH hosts shared keys in a vulnerable matter, from a total number
of 5.8 million unique TLS certificates from 12.8 million hosts and 6.2 million
unique SSH host keys from 10.2 million hosts.

The approach in our paper was focusing on consequences of RSA issues that
someone might find with enough super-computing power and experiment with
various GCD implementations, using existing databases of RSA keys such as
continuous scan of HTTPS Ecosystem between 2012 and 2013 [16] or dataset
done by EFF SSL Observatory [5] in 2010.

The first analysis in our study was a sanity check session on 512-bit and
1024-bit RSA public keys from amongst 43 million unique certificates dumped
from a regular and continuous scan of HTTPS Ecosystem between 2012 and 2013
Sects. 2 and 3 will describe this problems and how a simple nmap on port 443 can
be done to obtain a certificate. This shows a simple Linux userspace approach
to extract X.509 certificates that was used in [16]. These keys are considered the
most vulnerable, that even ransomware viruses choose 2048-bit RSA length for
their keys. Also, the default length used in OpenSSH for RSA key generation
is 2048-bit. Section 5 will describe more of our results, using multiple common
divisor approaches.

The next focus in our study was to find if there are vulnerable Github public keys or not. Many Github users usually use OpenSSH in Linux (command
ssh-keygen) or Putty to generate their pair of public/private keys and upload
the public key on Github. By using a simple HTTP Request to Github API
one can extremely easily retrieve the SSH public keys of an user by using either
a link like https://github.com/torvalds.keys or https://api.github.com/users/
torvalds/keys.

About 97.7 % public keys on Github are `ssh-rsa`, while the rest of them are `ssh-dsa`. A similar effort was done by Cryptosense company. Their focus was on 2048-bit RSA keys (the most common amongst Github users), as these are 93.3 % from all the keys and only 4.2 % are 1024-bit length. In June 2015 from all Github keys there were also public keys with major vulnerability due to length: 2 keys with 256 bits to them and 7 that have 512 bit [1]. While crawling on Github, we did not manage to find these keys so the users might have got the warning and managed to retract them in time. Section 4 will detail our procedure to scan Github keys. The study from Cryptosense used an implementation of GMP-ECM (Elliptic Curve Method for Integer Factorization) [12] but there is no clear disclosure of their results [10].

In 2013, it was reported that an attacker can efficiently factor 184 distinct RSA keys out of more than two million 1024-bit RSA keys downloaded from Taiwan's national *Citizen Digital Certificate* database. The Ministry of Interior Certificate Authority (MOICA) from Taiwan confirmed that these keys were generated, using a low-quality hardware random number generator, by Renesas HD65145C1 chips inside Chunghwa Telecom HICOS PKI Smart Card and also no run-time sanity check was performed. [13] That is why, in Sect. 3 we describe briefly how we took a look at Estonia Electronic ID.

Lastly, another focus in our research was the ransomware virus. Ransomware represents the mechanism through which a hacker locks a resource owned by a user and demands a ransom in return for unlocking that resource. The resource locking is usually done through encryption. A cryptographic ransomware is capable of encrypting an entire filesystem using AES and then encrypt the AES password using RSA. Usually these viruses do not store the RSA public key on the victim's computer due to the known facts about RSA problems that they might have.

2   Background

2.1   Scanning for X.509 Certificates

A potential methodology for scanning HTTPS TCP port 443 in Linux can be described as follows:

- discover hosts with HTTPS (443) port activated. One can easily achieve this by using `nmap` command, similar to the following execution:

```
u@linux: ~ $ nmap --script=ssl-cert.nse -p 443 www.google.com
```

- completing a TLS handshake with responsive addresses and collecting the presented certificate chains. This can be achieved in Linux command line by using the `openssl` suite:

```
u@linux: ~ $ openssl s_client -crlf -connect www.example.net:443
```

- parse and validate certificate. A full C example of how this can be done using OpenSSL library is described in [11].

2.2 RSA Background

RSA is one of the most well known and most used asymmetric cryptographic algorithm which uses two keys for the encryption and decryption process: a public key and a private key. The public key is represented by an exponent e and by a modulus N. The modulus is computed as the product of two randomly private generated prime numbers p and q. The private key d can be computed using the following formula:

$$d = e^-1 \mod (p-1)(q-1)$$

Since p and q are unknown the best way to calculate the private key is to factor the modulus N and obtain the two prime numbers. However, this kind of attack can be unfeasible given a certain RSA key length. A better approach is to try to find if the moduli from multiple RSA public keys have a common factor.

2.3 GCD Algorithms

For running the initial sanity check session on 512 and 1024 bit length RSA keys we used the C language with the OpenMP support for easy multi-threading enablement in order to use at maximum an AMD multi-core architecture we had. Because C does not have built-in support for big numbers, which was a requirement for our application, we used an arbitrary precision (bignum) library.

We decided to use GMP (GNU Multiple Precision Arithmetic Library) [6], as it has support for integer and rational numbers, can do computations in finite fields, aiming at speed and supporting numerical algorithms such as greatest common divisor, extended euclidean algorithm for inverse modulo n and other useful cryptographic computations.

The brute-force approach to find the prime factors of a number n is to check against all the prime numbers in the interval $[2, \sqrt{n}]$. Because this is not feasible for big numbers (larger than 2^{100}), another approach has to be chosen, such as batch GCD.

The approach we used was to compute the GCD using Euclid's algorithm on all the possible pairs in a set of numbers. This way, instead of storing a large database of prime numbers, we only store the set of numbers to be checked.

```
for i = 0 to m-1
    for j = i to m
        t = gcd(A[i], A[j])$
        if t != 1 and t != A[i]$
            print i:A[i]:t
            print j:A[j]:t
```

The idea behind batch GCD is very simple: Given a sequence X of positive integers, the algorithm computes the sequence

- $gcd(X_0,\ X_1 \cdot X_2 \cdot X_3 \ldots)$
- $gcd(X_1,\ X_0 \cdot X_2 \cdot X_3 \cdot \ldots)$
- $gcd(X_2,\ X_0 \cdot X_1 \cdot X_3 \cdot \ldots)$
- etc. ...

It shows which integers share primes with other integers in the sequence. Because one only wants to know if a key is compromised, not with which key has a common divisor. The initial development of algorithm was done in [3]. The algorithm can be described using the following steps

- Input: $N_1, \ldots, N_m$ RSA public keys
- Compute: $P = \prod_{i=1}^{m} N_i$ (use product tree)
- Compute $z_i = (P \mod N_i^2), \forall i = 1, \ldots, m$ (use remainder tree)
- Output: $gcd(N_i, z_i/N_i), \forall i = 1, \ldots, m$

The final output is the GCD of each modulus N_i with the product of all the other N. Interest is in those for which this GCD is not 1.

2.4 Ransomware

The ransomware techniques can be classified into two categories: locker ransomware and crypto ransomware.

Locker ransomware denies access to computing resources by usually locking the device's user interface. It then asks the user for a ransom in order to restore access. In general the user interface will contain only the ransomware interface through which he will make the payment. Access to the mouse is disabled and access is granted only to the numerical keys on the keyboard. Locker ransomware just locks the access to a system, it does not modify anything in the system (filesystem data). This type of ransomware is among the least destructive types since it can be removed cleanly without affecting the system, by using various tools provided by security vendors.

Crypto ransomware is the most destructive type of ransomware. It is capable of encrypting data on a device through an encryption process. It usually runs under the radar, it tries to search and encrypt as much as files as possible notifying the user and demanding a ransom in return afterwards. The user can regain access to his data only if he pays the ransom or if the user is capable of computing the decryption key necessary to decrypt the ransomed data.

The modern cryptographic ransomware techniques usually use both symmetric and asymmetric cryptographic algorithms. A symmetric algorithm uses the same key for the encryption and the decryption process. This key can be either generated locally (on the infected device) and sent back to the attacker or it can be generated by the attacker (C&C server). An important observation is that after the files were encrypted this key needs to be erased from the user's system since it can be tracked and used to decrypt the files. The advantage in using a symmetric encryption algorithm is that it is faster than an asymmetric encryption algorithm. Depending on how many files the ransomware tool encrypts, the encryption process can take a significant amount of time. Using a symmetric key can boost the speed of the encryption process and prevent the user from detecting on time that files are being encrypted.

An asymmetric algorithm uses a pair of keys: a public one for data encryption and a private one for data decryption. In ransomware techniques the public key is used to encrypt the files whereas the private key is held by the C&C server and will be used once the ransom is paid by the infected user. Having the public key stored on the infected device does not generally affect the security of the key pair used for ransom. A significant drawback of this algorithm is that it is slow and it can expose the encryption process to the user.

Depending on where the cryptographic keys are stored there are multiple ransomware families:

- downloaded public key - the files are encrypted with an AES symmetric key that is generated on the infected device. The symmetric key is encrypted with a public key that is downloaded from the C&C server. The encrypted symmetric key is stored in each encrypted file and cannot be decrypted since the private key is held by the server. A significant drawback for this method is that if the C&C server cannot be accessed because of a firewall or because of having no internet connection then this ransomware attack will fail. An example of a ransomware virus that behaves this way is Trojan.Cryptodefense.
- embedded public key - the ransomware virus includes an embedded RSA public key which will be used to encrypt a locally generated AES symmetric key. The advantage of this method is that there is no need to contact the C&C server. The drawback is that the ransomware virus needs to have a different public key every time it infects a device. If it is not different then once the private key has been determined the ransomware virus will become obsolete. An example of such a virus is CTBlocker.
- embedded symmetric key - the ransomware virus includes an embedded AES symmetric key which will be used to directly encrypt the files. There are no asymmetric keys used in this technique. The advantage is that the virus does not have to contact the C&C server, but the weakness is that once the secret key has been determined all the files can be decrypted. An example of a virus from this family is represented by Android.Simplelocker, a virus for Android mobile devices.

User devices usually end up being infected with ransomware viruses through unscanned downloads from spam e-mails, from exploit kits, bot infections and even from social engineering attacks. [7]

3 Mining After Public Keys

3.1 Extracting Github Keys

Previous attempts, such as the one performed by Cryptosense company [10] used OCaml to implement batch GCD, but no disclosure of how Github API was used to extract the public keys. It is important to note that Github API only shows information of users that exist and does not include the users whose accounts have been deleted or IDs of private organizations. Listed users obtained after a HTTP request to Github API can be of type *User* or type *Organization*. Organizations are also regular Github users with some particularities.

In our approach, we developed a method to extract keys using Python and HTTP requests to Github API. The first issue we ran into was that Github has rate limiting for API queries, allowing only 60 HTTP requests per hour for unregistered scripts. We have generated a token so that we were able to make 5000 calls per hour.

Another lesson learned while crawling the keys was that instead of using Github API to extract a user's public keys, using a HTTP request to
https://api.github.com/users/torvalds/keys
we found that we could do a simple HTTP request to
https://github.com/torvalds.keys
which did not cost us any API calls, and in 1 h we were able to process more users and make timeouts smaller.

For extracting the public keys we just estimated the total number of Github users (a statistic done by Prajan Mittal determined 10492402 valid accounts in 11 January 2015 [2]) and at each iteration retained the last valid ID of user and get the next 30 registered users, as there is no way to list all the Github users using only one HTTP request. The only accepted method is listing a chunk of users by querying https://api.github.com/users?since=111. Using this method we can list all the users, in the order that they signed up on Github and pagination is powered exclusively by the `since` parameter - this parameter expects a valid ID number.

Because of the timeouts after 5000 hits due to Github API rate limiting and because of the low computing powers required (all we needed was a hard drive and a computer connected to Internet), we did this key mining on a Raspberry PI platform connected via USB to a hard- drive with external 5.1 V DC input voltage.

3.2   Extracting Estonia Certificates

Estonia uses a nation-wide database to store the citizen's identification data and cryptographic certificates, which can be queried using LDAP. The certificates store 1024-bit long RSA public keys. To protect against crawlers, they limit the number of queries a host can do in a certain time-frame, and limit the possible LDAP queries to two types: general queries (returning a maximum of 50 identities at a time) and targeted queries (assuming the personal ID number is known).

To crawl this database beyond the 50 initial identities, we had to generate queries with valid ID numbers. The Estonian ID numbers can be easily brute-forced, as they contain seven digits for the date of birth and gender information, three digits as serial numbers and one checksum digit. To get the certificates of every citizen born in the same day, only 2000 queries are needed.

To do such a query, the following command is used:

```
ldapsearch -x -h ldap.sk.ee -b c=EE "(serialNumber=$ID_NUMBER)"
```

Unfortunately, after the first hundred of requests, time-based restrictions kick in, blocking further requests until a timeout expires. Among the gathered certificates, no weak keys were found.

3.3   Ransomware

In early 2015 a ransomware virus named SleeperLocker has silently infected the workstations of thousands of employees, but it hadn't triggered at all until the midnight of 25th of May 2015. According to [9] a possible source for the ransomware spread was a corrupted installer of the game Minecraft.

The locker uses Windows services to encrypt using an RSA key files with different extensions (.doc, .docx, .jpg, etc.). It does not change the file extensions since the operating system would notify the user of the appearance of corrupted files. Apparently, the locker will terminate if it detects that the system it was installed on is a virtual machine. Also, it deletes the volume copies from C:\shadow which contains snapshots of the C drive at certain moments of time. In order to have its files decrypted, the user had to pay 0.1 bitcoins.

The unthinkable happened on 30 May 2015. Apparently the author of the locker ransomware apologized for what his tool has caused and uploaded a database containing bitcoin addresses, public keys and private keys. Afterwards, on the 2nd of June the author issued a command to have the locker ransomware decrypt all files.

We managed to find the database dump on [4]. This dump was written in an XML format used in .NET applications. As a matter of fact, according to a post belonging to the author of the ransomware all the RSA key-pairs were generated using the RSACryptoServiceProvider class from the .NET framework and all the AES keys were generated using the RijndaelManaged class.

The database has 62703 rows and each row of the database contains its data encoded in the base64 format. The data contains the following information:

- the public key - represented by the moduli N and the public exponent e
- the private key - represented by the prime numbers p and q whose product gives N. It also contains the values of dP, dQ and Q^{-1}. These keys contain the necessary elements that can be used in Chinese Remainder's Theorem for decrypting the private key. Lastly the row also contains the private exponent d.

All the generated keys have a 2048 length. An interesting observation is that all the keys have the same public exponent $AQAB$ in BASE64 format or 65537 in decimal format. This exponent is the standard one used because it is a compromise between being a high enough number in order for the key to be secure and the computational cost of performing an exponentiation. Another reason is due to it being a Fermat prime number which makes exponentiation a lot faster (Table 1).

4   Scenarios and Results

Table 2 shows the results extracted from database provided by [16] which contained a total number of 44474713 keys. The results from the 512-bit length keys was done using the naive approach (to demonstrate how weak 512-bit RSA is) by computing all-pairs GCD using Euclid's algorithm. Using an AMD quad-core x86_64 CPU, running at 3.9 GHz, with 6 GB RAM we were able to perform $720k$ GCD computations per second for 512-bit length RSA. We also used this approach for some of the 1024-bit length RSA keys using two approaches: exhaustive search for matches on a set of $100k$ keys (phase I) and trying to match the 2 divisors from the previous set against the full dataset (phase II). The two phases from naive approach took 48 h for 1024-bit RSA and about 8 h for 512-bit RSA.

Table 1. Results of RSA keys from 2012–2013 scan of X.509 certificates

Len/Ph	Total keys	Pairs	GCDs	Broken
512-bit	323338	52273246116	4717	12209 (3.7 %)
1024 (ph I)	100000	4999850001	2	6 (0.0006 %)
1024 (ph II)	26177420	53738048	6806	13617 (0.05 %)

The third approach (phase III) on 1024-bit RSA was to use the fast GCD implementation done by [18]. Because of the limited amount of RAM of our systems we broke the 26177420 (which is 60 %) total number of 1024-bit keys from the dataset in chunks of 800000, thus comparing a key with the product of the other 799999 keys, and used 8 threads. Using this approach computation took only 18944.7 s. In this third approach there was no pairs approach. Out of 26177420 keys tested, about 0.25 % (meaning 63502) keys were found to be broken.

During two weeks of Github crawling between 22 December 2015 and 7 January 2016 we managed to discover that only 26 % of the users we processed (approximatively 3 million Github users) had public SSH-RSA keys configured. 1 key was 512-bit length and only 12 keys were 16384-bit length. 0.51 % were 1024-bit length,

The single 512-bit RSA key discovered through Github crawling was ran against our set of databases and was found to be broken. For the other lengths, by comparing keys between them, no vulnerability was found. It is needed now a smarter method to compare the 1024 and 2048 bit lengths with databases available.

Regarding Estonia LDAP with RSA IDs a big limitation was the restrictions on the number of queries. Thus we were not able to extract a relevant number of keys to find vulnerabilities.

Overall, the generated public keys for ransomware virus from [4] seemed to be secure due to their length (2048-bit). Comparing the keys between them, the

Table 2. Results of Github scanned keys

Len	Percent keys
512	1 key
1024	0.51 %
2048	55,5 %
4096	3 %
8192	0.01 %
Other	41 %

entropy did not raise any concern, as no vulnerability was discovered by any of our GCD approaches.

5   Conclusion and Further Work

The results and facts presented in this paper should discourage the use of RSA keys having lengths less or equal to 1024 bits and force readers to use at least 2048-bit long keys, pay more attention to random number generators in their system (if they used Debian or derivates in 2008–2009 to generate RSA keys, they should re-generate a new pair and revocate the keys that might be compromised). Multiple online tools such as the ones by [10] have been developed for fast, local sanity checks, of freshly-generated RSA keys, but this is not enough. Users should be aware that, when using RSA, there is always a hacker with enough computing power and patience crawling for public keys and searching for vulnerabilities.

Acknowledgments. This work partially supported by the Romanian National Authority for Scientific Research (CNCSUEFISCDI) under the project PN-II-PT-PCCA-2013-4-1651.

References

1. Cox, B.: Auditing Github Users' SSH Key Quality. https://blog.benjojo.co.uk/post/auditing-github-users-keys
2. Cryptosense - Batch-GCDing Github SSH Keys. https://cryptosense.com/batch-gcding-github-ssh-keys/
3. Bernstein, D.J., Heninger, N., Lange, T.: FACTHACKS - RSA Factorization in the Real World. http://facthacks.cr.yp.to/batchgcd.html
4. Database with Ransomware Public Keys (from the author of the virus). https://archive.org/download/locker-ransomware-database-dump
5. Eckersley, P., Burns, J.: An observatory for the SSLiverse. Talk at Defcon 18 (2010). https://www.eff.org/files/DefconSSLiverse.pdf
6. GMP Library. https://gmplib.org/. Accessed 11 June 2015
7. Savage, K., Coogan, P., Lau, H.: The evolution of ransomware. http://www.symantec.com/content/en/us/enterprise/media/security_response/whitepapers/the-evolution-of-ransomware.pdf

8. Bello, L.: Bug DSA-1571-1 OpenSSL Predictable Random Number Generator. http://www.debian.org/security/2008/dsa-1571

9. Sjouwerman, S.: Is Your Network Infected with Sleeper Ransomware? https://blog.knowbe4.com/is-your-network-infected-with-sleeper-ransomware

10. Total Number of Github User Accounts. http://tech.pranjalmittal.in/blog/2015/01/10/github-api-calculating-total-users-on-github/

11. Durumeric, Z.: Certificate Parsing with OpenSSL and C. https://zakird.com/2013/10/13/certificate-parsing-with-openssl/

12. Zimmerman, P., et al.: GMP-ECM (Elliptic Curve Method for Integer Factorization). https://gforge.inria.fr/projects/ecm/

13. Bernstein, D.J., Chang, Y.-A., Cheng, C.-M., Chou, L.-P., Heninger, N., Lange, T., van Someren, N.: Factoring RSA keys from certified smart cards: Coppersmith in the wild. In: Sako, K., Sarkar, P. (eds.) ASIACRYPT 2013, Part II. LNCS, vol. 8270, pp. 341–360. Springer, Heidelberg (2013). http://dx.doi.org/10.1007/978-3-642-42045-0_18

14. Cavallar, S., et al.: Factorization of a 512-bit RSA modulus. In: Preneel, B. (ed.) EUROCRYPT 2000. LNCS, vol. 1807, pp. 1–18. Springer, Heidelberg (2000). http://dl.acm.org/citation.cfm?id=1756169.1756171

15. Dorrendorf, L., Gutterman, Z., Pinkas, B.: Cryptanalysis of the windows random number generator. In: Proceedings of 14th ACM Conference on Computer and Communications Security, CCS 2007, pp. 476–485. ACM, New York (2007). http://doi.acm.org/10.1145/1315245.1315304

16. Durumeric, Z., Kasten, J., Bailey, M., Halderman, J.A.: Analysis of the HTTPS certificate ecosystem. In: Proceedings of 13th Internet Measurement Conference, October 2013

17. Gutmann, P.: Software generation of practically strong random numbers. In: Proceedings of 7th USENIX Security Symposium, San Antonio, Texas, 26–29 January 1998. USENIX, New York (1998)

18. Heninger, N., Durumeric, Z., Wustrow, E., Halderman, J.A.: Mining your Ps and Qs: detection of widespread weak keys in network devices. In: Proceedings of 21st USENIX Security Symposium, August 2012

19. Kleinjung, T., et al.: Factorization of a 768-Bit RSA modulus. In: Rabin, T. (ed.) CRYPTO 2010. LNCS, vol. 6223, pp. 333–350. Springer, Heidelberg (2010). http://dl.acm.org/citation.cfm?id=1881412.1881436

20. Lenstra, A.K., Hughes, J.P., Augier, M., Kleinjung, T., Wachter, C.: Ron was wrong, Whit is right. Technical report (2012)

A Tweak for a PRF Mode of a Compression Function and Its Applications

Shoichi Hirose[1](✉) and Atsushi Yabumoto[2]

[1] Faculty of Engineering, University of Fukui, Fukui, Japan
hrs_shch@u-fukui.ac.jp
[2] Graduate School of Engineering, University of Fukui, Fukui, Japan

Abstract. We discuss a tweak for the domain extension called Merkle-Damgård with Permutation (MDP), which was presented at ASI-ACRYPT 2007. We first show that MDP may produce multiple independent pseudorandom functions (PRFs) using a single secret key and multiple permutations if the underlying compression function is a PRF against related key attacks with respect to the permutations. Using this result, we then construct a hash-function-based MAC function, which we call FMAC, using a compression function as its underlying primitive. We also present a scheme to extend FMAC so as to take as input a vector of strings.

Keywords: Compression function · MAC · Provable security · Pseudo-random function · Vector-input PRF

1 Introduction

Background. HMAC [3] is the widely deployed function for message authentication (MAC function) constructed from a cryptographic hash function. HMAC is defined with a hash function H as follows:

$$\mathsf{HMAC}(K, M) = H((K \oplus \mathsf{opad}) \| H((K \oplus \mathsf{ipad}) \| M)) \ ,$$

where K is a secret key, M is an input message, $\|$ represents concatenation, $\oplus$ represents bitwise XOR, $\mathsf{ipad} = \mathsf{0x3636 \cdots 36}$ and $\mathsf{opad} = \mathsf{0x5c5c \cdots 5c}$.

Due to the length extension property of standardized hash functions such as SHA-1, SHA-256 and SHA-512 [14], HMAC invokes the underlying hash function twice. The drawback of the adoption of this structure is inefficiency for short messages. Inefficiency of HMAC may also come from the padding of the underlying hash function based on the Merkle-Damgård strengthening. More efficient scheme is expected to be constructed if a compression function of a hash function is used as an underlying primitive instead of the hash function itself.

Recently, an approach attracts a lot of interest to construct symmetric-key schemes using a public permutation. It is emerged from the sponge construction [7], which is the basis of the SHA-3 hash function [15]. Following the approach, methods to construct authenticated encryption schemes and pseudorandom generators are proposed [8]. The Even-Mansour cipher [12,13], which is constructed from a public permutation, also attracts renewed interest, and schemes

© Springer International Publishing AG 2016
I. Bica and R. Reyhanitabar (Eds.): SECITC 2016, LNCS 10006, pp. 103–114, 2016.
DOI: 10.1007/978-3-319-47238-6_7

for encryption, message authentication and authenticated encryption are proposed based on it [19–21,27]. Chaskey is a recently proposed MAC function based on a permutation [23].

The approach to construct secret-key schemes using a compression function is not new. In the context of multi-property preservation [6], some schemes are proposed such as EMD [6] and MDP [16], which may produce PRFs with some appropriate keying strategies. Yasuda [28] also presents a novel PRF mode of a compression function, which almost maximizes the efficiency of the Merkle-Damgård iteration. The recent proposal OMD [11] for authenticated encryption is constructed with a compression function.

Our Contribution. This paper extends the MDP domain extension [16] to construct efficient pseudorandom functions (PRFs). It is first shown that the MDP domain extension with a single key and multiple permutations may produce multiple independent PRFs if the underlying compression function is PRF against related key attacks with respect to the permutations. Based on this result, a PRF with minimum padding is proposed, which is called FMAC (compression-Function-based MAC). We say that padding is minimum if the produced message blocks does not include message blocks only with the padding sequence for any non-empty input message. Finally, a vector-input PRF is constructed with FMAC, which is called vFMAC. A vector-input PRF (vPRF) takes as input a vector of strings. For vFMAC, the number of the components in an input vector is bounded from above and the upper bound is determined by the number of the permutations used in vFMAC.

Related Work. It is shown that HMAC is a PRF if the compression function of the underlying hash function is a PRF with respect to two keying strategies [1]. In particular, for one of the keying strategies, the compression function is required to be a PRF against related key attacks with respect to `ipad` and `opad`.

Yasuda [30] presented a secure HMAC variant without the second key, which is called H^2-MAC. It is shown to be a PRF on the assumption that the underlying compression function is a PRF even if an adversary is allowed to obtain a piece of information on the secret key.

AMAC [2] is a MAC function using a hash function encapsulated with an unkeyed output function. Typical candidates for the output function are truncation and the mod function. AMAC is more efficient than HMAC especially for short messages. It is shown that AMAC is a PRF if the underlying compression function remains a PRF under leakage of the key by the output function.

The plain Merkle-Damgård cascade is shown to be a PRF against adversaries making prefix-free queries if the underlying compression function is a PRF [4].

Yasuda's PRF mode of a compression function in [28] is shown to be a PRF if the underlying compression function is a PRF against a kind of related key attacks.

Sandwich construction for an iterated hash function is shown to produce a PRF if the underlying compression function is a PRF with respect to two keying strategies [29].

Minimum padding is already common among block-cipher-based MAC functions such as CMAC [25] and PMAC [10]. CMAC, which is based on OMAC (One-key CBC-MAC) [17], originated from XCBC [9]. The idea to finalize the iteration with multiple permutations is used in the secure CBC-MAC variants GCBC1 and GCBC2 [24].

Rogaway and Shrimpton [26] introduced the notion of vPRF. They also presented a generic scheme to construct a vPRF from a common PRF taking a single string as input. Minematsu [22] also proposed a vPRF using his universal hash function based on bit rotation.

Organization. Sect. 2 gives notations and definitions used in the remaining parts of the paper. It is shown in Sect. 3 that the MDP domain extension may produce multiple independent PRFs with a single secret key and multiple permutations. Based on the result in Sect. 3, FMAC and vFMAC is presented and their security is confirmed in the manner of provable security in Sect. 4. Section 5 concludes the paper.

2 Preliminaries

2.1 Notations and Definitions

Let $\Sigma = \{0, 1\}$. For any non-negative integer l, Σ^l is identified with the set of all Σ-sequences of length l. Σ^0 is the set of the empty sequence ε. Σ^1 is identified with Σ. For $l \geq 1$, let $(\Sigma^l)^* = \bigcup_{i \geq 0}(\Sigma^l)^i$ be the set of all Σ-sequences whose lengths are multiples of l. Let $(\Sigma^l)^+ = (\Sigma^l)^* \setminus \{\varepsilon\}$. For $k_1 \leq k_2$, let $(\Sigma^l)^{[k_1, k_2]} = \bigcup_{i=k_1}^{k_2}(\Sigma^l)^i$.

For $x \in \Sigma^*$, the length of x is denoted by $|x|$. The concatenation of x_1 and x_2 in Σ^* is denoted by $x_1 \| x_2$.

The operation of selecting element s from set S uniformly at random is denoted by $s \leftarrow S$.

Let $f : \mathcal{K} \times \mathcal{D} \to \mathcal{R}$ be a family of functions from $\mathcal{D}$ to $\mathcal{R}$ indexed by keys in $\mathcal{K}$. Then, $f(K, \cdot)$ is a function from $\mathcal{D}$ to $\mathcal{R}$ for each key $K \in \mathcal{K}$ and is often denoted by $f_K(\cdot)$.

Let $\mathbf{F}(\mathcal{D}, \mathcal{R})$ denote the set of all functions from $\mathcal{D}$ to $\mathcal{R}$. Let $\mathbf{P}(\mathcal{D})$ denote the set of all permutations on $\mathcal{D}$. *id* represents an identity permutation.

2.2 Pseudorandom Functions

For $f : \mathcal{K} \times \mathcal{D} \to \mathcal{R}$, let A be an adversary trying to distinguish f_K from a function ρ, where K and ρ are chosen uniformly at random from $\mathcal{K}$ and $\mathbf{F}(\mathcal{D}, \mathcal{R})$, respectively. A is given access to f_K or ρ as an oracle and makes adaptive queries in $\mathcal{D}$ and obtains the corresponding outputs. The prf-advantage of A against f is defined as

$$\mathrm{Adv}_f^{\mathrm{prf}}(A) = \left| \Pr\left[A^{f_K} = 1 \right] - \Pr\left[A^{\rho} = 1 \right] \right| ,$$

where $K \leftarrow \mathcal{K}$ and $\rho \leftarrow F(\mathcal{D}, \mathcal{R})$. In this notation, adversary A is regarded as a random variable.

f is called a pseudorandom function, or PRF in short, if no efficient adversary A can have any significant prf-advantage against f.

The definition of the prf-advantage can naturally be extended to adversaries with multiple oracles. The prf-advantage of adversary A with access to m oracles is defined as

$$\mathrm{Adv}_f^{m\text{-prf}}(A) = \left| \Pr[A^{F_{K_1}, \dots, F_{K_m}} = 1] - \Pr[A^{\rho_1, \dots, \rho_m} = 1] \right| ,$$

where $(K_1, \dots, K_m) \leftarrow \mathcal{K}^m$ and $(\rho_1, \dots, \rho_m) \leftarrow F(\mathcal{D}, \mathcal{R})^m$.

The following lemma is a paraphrase of Lemma 3.3 in [4]:

Lemma 1. *Let A be any adversary against f with access to m oracles. Then, there exists an adversary B against f such that*

$$\mathrm{Adv}_f^{m\text{-prf}}(A) \leq m \cdot \mathrm{Adv}_f^{\mathrm{prf}}(B) .$$

The run time of B is approximately total of that of A and the time required to compute f to answer to the queries made by A. The number of the queries made by B is at most $\max\{q_i \mid 1 \leq i \leq m\}$, where q_i is the number of the queries made by A to its i-th oracle.

2.3 PRFs Under Related-Key Attacks

The notion of PRF under related-key attacks is formalized by Bellare and Kohno [5]. Let $\Phi \subset F(\mathcal{K}, \mathcal{K})$. Let key $\in F(\Phi \times \mathcal{K}, \mathcal{K})$ be a function such that $\mathrm{key}(\varphi, K) = \varphi(K)$. Adversary A has oracle access to $g(\mathrm{key}(\cdot, K), \cdot)$, where $g \in F(\mathcal{K} \times \mathcal{D}, \mathcal{R})$. The oracle accepts $(\varphi, x) \in \Phi \times \mathcal{D}$ as a query and returns $g(\varphi(K), x)$. To simplify the notation, $g(\mathrm{key}(\cdot, K), \cdot)$ is denoted by $g[K]$. The prf-rka-advantage of A against $f \in F(\mathcal{K} \times \mathcal{D}, \mathcal{R})$ with a Φ-restricted related-key attack (Φ-RKA) is given by

$$\mathrm{Adv}_{\Phi,f}^{\mathrm{prf\text{-}rka}}(A) = \left| \Pr[A^{f[K]} = 1] - \Pr[A^{\rho[K]} = 1] \right| ,$$

where $K \leftarrow \mathcal{K}$ and $\rho \leftarrow F(\mathcal{K} \times \mathcal{D}, \mathcal{R})$.

The prf-rka-advantage can naturally be extended to adversaries with multiple oracles as well as the prf-advantage. The prf-rka-advantage of adversary A with access to m oracles launching a Φ-RKA is defined as

$$\mathrm{Adv}_{\Phi,f}^{m\text{-prf\text{-}rka}}(A) = \left| \Pr[A^{f[K_1], \dots, f[K_m]} = 1] - \Pr[A^{\rho_1[K_1], \dots, \rho_m[K_m]} = 1] \right| ,$$

where $(K_1, \dots, K_m) \leftarrow \mathcal{K}^m$ and $(\rho_1, \dots, \rho_m) \leftarrow F(\mathcal{K} \times \mathcal{D}, \mathcal{R})^m$.

2.4 MDP Domain Extension

The MDP domain extension is a variant of the plain Merkle-Damgård iteration of a compression function [16]. It finalizes the iteration of the compression function by permuting the chaining variable fed into the final compression function with a permutation.

Let $F : \Sigma^n \times \Sigma^w \to \Sigma^n$ be a compression function. Let π be a permutation on Σ^n. The MDP domain extension of F with π is defined by the function $I^{F,\pi} : \Sigma^n \times (\Sigma^w)^+ \to \Sigma^n$ such that

$$I^{F,\pi}(Y_0, X_1 \| X_2 \| \cdots \| X_x) = Y_x$$

for any $Y_0 \in \Sigma^n$ and $X_1, X_2, \ldots, X_x \in \Sigma^w$, where

$$Y_i \leftarrow \begin{cases} F(Y_{i-1}, X_i) & \text{if } 1 \leq i \leq x-1 \\ F(\pi(Y_{x-1}), X_x) & \text{if } i = x \ . \end{cases}$$

$X_1, X_2, \ldots, X_x$ are called blocks. $I^{F,\pi}$ is also depicted in Fig. 1.

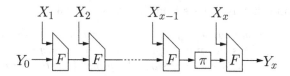

Fig. 1. MDP domain extension $I^{F,\pi}(Y_0, X_1 \| X_2 \| \cdots \| X_x) = Y_x$

3 Multiple PRFs Based on MDP

It is shown in this section that the MDP domain extension may produce multiple independent PRFs with a single compression function, a single secret key and multiple permutations.

For compression function $F : \Sigma^n \times \Sigma^w \to \Sigma^n$ and set of permutations $\Pi = \{\pi_1, \pi_2, \ldots, \pi_d\} \subset \boldsymbol{P}(\Sigma^n) \setminus \{id\}$, let $I^{F,\Pi} = \{I^{F,\pi_1}, I^{F,\pi_2}, \ldots, I^{F,\pi_d}\}$.

Let A be an adversary against $I^{F,\Pi}$. The advantage of A is defined by

$$\mathrm{Adv}^{\mathrm{prfs}}_{I^{F,\Pi}}(A) = \left| \Pr\left[A^{I_K^{F,\pi_1}, I_K^{F,\pi_2}, \ldots, I_K^{F,\pi_d}} = 1\right] - \Pr\left[A^{\rho_1, \rho_2, \ldots, \rho_d} = 1\right] \right| \ ,$$

where $K \leftarrow \Sigma^n$ and $(\rho_1, \rho_2, \ldots, \rho_d) \leftarrow \boldsymbol{F}((\Sigma^w)^+, \Sigma^n)^d$. Notice that the setting is different from that of PRF for an adversary with multiple oracles in Sect. 2.2. $I_K^{F,\pi_1}, I_K^{F,\pi_2}, \ldots, I_K^{F,\pi_d}$ use a single key K.

For Π, let

$$p_\Pi = \Pr\left[\pi(X) = \pi'(X) \text{ for some distinct } \pi, \pi' \in \Pi \cup \{id\}\right] \ ,$$

where X is a random variable with uniform distribution over Σ^n.

The following theorem states that $I^{F,\Pi}$ may produce multiple independent PRFs with a single key under the assumption that F is a PRF against related-key attacks restricted by $\Pi \cup \{id\}$.

Theorem 1. *Let A be any adversary against $I^{F,\Pi}$ running in time at most t and making at most q queries in total. Suppose that each query consists of at most ℓ blocks. Then, there exists an adversary B against F such that*

$$\mathrm{Adv}_{I^{F,\Pi}}^{\mathrm{prfs}}(A) \le \ell q \left(\mathrm{Adv}_{\Pi \cup \{id\}, F}^{\mathrm{prf\text{-}rka}}(B) + p_\Pi \right) \ .$$

B runs in time at most $t + O(\ell q T_F)$, and makes at most q queries. T_F is the time required to compute F.

Remark 1. Theorem 1 extends Theorem 2 in [16] in two ways. First, Theorem 1 deals with multiple instances of $I^{F,\pi}$, while the latter shows the PRF security of a single instance. Second, Theorem 1 covers the case that $p_\Pi \ne 0$. Theorem 2 in [16] only covers the case that $p_{\{\pi\}} = 0$ for $\pi \in \boldsymbol{P}(\Sigma^n)$.

Remark 2. The probability p_Π should be negligibly small for $\Pi = \{\pi_1, \pi_2, \ldots, \pi_d\}$. Let $c_1, c_2, \ldots, c_d$ be distinct nonzero constants in Σ^n.

- Suppose that $\pi_i(x) = x \oplus c_i$ for $1 \le i \le d$. Then, $p_\Pi = 0$.
- Suppose that $\pi_i(x) = c_i \cdot x$ and $c_i \ne 1$ for $1 \le i \le d$. Then, $p_\Pi = 1/2^n$.

Theorem 1 immediately follows from Lemmas 2 and 3.

Lemma 2. *Let A be any adversary against $I^{F,\Pi}$ running in time at most t and making at most q queries in total. Suppose that each query consists of at most ℓ blocks. Then, there exists an adversary B against F with access to q oracles such that*

$$\mathrm{Adv}_{I^{F,\Pi}}^{\mathrm{prfs}}(A) \le \ell \left(\mathrm{Adv}_{\Pi \cup \{id\}, F}^{q\text{-}\mathrm{prf\text{-}rka}}(B) + q p_\Pi \right) \ .$$

B runs in time at most $t + O(\ell q T_F)$ and makes at most q queries.

Proof. Let $X = X_1 \| X_2 \| \cdots \| X_l$, where $|X_i| = w$ for $1 \le i \le l$ and $l \le \ell$. For $1 \le i_1 \le i_2 \le l$, let $X_{[i_1, i_2]} = X_{i_1} \| X_{i_1+1} \| \cdots \| X_{i_2}$. For $i \in \{0, 1, \ldots, \ell\}$ and two functions $\mu : (\Sigma^w)^{[1,\ell]} \to \Sigma^n$ and $\xi : (\Sigma^w)^{[0,\ell]} \to \Sigma^n$, let $R[i]_{\mu,\xi}^{F,\pi} : (\Sigma^w)^{[1,\ell]} \to \Sigma^n$ be a function such that

$$R[i]_{\mu,\xi}^{F,\pi}(X) = \begin{cases} \mu(X) & \text{if } l \le i, \\ I^{F,\pi}(\xi(X_{[1,i]}), X_{[i+1,l]}) & \text{if } l \ge i+1, \end{cases}$$

where $X_{[1,i]} = \varepsilon$ if $i = 0$. We define

$$P_i = \Pr \left[A^{R[i]_{\mu_1,\xi}^{F,\pi_1}, R[i]_{\mu_2,\xi}^{F,\pi_2}, \ldots, R[i]_{\mu_d,\xi}^{F,\pi_d}} = 1 \right] \ ,$$

where $(\mu_1, \ldots, \mu_d) \leftarrow \boldsymbol{F}((\Sigma^w)^{[1,\ell]}, \Sigma^n)^d$ and $\xi \leftarrow \boldsymbol{F}((\Sigma^w)^{[0,\ell]}, \Sigma^n)$. Then, the advantage of A is

$$\mathrm{Adv}_{I^{F,\Pi}}^{\mathrm{prfs}}(A) = |P_0 - P_\ell| \ .$$

The algorithm of an adversary B against F with q oracles is described below. Let the oracles $(g_1, \ldots, g_q)$ of B be either $(F[K_1], F[K_2], \ldots, F[K_q])$ or $(\tilde{\rho}_1, \tilde{\rho}_2, \ldots, \tilde{\rho}_q)$ such that $(K_1, \ldots, K_q) \leftarrow (\Sigma^n)^q$ and $(\tilde{\rho}_1, \tilde{\rho}_2, \ldots, \tilde{\rho}_q) \leftarrow \boldsymbol{F}((\Pi \cup \{id\}) \times \Sigma^w, \Sigma^n)^q$. B uses A as a subroutine.

1. B selects r from $\{1, \ldots, \ell\}$ uniformly at random.
2. If $r \geq 2$, then B selects functions $(\tilde{\mu}_1, \ldots, \tilde{\mu}_d)$ from $\boldsymbol{F}((\Sigma^w)^{[1, r-1]}, \Sigma^n)^d$ uniformly at random.
3. B runs A. Finally, B outputs the output of A.

For $1 \leq k \leq q$ and $1 \leq l \leq \ell$, let $X = X_1 \| X_2 \| \cdots \| X_l$ be the k-th query made by A during the execution of A. Suppose that X is given to the j-th oracle. If $l \geq r$, then B makes a query to the $idx(k)$-th oracle, where $idx : \{1, \ldots, q\} \to \{1, \ldots, q\}$ is a function such that

- $idx(k) = idx(k')$ if there exists a previous k'-th query X' ($k' < k$) such that $X'_{[1, r-1]} = X_{[1, r-1]}$, and
- $idx(k) = k$ otherwise.

The query made by B is (π_j, X_r) if $l = r$ and (id, X_r) if $l \geq r + 1$. The answer of B to X is

$$
\begin{cases}
\tilde{\mu}_j(X) & \text{if } l \leq r - 1, \\
g_{idx(k)}(\pi_j, X_r) & \text{if } l = r, \\
I^{F, \pi_j}(g_{idx(k)}(id, X_r), X_{[r+1, l]}) & \text{if } l \geq r + 1.
\end{cases}
$$

Now, suppose that B is given oracles $(F[K_1], \ldots, F[K_q])$. Then, the answer of B to X is

$$
\begin{cases}
\tilde{\mu}_j(X) & \text{if } l \leq r - 1, \\
F_{\pi_j(K_{idx(k)})}(X_r) & \text{if } l = r, \\
I^{F, \pi_j}(F_{K_{idx(k)}}(X_r), X_{[r+1, l]}) & \text{if } l \geq r + 1.
\end{cases}
$$

$K_{idx(k)}$ can be regarded as an output of a function chosen uniformly at random from $\boldsymbol{F}((\Sigma^w)^{r-1}, \Sigma^n)$ since $idx(k)$ depends on $X_{[1, r-1]}$ and $K_{idx(k)}$ is chosen uniformly at random from Σ^n. Thus, B provides A with the oracle $R[r-1]^{F, \pi_j}_{\mu_j, \xi}$, and

$$
\Pr\left[B^{F[K_1], \ldots, F[K_q]} = 1 \right]
$$

$$
= \sum_{i=1}^{\ell} \Pr\left[r = i \wedge B^{F[K_1], \ldots, F[K_q]} = 1 \right] = \frac{1}{\ell} \sum_{i=1}^{\ell} \Pr\left[B^{F[K_1], \ldots, F[K_q]} = 1 \,\middle|\, r = i \right]
$$

$$
= \frac{1}{\ell} \sum_{i=1}^{\ell} \Pr\left[A^{R[i-1]^{F, \pi_1}_{\mu_1, \xi}, R[i-1]^{F, \pi_2}_{\mu_2, \xi}, \ldots, R[i-1]^{F, \pi_d}_{\mu_d, \xi}} = 1 \right] = \frac{1}{\ell} \sum_{i=1}^{\ell} P_{i-1} .
$$

Suppose that B is given oracles $(\tilde{\rho}_1, \ldots, \tilde{\rho}_q)$. Then, the answer of B to X is

$$
\begin{cases}
\tilde{\mu}_j(X) & \text{if } l \leq r - 1, \\
\tilde{\rho}_{idx(k)}(\pi_j, X_r) & \text{if } l = r, \\
I^{F, \pi_j}(\tilde{\rho}_{idx(k)}(id, X_r), X_{[r+1, l]}) & \text{if } l \geq r + 1.
\end{cases}
$$

Notice that $\tilde{\rho}_{idx(k)}(\pi_1, \cdot), \ldots, \tilde{\rho}_{idx(k)}(\pi_d, \cdot)$ and $\tilde{\rho}_{idx(k)}(id, \cdot)$ are independent of each other. Thus, B provides A with the oracle $R[r]^{F,\pi_j}_{\mu_j,\xi}$, and

$$\Pr[B^{\tilde{\rho}_1,\ldots,\tilde{\rho}_q} = 1] = \frac{1}{\ell}\sum_{i=1}^{\ell} P_i \ .$$

Thus,

$$\left|\Pr\left[B^{F[K_1],\ldots,F[K_q]} = 1\right] - \Pr\left[B^{\tilde{\rho}_1,\ldots,\tilde{\rho}_q} = 1\right]\right| = \left|\frac{1}{\ell}\sum_{i=1}^{\ell} P_{i-1} - \frac{1}{\ell}\sum_{i=1}^{\ell} P_i\right|$$

$$= \frac{|P_0 - P_\ell|}{\ell} = \frac{1}{\ell}\operatorname{Adv}^{\mathrm{prf}}_{I^F,\Pi}(A) \ .$$

Now, let $(\rho_1, \rho_2, \ldots, \rho_q) \twoheadleftarrow \boldsymbol{F}(\Sigma^n \times \Sigma^w, \Sigma^n)^q$. Then,

$$\left|\Pr\left[B^{F[K_1],\ldots,F[K_q]} = 1\right] - \Pr\left[B^{\tilde{\rho}_1,\ldots,\tilde{\rho}_q} = 1\right]\right|$$

$$\leq \left|\Pr\left[B^{F[K_1],\ldots,F[K_q]} = 1\right] - \Pr\left[B^{\rho_1[K_1],\ldots,\rho_q[K_q]} = 1\right]\right|$$

$$+ \left|\Pr\left[B^{\rho_1[K_1],\ldots,\rho_q[K_q]} = 1\right] - \Pr\left[B^{\tilde{\rho}_1,\ldots,\tilde{\rho}_q} = 1\right]\right|$$

$$= \operatorname{Adv}^{q\text{-prf-rka}}_{\Pi\cup\{id\},F}(B) + \left|\Pr\left[B^{\rho_1[K_1],\ldots,\rho_q[K_q]} = 1\right] - \Pr\left[B^{\tilde{\rho}_1,\ldots,\tilde{\rho}_q} = 1\right]\right| \ .$$

$(\rho_1[K_1], \ldots, \rho_q[K_q])$ and $(\tilde{\rho}_1, \ldots, \tilde{\rho}_q)$ are identical as long as $\pi(K_i) \neq \pi'(K_i)$ for any distinct $\pi, \pi' \in \Pi \cup \{id\}$ for $1 \leq i \leq q$. Thus,

$$\left|\Pr\left[B^{\rho_1[K_1],\ldots,\rho_q[K_q]} = 1\right] - \Pr\left[B^{\tilde{\rho}_1,\ldots,\tilde{\rho}_q} = 1\right]\right| \leq qp_\Pi \ .$$

To answer to the queries made by A, B may compute $I^{F,\pi_1}, \ldots, I^{F,\pi_d}$ and simulate $\tilde{\mu}$. It approximately costs at most ℓq evaluations of F. $\square$

Lemma 3. *Let A be any adversary with m oracles against F running in time at most t, and making at most q queries. Then, there exists an adversary B against F such that*

$$\operatorname{Adv}^{m\text{-prf-rka}}_{\Pi\cup\{id\},F}(A) \leq m \cdot \operatorname{Adv}^{\mathrm{prf\text{-}rka}}_{\Pi\cup\{id\},F}(B) \ .$$

B runs in time at most $t + O(qT_F)$ and makes at most q queries, where T_F represents the time required to compute F.

Lemma 3 is a generalized version of Lemma 4 in [16], which only covers the case that $|\Pi| = 1$. The proof of Lemma 3 is omitted since it is standard and similar to that of Lemma 4 in [16].

4 Applications

4.1 PRF with Minimum Padding

The proposed MAC function FMAC consists of a compression function F : $\Sigma^n \times \Sigma^w \to \Sigma^n$ and distinct permutations π_1 and π_2 on Σ^n.

The padding function used in FMAC is defined as follows: For any $M \in \Sigma^*$,

$$\mathsf{pad}(M) = \begin{cases} M & \text{if } |M| > 0 \text{ and } |M| \equiv 0 \pmod{w} \\ M\|10^l & \text{if } |M| = 0 \text{ or } |M| \not\equiv 0 \pmod{w} , \end{cases}$$

where l is the minimum non-negative integer such that $|M|+1+l \equiv 0 \pmod{w}$. In particular, $\mathsf{pad}(\varepsilon) = 10^{w-1}$.

For any M, $|\mathsf{pad}(M)|$ is the minimum positive multiple of w, which is greater than or equal to $|M|$. Let $\mathsf{pad}(M) = \bar{M}_1\|\bar{M}_2\|\cdots\|\bar{M}_m$, where $|\bar{M}_i| = w$ for every i such that $1 \leq i \leq m$. $m = 1$ if $|M| = 0$, and $m = \lceil|M|/w\rceil$ if $|M| > 0$. $\bar{M}_i$ is called the i-th block of $\mathsf{pad}(M)$.

FMAC is the MAC function $C^{F,\{\pi_1,\pi_2\}} : \Sigma^n \times \Sigma^* \to \Sigma^n$ defined by

$$C^{F,\{\pi_1,\pi_2\}}(K, M) = \begin{cases} I^{F,\pi_1}(K, \mathsf{pad}(M)) & \text{if } |M| > 0 \text{ and } |M| \equiv 0 \pmod{w} \\ I^{F,\pi_2}(K, \mathsf{pad}(M)) & \text{if } |M| = 0 \text{ or } |M| \not\equiv 0 \pmod{w} . \end{cases}$$

$C^{F,\{\pi_1,\pi_2\}}$ is shown to be a PRF under the assumptions that F is a PRF against related-key attacks with respect to permutations π_1 and π_2 and that $p_{\{\pi_1,\pi_2\}}$ is negligibly small. The proof is omitted due to the page limit.

Corollary 1. *Let π_1 and π_2 be permutations on Σ^n. Let A be any adversary against $C^{F,\{\pi_1,\pi_2\}}$ running in time at most t and making at most q queries. Suppose that the length of each query is at most ℓw. Then, there exists an adversary B against F such that*

$$\mathrm{Adv}^{\mathrm{prf}}_{C^{F,\{\pi_1,\pi_2\}}}(A) \leq \ell q \left(\mathrm{Adv}^{\mathrm{prf\text{-}rka}}_{\{id,\pi_1,\pi_2\},F}(B) + p_{\{\pi_1,\pi_2\}} \right) .$$

B runs in time at most $t + O(\ell q T_F)$, and makes at most q queries. T_F is the time required to compute F.

4.2 Vector-Input PRF

A scheme is proposed to construct a vector-input PRF (vPRF) using instances of FMAC. In the original formalization [26], a vPRF accepts vectors with any number of components as inputs. In contrast, the proposed scheme has a parameter which specifies the maximum number of the components in an input vector.

Let d be a positive integer, which is the maximum number of the components in an input vector. Let $F : \Sigma^n \times \Sigma^w \to \Sigma^n$ and $\Pi = \{\pi_1, \pi_2, \ldots, \pi_{2d+2}\} \subseteq P(\Sigma^n)$. The proposed vector-input function vFMAC $V^{F,\Pi} : \Sigma^n \times (\Sigma^*)^{[0,d]} \to$

Σ^n is defined as follows: For an s-component vector $(S_1, S_2, \ldots, S_s)$ such that $0 \le s \le d$,

$$V^{F,\Pi}(K, (S_1, S_2, \ldots, S_s))$$
$$= \begin{cases} C_K^{F,\{\pi_{2d+1}, \pi_{2d+2}\}}(\varepsilon) & \text{if } s = 0, \\ C_K^{F,\{\pi_{2d+1}, \pi_{2d+2}\}}\left(\bigoplus_{i=1}^s C_K^{F,\{\pi_{2i-1}, \pi_{2i}\}}(S_i)\right) & \text{if } s \ge 1. \end{cases}$$

It is shown that $V^{F,\Pi}$ is a vPRF if F is a PRF against related-key attacks with respect to permutations in Π and p_Π is negligibly small.

Corollary 2. *Let* $\Pi = \{\pi_1, \pi_2, \ldots, \pi_{2d+2}\} \subset P(\Sigma^n) \backslash \{id\}$. *Let* A *be any adversary against* $V^{F,\Pi}$ *running in time at most* t *and making at most* q *queries. Suppose that the length of each vector component in queries is at most* ℓw *and that the total number of the vector components in all of the queries is at most* $\sigma(\ge q - 1)$. *Then, there exists an adversary* B *against* F *such that*

$$\text{Adv}_{V^{F,\Pi}}^{\text{prf}}(A) \le \ell(\sigma + q)\left(\text{Adv}_{\Pi \cup \{id\}, F}^{\text{prf-rka}}(B) + p_\Pi\right) + \frac{q(q-1)}{2^{n+1}} \ .$$

B *runs in time at most* $t + O(\ell\sigma T_F)$, *and makes at most* $(\sigma + q)$ *queries.* T_F *is the time required to compute* F.

Corollary 2 directly follows from Lemmas 4 and 5. The proofs are omitted.

Lemma 4. *Let* $\Pi = \{\pi_1, \pi_2, \ldots, \pi_{2d+2}\} \subset P(\Sigma^n) \backslash \{id\}$. *Let* A *be any adversary against* $\left\{C^{F,\{\pi_{2i-1}, \pi_{2i}\}} \mid 1 \le i \le d+1\right\}$ *running in time at most* t *and making at most* q *queries in total. Suppose that the length of each query is at most* ℓw. *Then, there exists an adversary* B *against* F *such that*

$$\text{Adv}_{\left\{C^{F,\{\pi_{2i-1}, \pi_{2i}\}} \mid 1 \le i \le d+1\right\}}^{\text{prfs}}(A) \le \ell q\left(\text{Adv}_{\Pi \cup \{id\}, F}^{\text{prf-rka}}(B) + p_\Pi\right) \ .$$

B *runs in time at most* $t + O(\ell q T_F)$, *and makes at most* q *queries.* T_F *is the time required to compute* F.

Lemma 5. *Let* $\Pi = \{\pi_1, \pi_2, \ldots, \pi_{2d+2}\} \subset P(\Sigma^n) \backslash \{id\}$. *Let* A *be any adversary against* $V^{F,\Pi}$ *running in time at most* t *and making at most* q *queries. Suppose that the length of each vector component in queries is at most* ℓw *and that the total number of the vector components in all of the queries is at most* σ. *Then, there exists an adversary* B *against* $\left\{C^{F,\{\pi_{2i-1}, \pi_{2i}\}} \mid 1 \le i \le d+1\right\}$ *such that*

$$\text{Adv}_{V^{F,\Pi}}^{\text{prf}}(A) \le \text{Adv}_{\left\{C^{F,\{\pi_{2i-1}, \pi_{2i}\}} \mid 1 \le i \le d+1\right\}}^{\text{prfs}}(B) + \frac{q(q-1)}{2^{n+1}} \ .$$

B *runs in time at most* t *and makes at most* $(\sigma + q)$ *queries in total. The length of each query is at most* ℓw.

5 Conclusion

We have presented a MAC function called FMAC, which is cascade of a compression function based on the MDP domain extension. We have also extended FMAC so as to take as input a vector of strings. We have confirmed their security as PRF on the assumption that the underlying compression function is PRF under related-key attacks. Future work is to evaluate their security as PRF in the multi-user setting.

Acknowledgements. This work was supported in part by JSPS KAKENHI Grant Number JP16H02828.

References

1. Bellare, M.: New proofs for NMAC and HMAC: security without collision-resistance. In: Dwork, C. (ed.) CRYPTO 2006. LNCS, vol. 4117, pp. 602–619. Springer, Heidelberg (2006). doi:10.1007/11818175_36
2. Bellare, M., Bernstein, D.J., Tessaro, S.: Hash-function based PRFs: AMAC and its multi-user security. Cryptology ePrint Archive, Report 2016/142 (2016). http://eprint.iacr.org/
3. Bellare, M., Canetti, R., Krawczyk, H.: Keying hash functions for message authentication. In: Koblitz, N. (ed.) CRYPTO 1996. LNCS, vol. 1109, pp. 1–15. Springer, Heidelberg (1996). doi:10.1007/3-540-68697-5_1
4. Bellare, M., Canetti, R., Krawczyk, H.: Pseudorandom functions revisited: the cascade construction and its concrete security. In: Proceedings of the 37th IEEE Symposium on Foundations of Computer Science, pp. 514–523 (1996)
5. Bellare, M., Kohno, T.: A theoretical treatment of related-key attacks: RKA-PRPs, RKA-PRFs, and applications. In: Biham, E. (ed.) EUROCRYPT 2003. LNCS, vol. 2656, pp. 491–506. Springer, Heidelberg (2003). doi:10.1007/3-540-39200-9_31
6. Bellare, M., Ristenpart, T.: Multi-property-preserving hash domain extension and the EMD transform. In: Lai, X., Chen, K. (eds.) ASIACRYPT 2006. LNCS, vol. 4284, pp. 299–314. Springer, Heidelberg (2006). doi:10.1007/11935230_20
7. Bertoni, G., Daemen, J., Peeters, M., Van Assche, G.: Sponge functions. In: ECRYPT Hash Workshop (2007)
8. Bertoni, G., Daemen, J., Peeters, M., Assche, G.: Duplexing the sponge: single-pass authenticated encryption and other applications. In: Miri, A., Vaudenay, S. (eds.) SAC 2011. LNCS, vol. 7118, pp. 320–337. Springer, Heidelberg (2012). doi:10.1007/978-3-642-28496-0_19
9. Black, J., Rogaway, P.: CBC MACs for arbitrary-length messages: the three-key constructions. In: Bellare, M. (ed.) CRYPTO 2000. LNCS, vol. 1880, pp. 197–215. Springer, Heidelberg (2000). doi:10.1007/3-540-44598-6_12
10. Black, J., Rogaway, P.: A block-cipher mode of operation for parallelizable message authentication. In: Knudsen, L.R. (ed.) EUROCRYPT 2002. LNCS, vol. 2332, pp. 384–397. Springer, Heidelberg (2002). doi:10.1007/3-540-46035-7_25
11. Cogliani, S., Maimut, D., Naccache, D., do Canto, R.P., Reyhanitabar, R., Vaudenay, S., Vizár, D.: OMD: a compression function mode of operation for authenticated encryption. In: Joux and Youssef [18], pp. 112–128

12. Even, S., Mansour, Y.: A construction of a cipher from a single pseudorandom permutation. In: Imai, H., Rivest, R.L., Matsumoto, T. (eds.) ASIACRYPT 1991. LNCS, vol. 739, pp. 210–224. Springer, Heidelberg (1993). doi:10.1007/3-540-57332-1_17

13. Even, S., Mansour, Y.: A construction of a cipher from a single pseudorandom permutation. J. Cryptology 10(3), 151–162 (1997)

14. FIPS PUB 180-4: secure hash standard (SHS), March 2012

15. FIPS PUB 202: SHA-3 standard: permutation-based hash and extendable-output functions (2015)

16. Hirose, S., Park, J.H., Yun, A.: A simple variant of the Merkle-Damgård scheme with a permutation. J. Cryptology 25(2), 271–309 (2012)

17. Iwata, T., Kurosawa, K.: OMAC: one-key CBC MAC. In: Johansson, T. (ed.) FSE 2003. LNCS, vol. 2887, pp. 129–153. Springer, Heidelberg (2003). doi:10.1007/978-3-540-39887-5_11

18. Joux, A., Youssef, A. (eds.): SAC 2014. LNCS, vol. 8781. Springer, Heidelberg (2014)

19. Kurosawa, K.: Power of a public random permutation and its application to authenticated-encryption. Cryptology ePrint Archive, report 2002/127 (2002). http://eprint.iacr.org/

20. Kurosawa, K.: Power of a public random permutation and its application to authenticated encryption. IEEE Trans. Inf. Theory 56(10), 5366–5374 (2010)

21. Mennink, B.: XPX: Generalized tweakable Even-Mansour with improved security guarantees. Cryptology ePrint Archive, Report 2015/476 (2015). http://eprint.iacr.org/

22. Minematsu, K.: A short universal hash function from bit rotation, and applications to blockcipher modes. In: Susilo, W., Reyhanitabar, R. (eds.) ProvSec 2013. LNCS, vol. 8209, pp. 221–238. Springer, Heidelberg (2013). doi:10.1007/978-3-642-41227-1_13

23. Mouha, N., Mennink, B., Herrewege, A.V., Watanabe, D., Preneel, B., Verbauwhede, I.: Chaskey: an efficient MAC algorithm for 32-bit microcontrollers. In: Joux and Youssef [18], pp. 306–323

24. Nandi, M.: Fast and secure CBC-type MAC algorithms. In: Dunkelman, O. (ed.) FSE 2009. LNCS, vol. 5665, pp. 375–393. Springer, Heidelberg (2009). doi:10.1007/978-3-642-03317-9_23

25. NIST Special Publication 800-38B: Recommendation for block cipher modes of operation: The CMAC mode for authentication (2005)

26. Rogaway, P., Shrimpton, T.: A provable-security treatment of the key-wrap problem. In: Vaudenay, S. (ed.) EUROCRYPT 2006. LNCS, vol. 4004, pp. 373–390. Springer, Heidelberg (2006). doi:10.1007/11761679_23

27. Sasaki, Y., Todo, Y., Aoki, K., Naito, Y., Sugawara, T., Murakami, Y., Matsui, M., Hirose, S.: Minalpher v1. Submission to CAESAR (Competition for Authenticated Encryption: Security, Applicability, and Robustness) (2014)

28. Yasuda, K.: Boosting Merkle-Damgård hashing for message authentication. In: Kurosawa, K. (ed.) ASIACRYPT 2007. LNCS, vol. 4833, pp. 216–231. Springer, Heidelberg (2007). doi:10.1007/978-3-540-76900-2_13

29. Yasuda, K.: "Sandwich" is indeed secure: how to authenticate a message with just one hashing. In: Pieprzyk, J., Ghodosi, H., Dawson, E. (eds.) ACISP 2007. LNCS, vol. 4586, pp. 355–369. Springer, Heidelberg (2007)

30. Yasuda, K.: HMAC without the "second" key. In: Samarati, P., Yung, M., Martinelli, F., Ardagna, C.A. (eds.) ISC 2009. LNCS, vol. 5735, pp. 443–458. Springer, Heidelberg (2009)

May-Ozerov Algorithm for Nearest-Neighbor Problem over $\mathbb{F}_q$ and Its Application to Information Set Decoding

Shoichi Hirose[(✉)]

Faculty of Engineering, University of Fukui, Fukui, Japan
hrs_shch@u-fukui.ac.jp

Abstract. May and Ozerov proposed an algorithm for the nearest-neighbor problem of vectors over the binary field at EUROCRYPT 2015. They applied their algorithm to the decoding problem of random linear codes over the binary field and confirmed the performance improvement. We describe a generalization of their algorithm for vectors over the finite field $\mathbb{F}_q$ with arbitrary prime power q. We also apply the generalized algorithm to the decoding problem of random linear codes over $\mathbb{F}_q$. It is observed by our numerical analysis of asymptotic time complexity that the May-Ozerov nearest-neighbor algorithm may not contribute to the performance improvement of the Stern information set decoding over $\mathbb{F}_q$ with $q \geq 3$.

Keywords: Code-based cryptography · Information set decoding · Nearest-neighbor problem · Random linear code

1 Introduction

Background. Decoding random linear codes is a well-known combinatorial problem in coding theory and cryptography. No efficient algorithm is found for this problem, and the intractability is used to construct various cryptographic schemes. In particular, different from public key cryptosystems based on factoring or discrete logarithms, public key cryptosystems based on codes such as McEliece PKC [11] are expected to remain secure even if large-scale quantum computers become available.

An $[n, k]$ linear code over the finite field $\mathbb{F}_q$ is a k-dimensional subspace of $\mathbb{F}_q^n$. n is the length of the code and k/n is called the rate. An $[n, k]$ linear code over $\mathbb{F}_q$ can be defined as a kernel of a matrix $\boldsymbol{H} \in \mathbb{F}_q^{(n-k) \times n}$ with rank $n - k$. $\boldsymbol{H}$ is called a parity check matrix. The distance d of an $[n, k]$ linear code is the minimum Hamming distance between its codewords.

A random parity check matrix $\boldsymbol{H} \in \mathbb{F}_q^{(n-k) \times n}$ specifies a random $[n, k]$ linear code. It is shown that, for large n, virtually all random linear $[n, k]$ codes over $\mathbb{F}_q$ achieve the Gilbert-Varshamov bound $k/n \leq 1 - H_q(d/n)$, where H_q is the q-ary entropy function [3]. Thus, it is assumed in this paper that d satisfies $k/n = 1 - H_q(d/n)$.

© Springer International Publishing AG 2016
I. Bica and R. Reyhanitabar (Eds.): SECITC 2016, LNCS 10006, pp. 115–126, 2016.
DOI: 10.1007/978-3-319-47238-6_8

An instance of the decoding problem of random linear codes is a pair of a random parity check matrix $\boldsymbol{H} \in \mathbb{F}_q^{(n-k) \times n}$ and a vector $\boldsymbol{x} \in \mathbb{F}_q^n$. The required answer is a codeword with minimum Hamming distance to $\boldsymbol{x}$. This setting is called the full distance decoding. The other setting, which is more typical in the application to cryptography, promises that there exists a codeword $\boldsymbol{c}$ such that $\boldsymbol{x} = \boldsymbol{c} + \boldsymbol{e}$ and the Hamming weight of $\boldsymbol{e}$ is less than or equal to $\lfloor (d-1)/2 \rfloor$, where d is the distance of the given code. This setting is called the bounded distance decoding, which will be focused on in this paper. In the bounded distance decoding, it is ensured that the answer $\boldsymbol{c}$ is unique.

Related Work. The important class of algorithms for decoding random linear codes is information set decoding (ISD), which was first suggested by Prange [14]. ISD consists of two steps: the first step is a permutation step and the second step is a search step. A successive execution of these steps is iterated until an answer is obtained. In its basic form by Lee and Brickell [8], in the first permutation step, one first permutes the columns of $\boldsymbol{H}$ randomly and transform the permuted $\boldsymbol{H}$ into $(\boldsymbol{R}\ \boldsymbol{I})$ with Gaussian elimination, where $\boldsymbol{R} \in \mathbb{F}_q^{(n-k) \times k}$ and $\boldsymbol{I}$ is the $(n-k)$-dimensional identity matrix. The Gaussian elimination is also applied to the syndrome $\boldsymbol{s} = \boldsymbol{H}\boldsymbol{x}$, which is transformed to $\tilde{\boldsymbol{s}}$. In the second search step, for some fixed p, one searches a linear combination of p columns of $\boldsymbol{R}$ whose Hamming distance to $\tilde{\boldsymbol{s}}$ is $w - p$. For such a linear combination, $\tilde{\boldsymbol{s}}$ is obtained by adding a linear combination of $w - p$ columns of $\boldsymbol{I}$ to the linear combination. Thus, one can recover $\boldsymbol{e}$ and obtain $\boldsymbol{c} = \boldsymbol{x} - \boldsymbol{e}$. p is chosen to optimize the time complexity.

Stern reduced the time complexity of ISD using the meet-in-the-middle approach for the search step [15]. The Stern ISD was the best algorithm in terms of time complexity for about twenty years. Recently, several proposals for the search step have been made to further reduce the time complexity. Bernstein, Lange and Peters introduced the ball-collision technique [2]. May, Meurer and Thomae [9] used the representation technique introduced by Howgrave-Graham and Joux [7] for the subset sum problem. Becker, Joux, May and Meurer [1] introduced an interesting tweak to the algorithm by May, et al. [9]. May-Ozerov devised an algorithm to find a pair of nearest neighbors [10].

The decoding problem of random linear codes is often discussed for codes over the binary field. Still, some work has been done to generalize ISD for codes over other finite fields. Coffey and Goodman [4] analyzed the complexity of the Prange ISD over $\mathbb{F}_q$. Peters [13] generalized the Stern ISD and its extension by Finiansz and Sendrier [5]. Meurer [12] generalized the BJMM ISD [1] and analyzed its time complexity. May and Ozerov [10] claimed that they did not see any obstacles in transferring their algorithm to $\mathbb{F}_q$. However, the generalization does not seem so straightforward as the generalization of the other algorithms.

Our Contribution. In this paper, the May-Ozerov algorithm for the nearest-neighbor problem is generalized to work over $\mathbb{F}_q$ with any prime power q. The time complexity of the algorithm is also analyzed. The analysis suggests that the May-Ozerov algorithm may not be practical even for small $q \geq 3$ due to the factors of the time complexity which does not appear in its $\tilde{O}$-notation. Then, the May-Ozerov algorithm is applied to the decoding problem of random linear codes over $\mathbb{F}_q$. The asymptotic time complexity of the Stern ISD with the May-Ozerov nearest-neighbor algorithm is analyzed by numerical optimization. It is observed by the analysis that the May-Ozerov nearest-neighbor algorithm may not contribute to the performance improvement of the Stern ISD over $\mathbb{F}_q$ with $q \geq 3$.

Organization. Section 2 gives some notations and definitions. The May-Ozerov algorithm for the nearest-neighbor problem over $\mathbb{F}_q$ is presented in Sect. 3. The application of the May-Ozerov algorithm to the Stern ISD over $\mathbb{F}_q$ is described in Sect. 4. Some numerical analyses of asymptotic time complexity of this algorithm is given in Sect. 5. A concluding remark is given in Sect. 6.

Most of the proofs are omitted due to the page limit. They are given in the full version [6].

2   Preliminaries

Notation. The q-ary entropy function is denoted by H_q. Namely,

$$H_q(x) = x \log_q(q-1) - x \log_q x - (1-x) \log_q(1-x).$$

The binary entropy function H_2 is often simply denoted by H.

Let $\mathbb{F}_q$ be the finite field for prime power q. $\mathbb{F}_q$ is also used to represent the set of elements of the field.

Let $\boldsymbol{w} \in \mathbb{F}_q^l$ be a vector. The Hamming weight of $\boldsymbol{w}$ is the number of its nonzero coordinates, which is denoted by $w_\mathrm{H}(\boldsymbol{w})$. The number of the coordinates of $\boldsymbol{w}$ is denoted by $|\boldsymbol{w}|$, that is, $|\boldsymbol{w}| = l$.

Multinomial Coefficient and Stirling's Formula. The multinomial coefficient

$$\binom{n}{n_1, n_2, \cdots, n_\tau} = \frac{n!}{n_1! n_2! \cdots n_\tau!}$$

is the number of ways to split n distinct elements into τ disjoint groups with the size of the i-th group n_i for $1 \leq i \leq \tau$, where $n = n_1 + n_2 + \cdots + n_\tau$ and $\tau \geq 2$.

We will often use Stirling's formula $n! = \sqrt{2\pi n}(n/e)^n e^{o(1)}$ and

$$\binom{\kappa n}{\mu n} = \sqrt{\frac{\kappa}{2\pi\mu(\kappa-\mu)}} 2^{\kappa H(\mu/\kappa)n - o(n)} = \tilde{\Theta}\left(2^{\kappa H(\mu/\kappa)n}\right).$$

Nearest-Neighbor Problem over $\mathbb{F}_q$. The nearest-neighbor (NN) problem over the binary field defined in [10] is generalized over other finite fields:

Definition 1 (Nearest-Neighbor Problem over $\mathbb{F}_q$). *Let q be a prime power. Let m be a positive integer. Let $0 < \gamma < 1/2$ and $0 < \lambda < 1$. The (m, γ, λ)-NN problem over $\mathbb{F}_q$ is defined as follows:*

Input $\mathcal{U}$, $\mathcal{V}$ and γ, where $\mathcal{U} \subset \mathbb{F}_q^m$, $\mathcal{V} \subset \mathbb{F}_q^m$ and $|\mathcal{U}| = |\mathcal{V}| = q^{\lambda m}$,
Output $\mathcal{C} \subset \mathcal{U} \times \mathcal{V}$ which have $(\boldsymbol{u}^*, \boldsymbol{v}^*)$ such that $w_{\mathrm{H}}(\boldsymbol{u}^* - \boldsymbol{v}^*) = \gamma m$ (if any).

It is also assumed that the vectors in $\mathcal{U}$ and $\mathcal{V}$ are chosen uniformly at random and pairwise independent.

To simplify the description of the May-Ozerov algorithm for the NN problem, the balancedness of a vector over $\mathbb{F}_q$ is defined:

Definition 2. *A vector in $\mathbb{F}_q^l$ is called balanced if the number of its coordinates equal to x is l/q for every element $x \in \mathbb{F}_q$.*

3   May-Ozerov Algorithm for Nearest-Neighbor Problem over $\mathbb{F}_q$

The May-Ozerov algorithm for the nearest-neighbor problem over $\mathbb{F}_2$ [10] is generalized to work over $\mathbb{F}_q$ with arbitrary prime power q. The generalized algorithm is given in Algorithm 1. An overview of the algorithm is given below.

For a given pair of lists, $\mathcal{U}$ and $\mathcal{V}$, the May-Ozerov NN algorithm creates exponentially many pairs of sublists with sizes expected polynomial so that at least one of the pairs of sublists contain an unknown solution with overwhelming probability. Since the sizes of the sublists are expected to be polynomial, the naive search is carried out to find the unknown solution.

All the vectors in the given lists first randomized with a random permutation matrix $\boldsymbol{P}$ and a random vector $\boldsymbol{r}$. This randomization plays an important role in the algorithm. In the description of Algorithm 1,

$$\boldsymbol{P}\mathcal{U} + \boldsymbol{r} = \{\boldsymbol{u}' \mid \boldsymbol{u}' = \boldsymbol{P}\boldsymbol{u} + \boldsymbol{r}, \ \boldsymbol{u} \in \mathcal{U}\},$$

and $\boldsymbol{P}\mathcal{V} + \boldsymbol{r}$ is defined similarly. $\boldsymbol{P}$ is used for random transposition of coordinates of each vector.

Each pair of sublists are created first by choosing some of the coordinates of the vectors at random. Let A be the set of the chosen coordinates with $|A| = \beta m$ for $0 < \beta < 1$. Then, a pair of sublists consist of vectors satisfying that the number of coordinates in A equal to $x \in \mathbb{F}_q$ is $h_x \beta m$, where h_x's are positive and $\sum_{x \in \mathbb{F}_q} h_x = 1$. Actually, the vectors are filtered gradually with recursive calls to the procedure NNR. Each vector is divided into t pieces with the size of the i-th piece $\alpha_i m$, where α_i's are positive and $\alpha_1 + \alpha_2 + \cdots + \alpha_t = 1$. A is a union of disjoint sets $A_1, A_2, \ldots, A_t$, where the coordinates in A_i are from the i-th piece and $|A_i| = \beta \alpha_i m$ for $1 \leq i \leq t$. The pair of sublists consist of vectors satisfying that the number of coordinates in A_i equal to $x \in \mathbb{F}_q$ is $h_x \beta \alpha_i m$ for $1 \leq i \leq t$.

The recursive calls to the procedure NNR form a tree structure with the root corresponding to the call from MO-NN. The last argument i of NNR represents the depth of the call in the tree, where the depth of the root is 1 and the depth of a leaf is $t + 1$.

Algorithm 1. May-Ozerov Algorithm for (m, γ, λ)-NN problem over $\mathbb{F}_q$

1: **procedure** MO-NN$(\mathcal{U}, \mathcal{V}, \gamma)$
2: $\quad y \leftarrow (1 - \gamma) \left(H_q(\beta) - \frac{1}{q} \sum_{x \in \mathbb{F}_q} H_q \left(\frac{qh_x - \gamma}{1 - \gamma} \beta \right) \right)$
3: $\quad$ Select $\varepsilon > 0$
4: $\quad t \leftarrow \lceil (\log_2(y - \lambda + \varepsilon/2) - \log_2(\varepsilon/2))/(\log_2 y - \log_2 \lambda) \rceil$
5: $\quad \alpha_1 \leftarrow (y - \lambda + \varepsilon/2)/y$
6: $\quad \alpha_i \leftarrow (\lambda/y)\alpha_{i-1}$ for $2 \leq i \leq t$
7: $\quad$ **for** $m^{O(1)}$ times **do**
8: $\qquad$ Select a permutation matrix $P \in \{0,1\}^{m \times m}$ u.a.r. (uniformly at random)
9: $\qquad$ Select u.a.r. $r = (r_1, \ldots, r_t) \in \mathbb{F}_q^m$ s.t. $r_i \in \mathbb{F}_q^{\alpha_i m}$ is balanced for $1 \leq i \leq t$
10: $\qquad \tilde{\mathcal{U}} \leftarrow \{\tilde{u} \,|\, \tilde{u} = (\tilde{u}_1, \ldots, \tilde{u}_t) \in P\mathcal{U} + r \wedge \forall j.(\tilde{u}_j \in \mathbb{F}_q^{\alpha_j m}$ is balanced$)\}$
11: $\qquad \tilde{\mathcal{V}} \leftarrow \{\tilde{v} \,|\, \tilde{v} = (\tilde{v}_1, \ldots, \tilde{v}_t) \in P\mathcal{V} + r \wedge \forall j.(\tilde{v}_j \in \mathbb{F}_q^{\alpha_j m}$ is balanced$)\}$
12: $\qquad$ **return** NNR$(\tilde{\mathcal{U}}, \tilde{\mathcal{V}}, m, t, \gamma, \lambda, \alpha_1, \ldots, \alpha_t, y, \varepsilon, 1)$
13: $\quad$ **end for**
14: **end procedure**

15: **procedure** NNR$(\tilde{\mathcal{U}}, \tilde{\mathcal{V}}, m, t, \gamma, \lambda, \alpha_1, \ldots, \alpha_t, y, \varepsilon, i))$
16: $\quad$ **if** $i = t + 1$ **then**
17: $\qquad \mathcal{C} \leftarrow \{(\tilde{u}, \tilde{v}) \,|\, (\tilde{u}, \tilde{v}) \in \tilde{\mathcal{U}} \times \tilde{\mathcal{V}} \wedge w_{\mathrm{H}}(\tilde{u} - \tilde{v}) = \gamma m\}$ $\quad \triangleright$ The naive algo. is used.
18: $\quad$ **end if**
19: $\quad$ **for** $\tilde{\Theta}(q^{y\alpha_i m})$ times **do**
20: $\qquad$ Select $A_i \subset \left\{ (\sum_{j=1}^{i-1} \alpha_j)m + 1, \ldots, (\sum_{j=1}^{i} \alpha_j)m \right\}$ s.t. $|A_i| = \beta\alpha_i m$ u.a.r.
21: $\qquad \mathcal{U}' \leftarrow \{u \,|\, u \in \tilde{\mathcal{U}}$ s.t. # of coordinates in A_i equal to $x \in \mathbb{F}_q$ is $h_x \beta \alpha_i m\}$
22: $\qquad \mathcal{V}' \leftarrow \{v \,|\, v \in \tilde{\mathcal{V}}$ s.t. # of coordinates in A_i equal to $x \in \mathbb{F}_q$ is $h_x \beta \alpha_i m\}$
23: $\qquad$ **if** $|\mathcal{U}'|$ and $|\mathcal{V}'|$ are $\tilde{O}\left(q^{(\lambda(1 - \sum_{j=1}^{i} \alpha_j) + \varepsilon/2)m} \right)$ **then**
24: $\qquad\quad \mathcal{C} \leftarrow \mathcal{C} \cup \mathrm{NNR}(\mathcal{U}', \mathcal{V}', m, t, \gamma, \lambda, \alpha_1, \ldots, \alpha_t, y, \varepsilon, i + 1)$
25: $\qquad$ **end if**
26: $\quad$ **end for**
27: $\quad$ **return** $\mathcal{C}$
28: **end procedure**

The time complexity of the May-Ozerov NN algorithm over $\mathbb{F}_q$ in Algorithm 1 is given by Theorem 1, which follows from Lemmas 1, 2, 3 and 4. The proof proceeds in the same way as the proof of Theorem 1 in [10].

Theorem 1. *Let q be any prime power. Let γ be any real such that $0 < \gamma < 1/2$. Let β be any real such that $0 < \beta < 1$. Let ε be any positive real and λ be any real such that*

$$\lambda \leq H_q(\beta) - \frac{1}{q} \sum_{x \in \mathbb{F}_q} H_q(qh_x\beta) \tag{1}$$

with $\sum_{x \in \mathbb{F}_q} h_x = 1$ and $\gamma/q \leq h_x \leq \gamma/q + (1 - \gamma)/(q\beta)$ for every $x \in \mathbb{F}_q$. Let

$$y = (1 - \gamma)\left(H_q(\beta) - \frac{1}{q} \sum_{x \in \mathbb{F}_q} H_q \left(\frac{qh_x - \gamma}{1 - \gamma} \beta \right) \right). \tag{2}$$

Then, the May-Ozerov algorithm solves the (m, γ, λ)-NN problem over $\mathbb{F}_q$ with overwhelming probability in time $\tilde{O}(q^{(y+\varepsilon)m})$.

Lemma 1. *Let $(\mathcal{U}, \mathcal{V}, \gamma)$ be an instance of the (m, γ, λ)-NN problem with unknown solution $(\boldsymbol{u}^*, \boldsymbol{v}^*) \in \mathcal{U} \times \mathcal{V}$ such that $w_{\mathrm{H}}(\boldsymbol{u}^* - \boldsymbol{v}^*) = \gamma m$. Let $\boldsymbol{z}^* = \boldsymbol{u}^* - \boldsymbol{v}^*$. Let t be a constant integer. Let $\alpha_1, \alpha_2, \ldots, \alpha_t$ be positive reals satisfying $\alpha_1 + \cdots + \alpha_t = 1$. Let $\boldsymbol{P}$ be a permutation matrix chosen uniformly at random from $\{0,1\}^{m \times m}$. Let $\boldsymbol{r} \in \mathbb{F}_q^m$ be a vector chosen uniformly at random such that $\boldsymbol{r} = (\boldsymbol{r}_1, \ldots, \boldsymbol{r}_t)$ with $\boldsymbol{r}_i \in \mathbb{F}_q^{\alpha_i m}$ balanced for every $1 \le i \le t$. Let*

$$\tilde{\boldsymbol{u}}^* = \boldsymbol{P}\boldsymbol{u}^* + \boldsymbol{r} = (\tilde{\boldsymbol{u}}_1^*, \tilde{\boldsymbol{u}}_2^*, \ldots, \tilde{\boldsymbol{u}}_t^*),$$
$$\tilde{\boldsymbol{v}}^* = \boldsymbol{P}\boldsymbol{v}^* + \boldsymbol{r} = (\tilde{\boldsymbol{v}}_1^*, \tilde{\boldsymbol{v}}_2^*, \ldots, \tilde{\boldsymbol{v}}_t^*),$$
$$\tilde{\boldsymbol{z}}^* = \tilde{\boldsymbol{u}}^* - \tilde{\boldsymbol{v}}^* = \boldsymbol{P}\boldsymbol{z}^* = (\tilde{\boldsymbol{z}}_1^*, \tilde{\boldsymbol{z}}_2^*, \ldots, \tilde{\boldsymbol{z}}_t^*),$$

where $\tilde{\boldsymbol{u}}_i^* \in \mathbb{F}_q^{\alpha_i m}$, $\tilde{\boldsymbol{v}}_i^* \in \mathbb{F}_q^{\alpha_i m}$ and $\tilde{\boldsymbol{z}}_i^* \in \mathbb{F}_q^{\alpha_i m}$ for every $1 \le i \le t$. Then, the probability that both $\tilde{\boldsymbol{u}}_i^*$ and $\tilde{\boldsymbol{v}}_i^*$ are balanced and $w_{\mathrm{H}}(\tilde{\boldsymbol{z}}_i^*) = \gamma \alpha_i m$ for every $1 \le i \le t$ is

$$1/O\left(m^{\frac{(q-1)^2(q+1)t+t-1}{2}}\right).$$

Proof. For $\tilde{\boldsymbol{u}}_i^*$ and $\tilde{\boldsymbol{v}}_i^*$, let $\mathtt{Bal}_i$ be the event that both of $\tilde{\boldsymbol{u}}_i^*$ and $\tilde{\boldsymbol{v}}_i^*$ are balanced. Let $\tilde{\boldsymbol{u}}_i^* - \boldsymbol{r}_i = (\hat{u}_{i,1}^*, \hat{u}_{i,2}^*, \ldots, \hat{u}_{i,\alpha_i m}^*)$ and $\tilde{\boldsymbol{v}}_i^* - \boldsymbol{r}_i = (\hat{v}_{i,1}^*, \hat{v}_{i,2}^*, \ldots, \hat{v}_{i,\alpha_i m}^*)$. Let $\hat{S}_{x,y} = \{j \mid (\hat{u}_{i,j}^* = x) \wedge (\hat{v}_{i,j}^* = y)\}$ for $(x, y) \in \mathbb{F}_q^2$. Then, $\mathtt{Bal}_i$ occurs if $\boldsymbol{r}_i$ is balanced on the coordinates in $\hat{S}_{x,y}$ for every $(x, y) \in \mathbb{F}_q^2$. Thus,

$$\Pr[\mathtt{Bal}_i] \ge \binom{\alpha_i m}{\alpha_i m/q, \ldots, \alpha_i m/q}^{-1} \prod_{(x,y) \in \mathbb{F}_q^2} \binom{|\hat{S}_{x,y}|}{|\hat{S}_{x,y}|/q, \ldots, |\hat{S}_{x,y}|/q}$$

$$\approx \left(\frac{q^q}{(2\pi)^{q-1}}\right)^{\frac{(q-1)(q+1)}{2}} \left(\alpha_i m / \prod_{(x,y) \in \mathbb{F}_q^2} |\hat{S}_{x,y}|\right)^{\frac{q-1}{2}} = 1/O\left(m^{\frac{(q-1)^2(q+1)}{2}}\right).$$

For $\tilde{\boldsymbol{z}}^*$, since $\boldsymbol{P}$ is chosen uniformly at random,

$$\Pr\left[\bigwedge_{i=1}^t (w_{\mathrm{H}}(\tilde{\boldsymbol{z}}_i^*) = \gamma \alpha_i m)\right] = \binom{m}{\gamma m}^{-1} \prod_{i=1}^t \binom{\alpha_i m}{\gamma \alpha_i m} = 1/\Theta\left(m^{\frac{t-1}{2}}\right).$$

Since $\boldsymbol{P}$ and $\boldsymbol{r}$ are independent of each other,

$$\Pr\left[\bigwedge_{i=1}^t ((w_{\mathrm{H}}(\tilde{\boldsymbol{z}}_i^*) = \gamma \alpha_i m) \wedge \mathtt{Bal}_i)\right] = 1/O\left(m^{\frac{(q-1)^2(q+1)t+t-1}{2}}\right).$$

$\square$

From Lemma 1, with $O\left(m^{\frac{(q-1)^2(q+1)t+t-1}{2}}\right)$ executions of the for-loop from the line 7 to the line 13, the randomized unknown solution satisfying the conditions in Lemma 1 is given to the procedure NNR with overwhelming probability. Notice that the condition $w_H(\tilde{z}_i^*) = \gamma\alpha_i m$ for $1 \leq i \leq t$ cannot be checked since the solution is unknown. The proof of Lemma 1 validates the algorithm only if each piece of vectors has at least q^3 coordinates.

Lemma 2. *For a recursive call to the procedure NNR in the May-Ozerov algorithm, suppose that, for input $(\tilde{\mathcal{U}}, \tilde{\mathcal{V}}, m, t, \gamma, \lambda, \alpha_1, \ldots, \alpha_t, y, \varepsilon, i)$, $\tilde{\mathcal{U}} \times \tilde{\mathcal{V}}$ includes a (randomized) unknown solution $(\tilde{u}^*, \tilde{v}^*)$. Then, the probability that the input $\mathcal{U}' \times \mathcal{V}'$ to the next call also includes $(\tilde{u}^*, \tilde{v}^*)$ is $1/\tilde{O}(q^{y\alpha_i m})$ if A_i is chosen uniformly at random.*

Proof. From Lemma 1 and its proof, it is assumed that $\tilde{u}_i^*$ and $\tilde{v}_i^*$ satisfy the conditions in Lemma 1 and that r_i is balanced on the coordinates in $\tilde{S}_{x,y}$ for every $(x,y) \in \mathbb{F}_q^2$. Let $\tilde{u}_i^* = (\tilde{u}_{i,1}^*, \tilde{u}_{i,2}^*, \ldots, \tilde{u}_{i,\alpha_i m}^*)$ and $\tilde{v}_i^* = (\tilde{v}_{i,1}^*, \tilde{v}_{i,2}^*, \ldots, \tilde{v}_{i,\alpha_i m}^*)$. Let $\tilde{S}_{x,y} = \{j \mid (\tilde{u}_{i,j}^* = x) \wedge (\tilde{v}_{i,j}^* = y)\}$ for $(x,y) \in \mathbb{F}_q^2$.

Since $w_H(\tilde{u}_i^* - \tilde{v}_i^*) = \gamma\alpha_i m$ and r_i is balanced on the coordinates in $\hat{S}_{x,x}$ for every $x \in \mathbb{F}_q$, $|\tilde{S}_{x,x}| = (1-\gamma)\alpha_i m/q$ and

$$\sum_{y \in \mathbb{F}_q \setminus \{x\}} |\tilde{S}_{x,y}| = \sum_{y \in \mathbb{F}_q \setminus \{x\}} |\tilde{S}_{y,x}| = \frac{\alpha_i m}{q} - \frac{(1-\gamma)\alpha_i m}{q} = \frac{\gamma\alpha_i m}{q}$$

for every $x \in \mathbb{F}_q$.

For $x \in \mathbb{F}_q$, let h_x be positive reals such that $\sum_{x \in \mathbb{F}_q} h_x = 1$. The number of x in coordinates of $\tilde{u}^*$ in A_i is $h_x \beta\alpha_i m$ if $|A_i \cap \tilde{S}_{x,y}| = \beta|\tilde{S}_{x,y}|$ for every $y \in \mathbb{F}_q \setminus \{x\}$ and $|A_i \cap \tilde{S}_{x,x}| = h_x \beta\alpha_i m - \sum_{y \in \mathbb{F}_q \setminus \{x\}} \beta|\tilde{S}_{x,y}|$. Thus,

$$\Pr\left[\bigwedge_{x \in \mathbb{F}_q}\left(\left|A_i \cap \bigcup_{y \in \mathbb{F}_q} \tilde{S}_{x,y}\right| = h_x \beta\alpha_i m\right)\right]$$

$$\geq \binom{\alpha_i m}{\beta\alpha_i m}^{-1} \prod_{x \in \mathbb{F}_q}\left(\binom{|\tilde{S}_{x,x}|}{h_x\beta\alpha_i m - \sum_{y \in \mathbb{F}_q \setminus \{x\}}\beta|\tilde{S}_{x,y}|}\prod_{y \in \mathbb{F}_q \setminus \{x\}}\binom{|\tilde{S}_{x,y}|}{\beta|\tilde{S}_{x,y}|}\right)$$

$$= 1/\tilde{\Theta}\left(2^{(1-\gamma)\left(H(\beta) - \frac{1}{q}\sum_{x \in \mathbb{F}_q} H\left(\frac{qh_x - \gamma}{1-\gamma}\beta\right)\right)\alpha_i m}\right)$$

$$= 1/\tilde{\Theta}\left(q^{y\alpha_i m}\right),$$

where

$$y = (1-\gamma)\left(H_q(\beta) - \frac{1}{q}\sum_{x \in \mathbb{F}_q} H_q\left(\frac{qh_x - \gamma}{1-\gamma}\beta\right)\right).$$

Since $0 \leq \frac{qh_x - \gamma}{1-\gamma}\beta \leq 1$, $\gamma/q \leq h_x \leq \gamma/q + (1-\gamma)/(q\beta)$ for every $x \in \mathbb{F}_q$.
    Notice that, if

– $\left|A_i \cap \tilde{S}_{x,y}\right| = \beta\left|\tilde{S}_{x,y}\right|$ for every $(x,y) \in \mathbb{F}_q^2$ such that $x \neq y$, and
– $\left|A_i \cap \tilde{S}_{x,x}\right| = h_x \beta \alpha_i m - \sum_{y \in \mathbb{F}_q \setminus \{x\}} \beta\left|\tilde{S}_{x,y}\right|$ for every $x \in \mathbb{F}_q$,

the number of x in coordinates of $\tilde{v}^*$ in A_i is also $h_x \beta \alpha_i m$ for every $x \in \mathbb{F}_q$.   □

Lemma 3. *For the (m, γ, λ)-NN problem over $\mathbb{F}_q$, suppose that*

$$\lambda \leq H_q(\beta) - \frac{1}{q} \sum_{x \in \mathbb{F}_q} H_q(qh_x\beta),$$

where $\sum_{x \in \mathbb{F}_q} h_x = 1$ and $\gamma/q \leq h_x \leq \gamma/q + (1-\gamma)/(q\beta)$ for every $x \in \mathbb{F}_q$. For a recursive call to NNR with depth i in the May-Ozerov algorithm, if the input lists $\tilde{U} \times \tilde{V}$ include a (randomized) unknown solution, then the probability that $|U'|$ and $|V'|$ are $\tilde{O}\left(q^{\left(\lambda\left(1-\sum_{j=1}^i \alpha_j\right)+\varepsilon/2\right)m}\right)$ is at least $1 - 1/q^{\varepsilon m}$ for the input lists U' and V' to the next call which include the (randomized) unknown solution.

Lemma 4. *Let q be any prime power. Let γ be any real such that $0 < \gamma < 1/2$. Let β be any real such that $0 < \beta < 1$. Then,*

$$H_q(\beta) - \frac{1}{q} \sum_{x \in \mathbb{F}_q} H_q(qh_x\beta) \leq (1-\gamma)\left(H_q(\beta) - \frac{1}{q} \sum_{x \in \mathbb{F}_q} H_q\left(\frac{qh_x - \gamma}{1 - \gamma}\beta\right)\right)$$

for all h_x's such that $\sum_{x \in \mathbb{F}_q} h_x = 1$ and $\gamma/q \leq h_x \leq \gamma/q + (1-\gamma)/(q\beta)$ for every $x \in \mathbb{F}_q$. The equality is satisfied iff $h_x = 1/q$ for every $x \in \mathbb{F}_q$. In this case, both sides are equal to 0.

4   Stern ISD Using May-Ozerov NN Algorithm over $\mathbb{F}_q$

May and Ozerov applied their algorithm for the nearest-neighbor problem to the Stern ISD for linear codes over $\mathbb{F}_2$ [10]. It is quite straightforward to generalize it for linear codes over other finite fields with the algorithm presented in the previous section. The generalized decoding algorithm is given in Algorithm 2. As was mentioned earlier, the bounded distance decoding is considered. It is also assumed that, for a given instance (n, k, H, x), the distance d satisfies $k/n = 1 - H_q(d/n)$ and the distance between x and the closest codeword is $w = \lfloor (d-1)/2 \rfloor$.

Theorem 2. *For any $\varepsilon > 0$, the Stern ISD with the May-Ozerov NN algorithm solves the decoding problem of random $[n, k]$ linear codes over $\mathbb{F}_q$ with overwhelming probability in time*

$$\min_{p, \beta, \{h_x \,|\, x \in \mathbb{F}_q\}} \tilde{O}\left(q^{g(q, n, k, w, p, \beta, \{h_x \,|\, x \in \mathbb{F}_q\}, \varepsilon)}\right),$$

where

$$g(q, n, k, w, p, \beta, \{h_x \,|\, x \in \mathbb{F}_q\}, \varepsilon) =$$
$$(\log_q 2)\left(nH\left(\frac{w}{n}\right) - kH\left(\frac{p}{k}\right) - (n-k)H\left(\frac{w-p}{n-k}\right)\right) + (y + \varepsilon)(n - k)$$

Algorithm 2. Stern ISD with May-Ozerov Nearest-Neighbor Algorithm over $\mathbb{F}_q$

1: **procedure** ISD$(n, k, \boldsymbol{H}, \boldsymbol{x})$ $\triangleright\ \boldsymbol{H} \in \mathbb{F}_q^{(n-k) \times n},\ \boldsymbol{x} \in \mathbb{F}_q^n$
2:   $\boldsymbol{s} \leftarrow \boldsymbol{H} \boldsymbol{x}$
3:   $d \leftarrow H_q^{-1}(1 - k/n) \cdot n$
4:   $w \leftarrow \lfloor (d-1)/2 \rfloor$
5:   Select p $\triangleright\ \max\{1, w+k-n\} \le p \le \min\{k, w\}$
6:   **repeat**
7:    **repeat**
8:     Select a permutation matrix $\boldsymbol{P} \in \{0,1\}^{n \times n}$ u.a.r.
9:     $(\ \cdot\ \boldsymbol{Q}) \leftarrow \boldsymbol{H} \boldsymbol{P}$
10:    **until** $\boldsymbol{Q}$ is non-singular
11:    $\tilde{\boldsymbol{H}} \leftarrow \boldsymbol{Q}^{-1} \boldsymbol{H} \boldsymbol{P}$
12:    $\tilde{\boldsymbol{s}} \leftarrow \boldsymbol{Q}^{-1} \boldsymbol{s}$
13:    $\mathcal{U} \leftarrow \{\boldsymbol{u} \,|\, \boldsymbol{u} = \tilde{\boldsymbol{H}} \boldsymbol{e}_1$ for $\boldsymbol{e}_1 \in \mathbb{F}_q^{k/2} \times \{0\}^{k/2} \times \{0\}^{n-k}$ s.t. $w_{\mathrm{H}}(\boldsymbol{e}_1) = p/2\}$
14:    $\mathcal{V} \leftarrow \{\boldsymbol{v} \,|\, \boldsymbol{v} = \tilde{\boldsymbol{H}} \boldsymbol{e}_2 + \tilde{\boldsymbol{s}}$ for $\boldsymbol{e}_2 \in \{0\}^{k/2} \times \mathbb{F}_q^{k/2} \times \{0\}^{n-k}$ s.t. $w_{\mathrm{H}}(\boldsymbol{e}_2) = p/2\}$
15:    $\mathcal{C} \leftarrow$ MO-NN$(\mathcal{U}, \mathcal{V}, (w-p)/(n-k))$ $\triangleright$ Run the May-Ozerov NN algorithm
   over $\mathbb{F}_q$
16:   **until** there exists $(\boldsymbol{u}^*, \boldsymbol{v}^*) \in \mathcal{C}$ s.t. $w_{\mathrm{H}}(\boldsymbol{u}^* - \boldsymbol{v}^*) = w - p$
17:   **return** $\boldsymbol{P}(\boldsymbol{e}_1^* - \boldsymbol{e}_2^* - (0^k \| (\boldsymbol{u}^* - \boldsymbol{v}^*)))$ $\triangleright\ \boldsymbol{u}^* = \tilde{\boldsymbol{H}} \boldsymbol{e}_1^*$ and $\boldsymbol{v}^* = \tilde{\boldsymbol{H}} \boldsymbol{e}_2^* + \tilde{\boldsymbol{s}}$
18: **end procedure**

---

and

$$y = (1 - \gamma) \left(H_q(\beta) - \frac{1}{q} \sum_{x \in \mathbb{F}_q} H_q \left(\frac{q h_x - \gamma}{1 - \gamma} \beta \right) \right)$$

with $\gamma = (w - p)/(n - k)$. The conditions on p, β and $\{h_x \,|\, x \in \mathbb{F}_q\}$ for minimization are

- $\max\{1, w+k-n\} \le p \le \min\{k, w\}$,
- $0 < \beta < 1$,
- $\displaystyle\sum_{x \in \mathbb{F}_q} h_x = 1$,
- $\gamma/q \le h_x \le \gamma/q + (1 - \gamma)/(q\beta)$, *and*
- $\dfrac{(k/2) H_q(p/k)}{n - k} < H_q(\beta) - \dfrac{1}{q} \displaystyle\sum_{x \in \mathbb{F}_q} H_q(q h_x \beta)$.

5   Numerical Analysis of Time Complexity

Some numerical analyses are given to the asymptotic time complexity of the Stern ISD using the May-Ozerov NN algorithm over $\mathbb{F}_q$.

For the time complexity of the Stern ISD with May-Ozerov NN algorithm over $\mathbb{F}_q$, let

$$T(q, n, k, w) = \min_{p, \beta, \{h_x \,|\, x \in \mathbb{F}_q\}} q^{g(q, n, k, w, p, \beta, \{h_x \,|\, x \in \mathbb{F}_q\}, \varepsilon)}.$$

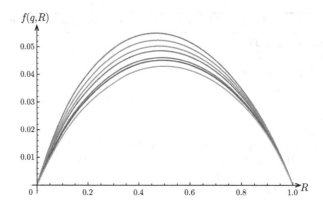

Fig. 1. Asymptotic time complexity of the Stern ISD with the May-Ozerov NN algorithm over $\mathbb{F}_q$. $q = 2, 3, 4, 5, 7, 8, 11$ in the decreasing order.

Then, $\lim_{n\to\infty} \frac{1}{n} \log_q T(q, n, k, w)$ is a function of q and $R = k/n$. Let us denote it by $f(q, R)$. The asymptotic time complexity is evaluated with $f(q, R)$. Since $\varepsilon > 0$ is arbitrary from Theorem 2, it is neglected in the analysis given below.

To obtain the values of $f(q, R)$, the numerical optimization problem given in Theorem 2 is solved for $q = 2, 3, 4$. For $q = 3, 4$, the optimal values are obtained for h_x's such that all but one of them have the same value. Thus, for some larger values of q, the optimization problem is solved on the assumption that all but one of h_x's are equal to each other.

The curves of $f(q, R)$ for $q = 2, 3, 4, 5, 7, 8, 11$ are given in Fig. 1. $f(q, R)$ gets smaller as q gets larger.

Table 1. Asymptotic time complexity of worst cases for bounded distance decoding. $\Delta = f(q, R_w) - f_S(q, R'_w)$. For Stern-MO, all but one of h_x's are equal to h.

	Stern-MO					Stern		
q	$f(q, R_w)$	R_w	p/n	β	h	$f_S(q, R'_w)$	R'_w	Δ
2	.05498	.4663	.003848	.4998	.3981	.05563	.4655	−.00065
3	.05242	.4736	.002979	.1792	.2322	.05217	.4742	.00025
4	.05032	.4796	.002201	.0932	.1644	.04987	.4801	.00045
5	.04864	.4843	.001704	.0593	.1279	.04815	.4844	.00049
7	.04614	.4909	.001164	.0326	.0893	.04571	.4907	.00043
8	.04519	.4933	.001006	.0263	.0778	.04478	.4931	.00041
11	.04299	.4989	.000727	.0166	.0563	.04266	.4985	.00033

Table 1 presents the asymptotic time complexity of the worst cases for bounded distance decoding. In this table, Stern-MO represents the Stern ISD with the May-Ozerov NN algorithm, and Stern represents the Stern ISD given in Algorithm 3. $f_S(q, R)$ is defined for the Stern ISD similarly to $f(q, R)$. The results for $q = 2$ are consistent with the results by May and Ozerov in [10]. It is shown that, in this analysis, the Stern-MO algorithm outperforms the Stern algorithm only over $\mathbb{F}_2$. For $q \geq 5$, as q gets larger, the degradation of the Stern-MO algorithm gets smaller.

Algorithm 3. Stern ISD over $\mathbb{F}_q$

1: **procedure** ISD$(n, k, \boldsymbol{H}, \boldsymbol{x})$ $\triangleright$ $\boldsymbol{H} \in \mathbb{F}_q^{(n-k)\times n}$, $\boldsymbol{x} \in \mathbb{F}_q^n$
2:     $\boldsymbol{s} \leftarrow \boldsymbol{H}\boldsymbol{x}$
3:     $d \leftarrow H_q^{-1}(1 - k/n) \cdot n$
4:     $w \leftarrow \lfloor (d-1)/2 \rfloor$
5:     Select p and ℓ $\triangleright$ $0 \leq \ell \leq n - k$ and $\max\{0, k + w + \ell - n\} < p < \min\{k, w\}$
6:     **repeat**
7:        **repeat**
8:           Select a permutation matrix $\boldsymbol{P} \in \{0, 1\}^{n \times n}$ u.a.r.
9:           $(\cdot \; \boldsymbol{Q}) \leftarrow \boldsymbol{H}\boldsymbol{P}$
10:        **until** $\boldsymbol{Q}$ is non-singular
11:        $\tilde{\boldsymbol{H}} \leftarrow \boldsymbol{Q}^{-1}\boldsymbol{H}\boldsymbol{P}$
12:        $\tilde{\boldsymbol{s}} \leftarrow \boldsymbol{Q}^{-1}\boldsymbol{s}$
13:        $\mathcal{U} \leftarrow \{\boldsymbol{u} \mid \boldsymbol{u} = \tilde{\boldsymbol{H}}\boldsymbol{e}_1$ for $\boldsymbol{e}_1 \in \mathbb{F}_q^{k/2} \times \{0\}^{k/2} \times \{0\}^{n-k}$ s.t. $w_H(\boldsymbol{e}_1) = p/2\}$
14:        $\mathcal{V} \leftarrow \{\boldsymbol{v} \mid \boldsymbol{v} = \tilde{\boldsymbol{H}}\boldsymbol{e}_2 + \tilde{\boldsymbol{s}}$ for $\boldsymbol{e}_2 \in \{0\}^{k/2} \times \mathbb{F}_q^{k/2} \times \{0\}^{n-k}$ s.t. $w_H(\boldsymbol{e}_2) = p/2\}$
15:        sort the vectors in $\mathcal{U}$ with respect to the last ℓ coordinates
16:        sort the vectors in $\mathcal{V}$ with respect to the last ℓ coordinates
17:        **for all** $(\boldsymbol{u}, \boldsymbol{v}) \in \mathcal{U} \times \mathcal{V}$ s.t. $\boldsymbol{u}$ and $\boldsymbol{v}$ are equal in the last ℓ coordinates **do**
18:           check if $w_H(\boldsymbol{u} - \boldsymbol{v}) = w - p$
19:        **end for**
20:     **until** there exists $(\boldsymbol{u}^*, \boldsymbol{v}^*) \in \mathcal{U} \times \mathcal{V}$ s.t. $w_H(\boldsymbol{u}^* - \boldsymbol{v}^*) = w - p$
21:     **return** $\boldsymbol{P}(\boldsymbol{e}_1^* - \boldsymbol{e}_2^* - (0^k \| (\boldsymbol{u}^* - \boldsymbol{v}^*)))$ $\triangleright$ $\boldsymbol{u}^* = \tilde{\boldsymbol{H}}\boldsymbol{e}_1^*$ and $\boldsymbol{v}^* = \tilde{\boldsymbol{H}}\boldsymbol{e}_2^* + \tilde{\boldsymbol{s}}$
22: **end procedure**

---

6 Conclusion

The paper have shown a generalization of the May-Ozerov NN algorithm over $\mathbb{F}_q$ with any prime power q. The complexity analysis suggests that the May-Ozerov NN algorithm over $\mathbb{F}_q$ may not be practical even for small prime $q \geq 3$ due to the huge polynomial which does not appear in the $\tilde{O}$ notation of its time complexity. It is an open problem if more rigorous analysis or some other generalization over $\mathbb{F}_q$ reduces the time complexity. It is also left as future work to analyze the complexity of the BJMM information set decoding with the May-Ozerov NN algorithm over $\mathbb{F}_q$.

Acknowledgments. This work was supported in part by JSPS KAKENHI Grant Numbers JP25330152 and JP16H02828.

References

1. Becker, A., Joux, A., May, A., Meurer, A.: Decoding random binary linear codes in $2^{n/20}$: how $1 + 1 = 0$ improves information set decoding. In: Pointcheval, D., Johansson, T. (eds.) EUROCRYPT 2012. LNCS, vol. 7237, pp. 520–536. Springer, Heidelberg (2012)
2. Bernstein, D.J., Lange, T., Peters, C.: Smaller decoding exponents: ball-collision decoding. In: Rogaway, P. (ed.) CRYPTO 2011. LNCS, vol. 6841, pp. 743–760. Springer, Heidelberg (2011)
3. Coffey, J.T., Goodman, R.M.: Any code of which we cannot think is good. IEEE Trans. Inf. Theory **36**(6), 1453–1461 (1990)
4. Coffey, J.T., Goodman, R.M.: The complexity of information set decoding. IEEE Trans. Inf. Theory **36**(5), 1031–1037 (1990)
5. Finiasz, M., Sendrier, N.: Security bounds for the design of code-based cryptosystems. In: Matsui, M. (ed.) ASIACRYPT 2009. LNCS, vol. 5912, pp. 88–105. Springer, Heidelberg (2009)
6. Hirose, S.: May-Ozerov algorithm for nearest-neighbor problem over $\mathbb{F}_q$ and its application to information set decoding. IACR Cryptology ePrint Archive, Report 2016/237 (2016)
7. Howgrave-Graham, N., Joux, A.: New generic algorithms for hard knapsacks. In: Gilbert, H. (ed.) EUROCRYPT 2010. LNCS, vol. 6110, pp. 235–256. Springer, Heidelberg (2010)
8. Lee, P.J., Brickell, E.F.: An observation on the security of McEliece's public-key cryptosystem. In: Günther, C.G. (ed.) EUROCRYPT 1988. LNCS, vol. 330, pp. 275–280. Springer, Heidelberg (1988)
9. May, A., Meurer, A., Thomae, E.: Decoding random linear codes in $\tilde{\mathcal{O}}(2^{0.054n})$. In: Lee, D.H., Wang, X. (eds.) ASIACRYPT 2011. LNCS, vol. 7073, pp. 107–124. Springer, Heidelberg (2011)
10. May, A., Ozerov, I.: On computing nearest neighbors with applications to decoding of binary linear codes. In: Oswald, E., Fischlin, M. (eds.) EUROCRYPT 2015. LNCS, vol. 9056, pp. 203–228. Springer, Heidelberg (2015)
11. McEliece, R.J.: A public-key cryptosystem based on algebraic coding theory. Jet Propulsion Laboratory DSN Progress Report 4244 (1978)
12. Meurer, A.: A coding-theoretic approach to cryptanalysis. Ph.D. thesis, Ruhr-University Bochum (2012)
13. Peters, C.: Information-set decoding for linear codes over $\mathbf{F}_q$. In: Sendrier, N. (ed.) PQCrypto 2010. LNCS, vol. 6061, pp. 81–94. Springer, Heidelberg (2010)
14. Prange, E.: The use of information sets in decoding cyclic codes. IRE Trans. Inf. Theory **8**(5), 5–9 (1962)
15. Stern, J.: A method for finding codewords of small weight. In: Cohen, G.D., Wolfmann, J. (eds.) Coding Theory and Applications. LNCS, vol. 388, pp. 106–113. Springer, Heidelberg (1988)

A Cryptographic Approach for Implementing Semantic Web's Trust Layer

Bogdan Iancu[1(✉)] and Cristian Sandu[2]

[1] The Bucharest University of Economic Studies,
Bucharest, Romania
bogdan.iancu@ie.ase.ro
[2] Cegeka, Blockchain Team, Bucharest, Romania
cristian.sandu@cegeka.com

Abstract. Even if the core technologies for the semantic web are in place, it still lacks some layers that prevent it from being a fully implemented system. One of these layers is the trustworthiness one. In this paper we propose a way to implement trust by the usage of the technology that stays behind the cryptocurrencies. After an analysis of the existing blockchains, an example is built on top of Openchain in order to demonstrate our approach.

Keywords: Semantic web · Trust layer · Bitcoin · Blockchain · Cryptocurrency

1   Introduction

The semantic web or web 3.0 is soon to be the newest version of the world wide web. Based especially on meta-data, this new web allows some specific designed software agents to understand the content of web pages, content that was comprehensible until now only for humans. In order to do so, it organizes all its data into the so called ontologies. Even if most of the key technologies for implementing the semantic web are in place and already standardized by the W3C Consortium [1] (technologies like RDF, RDFS, OWL, SPARQL, etc.), there is still one area that is work in progress. This area, or layer according to the semantic web technologies cake (Fig. 1), is the trust. In order to create a complete semantic web application or at least a secure one, we need trust on top of everything. Even if they are some ideas for modeling this layer, ideas based on user feedback [2] or different types of certificates [3], those couldn't stand against a day by day worldwide spread semantic web (the first case) or want to apply some old technologies for securing an out of the box one (the second case). In this paper we present a new approach for dealing with ontology trustworthiness by using a new technology stack from the cryptography domain called blockchain system.

© Springer International Publishing AG 2016
I. Bica and R. Reyhanitabar (Eds.): SECITC 2016, LNCS 10006, pp. 127–136, 2016.
DOI: 10.1007/978-3-319-47238-6_9

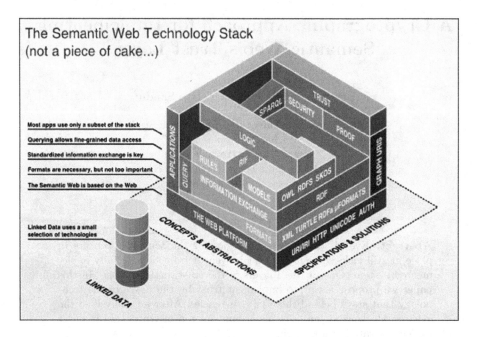

Fig. 1. The semantic web, not a piece of cake (Source: http://bnode.org/blog/2009/ 07/08/the-semantic-web-not-a-piece-of-cake)

2 Blockchain Systems

2.1 Bitcoin

In order to talk about block chain systems (or blockchain) we need to talk in the first place about the idea that generated everything: the Bitcoin electronic cash system. Bitcoin was introduced to the world in the year 2008, in an anonymous paper signed with the now famous pseudonym "Satoshi Nakamoto".

Bitcoin's goal was to offer a way to transfer money from user to user without going through a financial institution or any central entity for that matter. To achieve this goal the system uses digital signatures to seal transactions and an algorithm called proof-of-work for making the system resilient against attacks. The creator of the Bitcoin system describes the system in the following words:

> "The network timestamps transactions by hashing them into an ongoing chain of hash-based proof-of-work, forming a record that cannot be changed without redoing the proof-of-work. The longest chain not only serves as proof of the sequence of events witnessed, but proof that it came from the largest pool of CPU power. As long as a majority of CPU power is controlled by nodes that are not cooperating to attack the network, they'll generate the longest chain and outpace attackers" [4].

The chain of hashes referenced here is in fact the block chain that we will be talking about in this section of our paper. Whether Bitcoin (BTC) has succeeded in creating this perfect distributed network for transacting electronic money is debatable. A later paper [5] argues that it has failed in a few key points, like providing a democratic system where one CPU is one vote when processing transactions. That is however not the object of this paper.

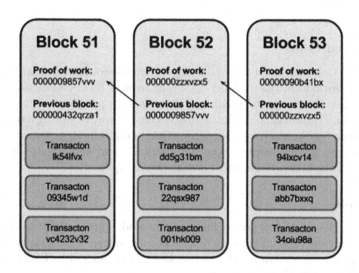

Fig. 2. The transaction ledger (Source: http://www.ybrikman.com/writing/2014/04/24/bitcoin-by-analogy/)

The block chain is used in the Bitcoin network solely for storing BTC transactions. That is why we sometimes refer to the a block chain as a "transaction ledger". To safeguard the data stored on a blockchain when a new block is introduced to the chain, this new block will also contain the previous block's hash (as seen in Fig. 2). If we were to tamper with the transaction data stored in previous blocks the chain would "break", making all following hashes and blocks invalid. If we would try to publish this corrupted data to the network, the other participants would reject it. The software nodes participating in the Bitcoin network in this fashion are known as "miners". The incentive for participating in the network is the fact that when a new block is found (the proof-of-work according to [4] is completed) by a miner, he gets a reward of 25 BTC (used to be 50).

2.2 From Bitcoin to Blockchain

Whether Bitcoin will succeed in being an universal and democratic electronic cash solution is probably a philosophical debate at this point. However, the technology behind it, the blockchain, has been picked up by a diverse group of companies that are looking to revolutionize both financial and administrative intuitions.

Blockchains are interesting systems because they propose that the trust should be placed in a technology (or a software protocol) instead of a certified entity like a bank or a notary. The software of course needs to be open source in order to inspire confidence and assure that no person is controlling it.

In the next part of this section we present a few of these blockchain based technologies.

2.3 Colored Coins

The Colored Coins protocol works directly on the Bitcoin blockchain by adding additional information (meta-data) on top of regular BTC transactions (something that the Bitcoin protocol allows). It is as such possible to give a special meaning to any transaction. A transaction becomes a way of storing data directly on the Bitcoin blockchain (like a property title or a digitally signed document) [6].

Data stored in this manner becomes read-only and permanent (or at least until the Bitcoin network disbands, if that ever happens).

2.4 Ripple

Ripple Labs (formerly Opencoin) has implemented a protocol for trading both virtual currencies (called crypto-currencies because of the cryptography involved in hashing and signing transactions) and FIAT currencies (like USD, EUR) on top of a Bitcoin-like software network.

The Ripple protocol diverges from Bitcoin in a few key points:

- The proof-of-work no longer needs to be computed, the network operates instead on a consensus based protocol, in which it is enough for 80 % of a set of trusted nodes to agree upon the next block of transactions [7]
- The embedded virtual currency, called XRP (ripples), is sourced from a root account that contains the entire volume to be used during the lifetime of the network (XRP is never issued)
- A special construction called a trust line allows the users to send FIAT currency transactions on the network, not just XRP. This is similar to how banks function, having in consideration that the virtual FIAT currency is issued by a trusted entity called Gateway. A user A can send FIAT currency to user B, if and only if a trust line path can be found between them. In simple terms, this only works if the entities that issued our currency trust each other (like banks).

Ripple demonstrated that the interaction between classical financial institutions and crypto-currency based systems is possible [8].

2.5 Stellar

Like Ripple, Stellar drops the proof-of-work algorithm and goes for a consensus protocol. However, the Stellar consensus protocol (a FBA - Federated Byzantine Agreement - model) differs from Ripple's implementation. The main difference is the usage of quorum slices. They describe their model as:

"By agreeing on what updates to apply, nodes avoid contradictory, irreconcilable states. We identify each update by a unique slot from which inter-update dependencies can be inferred. For instance, slots may be consecutively numbered positions in a sequentially applied log. In a consensus protocol, nodes exchange messages asserting statements about slots. We assume such assertions cannot be forged, which can be guaranteed if nodes are named by public key and they digitally sign messages. When a node hears a sufficient set of nodes assert a statement, it assumes no functioning node will ever contradict that statement. We call such a sufficient set a quorum slice, or, more concisely, just a slice. To permit progress in the face of node failures, a node may have multiple slices, any one of which is sufficient to convince it of a statement. At a high level, then, an FBA system consists of a loose confederation of nodes each of which has chosen one or more slice" [9].

2.6   Permissioned Blockchains

All the systems discussed so far are "unpermissioned" - anyone can submit transactions on the public network without any restrictions. In a permissioned system, the protocol allows for limiting the actions that a participant can take on a given object (not to be confused with a transaction, anyone can still submit transactions but they will fail if the transaction affects an object which the user doesn't have access to). The best examples are the smart contract oriented blockchain systems which we will present in detail in the next paragraphs.

Ethereum takes a different approach than previously discussed systems. It works on the premise that a blockchain is after all a storage engine and pretty much anything can be encoded as a transaction [10].

The declared purpose of Ethereum is to offer a framework for creating "smart contracts". A smart contract is set of rules defined as a class (a concept borrowed from object oriented programming languages like Java, C++, C#, etc.) which model an interaction between a set of users of the blockchain (each user is identified by a public key).

Like Ripple and Bitcoin, Ethereum relies on a cryptocurrency which is used for paying for actions within the network, as well as rewarding miners (nodes that validate transactions). The fact that users have to pay for actions also protects the network against spam. Ethereum currently uses a proof-of-work algorithm.

Theoretically, this system can be used for a large set of applications, not just financial transactions, like regulating property deed transfers (like a virtual notary), inter-mediating international trading, controlling signed documents and much more.

Because interactions between users on Ethereum can be moderated via a smart contract, Ethereum is a permissioned blockchain system. Ethereum also allows for crypto-currency transfer using its embedded coin, the "ether".

Tendermint takes the general purpose blockchain a step further and strips the application layer from the blockchain and offers only the basic functions of a blockchain:

– Storage of data on the blockchain
– A protocol for communicating transactions and proposed blocks between peers
– A consensus based protocol for verifying transactions

Everything else is up to the user. Including what it means for a transaction to be valid. Using Tendermint API you can build Ethereum like systems or pretty much everything else.

Tendermint wants to position itself at the bottom of the software stack of a blockchain based application, leaving the logic of the application entirely up to third party developers. This however, opens up some trust issues because the source of the software becomes more fragmented [11].

Sidechains or "two-way pegged sidechains" are a method of using the Bitcoin main blockchain for operating with more advanced altcoins, without modifying the proven Bitcoin protocol. They propose to do this by first locking an amount of Bitcoin on the main chain which then gets created with the same value on a secondary blockchain, gets transacted using a protocol of the blockchain's designer's choice and then gets put back on the Bitcoin blockchain (the BTC gets unlocked) [12].

As of now there is no proper implementation, with a company named Blockstream (https://blockstream.com/) working on the first such sidechain.

While the current sidechain efforts are geared towards the Bitcoin network, a sidechain can, in theory, be built for any pre-existing blockchain. As long as one can construct a protocol for associating transactions from his blockchain to transactions on the main blockchain.

A common way to do this is to publish a hash of a block in one's blockchain as a transaction on the main blockchain. In general, the main blockchain is considered the more secure one and is used to ensure the immutability of the smaller sidechain. This, however, is actually a "one-way pegged" strategy (so not a proper sidechain) because the original transactions of the sidechain cannot be recovered from the data on the main blockchain; for the proper way to do sidechains see the first paragraph of this section.

Openchain, the solution discussed in the next section, implements this simplified one-way sidechain strategy.

Openchain is an initiative by Coinprism (https://www.coinprism.com/), who have experience with Colored Coins [6]. Their focus is transacting digital assets (like on colored coins) within the context of enterprise applications. Also, according to their published documents [13], transactions are validated by a centralized server deployed in a trusted enterprise environment.

Openchain however is not a "blockchain" per se because it directly chains transactions instead of grouping them into blocks to provide instant validation. In order to get the same benefits as a traditional blockchain implementation,

Openchain uses the Bitcoin blockchain to periodically (on each BTC block) save a hash of its entire chain in a BTC transaction.

3   A New Way to Provide Trust

Blockchains are, at their core, a secure and immutable database where transactions are signed read-only entries (or rows in DB lingo).

All blockchain implementations allow for storing meta-data (sometimes called memos) on a transaction. While the initial purpose of transactions was to send value from one address (user) to another, the systems quickly evolved to store all kinds of data. For example, Ethereum stores code and changes on that code using transactions on a blockchain while colored coins was demonstrated as a way to store safely land ownership bills.

Using this logic we can infer that any object can be stored on a blockchain, the advantages being:

- Data is secured using cryptography - all inserts (transactions) are signed using an ECDSA (secp256k1 curve) key-pair
- Data is immutable - once a transaction is final, it's data is stored forever on the chain
- We can build a system where all signed data can be traced back to a real person (the holder of the public key) - similar to digital certificates

Those being said we can infer that ontologies (which are in fact meta-data) can be securely stored in a blockchain. More than that we can certify and track each ontology statement (usually expressed as a Subject-Property-Object declaration) back to its creator. Even if we talk about domain specific ontologies or general ones, each and every change in the ontology will be saved in the blockchain. If the ontology is domain-specific then the blockchain system should probably be a permissioned one, otherwise an unpermissioned blockchain is enough. The idea is quite new with a small amount of related work [14]. In the next section we present a study case built on top of Openchain that puts our theory (blockchains as the trust layer of the semantic web technologies) to the test.

4   Using the Blockchain as a Trust Layer

Let's say that "The John Lennon Museum" wants to create an ontology about John Lennon. They start by creating a simple ontology that uses the DBpedia URI as an identifier and offers some simple information like date of birth and spouse (ontology inspired by the example presented at http://json-ld.org/). They decide to store the information by using the RDF standard and to encode it in the JSON-LD format. In order to do so, they create an account on the Openchain's official site (https://wallet.openchain.org/) and they issue their own digital asset with the short name JLM. They store the JSON-LD from bellow in the digital asset's definition. Additionally, the Openchain server will take care of periodically securing its chain via storing a snapshot of its data on the Bitcoin public blockchain. To store data on an asset in Openchain the user should modify its [DATA] asdef (asset definition) entry via a transaction signed by the owner of that asset. Again, all changes (transactions) are signed and can be traced back to their creator.

The initial stored data is:

```
{"name":"The John Lennon Museum",
  "name_short":"JLM",
  "icon_url":"",
      "metadata":{
          "@context": "http://schema.org/",
          "@type": "Person",
          "@id": "http://dbpedia.org/resource/John_Lennon",
          "name": "John Lennon",
          "born": "1940-10-09",
          "spouse": "http://dbpedia.org/resource/Cynthia_Lennon"
      }
}
```

We can inspect the data by using a browser based Openchain client and confirm that it is stored (Fig. 3):

Fig. 3. The initial asset definition

After that, let's say that the Virgin Books Publishing House, which published "The John Lennon Encyclopedia", wants to add that John Lennon was also married to Yoko Ono. In order to do so they create their own asset on the Openchain platform with the short name VBP. They store the JSON-LD from bellow in the digital asset's definition.

```
{"name":"Virgin Books Publishing House",
  "name_short":"VBP",
  "icon_url":"",
      "metadata":{
          "@context": "http://schema.org/",
          "@type": "Person",
          "@id": "http://dbpedia.org/resource/John_Lennon",
          "spouse": "http://dbpedia.org/resource/Yoko_Ono"
      }
}
```

After some time, let's assume that Daily Mail, which is known for its not-so-verified news, finds out from an obscure source that John Lennon was also married in secret with Brian Epstein. They proceed with the creation of a new asset with the short name DMN. After that, they store their own JSON-LD in the Openchain system. Their digital asset's definition can look like the one from below:

```
{"name":"Daily Mail Newspaper",
  "name_short":"DMN",
  "icon_url":"",
      "metadata":{
          "@context": "http://schema.org/",
          "@type": "Person",
          "@id": "http://dbpedia.org/resource/John_Lennon",
          "spouse": "http://dbpedia.org/resource/Brian_Epstein"
      }
}
```

Now anyone who is interested in John Lennon's personal relationships can follow all the changes done to the ontology (and the makers of these changes) by looking at the related transactions. A serious researcher interested about John Lennon's personal life will probably take into consideration the first two transactions because they came from trustworthy sources and will ignore the third one because the asset issuer is not a trustworthy source.

5   Conclusions

In this paper we presented a new approach for providing a trust layer for the semantic web technologies by the usage of blockchain systems. The blockchain systems appeared together with the revolutionary idea that generated everything: The Bitcoin. We presented a short history of the blockchain systems together with a classification based on permissions. In the final part we explained with an example how the blockchain systems can act as a trust layer for the semantic web.

Acknowledgments. We would like to address some special thanks to all the members of the Cegeka's Blockchain team: Alexandru Baloc, Andrei Grigoriu, Gabriel Purcaru and Alexandru Gherghe. Without their help this paper would not have been possible.

References

1. Semantic Web - W3C. https://www.w3.org/standards/semanticweb/
2. Ceravolo, P., Damiani, G., Viviani, M.: Adding a trust layer to semantic web metadata. In: Herrera-Viedma, E., Pasi, G., Crestani, F. (eds.) Soft Computing in Web Information Retrieval. SFSC, vol. 197, pp. 87–104. Springer, Berlin (2006)
3. Leuf, B.: The Semantic Web: Crafting Infrastructure for Agency. Wiley, Chichester (2006)
4. Nakamoto, S.: Bitcoin: A Peer-to-Peer Electronic Cash System (2008). https://bitcoin.org/bitcoin.pdf
5. Saberhagen, N.: CryptoNote v 2.0 (2013). https://downloads.getmonero.org/whitepaper_annotated.pdf
6. Rosenfeld, M.: Overview of Colored Coins (2012). https://bitcoil.co.il/BitcoinX.pdf
7. Schwartz, D., Youngs, N., Britto, A.: The Ripple Protocol Consensus Algorithm. Ripple Labs Inc White Paper (2014). http://www.theblockchaininfo.com/wp-content/uploads/2015/07/ripple_consensus_whitepaper.pdf
8. Liu, A.: Ripple Labs Signs First Two US Banks (2014). https://ripple.com/insights/ripple-labs-signs-first-two-us-banks
9. Mazieres, D.: The Stellar Consensus Protocol: A Federated Model for Internet-level Consensus. Draft, Stellar Development Foundation (2016). https://www.stellar.org/papers/stellar-consensus-protocol.pdf
10. Wood, G.: Ethereum: A Secure Decentralised Generalised Transaction Ledger. Homestead Draft (2014). http://gavwood.com/paper.pdf
11. Kwon, J.: Tendermint: Consensus Without Mining (2014). http://tendermint.com/docs/tendermint.pdf
12. Back, A., Corallo, M., Dashjr, L., et al.: Enabling Blockchain Innovations with Pegged Sidechains (2014). https://www.blockstream.com/sidechains.pdf
13. Openchain: Openchain 0.5 Documentation (2015). https://docs.openchain.org/en/latest/
14. ISITC Europe: Blockchain Work Stream Inaugural Meeting (2016). http://www.isitc-europe.com/files/documents/Complete-presentation-for-Blockchain-Event-FINAL.pdf

Schnorr-Like Identification Scheme Resistant to Malicious Subliminal Setting of Ephemeral Secret

Łukasz Krzywiecki[(✉)]

Faculty of Fundamental Problems of Technology, Department of Computer Science,
Wrocław University of Technology, Wrocław, Poland
lukasz.krzywiecki@pwr.wroc.pl

Abstract. In this paper we propose a modification of the Schnorr *Identification Scheme* (IS), which is immune to malicious subliminal setting of ephemeral secret. We introduce a new strong security model in which, during the *query stage*, we allow the adversary verifier to set random values used on the prover side in the commitment phase. We define the IS scheme to be secure if such a setting will not enable the adversary to impersonate the prover later on. Subsequently we prove the security of the modified Schnorr IS in our strong model. We assume the proposition is important for scenarios in which we do not control the production process of the device on which the scheme is implemented, and where the erroneous pseudo-random number generators make such attacks possible.

Keywords: Identification scheme · Ephemeral secret setting · Ephemeral secret leakage · Deniability · Simulatability

1 Introduction

An identification scheme enables one party - a *prover* - to prove its identity in front of another party - a *verifier*. In many *public key* IS constructions the prover has a long term secret key, and proves its knowledge in such a way, that the verifier, provided with the corresponding public key of the prover, is convince about that fact but gets no information about the prover's secret. Typically the proving protocol consists of three rounds: a *commitment*, a *challenge*, and a *response*. In the *commitment* the prover sends to the verifier a commitment to some random ephemeral value (so called the ephemeral secret). In the *challenge* the verifier sends back to the prover some random unpredictable value. In the *response* the prover send to the verifier the result of some computations, involving the received challenge, and its long term secret key masked by the ephemeral value committed in the first message. The prover is accepted if the response "agrees" with the computation on the verifier side involving the commitment, the challenge, the response and the public key of the prover.

Partially supported by funding from Polish NCN contract number DEC-2013/09/D/ST6/03927.

I. Bica and R. Reyhanitabar (Eds.): SECITC 2016, LNCS 10006, pp. 137–148, 2016.
DOI: 10.1007/978-3-319-47238-6_10

Problem Statement. The problem with this construction arises in systems (protocol implementations), where the ephemeral secrets may be leaked. Usually the masking method in the *response* is such, that the security of the long term key relies on the secrecy of the ephemeral key - e.g. the response value is a linear combination of the challenge, the committed ephemeral secret, and the long term secret. Thus, once the ephemeral secrets is leaked the long term secret is also compromised.

The leakage of the ephemeral secret can be archived by some malicious implementation of the device which is used to perform computation on the prover side. Such a device usually has a *High Secure Memory* module (HSM), where long term secrets are kept securely and accessed (indirectly) only via predefined interfaces. A less secure area is used for scheme program computations, including random numbers sampling. Especially implementations of the pseudo-random number generators are vulnerable to attacks. If the adversary can somehow learn their state, it can also learn random values (and ephemerals) produced by those generators. Sometimes even a subtle subliminal adversarial interference, such as the reset of the internal state and/or randomization source of the prover device, can have influence on the produced values.

Therefore in this paper we want to address this issue, and strengthen the security model for the ephemeral secrets even further. We say that scheme should stay secure even if the adversary injects the malicious ephemeral values of its choice to the device of the prover. When using some subliminal channel this could happen even without the prover knowledge and against its will. In our security model, such ephemerals used by the prover during its interaction with the malicious verifier should not help the adversary to impersonate the prover subsequently. In this paper we concentrate on the Schnorr IS [1]. This particular scheme is one of the fundamental cryptographic building block, which security relies on the hardness of discrete logarithm problem (DLP). As such it can be used as a compatible part of more complex constructions, based on similar computational assumptions. E.g. authenticated key establishment protocols based on Diffie-Hellman key exchange. The regular Schnorr IS is vulnerable to the ephemeral injecting attack, and ephemeral leakage. Thus we propose the modification of that scheme, which becomes secure in our proposed model.

Contribution. The contribution of the paper is the following:

- We introduce a new strong security model for identification schemes in which we allow the *adversary verifier* to set random values used on the prover side in the commitment phase of the protocol. We define the IS scheme to be secure if such a setting in *query stage* of the security experiment, will not enable the adversary to impersonate the prover later in the *impersonate stage*.
- We propose a modification of Schnorr authentication protocol [1], which becomes immune to malicious setting of the ephemeral key by the adversary. Such a setting neither leads to subsequent leakage of long term secret key of the prover, nor help the adversary to impersonate the prover later on. Subsequently we prove the security of the modified Schnorr IS in our strong model.

We argue that our proposition is especially applicable in the systems where the regular Schnorr IS is used, but where the scenarios of the ephemeral leakage could be taken under consideration. PACEAA protocol from [2] is such an example, where regular Schnorr IS is a part of deniable authentication process, and where it can be replaced by our modified version.

Previous Work. There are many fundamental identification schemes proposed so far, e.g. RSA based: [3] of Fiat and Shamir, [4] of Feige, Fiat and Shamir, or [5] of Guillou and Quisquater. In [1] Schnorr introduced DLP based construction, followed by [6] of Okamoto. There are also specialized identity based IS e.g. [7] provably secure in the standard model, or [8] secure against concurrent man-in-the-middle attack without random oracles by using a variant of BB signature scheme. Problem of the leakage of secret bits of the long term key of the prover, in Bounded Retrieval Model, was analyzed in [9]. The problem of the security of IS schemes under reset attacks on ephemeral secrets was raised in [10] in the context of zero-knowledge proofs. Later in [11] constructions for making the IS protocols immune against *reset attacks* were shown: the reset-secure identification protocols based on a deterministic, stateless digital signature scheme (as such that proposition is not deniable); the reset-secure identification protocols based on a CCA secure asymmetric encryption scheme (not naturally compatible with the Diffie-Hellman key exchange protocols initiated with the prover ephemeral public key); the reset-secure identification schemes based on pseudorandom functions and trapdoor commitments (has more than 3 rounds). Comparing with [11] our solution preserves the characteristic of the original Schnorr IS: (1) it is defined in groups suitable for Diffie-Helman key exchange; (2) it has three rounds - the first one is initiated with the prover's commitment; (3) it is deniable for the prover - i.e. it is simulatable by the verifier without the secret key of the prover.

The paper is organized in the following way. In Sect. 2 we recall the Schnorr identification protocol. In Sect. 3 we introduce our stronger security model which addresses the problem of the ephemeral setting by the active malicious adversary. In Sect. 4 we propose the modified version of Schnorr IS, and prove its security in our model.

2   Schnorr Identification Scheme

2.1   Preliminaries and Notation

We loosely follow the notation from [9]. Let $x_1, \ldots, x_n \leftarrow_R X$ denotes that each x_i is sampled uniformly at random from the set X. Let $\mathcal{G}(1^\lambda)$ be a group generation algorithm that takes as an inputs 1^λ, and outputs a tuple $\mathbb{G} = (p, q, g, G)$, where $p, q \in PRIMES$ s.t. $q|p-1$, $\mathbb{Z}_p^*$ be a multiplicative group modulo p, and $\langle g \rangle = G$ be a subgroup of $\mathbb{Z}_p^*$ of order q. Let $\mathcal{H} : \{0,1\}^* \to G$ be a hash function. We will use it to compute another element of G denoted by $\hat{g}$. We assume the following:

Bilinear Map: Let G_T be another group of a prime order q. We assume that $\hat{e} : G \times G \to G_T$ is a bilinear map s.t. following condition holds:

(1) *Bilinearity:* $\forall a, b \in \mathbb{Z}_q^*, \forall g, g \in G: \hat{e}(g^a, g^b) = \hat{e}(g, g)^{ab}$.
(2) *Non-degeneracy:* $\hat{e}(g, g) \neq 1$.
(3) *Computability:* $\hat{e}$ is efficiently computable.

The *Discrete Logarithm* (DL) Assumption: For any probabilistic polynomial time (PPT) algorithm $\mathcal{A}_{DL}$ it holds that:

$$\Pr[\mathcal{A}_{DL}(\mathbb{G}, g^x) = x \mid \mathbb{G} \leftarrow_R \mathcal{G}(1^\lambda), x \leftarrow_R \mathbb{Z}_q^*] \leq \epsilon_{DL}(\lambda),$$

where $\epsilon_{DL}(\lambda)$ is negligible.

The *Computational Diffie-Hellman* (CDH) Assumption: For any probabilistic polynomial time (PPT) algorithm $\mathcal{A}_{CDH}$ it holds that:

$$\Pr[\mathcal{A}_{CDH}(\mathbb{G}, g^x, g^y) = g^{xy} \mid \mathbb{G} \leftarrow_R \mathcal{G}(1^\lambda), x \leftarrow_R \mathbb{Z}_q^*, y \leftarrow_R \mathbb{Z}_q^*] \leq \epsilon_{CDH}(\lambda),$$

where $\epsilon_{CDH}(\lambda)$ is negligible.

The *Decisional Diffie-Hellman* Oracle ($\mathcal{O}_{DDH}$) denotes the (PPT) algorithm, which for $\mathbb{G} \leftarrow_R \mathcal{G}(1^\lambda), x \in \mathbb{Z}_q^*, y \in \mathbb{Z}_q^*, z \in \mathbb{Z}_q^*$

$$\mathcal{O}_{DDH}(\mathbb{G}, g^x, g^y, g^z) = 1 \text{ iff } z = xy \mod q.$$

The *Gap Computational Diffie-Hellman* (GDH) Assumption: For any probabilistic polynomial time (PPT) algorithm $\mathcal{A}_{GDH}^{\mathcal{O}_{DDH}}$ that has access to decisional Diffie-Hellman oracle $\mathcal{O}_{DDH}$ it holds that:

$$\Pr[\mathcal{A}_{GDH}^{\mathcal{O}_{DDH}}(\mathbb{G}, g^x, g^y) = g^{xy} \mid \mathbb{G} \leftarrow_R \mathcal{G}(1^\lambda), x \leftarrow_R \mathbb{Z}_q^*, y \leftarrow_R \mathbb{Z}_q^*] \leq \epsilon_{GDH}(\lambda),$$

where $\epsilon_{GDH}(\lambda)$ is negligible.

2.2   Identification Schemes

An identification scheme is a system in which a prover proves its identity to a verifier. More formally we define the following:

Definition 1 (Identification Scheme). *An identification scheme* IS *is a system which consists of four algorithms* (ParGen, KeyGen, $\mathcal{P}$, $\mathcal{V}$) *and a protocol π:*

params $\leftarrow$ ParGen(1^λ): *inputs the security parameter λ, and outputs public parameters available to all users of the system (we omit them from the rest of the description).*
(sk, pk) $\leftarrow$ KeyGen(): *outputs the secret key* sk *and corresponding public key* pk.
$\mathcal{P}$(pk, sk): *denotes the prover – an ITM which interacts with the verifier $\mathcal{V}$ in the protocol π.*
$\mathcal{V}$(pk): *denotes the verifier – an ITM which interacts with the prover $\mathcal{V}$ in the protocol π.*
$\pi(\mathcal{P}, \mathcal{V})$: *denotes the protocol between the prover and the verifier.*

We distinguish two stages of the scheme:

- *Initialization: In this stage parameters are generated:* params $\leftarrow$ ParGen(1^λ), *and users are registered, e.g. on behalf of the user of identity $\hat{A}$ the procedure* $(a, A) \leftarrow$ KeyGen() *generates the pair of the secret key and the corresponding public key, denoted by a and A respectively.*
- *Operation: In this stage any user, e.g. $\hat{A}$, demonstrates its identity to a verifier by performing the protocol $\pi(\hat{A}(a, A), \mathcal{V}(A))$ related to the keys a, A. Finally the verifier outputs 1 for "accept" or 0 for "reject". For simplicity we denote $\pi(\mathcal{P}, \mathcal{V}) \to 1$ if $\mathcal{P}$ was accepted by $\mathcal{V}$ in π.*

We require that the scheme is <u>complete</u> *i.e. protocol $\pi(\mathcal{P}(\mathsf{sk}, \mathsf{pk}), \mathcal{V}(\mathsf{pk})) \to 1$ for any pair* $(\mathsf{sk}, \mathsf{pk}) \leftarrow$ KeyGen().

There are many security modes for identification schemes. Intuitively the scheme is regarded as secure if it is impossible for any adversary prover algorithm $\mathcal{A}$, to be accepted, e.g. as identity $\hat{A}$, by the verifier given the public key A, without the input of the appropriate secret key $\mathsf{sk} = a$. That is we require that probability $\Pr[\pi(\mathcal{P}(\mathsf{sk}, \mathsf{pk}), \mathcal{V}(\mathsf{pk})) \to 1]$ is negligible. Now we denote formally the *passive adversary* mode that is used for the regular Schnorr identification. In this mode the adversary passively listens to the polynomial number ℓ of the protocol executions between the prover and the verifier, $\pi(\mathcal{P}(\mathsf{sk}, \mathsf{pk}), \mathcal{V}(\mathsf{pk}))$, hoping that these observations will, later on, help him to impersonate the prover (without the prover secret key), to the verifier. We denote the view $\mathsf{v}^{\mathcal{P}, \mathcal{V}, \ell} = \{T_1, \dots, T_\ell\}$ as the total knowledge $\mathcal{A}$ can gain after the ℓ runs of $\pi(\mathcal{P}(\mathsf{sk}, \mathsf{pk}), \mathcal{V}(\mathsf{pk}))$, where T_i is the transcript of the protocol messages in ith execution.

Definition 2 (Passive Adversary (PA)). *Let* IS $=$ (ParGen, KeyGen, $\mathcal{P}$, $\mathcal{V}$, π) *is an identification scheme. We define security experiment* $\mathrm{Exp}_{\mathsf{IS}}^{\mathrm{PA}, \lambda, \ell}$:

Init stage : *Let* params $\leftarrow$ ParGen(1^λ), $(\mathsf{sk}, \mathsf{pk}) \leftarrow$ KeyGen(). *Let the adversary $\mathcal{A}$, be the malicious algorithm given the public key* pk.

Query stage : $\mathcal{A}$ *passively observes a polynomial number ℓ of executions of the protocol $\pi(\mathcal{P}(\mathsf{sk}, \mathsf{pk}), \mathcal{V}(\mathsf{pk}))$. Let $\mathsf{v}^{\mathcal{P}, \mathcal{V}, \ell} = \{T_1, \dots, T_\ell\}$ is the view $\mathcal{A}$ gains after the ℓ runs of $\pi(\mathcal{P}(\mathsf{sk}, \mathsf{pk}), \mathcal{V}(\mathsf{pk}))$, where T_i is the transcript of ith execution.*

Impersonation stage : $\mathcal{A}$ *runs the protocol $\pi(\mathcal{A}(\mathsf{pk}, \mathsf{v}^{\mathcal{P}, \mathcal{V}, \ell}), \mathcal{V}(\mathsf{pk}))$ with the honest verifier.*

We define the advantage of $\mathcal{A}$ in the experiment $\mathrm{Exp}_{\mathsf{IS}}^{\mathrm{PA}, \lambda, \ell}$ *as probability of acceptance in the last stage:*

$$\mathbf{Adv}(\mathcal{A}, \mathrm{Exp}_{\mathsf{IS}}^{\mathrm{PA}, \lambda, \ell}) = \Pr[\pi(\mathcal{A}(\mathsf{pk}, \mathsf{v}^{\mathcal{P}, \mathcal{V}, \ell}), \mathcal{V}(\mathsf{pk})) \to 1].$$

We say that the identification scheme IS is secure if $\mathbf{Adv}(\mathcal{A}, \mathrm{Exp}_{\mathsf{IS}}^{\mathrm{PA}, \lambda, \ell})$ *is negligible in λ.*

2.3   Regular Schnorr Identification Scheme

Let us recall the Schnorr identification scheme from [1].

---

params $\leftarrow$ ParGen(1^λ): Let $\mathbb{G} = (p, q, g, G) \leftarrow \mathcal{G}(1^\lambda)$, s.t. DL assumption holds. Set
    params $= (p, q, g, G)$.

KeyGen(): sk $= a \leftarrow \mathbb{Z}_q^*$, pk $= A = g^a$. Output (sk, pk).

$\pi(\mathcal{P}(a, A), \mathcal{V}(A))$: The prover $\mathcal{P}(a, A)$ with identity $\hat{A}$ runs with the verifier $\mathcal{V}(A)$ the
    folowing protocol:
1. $\mathcal{P}$: computes $x \in_R \mathbb{Z}_q^*$, $X = g^x$ and sends X to the verifier $\mathcal{V}$.
2. $\mathcal{V}$: choses $c \in_R \mathbb{Z}_q^*$, and sends c to the prover $\mathcal{P}$.
3. $\mathcal{P}$: computes $s = x + ac$ and sends s to the verifier $\mathcal{V}$.
4. $\mathcal{V}$: accepts the verification iff $g^s == XA^c$.

Fig. 1. The Schnorr identification scheme.

Protocol Simulation: The eavesdropping passive adversary learns transcript tuple $T = (X, c, s)$. The random variables X, c, s are uniformly distributed on their domains. In the protocol variables $x = \log_g X, c$ are mutually independent, and together determine $s = x + ac$ for the fixed a. On the other hand the protocol transcript can be efficiently simulated by choosing $\tilde{s}, \tilde{c}$ first and subsequently computing $\tilde{X} = (g^{\tilde{s}}/A^{\tilde{c}})$. Then the simulator algorithm, denoted by $\mathcal{S}_{\mathsf{IS}}^\pi(\tilde{c} \leftarrow_R \mathbb{Z}_q^*, \tilde{s} \leftarrow_R \mathbb{Z}_q^*)$, can replay the precomputed transcript $\tilde{T} = (\tilde{X}, \tilde{c}, \tilde{s})$ in the correct order, thus simulating the interaction between the prover and the verifier. The tuples $T = (X, c, s)$ and $\tilde{T} = (\tilde{X}, \tilde{c}, \tilde{s})$ are identically distributed. As the immediate consequence of the *simulatability*, the security requirements for the above-mentioned protocol is that the challenge c is not know to the prover before it sends the commitment X to the verifier. This is especially crucial in the setups where the possible leakage on the verifier side is considered. In real implementation it must be ensured that the challenge value c is coined only after the verifier obtains the value X, but not earlier. Below we recall the security of Schnorr IS in PA model.

Rewinding Technique: The idea behind the proof is the following: If we have the efficient adversary algorithm $\mathcal{A}$ for which $\mathbf{Adv}(\mathcal{A}, \mathsf{Exp}_{\mathsf{IS}}^{\mathsf{PA}, \lambda, \ell})) = \epsilon$ is non-negligible, then, with also non-negligible probability $\epsilon(\epsilon - 1/q)$, it can be run twice and accepted, for the same fixed ephemeral x, but with different challenges c_1, c_2 resulting with different responses s_1, s_2. The ϵ factor denotes the probability of acceptance in the first run, while $\epsilon - 1/q$ is the probability of acceptance in the second run for $c_1 \neq c_2$. The two tuples $(x, c_1, s_1), (x, c_2, s_2)$ will help us to break the underlying DL problem.

Theorem 1. *Let* IS *denotes the Schnorr identification scheme (as of Fig. 1). IS is secure (in the sense of Definition 2), i.e. the advantage* $\mathbf{Adv}(\mathcal{A}, \mathsf{Exp}_{\mathsf{IS}}^{\mathsf{PA}, \lambda, \ell}))$ *is negligible in* λ*, for any PPT algorithm* $\mathcal{A}$*.*

Proof (Sketch). The proof is by contradiction. Suppose there is an adversary $\mathcal{A}$ for which the advantage $\mathbf{Adv}(\mathcal{A}, \mathsf{Exp}_{\mathsf{IS}}^{\mathsf{PA}, \lambda, \ell}))$ is non-negligible. Then it can be used as a subprocedure by the efficient algorithm $\mathcal{A}_{\mathsf{DL}}$ that breaks the DL assumption, computing e.g. $\log_g(A)$ for the given instance of DL problem $(\mathbb{G}, A)$, also with a non negligible probability, in the following way:

Init stage : Let params $\leftarrow \mathbb{G} = (p, q, g, G)$, pk $= A$. The adversary $\mathcal{A}$, is given the public key A.

Query stage : We simulate the view $\tilde{v}^{\mathcal{P}, \mathcal{V}, \ell} = \{\tilde{T}_1, \ldots, \tilde{T}_\ell\}$ of $\mathcal{A}$ in the ℓ executions of the protocol π, where each $\tilde{T}_i = (\tilde{X}_i, \tilde{c}_i, \tilde{s}_i)$ for $\tilde{X} = (g^{\tilde{s}}/A^{\tilde{c}})$ produced by the simulator $\mathcal{S}_{IS}^{\pi}()$.

Impersonation stage : We run the protocol $\pi(\mathcal{A}(\text{pk}, \tilde{v}^{\mathcal{P}, \mathcal{V}, \ell}), \mathcal{V}(\text{pk}))$ serving the role of the honest verifier. Then we use a *rewinding technique*: we fix the random value x used in $X = g^x$ by the algorithm $\mathcal{A}$, and let $\mathcal{A}$ interact twice with the verifier, choosing each time a different random c, say c_1 and c_2. These will result with x, c_1, s_1 and x, c_2, s_2 accordingly. If the verifier accepts in both cases we have $s_1 = x + ac_1$ and $s_2 = x + ac_2$. Thus we have $s_1 - s_2 = a(c_1 - c_2)$, so we can compute $a = (s_1 - s_2)/(c_1 - c_2)$.   □

3   New Stronger Security Model

In this section we propose the new strong security model for IS. In this model we assume that in the *learning phase* the adversary can influence the choices of ephemeral secrets of the prover in an adaptive manner. In the worst scenario, the malicious verifier denoted by $\tilde{\mathcal{V}}$, can choose ephemerals on behalf of $\mathcal{P}$, and inject them to $\mathcal{P}$, even against its will and without its knowledge, over some *subliminal* channel before the computation involving x on $\mathcal{P}$ side starts. Let $\bar{x}$ denotes the ephemeral secrets chosen by $\tilde{\mathcal{V}}$, and $\mathcal{P}^{\bar{x}}$ denotes the honest prover $\mathcal{P}$ with injected $\bar{x}$, which uses this value as the random ephemeral during the protocol execution. Furthermore, we assume the subsequent choices of $\tilde{\mathcal{V}}$ can be adjusted according to responses from $\mathcal{P}^{\bar{x}}$ during the subsequent protocol executions. We denote the protocol execution in which the ephemeral secrets $\bar{x}$ was chosen by $\tilde{\mathcal{V}}$ and $\mathcal{P}$ was forced to use it, as $\pi(\mathcal{P}^{\bar{x}}(\text{sk}, \text{pk}), \tilde{\mathcal{V}}(\text{pk}, \bar{x}))$. We denote the view $v^{\mathcal{P}, \tilde{\mathcal{V}}, \bar{x}(\ell)}$ as the total knowledge $\tilde{\mathcal{V}}$ can gain after the polynomial number ℓ of executions $\pi(\mathcal{P}^{\bar{x}}(\text{sk}, \text{pk}), \tilde{\mathcal{V}}(\text{pk}, \bar{x}))$, where $\bar{\boldsymbol{x}}(\ell) = \{\bar{x}_1, \ldots, \bar{x}_\ell\}$ are the adaptive choices of $\tilde{\mathcal{V}}$.

Definition 3 (Chosen Prover Ephemeral – (CPE)). *Let* IS $=$ (ParGen, KeyGen, $\mathcal{P}$, $\mathcal{V}$, π) *is an identification scheme. We define security experiment* $\text{Exp}_{IS}^{CPE, \lambda, \ell}$:

Init stage : *Let* params $\leftarrow$ ParGen(1^λ), (sk, pk) $\leftarrow$ KeyGen(). *Let the adversary $\mathcal{A}$, be the coalition of malicious algorithms* $(\tilde{\mathcal{P}}, \tilde{\mathcal{V}})$ *given the public key* pk.

Query stage : *$\mathcal{A}$ runs a polynomial number ℓ of executions of the protocol* $\pi(\mathcal{P}^{\bar{x}_i}(\text{sk}, \text{pk}), \tilde{\mathcal{V}}(\text{pk}, \bar{x}_i)$ *with the honest prover* $\mathcal{P}^{\bar{x}_i}$, *collecting* $v^{\mathcal{P}, \tilde{\mathcal{V}}, \bar{x}(\ell)}$, *where $\bar{x}_i \in \{\bar{x}_1, \ldots, \bar{x}_\ell\}$ denotes the adaptive choices of $\tilde{\mathcal{V}}$ injected as ephemerals to the prover $\mathcal{P}^{\bar{x}_i}$ in the ith execution.*

Impersonation stage : *$\mathcal{A}$ runs the protocol* $\pi(\tilde{\mathcal{P}}(\text{pk}, v^{\mathcal{P}, \tilde{\mathcal{V}}, \bar{x}(\ell)}), \mathcal{V}(\text{pk}))$ *with the honest verifier.*

We define the advantage of $\mathcal{A}$ in the experiment $\text{Exp}_{IS}^{CPE, \lambda, \ell}$ *as probability of acceptance in the last stage:*

$$\mathbf{Adv}(\mathcal{A}, \text{Exp}_{IS}^{CPE, \lambda, \ell}) = \Pr[\pi(\tilde{\mathcal{P}}(\text{pk}, v^{\mathcal{P}, \tilde{\mathcal{V}}, \bar{x}(\ell)}), \mathcal{V}(\text{pk})) \rightarrow 1].$$

We say that the identification scheme is secure if $\mathbf{Adv}(\mathcal{A}, \mathrm{Exp}_{\mathsf{IS}}^{\mathsf{CPE},\lambda,\ell})$ is negligible in λ.

It is easy to check that the regular Schnorr IS is not secure in the proposed CPE model. The adversary with the injected $\bar{x}$ can easily compute the secret key $a = (s - \bar{x})/c$, and impersonate the prover $\hat{A}$ later on.

4   Modified Schnorr Identification Scheme

The idea behind the modification is the following. We want to address the threat that the adversary with the knowledge of c, $s = x + ac$ and the leaked x computes static secret a. Therefore instead of sending s in plain-text, the prover will send s hidden in the exponent $S = \hat{g}^s$, where the new generator $\hat{g} = \mathcal{H}(X|c)$ is obtained with the hash function $\mathcal{H}$. Now even if the ephemeral value x is leaked, the adversary should face DLP to obtain the value a from S. On the other hand we use the bilinear map $\hat{e}$ on the verifier side to check the linear equation $s = x + ac$ in the exponent. Indeed it holds that $\hat{e}(S, g) = \hat{e}(\mathcal{H}(X|c)), XA^c)$ due to the fact that $\hat{e}(\mathcal{H}(X|c), XA^c) = \hat{e}(\mathcal{H}(X|c)^{x+ac}, g)$.

The proposed modified Schnorr IS is depicted in Fig. 2.

---

params ← ParGen(1^λ): Let $p, q, g, G, G_T \leftarrow \mathcal{G}(1^\lambda)$. Let $\mathcal{H} : \{0, 1\}^* \to G$ be a hash function. Let $\hat{e} : G \times G \to G_T$ be a bilinear map. We assume that GDH holds in G, where $\hat{e}$ plays a role of $\mathcal{O}_{\mathsf{DDH}}$ oracle. Set params $= (p, q, g, G, G_T, \mathcal{H}, \hat{e})$.

KeyGen(): sk $= a \leftarrow \mathbb{Z}_q^*$, pk $= A = g^a$. Output (sk, pk).

$\pi(\mathcal{P}(a, A), \mathcal{V}(A))$: The prover $\mathcal{P}(a, A)$ with identity $\hat{A}$ runs with the verifier $\mathcal{V}(A)$ the folowing protocol:

    1. $\mathcal{P}$: computes $x \in_R \mathbb{Z}_q^*$, $X = g^x$ and sends X to the verifier $\mathcal{V}$.

    2. $\mathcal{V}$: choses $c \in_R \mathbb{Z}_q^*$, and sends c to the prover $\mathcal{P}$.

    3. $\mathcal{P}$: computes $\hat{g} = \mathcal{H}(X|c)$, $S = \hat{g}^{x+ac}$ and sends S to the verifier $\mathcal{V}$.

    4. $\mathcal{V}$: computes $\hat{g} = \mathcal{H}(X|c)$, accepts the proof iff $\hat{e}(S, g) = \hat{e}(\mathcal{H}(X|c), XA^c)$.

Fig. 2. The modified Schnorr identification scheme

In Fig. 3 we depict side-by-side the differences between the original Schnorr and our modified version. In our proposition we have one exponentiation and one hashing more on provers side. On the other hand the verifier does not have extra exponentiation during the verification. Indeed it has even one explicit exponentiation less – does not have to compute g^s. Instead, additionally it has to compute the hash, and compare results of two bilinear functions.

4.1   Simulation in the *Passive Adversary* Mode

The modified Schnorr IS preserves the simulatability property of its original version. In the weaker *passive adversary* model, the eavesdropping adversary

Regular Schnorr		Modified Schnorr	
$\mathcal{P}(a, A = g^a)$	$\mathcal{V}(A)$	$\mathcal{P}(a, A = g^a)$	$\mathcal{V}(A)$
$x \in_R \mathbb{Z}_q^*, X = g^x$		$x \in_R \mathbb{Z}_q^*, X = g^x$	
$\xrightarrow{\quad X \quad}$		$\xrightarrow{\quad X \quad}$	
	$c \in_R \mathbb{Z}_q^*$		$c \in_R \mathbb{Z}_q^*$
$\xleftarrow{\quad c \quad}$		$\xleftarrow{\quad c \quad}$	
		$\hat{g} = \mathcal{H}(X\|c)$	
$s = x + ac$		$S = \hat{g}^{x+ac}$	
$\xrightarrow{\quad s \quad}$		$\xrightarrow{\quad S \quad}$	
			$\hat{g} = \mathcal{H}(X\|c)$
	Accept iff		Accept iff
	$g^s = XA^c$		$\hat{e}(S, g) = \hat{e}(\hat{g}, XA^c)$

Fig. 3. Schnorr identification comparison

learns transcript tuple $T = (X, c, S)$, similarly as in the original Schnorr IS. The random variables X, c, S are uniformly distributed on their domains. In π variables $x = \log_g X, c$ are mutually independent, and together determine $S = \hat{g}^{x+ac}$ for the fixed a. On the other hand the protocol transcript can be efficiently simulated by choosing $\tilde{s}, \tilde{c}$ first, then subsequently computing $\tilde{X} = (g^{\tilde{s}}/A^{\tilde{c}})$, and only then $\hat{g} = \mathcal{H}(\tilde{X}|\tilde{c})$ and $\tilde{S} = \hat{g}^{\tilde{s}}$. Observe that for this transcript the verification holds: $\hat{e}(\tilde{S}, g) = \hat{e}(\mathcal{H}(\tilde{X}|\tilde{c}), \tilde{X}A^{\tilde{c}})$. Then the simulator algorithm, denoted by $\mathcal{S}_{IS}^{\pi}(\tilde{c} \leftarrow_R \mathbb{Z}_q^*, \tilde{s} \leftarrow_R \mathbb{Z}_q^*)$, can replay the precomputed transcript $\tilde{T} = (\tilde{X}, \tilde{c}, \tilde{s})$ in the correct order, thus simulating the interaction between the prover and the verifier. The tuples $T = (X, c, s)$ and $\tilde{T} = (\tilde{X}, \tilde{c}, \tilde{s})$ are identically distributed.

4.2 Simulation in the *Chosen Prover Ephemeral* Mode

The modified Schnorr IS is also simulatable in the proposed stronger *Chosen Prover Ephemeral* (CPE) model. Assuming programmable ROM (Random Oracle Model), we can simulate the protocol $\pi(\mathcal{P}^{\bar{x}}(\mathsf{pk}), \tilde{\mathcal{V}}^{\mathcal{O}_{\mathcal{H}}}(\mathsf{pk}, \bar{x})) \to 1$ on behalf of the prover $\mathcal{P}^{\bar{x}}(\mathsf{pk})$ without the secret key sk, using the injected ephemerals $\bar{x}$, and interacting with the active adversary $\tilde{\mathcal{V}}^{\mathcal{O}_{\mathcal{H}}}(\mathsf{pk}, \bar{x})$, which injects the ephemerals $\bar{x}$ to the prover and performs adaptive choices of challenges. Note that the adversary calls the oracle $\mathcal{O}_{\mathcal{H}}$ to compute the hash value for the queried input.

Theorem 2. *The modified Schnorr protocol (depicted in Fig. 2) is simulatable in the CPE model (of Definition 3).*

Proof. The simulator $\mathcal{S}_{IS}^{\mathsf{CPE},\pi}()$ is defined in the following way:

(1) **Hash queries $\mathcal{O}_{\mathcal{H}}$:** We setup ROM table for hash queries $\mathcal{O}_{\mathcal{H}}$. The table has three columns I, H, r: for the input, the output and the masked exponent respectively. On each query $\mathcal{O}_{\mathcal{H}}(I_i)$ we check if we have it already defined - if so we return the corresponding output H_i. Otherwise we choose $r_i \leftarrow_R \mathbb{Z}_q^*$, compute $H_i = g^{r_i}$, place a new row (I_i, H_i, r_i) in the ROM table, and return H_i.

(2) **Commitment** X: When injected ephemeral $\bar{x}$ we use it to compute $\tilde{X} = g^{\bar{x}}$. We send $\bar{X}$ to the verifier $\tilde{\mathcal{V}}^{\mathcal{O}_{\mathcal{H}}}(\mathsf{pk}, \bar{x})$ in the first message.

(3) **Proof** S: On receiving $\tilde{c}$ from the verifier, we call $\mathcal{O}_{\mathcal{H}}(\bar{X}|\tilde{c})$ We check $\mathcal{O}_{\mathcal{H}}$ table for the input $\bar{X}|c$, locate and retrieve the corresponding g^r and r. We set $\hat{g} = g^r$. We compute $S = \tilde{X}^r A^{rc} = \hat{g}^{\bar{x}+ac}$ for $\hat{g} \leftarrow \mathcal{O}_{\mathcal{H}}(\bar{X}|\tilde{c})$. Now verification on prover side holds: $\hat{e}(\tilde{S}, g) = \hat{e}(\hat{g}, \tilde{X}A^{\tilde{c}})$ for $\hat{g} \leftarrow \mathcal{O}_{\mathcal{H}}(\bar{X}|\tilde{c})$, and the *real* transcript tuple $T = (X, c, s)$, and the *simulated* $\tilde{T} = (\tilde{X}, \tilde{c}, \tilde{s})$ are identically distributed.   □

4.3 Security Analysis

We follow the same proving methodology as in the case of the original Schnorr IS. First we allow the adversary to gain some knowledge: we simulate the proofs on behalf of the prover (but without its secret key) interacting with malicious verifier, which injects the ephemerals for our usage. We are able to do this in ROM. Then, assuming that the advantage of the adversary is non-negligible, in the impersonation stage we use *rewinding technique* for obtaining two tuples (X, c_1, S_1), (X, c_2, S_2) which subsequently will help us to break the underlying hard problem - GDH in this case - also with non-negligible probability.

Theorem 3. *Let* IS *denotes the modified Schnorr identification scheme (as of Fig. 2). IS is secure (in the sense of Definition 3), i.e. the advantage* $\mathbf{Adv}(\mathcal{A}, \mathrm{Exp}_{\mathsf{IS}}^{\mathsf{CPE},\lambda,\ell})$) *is negligible in* λ*, for any PPT algorithm* $\mathcal{A}$*.*

Proof (Sketch). We use ROM for hash queries. The proof is by contradiction. Suppose there is an adversary $\mathcal{A} = (\tilde{\mathcal{P}}, \tilde{\mathcal{V}})$ for which $\mathbf{Adv}(\mathcal{A}, \mathrm{Exp}_{\mathsf{IS}}^{\mathsf{CPE},\lambda,\ell})$) is non-negligible. Then it can be used as a subprocedure by the efficient algorithm $\mathcal{A}_{\mathsf{GDH}}$ that breaks the GDH for the given instance g^α, g^β, computing $g^{\alpha\beta}$ also with non-negligible probability.

Init stage : Let params $\leftarrow \mathbb{G} = (p, q, g, G)$ s.t. CDH holds and (g^α, g^β) is GDH instance in $\mathbb{G}$. We set $\mathsf{pk} = g^\alpha$. The adversary $\mathcal{A}$, is given the public key $\mathsf{pk} = g^\alpha$. We setup ROM table for hash queries $\mathcal{O}_{\mathcal{H}}$. The table has three columns I, H, r for the input, the output and the masked exponent respectively. We will serve hash in the following way: in the Query stage we will use the simulator $\mathcal{S}_{\mathsf{IS}}^{\mathsf{CPE},\pi}$ (as in the proof of Theorem 2). In the Impersonation stage we will provide to the adversary the value $(g^\beta)^r$, where r is a random mask.

Query stage : We simulate in ROM a polynomial number ℓ of executions of the protocol $\pi(\mathcal{P}^{\bar{x}_i}(\mathsf{pk}), \tilde{\mathcal{V}}^{\mathcal{O}_{\mathcal{H}}}(\mathsf{pk}, \bar{x}_i)$ without the secret key, interacting with the active adversary verifier $\tilde{\mathcal{V}}^{\mathcal{O}_{\mathcal{H}}}(\mathsf{pk}, \bar{x}_i)$, which injects ephemerals $\bar{x}_i$ by running the simulator $\mathcal{S}_{\mathsf{IS}}^{\mathsf{CPE},\pi}$:

(1) **Serving Hash queries** $\mathcal{O}_{\mathcal{H}}$: On each query $\mathcal{O}_{\mathcal{H}}(I_i)$ we check if we have it already defined - if so we return the corresponding output H_i. Otherwise we choose $r_i \leftarrow_R \mathbb{Z}_q^*$, compute $H_i = g^{r_i}$, place a new row (I_i, H_i, r_i) in the ROM table, and return H_i.

(2) **Commitment** X: When injected ephemeral $\bar{x}$ we use it to compute $\tilde{X} = g^{\bar{x}}$. We send $\tilde{X}$ to the verifier $\tilde{\mathcal{V}}^{\mathcal{O}_{\mathcal{H}}}(\mathsf{pk}, \bar{x})$ in the first message.

(3) **Proof** S: On receiving $\tilde{c}$ from the verifier, we call $\mathcal{O}_{\mathcal{H}}(\tilde{X}|\tilde{c})$. We check $\mathcal{O}_{\mathcal{H}}$ table for the input $\tilde{X}|c$, locate and retrieve the corresponding g^r and r. We set $\hat{g} = g^r$. We compute $S = \tilde{X}^r A^{rc} = \hat{g}^{\bar{x}+ac}$ for $\hat{g} \leftarrow \mathcal{O}_{\mathcal{H}}(\tilde{X}|\tilde{c})$. Now verification on prover side holds: $\hat{e}(\tilde{S}, g) = \hat{e}(\hat{g}, \tilde{X}A^{\tilde{c}})$ for $\hat{g} \leftarrow \mathcal{O}_{\mathcal{H}}(\tilde{X}|\tilde{c})$. Observe that the *simulated* transcript tuple $\tilde{T} = (\tilde{X}, \tilde{c}, \tilde{s})$, and the tuple from the *real* protocol $T = (X, c, s)$ and are identically distributed. Let $\mathsf{v}^{\mathcal{P}, \tilde{\mathcal{V}}, \bar{x}(\ell)}$ be the view of the adversary collected in this stage, where $\bar{x}_i \in \{\bar{x}_1, \dots, \bar{x}_\ell\} = \bar{x}(\ell)$ denotes the adaptive choices of $\tilde{\mathcal{V}}$ injected as ephemerals to the prover $\mathcal{P}^{\bar{x}_i}$ in ith execution.

Impersonation stage : In ROM we run $\pi(\tilde{\mathcal{P}}^{\mathcal{O}_{\mathcal{H}}}(\mathsf{pk}, \mathsf{v}^{\mathcal{P}, \tilde{\mathcal{V}}, \bar{x}(\ell)}), \mathcal{V}(\mathsf{pk}))$ serving the role of the honest verifier. We use the *rewinding technique*: we fix the random value x used in $X = g^x$ by the algorithm $\tilde{\mathcal{P}}$, and let $\tilde{\mathcal{P}}$ interact twice with the verifier, choosing each time a different random challenge, c_1 and c_2, such that neither $X|c_1$ nor $X|c_2$ were the input to $\mathcal{O}_{\mathcal{H}}$ in **Query stage**, and setting $H_1 = \mathcal{O}_{\mathcal{H}}(X|c_1) \leftarrow (g^\beta)^{r_1}$, $H_2 = \mathcal{O}_{\mathcal{H}}(X|c_2) \leftarrow (g^\beta)^{r_2}$ for $r_1, r_2 \leftarrow_R \mathbb{Z}_q^*$. These will result with $(X, c_1, S_1, \hat{g}_1, r_1)$ and $(X, c_2, S_2, \hat{g}_2, r_2)$ accordingly. If we accept the adversary prover both times by checking: $\hat{e}(S_1, g) = \hat{e}(\hat{g}_1, XA^{c_1})$, and $\hat{e}(S_2, g) = \hat{e}(\hat{g}_2, XA^{c_2})$, we conclude: $S_1 = (g^{\beta r_1})^x (g^{\beta r_1})^{ac_1}$ and $S_2 = (g^{\beta r_2})^x (g^{\beta r_2})^{ac_2}$. Thus we have $S_1^{r_1^{-1}}/S_2^{r_2^{-1}} = (g^\beta)^{ac_1 - ac_2}$, so we can compute $g^{\alpha\beta} = (S_1^{r_1^{-1}}/S_2^{r_2^{-1}})^{(c_1 - c_2)^{-1}}$. $\qquad\square$

5   Conclusion

In this paper we modify the Schnorr IS from [1] in such a way that it becomes immune to the ephemeral key setting. Such a setting can be done e.g. by the malicious verifier who exploits the knowledge of the erroneous pseudo-random number generator implemented into the device of the prover. We observe that secret key of the prover, masked by the ephemeral values in the response message of the protocol, are no longer secure in such setups. Therefore the prover, in the response message, sends the fragile values hidden in the exponent. The verifier uses bilinear maps to check the equality of the equation in exponent on its side for the commitment and the public key of the prover. We introduce the new stronger security model to cover that scenario. We prove the security of the proposed scheme in our model.

References

1. Schnorr, C.P.: Efficient signature generation by smart cards. J. Cryptol. **4**(3), 161–174 (1991)
2. Bender, J., Dagdelen, Ö., Fischlin, M., Kügler, D.: The PACE—AA protocol for machine readable travel documents, and its security. In: Keromytis, A.D. (ed.) FC 2012. LNCS, vol. 7397, pp. 344–358. Springer, Heidelberg (2012). http://dx.doi.org/10.1007/978-3-642-32946-3_25

3. Fiat, A., Shamir, A.: How to prove yourself: practical solutions to identification and signature problems. In: Odlyzko, A.M. (ed.) CRYPTO 1986. LNCS, vol. 263, pp. 186–194. Springer, Heidelberg (1987). http://dx.doi.org/10.1007/3-540-47721-7_12

4. Feige, U., Fiat, A., Shamir, A.: Zero-knowledge proofs of identity. J. Cryptol. 1(2), 77–94. http://dx.doi.org/10.1007/BF02351717

5. Guillou, L.C., Quisquater, J.-J.: A practical zero-knowledge protocol fitted to security microprocessor minimizing both transmission and memory. In: Günther, C.G. (ed.) EUROCRYPT 1988. LNCS, vol. 330, pp. 123–128. Springer, Heidelberg (1988). http://dl.acm.org/citation.cfm?id=55554.55565

6. Okamoto, T.: Provably secure and practical identification schemes and corresponding signature schemes. In: Brickell, E.F. (ed.) CRYPTO 1992. LNCS, vol. 740, pp. 31–53. Springer, Heidelberg (1993). http://dx.doi.org/10.1007/3-540-48071-4_3

7. Kurosawa, K., Heng, S.-H.: Identity-based identification without random oracles. In: Gervasi, O., Gavrilova, M.L., Kumar, V., Laganà, A., Lee, H.P., Mun, Y., Taniar, D., Tan, C.J.K. (eds.) ICCSA 2005. LNCS, vol. 3481, pp. 603–613. Springer, Heidelberg (2005). http://dx.doi.org/10.1007/11424826_64

8. Kurosawa, K., Heng, S.-H.: The power of identification schemes. In: Yung, M., Dodis, Y., Kiayias, A., Malkin, T. (eds.) PKC 2006. LNCS, vol. 3958, pp. 364–377. Springer, Heidelberg (2006). http://dx.doi.org/10.1007/11745853_24

9. Alwen, J., Dodis, Y., Wichs, D.: Leakage-resilient public-key cryptography in the bounded-retrieval model. In: Halevi, S. (ed.) CRYPTO 2009. LNCS, vol. 5677, pp. 36–54. Springer, Heidelberg (2009). http://dx.doi.org/10.1007/978-3-642-03356-8_3

10. Canetti, R., Goldreich, O., Goldwasser, S., Micali, S.: Resettable zero-knowledge (extended abstract). In: Proceedings of the Thirty-Second Annual ACM Symposium on Theory of Computing, STOC 2000, pp. 235–244. ACM, New York (2000). http://doi.acm.org/10.1145/335305.335334

11. Bellare, M., Fischlin, M., Goldwasser, S., Micali, S.: Identification protocols secure against reset attacks. In: Pfitzmann, B. (ed.) EUROCRYPT 2001. LNCS, vol. 2045, pp. 495–511. Springer, Heidelberg (2001). http://dx.doi.org/10.1007/3-540-44987-6_30

Homomorphic Encryption Based on Group Algebras and Goldwasser-Micali Scheme

Cezar Pleşca[1,2], Mihai Togan[1,2(✉)], and Cristian Lupaşcu[1]

[1] Computer Science Department, Military Technical Academy, Bucharest, Romania
cezar.plesca@gmail.com, mihai.togan@gmail.com, clupascu8@gmail.com
[2] certSIGN, Research and Development Department, Bucharest, Romania

Abstract. The possibility of outsourcing computation to the cloud offers businesses and individuals substantial cost-savings, flexibility, and availability of computable resources, but potentially sacrifices privacy. Homomorphic encryption can help address this problem by allowing the user to upload encrypted data to the cloud, on which the cloud can then operate without having the secret key. The cloud can return encrypted outputs of computations to the user without decrypting the data, thus providing data hosting and services without compromising privacy.

First, we present a general framework introduced in [3] which extends a group homomorphic encryption scheme with respect to one operation towards a cryptosystem having homomorphic properties on both operations (i.e. addition and multiplication). Second, we describe the main contribution of this paper by showing how this framework can be applied to a well known homomorphic encryption scheme, Goldwasser-Micali, analyzing the proposed cryptosystem security and its possible applications.

Keywords: Homomorphic encryption · Group algebra · Probabilistic public-key cryptography · Quadratic residuosity problem

1 Introduction

The idea of efficient and secure algorithms to encrypt messages *and compute* efficiently any algebraic functions on encrypted data goes back to Rivest et al. [1]. Since then, many attempts to produce such encryption schemes have been made. Lately much of interest is drawn to this domain mainly due to two factors:

1. First, the use of a large database implies in practice to retrieve just partial information, so the need of doing what is called nowadays cloud computing is imperative.
2. Secondly, a partial progress in this direction has obtained a break-through by Gentry's result [2] on bootstrapable encryption schemes.

In the last two decades the researchers in the area of encryption and coding have been more and more divided into two main categories: researchers

© Springer International Publishing AG 2016
I. Bica and R. Reyhanitabar (Eds.): SECITC 2016, LNCS 10006, pp. 149–166, 2016.
DOI: 10.1007/978-3-319-47238-6_11

whose main goal are theoretical results and researchers who try to find practical approaches of these results. Gentry's result is of a theoretical nature and one can only implement what is called leveled fully homomorphic encryption with a relatively small efficiency.

From a practical point of view, Barcău and Paşol suggested in [3] that the efficiency of a homomorphic encryption scheme cannot just be considered as a function of the security parameters for which one can prove polynomial asymptotic. For this reason, the authors advise that the theoretical schemes proposed in the literature should be accompanied by explicit algorithms and tested for practical efficiency and security with a present day computer technology.

We build upon the theoretical work presented in [3] and propose a general framework able to construct a cryptosystem with homomorphic operations (i.e. addition and multiplication) based on a group homomorphic encryption scheme. Then, we apply this framework to a well known group homomorphic encryption scheme, namely Goldwasser-Micali [4], to produce and successfully implement a practical ring homomorphic encryption scheme.

1.1 State of the Art

One of the first algorithms which has the feature to perform algebraic computations on the encrypted data without revealing the encrypted information was proposed by Fellows and Koblitz in [5]. However, few years later, the algorithm proved to be insecure and no modifications of the algorithm could solve this inconvenient. In 1998, Hoffstein et al. [6] proposed a secure and efficient algorithm to encode messages called NTRU. It does have the same ring homomorphic feature, but it allows only a few operations (i.e. additions and multiplications) to be performed on the encrypted data. This *leveled* feature comes from the fact that the algorithm is an error-based one, so only circuits which keep the noise very low can be applied to the encrypted data.

A better use of the error-based encryption technique for the purpose of achieving fully homomorphic encryption scheme was proposed by Gentry in his Ph.D. thesis [2] where he used ideal lattices and latter in his work (together with his collaborators), Regev's learning with error theory to produce algorithms which accommodate a much larger number of computations on the encrypted data. He also proved that, if an algorithm has the capability of computing the polynomial corresponding to the extended decryption algorithm (i.e. bootstrapable encryption scheme), then one can use it in a limiting process to produce a fully homomorphic encryption scheme. The word limiting is important from the practical implementation point of view because, in this sense, one can achieve only leveled fully homomorphic encryption scheme, which means that one has to prescribe from the beginning, the degree (or the depth) of the polynomials to be computed on the encrypted data.

Since the Gentry's break-through, many improvements of the algorithms based on learning with errors theory have been published and a research team from IBM conducted by Halevi and Shoup proposed an implementation based on ideas found in [7–9]. The implementation, written in C++ and using the NTL library, is called Homomorphic-Encryption Library (HELib) [10].

Recently, the encryption community raised the question concerning the realization of at least a leveled fully homomorphic encryption scheme using algorithms that are not error-based. The error-based encryption algorithms have two major deficiencies: first, in order to accommodate the error, the fresh ciphertexts have to be quite large and secondly, by its nature, the algorithms produce only leveled encryption schemes and one needs the process of bootstrapping in order to accommodate the desired depth for computations, a process which proved to be extremely high resource-consuming.

In an attempt to answer this question, Barcău and Pașol [3] reused some ideas from Grigoriev and Ponomarenko's work [11] to propose a fully homomorphic encryption scheme using monoid or group algebras.

The basic idea is that if one has already an encryption scheme which supports an encrypted operation (and there exist many such encryption schemes in the literature), then, one can use the group algebra theory to obtain an encryption scheme which supports algebraic operations on the encrypted data. However, the algorithms described in [11] are not efficient and cannot be used to produce fully homomorphic encryption schemes. The blueprint in [3] is more general and flexible enough to overcome some of these drawbacks, proposing a general framework to produce fully homomorphic encryption schemes. We give in this paper one example based on Goldwasser-Micali cryptosystem [4], and analyze its security and efficiency properties.

The rest of this paper is organized as follows: first, we present the main definitions and mathematicals results about quadratic residues in Sect. 2, which are later used in the description of Goldwasser-Micali cryptosystem in Sect. 3. Then, Sect. 4 introduces the reader into the field of group algebras upon which our general framework for ring homomorphic schemes, described in Sect. 5, is built. The application of this framework to Goldwasser-Micali cryptosystem is presented in Sect. 6 and the analysis of its properties from a practical point of view is done in Sect. 7. Conclusions about the proposed general framework for ring homomorphic encryption together with some other directions for its practical application ends our paper.

2   Quadratic Residues, Legendre and Jacobi Symbols

Let $m, n \in \mathbb{Z}$ with $(m, n) = 1$. Then m is called a quadratic residue mod n if and only if $\exists x \in \mathbb{Z}$ such that $m \equiv x^2 \pmod{n}$; otherwise, m is called a quadratic non residue mod n. For odd prime p, it is easy to see that exactly half of the non-null residues mod p from $\mathbb{Z}_p^*$ are quadratic and the other half are not.

2.1   Legendre Symbol and Its Properties

For an odd prime p and $n \in \mathbb{Z}$, the **Legendre symbol** $\left(\frac{n}{p}\right)$ is defined as:

$$\left(\frac{n}{p}\right) = \begin{cases} 1 & \text{if } n \text{ is a quadratic residue mod } p \\ -1 & \text{if } n \text{ is a quadratic non residue mod } p \\ 0 & \text{if } p|n. \end{cases}$$

Hereafter, we recapitulate some important properties of the Legendre symbol. Let p be an odd prime and let $m, n \in \mathbb{Z}$. Then the following are true:

$$\left(\frac{mn}{p}\right) = \left(\frac{m}{p}\right)\left(\frac{n}{p}\right) \tag{1}$$

$$m \equiv n \pmod{p} \Rightarrow \left(\frac{m}{p}\right) = \left(\frac{n}{p}\right) \tag{2}$$

Let p be an odd prime and let $n \in \mathbb{Z}$ with $(n, p) = 1$. Starting from Fermat's Little Theorem: $n^{p-1} \equiv 1 \pmod{p}$, one can deduce that the all $p - 1$ non-null residues mod p are solutions of the equation $x^{p-1} = 1$ in $\mathbb{Z}_p$. One can use the factorization $x^{p-1} - 1 = (x^{(p-1)/2} - 1)(x^{(p-1)/2} + 1)$, and easily observe that quadratic residues from $\mathbb{Z}_p^*$ are roots of the polynomial $x^{(p-1)/2} - 1$.

Since the polynomial $x^{(p-1)/2} - 1$ can only have $(p - 1)/2$ distinct roots in $\mathbb{Z}_p$, it remains that all other $(p - 1)/2$ non quadratic residues from $\mathbb{Z}_p^*$ are roots for the other polynomial, namely $x^{(p-1)/2} + 1$. This leads us to the fundamental result about Legendre symbols, the Euler's Criterion: for an odd prime p and $n \in \mathbb{Z}$ with $(n, p) = 1$, we have:

$$\left(\frac{n}{p}\right) \equiv n^{\frac{p-1}{2}} \pmod{p}. \tag{3}$$

Plugging in various values for n into Eq. 3, one can get the following immediate consequences for an odd prime p:

$$\left(\frac{-1}{p}\right) = (-1)^{\frac{p-1}{2}}, \left(\frac{2}{p}\right) = (-1)^{\frac{p^2-1}{8}} \tag{4}$$

The law of quadratic reciprocity gives a relationship between the two Legendre symbols $\left(\frac{p}{q}\right)$ and $\left(\frac{q}{p}\right)$ for two distinct odd primes p and q [12]:

$$\left(\frac{p}{q}\right)\left(\frac{q}{p}\right) = (-1)^{\frac{p-1}{2} \cdot \frac{q-1}{2}} \tag{5}$$

2.2   Jacobi Symbol and Its Properties

The Jacobi symbol is a generalization of the Legendre symbol, defined in the previous subsection. Let $n > 1$ be an odd integer with prime factorization $n = p_1^{e_1} p_2^{e_2} \ldots p_k^{e_k}$. Then, for any integer a, the Jacobi symbol is defined as:

$$\left(\frac{a}{n}\right) = \left(\frac{a}{p_1}\right)^{e_1}\left(\frac{a}{p_2}\right)^{e_2} \ldots \left(\frac{a}{p_k}\right)^{e_k}$$

The Jacobi symbol $\left(\frac{a}{1}\right)$ is defined to be 1 for any integer a. As a consequence, the Jacobi symbol $\left(\frac{a}{n}\right) \in \{0, +1, -1\}$ and for an integer $n > 1$, we have:

$$\left(\frac{a}{n}\right) = \begin{cases} 0 & \text{if } \gcd(a, n) \neq 1 \\ \pm 1 & \text{if } \gcd(a, n) = 1 \end{cases}$$

It is easy to show the following properties of the Jacobi symbol. Let m, n be any positive odd integers and a, b be any integers. Then we have:

$$\left(\frac{ab}{n}\right) = \left(\frac{a}{n}\right)\left(\frac{b}{n}\right), \left(\frac{a}{mn}\right) = \left(\frac{a}{m}\right)\left(\frac{b}{n}\right), \left(\frac{a}{n}\right) = \left(\frac{a \bmod n}{n}\right) \quad (6)$$

$$\left(\frac{-1}{n}\right) = (-1)^{\frac{p-1}{2}}, \left(\frac{2}{n}\right) = (-1)^{\frac{n^2-1}{8}} \quad (7)$$

$$\left(\frac{m}{n}\right) = (-1)^{\frac{n-1}{2} \cdot \frac{m-1}{2}}\left(\frac{n}{m}\right), \left(\frac{m}{n}\right)\left(\frac{n}{m}\right) = (-1)^{\frac{n-1}{2} \cdot \frac{m-1}{2}} \quad (8)$$

The first three properties follow directly from the definition. Properties 7 and 8 could be deduced, by observing that, when all the primes p_i are odd, we have:

$$\left(\sum_{i=1}^{k} \frac{p_i^{e_i} - 1}{2} \bmod 2\right) = \left(\frac{p_1^{e_1} p_2^{e_2} \dots p_k^{e_k} - 1}{2} \bmod 2\right)$$

2.3   Computing Jacobi Symbol

The Jacobi symbol $\left(\frac{a}{n}\right)$ is easy to compute when the prime factorization of n is known. We now show how to compute it efficiently when this factorization is not known. This algorithm finds its importance in the next chapter where we'll describe the Goldwasser-Micali cryptosystem on which our proposal is based.

Let $n > 1$ be an odd integer and $a \in \mathbb{Z}_+^*$. Then we can write $a = 2^e \cdot n'$ with n' odd and $e \geq 0$, and we can write $n = qn' + a'$, with $0 \leq a' \leq n' - 1$. Then, from the properties of the Jacobi symbol described above, we obtain:

$$\left(\frac{a}{n}\right) = \left(\frac{2^e \cdot n'}{n}\right) = \left(\frac{2^e}{n}\right)\left(\frac{n'}{n}\right) = \left(\frac{2}{n}\right)^e \left(\frac{n'}{n}\right)$$

$$= (-1)^{\frac{e(n^2-1)}{8}}\left(\frac{n'}{n}\right) = (-1)^{e\frac{n^2-1}{8} + \frac{n-1}{2}\frac{n'-1}{2}}\left(\frac{n}{n'}\right)$$

$$= (-1)^{e\frac{n^2-1}{8} + \frac{n-1}{2}\frac{n'-1}{2}}\left(\frac{qn' + a'}{n'}\right) = (-1)^{e\frac{n^2-1}{8} + \frac{n-1}{2}\frac{n'-1}{2}}\left(\frac{a'}{n'}\right)$$

The important thing is that the value a' is strictly smaller than $|a|$. If we continue this process, we will ultimately obtain $a' = 0$, in which case the Jacobi symbol is trivial to evaluate. Let us define the following function:

$$f(e, n, n') = (-1)^{e\frac{n^2-1}{8} + \frac{n-1}{2} \cdot \frac{n'-1}{2}}$$

It is easy to show that the value $f(e, n, n')$ depends only on $e \bmod 2$, $n \bmod 8$ and $n' \bmod 4$. We thus have the two following rules that enable us to compute the Jacobi symbol:

$$\left(\frac{a}{n}\right) = f(e, n, n') \left(\frac{a'}{n'}\right)$$

$$\left(\frac{0}{n'}\right) = \begin{cases} 1 & \text{if } n' = 1 \\ 0 & \text{if } n' \neq 1 \end{cases}$$

A careful analysis very similar to the analysis done for Euclid's algorithm for computing the greatest common divisor, actually shows that the running time of the procedure suggested above is $O((\log a)(\log n))$. The Jacobi symbol $\left(\frac{a}{n}\right)$ can then be computed in time $O((\log a)(\log n))$.

3   Goldwasser-Micali Cryptosystem

The Goldwasser-Micali (GM) cryptosystem is an asymmetric key encryption algorithm developed by Shafi Goldwasser and Silvio Micali in 1982. GM has the distinction of being the first probabilistic public-key encryption scheme which is provably secure under standard cryptographic assumptions. However, it is not an efficient cryptosystem, as ciphertexts may be several hundred times larger than the initial plaintext. To prove the security properties of the cryptosystem, Goldwasser and Micali proposed the widely used definition of semantic security.

The GM cryptosystem is semantically secure based on the assumed intractability of the quadratic residuosity problem modulo a composite $N = pq$, where p and q are large primes. This assumption states that given the couple (x, N) it is difficult to determine whether x is a quadratic residue modulo N (i.e., $x = y^2 \bmod N$ for some y), when the Jacobi symbol for x is $+1$.

The quadratic residue problem is easily solved given the factorization of N, while new quadratic residues may be generated by any party, even without knowledge of this factorization. The GM cryptosystem leverages this asymmetry by encrypting individual plaintext bits as either random quadratic residues or non-residues modulo N, all with quadratic residue symbol $+1$. Recipients use the factorization of N as a secret key, and decrypt the message by testing the quadratic residuosity of the received ciphertext values.

Because Goldwasser-Micali produces a value of size approximately $|N|$ to encrypt every single bit of a plaintext, GM encryption results in substantial ciphertext expansion. To prevent factorization attacks, it is recommended that $|N|$ be several hundred bits or more. Because encryption is performed using a probabilistic algorithm, a given plaintext may produce very different ciphertexts, thus offering significant advantages, as it prevents an adversary from recognizing intercepted messages by comparing them to a dictionary of known ciphertexts.

GoldwasserMicali consists of 3 algorithms: a probabilistic key generation algorithm which produces a public and a private key, a probabilistic encryption algorithm, and a deterministic decryption algorithm. The scheme relies on deciding whether a given value x is a square mod N, given the factorization $N = pq$.

3.1 Key Generation

The modulus used in GoldwasserMicali encryption scheme is generated in the same manner as in the RSA cryptosystem.

1. Alice generates two distinct large prime numbers p and q, randomly and independently of each other, then computes $N = pq$.
2. She then finds some non-residue x such that the Legendre symbols satisfy $(x/p) = (x/q) = -1$ and hence the Jacobi symbol (x/N) is $+1$.

The value x can for example be found by selecting random values and testing the two Legendre symbols. If $p, q \equiv 3 \bmod 4$ (i.e., N is a Blum integer), then the value $N - 1$ is guaranteed to have the required property. The public key consists of (x, N), while the secret key is the factorization (p, q).

3.2 Message Encryption and Decryption

Encryption. Suppose Bob wishes to send a message m to Alice. Bob first encodes m as a string of bits $(m_1, ..., m_n)$. For every bit m_i, Bob generates a random value y_i from the group of units modulo N, or $\gcd(y_i, N) = 1$. He outputs the value $c_i = y_i^2 x^{m_i} \pmod{N}$. Bob sends the ciphertext $c = (c_1, ..., c_n)$.

Decryption. Alice receives $(c_1, ..., c_n)$. She can recover m using the following procedure: for each i, using the prime factorization (p, q), Alice determines whether the value c_i is a quadratic residue; if so, $m_i = 0$, otherwise $m_i = 1$. Alice outputs the message $m = (m_1, ..., m_n)$.

4 Group Algebras

In this section we describe how one can associate to any finite group $(G, \cdot)$ and any abelian ring $(R, +, \cdot)$ a group algebra noted as $R[G]$. Further, we will explore its properties and show that $R[G]$ has a commutative ring structure.

4.1 Notations and Properties

Every element $r \in R[G]$ has a unique representation given by:

$$r = \sum_{g \in G} r_g[g] \tag{9}$$

where $[g](g \in G)$ stands for a symbolic element from G and r_g are coefficients from the ring R. Otherwise, one can interpret such an element r as a vector from R^G whose coordinates r_g are indexed by an order defined over the entire set G. Over $R[G]$, one can define the addition operation which corresponds to the vector component-wise addition from R^G, as follows:

$$a = \sum_{g \in G} a_g[g], b = \sum_{g \in G} b_g[g] \quad a + b = \sum_{g \in G} (a_g + b_g)[g] \tag{10}$$

The multiplication over $R[G]$ is defined by the R-bilinear extension of $[x] \cdot [y] = [xy]$, thus the product of $a, b \in R[G]$ is given by:

$$a = \sum_{g \in G} a_g[g], b = \sum_{h \in G} b_h[h]$$

$$ab = \sum_{g,h \in G} a_g b_h[gh] = \sum_{f \in G} \left(\sum_{gh=f} a_g b_h \right) [f] \tag{11}$$

Enriched with the two operations previously defined, one can easily verify that $R[G]$ has a ring structure, having the following important identity elements:

$$Addition: \qquad 0 = \sum_{g \in G} 0[g]$$

$$Multiplication: \quad 1[e] = 1[e] + \sum_{g \in G \setminus \{e\}} 0[g] \tag{12}$$

In the previous formula, e is the identity element of G, 0 and 1 are the identity elements of R, with respect to addition and multiplication respectively. One can notice that the $R[G]$ algebra is commutative if and only if G is commutative.

4.2   Homomorphism Between Group Algebras

Let's consider two abelian groups, $(G, \cdot)$ and $(H, *)$ with a group homomorphism $\phi : G \to H$. Let's consider also a commutative ring R and the two algebras, $R[G]$ and $R[H]$, defined as above. Then ϕ induces an R-algebra homomorphism via the application $\phi^R : R[G] \to R[H]$, defined as follows:

$$\phi^R \left(\sum_{g \in G} r_g[g] \right) = \sum_{g \in G} r_g[\phi(g)] = \sum_{h \in H} \left(\sum_{\phi(g)=h} r_g \right) [h] \tag{13}$$

Notice that formula (13) defines ϕ^R as the R-linear extension of ϕ. The homomorphic property of ϕ^R with respect to addition operation is proven as follows:

$$\phi^R \left(\sum_{g \in G} a_g[g] + \sum_{g \in G} b_g[g] \right) = \phi^R \left(\sum_{g \in G} (a_g + b_g)[g] \right) = \sum_{g \in G} (a_g + b_g)[\phi(g)]$$

$$= \sum_{g \in G} a_g[\phi(g)] + \sum_{g \in G} b_g[\phi(g)] = \phi^R \left(\sum_{g \in G} a_g[g] \right) + \phi^R \left(\sum_{g \in G} a_g[g] \right) \tag{14}$$

The homomorphic property of ϕ^R with respect to multiplication operation is proven by the following two equations:

$$\phi^R \left(\sum_{g \in G} a_g[g] \cdot \sum_{h \in G} b_h[h] \right) = \phi^R \left(\sum_{f \in G} \left(\sum_{gh=f} a_g b_h \right) [f] \right)$$

$$= \sum_{f \in G} \left(\sum_{gh=f} a_g b_h \right) [\phi(f)] = \sum_{\phi(gh)} \left(\sum_{\phi(gh)=ct.} a_g b_h \right) [\phi(gh)] \tag{15}$$

$$\phi^R \left(\sum_{g \in G} a_g [g] \right) \cdot \phi^R \left(\sum_{h \in G} b_h [h] \right) = \sum_{g \in G} a_g [\phi(g)] \cdot \sum_{h \in G} b_h [\phi(h)]$$

$$= \sum_{\phi(g)*\phi(h)} \left(\sum_{\phi(gh)=ct.} a_g b_h \right) [\phi(g) * \phi(h)] = \sum_{\phi(gh)} \left(\sum_{\phi(gh)=ct.} a_g b_h \right) [\phi(gh)] \,(16)$$

Moreover, for any commutative ring R, there exists an evaluation map from $R[R]$ to R, that is the natural R-algebra homomorphism $\epsilon : R[R] \to R$ given by:

$$\epsilon \left(\sum_{x \in R} r_x [x] \right) = \sum_{x \in R} r_x x. \tag{17}$$

5   Ring Homomorphic Encryption Schemes

In this section we describe the ring homomorphic encryption schemes proposal presented in [3]. Let (G, H, E, D) be a group homomorphic encryption scheme, a commutative ring, R and a morphism $\chi : H \to (R, \cdot)$. We proceed by describing a ring encryption scheme $(R[G], R, \text{Enc}, \text{Dec})$, which we'll prove to be homomorphic in the sense that $\text{Dec} : R[G] \to R$ is a ring homomorphism.

Consider the image S of H in R through χ, and consider a fixed tuple $(r_1, \ldots, r_k) \in R^k$, where $k \geq 2$, such that the set containing elements of the form $\sum_{i=1}^k r_i s_i$ with $s_i \in S$ (not necessarily distinct) is the whole ring R. We'll explain later how and why this coverage property is important for the security scheme. It is important to note that the homomorphic application $\chi : H \to (R, \cdot)$ should not be trivial and allows us to find a fixed tuple $(r_1, \ldots, r_k) \in R^k$.

Encryption. The encryption algorithm is described by the following steps:

1. For a plaintext $m \in R$ consider one tuple $(s_1, \ldots, s_k) \in S^k$ such that:

$$m = \sum_{i=1}^k r_i s_i \tag{18}$$

2. Choose $(h_1, \ldots, h_k) \in H^k$ such that $\chi(h_i) = s_i, \forall i \in \{1, \ldots, k\}$
3. The encryption of the plaintext $m \in R$ is the following expression from $R[G]$:

$$\text{Enc}(m) := \sum_{i=1}^k r_i [E(h_i)] \tag{19}$$

Decryption. The decryption of an element from $R[G]$ is defined by the formula:

$$\text{Dec} \left(\sum_{g \in G} r_g [g] \right) := \sum_{g \in G} r_g \chi(D(g)). \tag{20}$$

5.1   Homomorphic Properties of the Encryption Scheme

As we have seen in Sect. 4, given the homomorphic properties of the χ mapping and the decryption function D (for the initial scheme), we'll get that $Dec : R[G] \rightarrow R$ is actually a ring homomorphism. More specifically, considering two cipher-texts a and b from $R[G]$, we have the following property:

$$Dec(a + b) = Dec \left(\sum_{g \in G} a_g[g] + \sum_{g \in G} b_g[g] \right) = Dec \left(\sum_{g \in G} (a_g + b_g)[g] \right)$$

$$= \sum_{g \in G} (a_g + b_g)[\chi(D(g))] = \sum_{g \in G} a_g[\chi(D(g))] + \sum_{g \in G} b_g[\chi(D(g))]$$

$$= Dec \left(\sum_{g \in G} a_g[g] \right) + Dec \left(\sum_{g \in G} b_g[g] \right) = Dec(a) + Dec(b) \quad (21)$$

The homomorphic property of the decryption function with respect to multiplication is done in a similar manner as shown previously by Eqs. 15 and 16. The security of the scheme is the same as the security of the group encryption scheme (G, H, E, D) since no information and no additional security was revealed or added through the steps describing the encryption algorithm.

5.2   Security Considerations

The choice to generate the set $(r_1, \ldots, r_k)$ as it was described earlier ensures the privacy of the encryption scheme in the sense that any plaintext has the same probability of being encrypted. An attacker having the cipher-text encoded as a vector $[r_i, g_i = E(h_i)], 1 \leq i \leq k$, could attempt to evaluate the plaintext as a linear combination of r_i elements of the form $\sum_{i=1}^{k} r_i s_i, s_i \in S$.

As guaranteed by the initial group encryption scheme security, the attacker could not know anything regarding h_i, henceforth he or she knows nothing about the $s_i \in S$. If all possible linear combinations of the form $\sum_{i=1}^{k} r_i s_i$ with $s_i \in S$ would not cover the entire set R, then at least the attacker could guess some information about the plaintext, i.e. knowing that certain plaintexts are for sure not encrypted in the given ciphertext. This is why we require the coverage property of R from the linear combinations of the form $\sum_{i=1}^{k} r_i s_i$ with $s_i \in S$.

A very important observation needs to be done: one should make the difference between the probability of plaintexts generated by choosing random elements in S and producing the plaintext $\sum_{i=1}^{k} r_i s_i$ and the probability of a certain plaintext to be encrypted. In essence, the choice of the set $(r_1, \ldots, r_k)$ ensures that no plaintext is left outside the encryption process.

Basically, the output of the encryption algorithm is a vector of GM-encryptions. Since the GM algorithm is a public-key encryption scheme, in order to decrypt the ciphertext, one has to decrypt each component of the vector. In other words, the security of the scheme is equivalent to the security of the GM-scheme.

5.3   Efficiency Considerations

In some cases, the choice of the of the generating set $(r_1, \ldots, r_k)$ could lead to a unique and deterministic choice for the $(s_1, \ldots, s_k)$, $s_i \in S$. Having such an efficient algorithm to find the unique linear combination of a plaintext obviously speeds up the encryption process. The bigger the set S is inside R the smaller the number k can be chosen (but not less than 2 if $S \subseteq R^*$ since for $k = 1$ the privacy will be breached by the fact that, in this case, the number 0 in the plaintext cannot be encrypted by a nonzero element in $R[G]$).

The parameter k has an impact over the length of ciphertexts, henceforth over the scheme efficiency. The efficiency of the encryption scheme is k times less the efficiency of the group homomorphic encryption scheme since basically the length of the ciphertext obtained by Enc is approximately $k \times$ (the length of a ciphertext obtained by E plus the length of the message) (by coding the couples $\{r_i, g_i\}$). The decryption algorithm Dec has the speed of the algorithm D in the group homomorphic encryption scheme divided by the ciphertext dimension, i.e. the number of couples $\{r_i, g_i\}$ from the ciphertext.

Having fixed the encryption scheme, the length of the ciphertexts obtained by performing algebraic computations is *finite* since all computations take place in $R[G]$ which is a finite ring. An addition operation will lead very often to a cipher text whose length is the sum of the operands' lengths, since for multiplication, the length will grow up to the product of the ciphertexts' lengths.

One has to be caution in implementing the above scheme in cloud computing for the following reason: even though the ciphertext resulted by computing a polynomial on ciphertexts remains finite, its length is growing up to a certain point exponentially. The maximal length of an element in $R[G]$ is often huge for practical purposes. Therefore, for implementation, one would need an additional process, called *sparsification* in which one has to ensure a practical finiteness of an output after an algebraic manipulation on ciphertexts. To conclude, all of the algebraic properties as well as the properties required in the privacy, efficiency and security problems are satisfied by the ring homomorphic encryption scheme constructed above if one starts with an efficient, private and secure group homomorphic encryption scheme.

6   Homomorphic Encryption Using GM Scheme

As we have seen in Sect. 5, given the homomorphic properties of the decryption function $D : G \rightarrow H$ of some scheme, one can build a ring homomorphic encryption system by means of a homomorphic mapping $\chi : H \rightarrow (R, \cdot)$, where R is the ring corresponding to the plaintext space.

It is worth to mention that many of the encryption schemes already treated in the literature are in fact group homomorphic schemes: RSA, ElGamal, Paillier, Goldwasser-Micali, Benaloh, Diffie-Hellman, etc. Practical encryption schemes require additional constraints on the algorithms KeyGen, Enc and Dec such that the encryption and decryption processes are both feasible, secure and efficient.

We will show how the homomorphic encryption scheme Goldwasser - Micali could be extended to a ring homomorphic encryption using the calculus already presented in Sect. 5. More exactly, for an odd prime m, we consider the ring $R = \mathbb{Z}_m$, with both addition and multiplication done modulo m.

Now we consider the group homomorphic encryption scheme (G, H, E, D) described in Sect. 3 specific to the Goldwasser-Micali scheme where $G = (\mathbb{Z}_N, \cdot)$ and $H = (\{-1, 1\}, \cdot)$. The value of N is chosen as the product of two distinct large prime numbers p and q. Then, one finds some non-residue x such that $(\frac{x}{p}) = (\frac{x}{q}) = -1$ and hence the Jacobi symbol $(\frac{x}{N})$ is $+1$. The encryption and decryption function for the lightly modified GM scheme, E and D respectively, are similar to the those already presented in Sect. 3:

1. **Encryption** of one bit $b \in \{-1, 1\}$ is done generating a random value y relative prime with N; the ciphertext is $c = E(b) = y^2 x^{(1-b)/2} \pmod{N}$.
2. **Decryption** of a ciphertext c is done by computing the Legendre symbol (x/p) using the prime factorization (p, q): $m = D(c) = (\frac{x}{p})$.

This GM cryptosystem inherits homomorphic properties, in the sense that if c_0, c_1 are the encryptions of bits $m_0, m_1 \in \{-1, 1\}$, then $c_0 c_1 \bmod N$ will be an encryption of $m_0 m_1$. We also need a homomorphic mapping $\chi : H \to (R, \cdot)$, which in our case is the identity application: $\chi(h) = h$. From Sect. 5, it is easy to observe that the set S, the image of χ in R, is $\{-1, 1\}$.

6.1   Plaintext Decomposition

The next step from the general framework described in the previous section, is to find a fixed tuple $(r_1, \ldots, r_k) \in \mathbb{Z}_m^k$, where $k \geq 2$, such that the set containing elements of the form $\sum_{i=1}^{k} \pm r_i$ covers the whole ring R. One can observe that we have at most 2^k elements generated by the previous sums, therefore $2^k \geq N$.

Suppose that the binary representation of m requires B bits, i.e. $B = \lceil log_2(m) \rceil$. We propose the choose of the following parameters: $k = B$ and the tuple $(r_1, \ldots, r_k)$ as the set $\{2^0, 2^1 \ldots, 2^{B-1}\} \subset \mathbb{Z}_m$. First, let's consider an odd residue modulus m written in its binary representation: $r = \overline{b_{B-1} \ldots b_1 b_0}, b_i \in \{0, 1\}$. Now consider the subset I of indexes from $B - 1$ to 0 corresponding to non null bits: $I = \{i | B - 1 \geq i \geq 0, b_i = 1\} = \{i_1 > i_2 > \ldots > i_f\}$ with $f = |I|$. Clearly, since r is odd, $i_f = 0$. Then, we have:

$$r = \sum_{0 \leq i < B} b_i 2^i = \sum_{i \in I} b_i 2^i = 2^{i_1} + \ldots + 2^{i_f} \tag{22}$$

Considering each term 2^{i_k} from the previous sum, separately, then for $k > 1$, it can be written in the following way:

$$2^{i_k} = 2^l - \left(\sum_{l > j \geq i_k} 2^j \right), l = i_{k-1} - 1 \tag{23}$$

One can observe that if the indexes i_k and i_{k-1} are consecutive numbers, then the Eq. 23 still holds, the sum in the paranthesis disappearing completely. Moreover, for the most significant bit, non null, from r binary representation (i.e. $k = 1$), we have a similar formula:

$$2^{i_1} = 2^{B-1} - \left(\sum_{B-1>j\geq i_1} 2^j \right) \tag{24}$$

Unifying the formulas 22, 23 and 24, one can observe that any odd residue $r \in \mathbb{Z}_m$ can be written in terms of $\sum \pm 2^i \bmod m, 0 \leq i \leq B - 1$, as follows:

$$r = \sum_{1\leq k\leq f} \left(2^l - \left(\sum_{l>j\geq i_k} 2^j \right) \right), l = \begin{cases} i_{k-1} - 1 & \text{if } k > 1 \\ B - 1 & \text{if } k = 1 \end{cases}$$

To better understand this decomposition in terms of $\sum \pm 2^i$, let's consider an example: $m = 61$ and $r = 23 = \overline{010111}_2$. The set of r_i is $\{2^5, 2^4, 2^3, 2^2, 2^1, 2^0\}$. Then, we have: $23 = 2^4 + 2^2 + 2^1 + 2^0 = 2^5 - 2^4 + 2^3 - 2^2 + 2^1 + 2^0$. To conclude, any odd residue from $\mathbb{Z}_m$ can be written in terms of the chosen set.

Let's consider now the case of an even residue r from $\mathbb{Z}_m{}^*$. Then, $m - r$ is an odd residue and therefore can be written as: $m - r = \sum s_i 2^i$, with $s_i \in \{-1, 1\}$. That means that: $r - m = \sum (-s_i) 2^i$. Reducing the two expressions modulus m, it gives us the following writing: $r = \sum (-s_i) 2^i \bmod m$, which corresponds to the decomposition of r in terms of the chosen set. The decomposition of the residue 0 from $\mathbb{Z}_m$, can be obtained from the writting of m (an odd number) just like in the same manner as all other odd residues from $\mathbb{Z}_m$.

Therefore, we know at this moment, a precise method to write any residue from $\mathbb{Z}_m$ as a sum of the form $\sum s_i r_i$, for the chosen set of $r_i = 2^i$. We'll explain further the key generation, the encryption and the decryption processes which derives naturally from the general framework described in Sect. 5.

6.2   Key Generation, Encryption and Decryption

Key Generation consists in the generation of two distinct large prime numbers p and q, randomly and independently of each other. One computes then $N = pq$. Further, one finds some non-residue x such that the Legendre symbols satisfy $\left(\frac{x}{p}\right) = \left(\frac{x}{q}\right) = -1$ and hence the Jacobi symbol $\left(\frac{x}{N}\right)$ is $+1$. The public key consists of (x, N), while the secret key is the factorization $N = pq$.

Encryption process is described by the following steps:

1. For a plaintext $r \in \mathbb{Z}_m$, one computes the tuple $(s_1, \ldots, s_B) \in \{-1, 1\}^k$ as described in Subsect. 6.1, such that: $r = \sum r_i s_i, 1 \leq i \leq B$.
2. For each $i \in \{1 \ldots B\}$, one generates a random value y_i relative prime to N and then encrypts s_i as $c_i = E(s_i) = y_i{}^2 x^{(1-s_i)/2} \pmod{N}$.

3. The encryption of the plaintext $r \in \mathbb{Z}_m$ is the following expression from the group algebra ring $\mathbb{Z}_m[\mathbb{Z}_N]$:

$$Enc(r) := \sum_{i=1}^{B} 2^{i-1}[c_i] \tag{25}$$

Decryption of an element from $\mathbb{Z}_m[\mathbb{Z}_N]$ is computed using the secret key (p, q) and is defined by the formula:

$$Dec\left(\sum_{c \in \mathbb{Z}_N} r_c[c]\right) := \sum_{c \in \mathbb{Z}_N} r_c D(c) = \left(\sum_{c \in \mathbb{Z}_N} r_c \left(\frac{c}{p}\right)\right) mod\ N \tag{26}$$

It is important to note that our scheme does NOT make a *bitwise encryption*. We can see that the plaintext space is $\mathbb{Z}_m$ and the encryption becomes homomorphic over both multiplicative and additive operations using the GM's multiplicative homomorphic properties. The GM scheme can be replaced within the above construction by any other encryption schemes, which have homomorphic properties with respect to the multiplication operation (e.g. Paillier encryption).

6.3   A Toy Example

To better understand the homomorphic encryption system based on GM scheme, let's consider a small example with the following parameters: $p = 7, q = 11$ and $N = pq = 77$. Therefore, N beeing a Blum number, i.e. $p \equiv q \equiv 3 \bmod 4$, we can choose $x = N - 1 = 76$; indeed, $\left(\frac{76}{7}\right) = \left(\frac{76}{11}\right) = -1$. The public key is the pair $(x = 76, N = 77)$ and the secret key is the factorization $(p = 7, q = 11)$.

Let's choose now $m = 7$, so the plaintext space is the ring $\mathbb{Z}_7$ and the B parameter from our scheme is $B = 3$. Suppose we want to encrypt two residues from $\mathbb{Z}_7$, namely 5 and 4. First, the decomposition of 5 is $5 = -1 + 2 + 4$ mod 7, so the set of coefficients s_i to be encrypted using GM is $\{-1, 1, 1\}$. Using the encryption algorithm described in Subsect. 6.2, we generates the 3 corresponding encryptions for $\{-1, 1, 1\}$ using the set of y_i as $\{2^2, 3^2, 5^2\}$; the encrypted values are $\{73, 9, 25\}$. Therefore, the encryption of 5 is as follows: $c_5 = Enc(5) = 1[73] + 2[9] + 4[25]$.

Second, the decomposition of 4 is the following: $4 = -3 = -1 + 2 - 4$ mod 7, so the set of coefficients s_i to be encrypted using GM is $\{-1, 1, -1\}$. Using the encryption algorithm described in Subsect. 6.2, we generates the 3 corresponding encryptions for $\{-1, 1, -1\}$ using the set of y_i as $\{4^2, 5^2, 1^2\}$; the encrypted values are $\{61, 25, 76\}$. Therefore, the encryption of 4 is as follows: $c_4 = Enc(4) = 1[61] + 2[25] + 4[76]$.

Now let's compute $c_4 + c_5$ and $c_4 c_5$ within the ciphertext space. In the next formulas we used the equations describing the group algebra operations from Sect. 4 together with the online tool [13] for computing Legendre symbols.

$$c_4 + c_5 = (1[73] + 2[9] + 4[25]) + (1[61] + 2[25] + 4[76])$$
$$= 1[73] + 2[9] + (4 + 2 \; mod \; 7)[25] + 1[61] + 4[76]$$
$$\boldsymbol{Dec(c_4 + c_5)} = 1\left(\frac{73}{7}\right) + 2\left(\frac{9}{7}\right) + 6\left(\frac{25}{7}\right) + 1\left(\frac{61}{7}\right) + 4\left(\frac{76}{7}\right) \; mod \; 7$$
$$= (-1 + 2 + 6 - 1 - 4) \; mod \; 7 = 2 = \boldsymbol{5 + 4 \; mod \; 7}$$

$$c_4 c_5 = (1[73] + 2[9] + 4[25]) \, (1[61] + 2[25] + 4[76])$$
$$= [73 \cdot 61] + 2[73 \cdot 25] + 4[73 \cdot 76] + 2[9 \cdot 61] + 4[9 \cdot 25] + [9 \cdot 76]$$
$$+ 4[25 \cdot 61] + [25 \cdot 25] + 2[25 \cdot 76]$$
$$= [64] + 2[54] + 4[4] + 2[10] + 4[71] + [68] + 4[62] + [9] + 2[52]$$
$$\boldsymbol{Dec(c_4 c_5)} = \left(\frac{64}{7}\right) + 2\left(\frac{54}{7}\right) + 4\left(\frac{4}{7}\right) + 2\left(\frac{10}{7}\right) + 4\left(\frac{71}{7}\right)$$
$$+ \left(\frac{68}{7}\right) + 4\left(\frac{62}{7}\right) + \left(\frac{9}{7}\right) + 2\left(\frac{52}{7}\right) \; mod \; 7$$
$$= (1 - 2 + 4 - 2 + 4 - 1 - 4 + 1 - 2) \; mod \; 7 = 6 = \boldsymbol{5 \cdot 4 \; mod \; 7}$$

7   Implementation and Experimental Results

The HE-GM is our implementation of the homomorphic encryption system presented in Sect. 6 of the paper. It has been written in C++ and is based on the NTL mathematical library [14]. The code includes the routines for GM scheme (GM-KeyGen, GM-Enc, GM-Dec) and the implementation of the homomorphic encryption system over group algebras (as described in Sect. 6.2).

The HE-GM can encrypt integer values of any B-bits lengths and get a fresh ciphertext with B terms each of them containing a GM encryption of one bit. The two basic homomorphic operations (addition and multiplication) have been implemented in the HE-GM at the ciphertext level. Using the HE-GM implementation we validated the correctness of the homomorphic encryption system. We made also various benchmarks that aim for time consumption necessary to achieve fresh data encryption/decryption, evaluation of add and multiply operations and the ciphertext sizes. The benchmarks have been carried out using different security levels for GM scheme (various sized key-parameters p, q).

Our experiments were conducted on a normal laptop having an Intel CPU (I7-4710HQ, 4 cores, 2.5 GHz, 3 GB RAM). The implementation is not multithreaded and it uses only one CPU core. The Table 1 presents the costs in terms of time and ciphertext size needed by a fresh encryption and decryption of an integer value with a binary representation length of 8 bits.

The Table 2 contains computation time measured during the evaluation of basis operations (adding and multiplying). The most time consuming operation is the multiplication, because in that case the number of terms from resulting ciphertext is the sum of terms contained by evaluated ciphertexts. We note that the growth factor for time spent for each additional multiplication with a fresh encrypted value is kept approximately constant.

Table 1. Fresh encryption and decryption of an integer value using HE-GM system

GM key-params p, q	Enc. time	Dec. time	Ciphertext size
$p, q = 1024$ bits	3.23 ms	0.8 ms	2072 bytes
$p, q = 2048$ bits	10 ms	2.3 ms	4120 bytes
$p, q = 4096$ bits	40 ms	6.5 ms	8216 bytes

Table 2. Time costs for HE-GM homomorphic operations

GM key-params p, q	$a + b$	$a * b$	$a * b * c$	$a * b * c * d$	$a * b * c * d * e$
$p, q = 1024$ bits	0.07 ms	0.8 ms	7.85 ms	64 ms	770 ms
$p, q = 2048$ bits	0.11 ms	2.205 ms	21 ms	163 ms	1637 ms
$p, q = 4096$ bits	0.15 ms	6.7 ms	67 ms	500 ms	4.5 s

Table 3 presents a comparison between our HE scheme implementation over GM (HE-GM) and the leveled implementation of HElib [10]. We used a 2048 bit length for the GM key. The values are calculated as an average execution time consumed by the implementation for multiplying integers of various length. The results show that for the case of small integers, our HE-GM system is considerable faster than HElib. Using the leveled variant of HElib, the time consumption in its case is relative constant. In the case of HE-GM, the number of multiplication operations has a polynomial growth for each additional multiplication.

Table 3. Timing costs for HE-GM and HElib in case of multiply operations

Number of bits	$a * b$		$a * b * c$		$a * b * c * d$		$a * b * c * d * e$	
	HE-GM	HElib	HE-GM	HElib	HE-GM	HElib	HE-GM	HElib
8 bits	0.8 ms	347 ms	7.85 ms	870 ms	64 ms	1 542 ms	770 ms	2 269 ms
16 bits	3.4 ms	336 ms	60 ms	851 ms	2193 ms	1 503 ms	510 s	2 374 ms
24 bits	7.8 ms	334 ms	241 ms	846 ms	44 060 ms	1 451 ms	107 min	2 205 ms

8   Conclusion

This paper builds on a general framework able to extend a group homomorphic encryption scheme with respect to one operation, towards a ring homomorphic cryptosystem. This new cryptosystem has homomorphic properties on two operations: addition and multiplication. We choose to apply the general framework to a well known homomorphic encryption scheme, Goldwasser-Micali, and analyze the resulted cryptosystem from the security and the efficiency point of view.

The security of the proposed scheme is the same as the security of the initial group encryption scheme (i.e. Goldwasser-Micali) since no information and no additional security was revealed or added through the steps describing the encryption process as described previously in Sect. 5.2. The GM cryptosystem is semantically secure based on the assumed intractability of the quadratic residuosity problem corresponding to a modulus product of two large large primes.

From the efficiency point of view, as illustrated by the experimental results, our scheme works well for the case of small integers (byte values) but shows its weakness for large integers, especially when the number of multiplications grows up. This is basically due first to the expansion introduced by Goldwasser-Micali on a bit level and second (more important) by the expansion given by operations on ciphertexts. As shown previously, the parameter k (i.e. the number of bits) has a direct (linear) impact over the length of fresh ciphertexts and the addition operation, while in the multiplication process the length of ciphertext will grow up to the product of the ciphertexts' lengths.

Therefore, one important perspective of our work regards the application of the general framework on schemes having smaller groups (i.e. smaller k) that contains the result of the encryption process. Another perspective concerns the application of the general framework to other encryption schemes known as group homomorphic schemes like RSA, ElGamal, Paillier, Diffie-Hellman, etc.

The blueprint of the above described encryption scheme opens the path of constructing new families of secure ring/fully-homomorphic encryption schemes which are NOT error-based. The efficiency issues are of different nature than those of error-based encryption schemes, and further improvements might bring better understanding of how far one can go in the attempt of realizing practical fully homomorphic encryption schemes.

Acknowledgments. This research was partially supported by the Romanian National Authority for Scientific Research (CNCS-UEFISCDI) under the project PN-II-PT-PCCA-2011-3 (ctr. 19/2012).

References

1. Rivest, R., Adleman, L., Dertouzos, M.: On data banks and privacy homomorphisms. In: Foundations of Secure Computation, pp. 169–179. Springer, Academia Press (1978)
2. Gentry, C.: A fully homomorphic encryption scheme. Ph.D. thesis, Stanford University (2009). http://crypto.stanford.edu/craig
3. Barcău, M., Paşol, V.: Fully Homomorphic Encryption from Monoid Algebras (2016)
4. Goldwasser, S., Micali, S.: Probabilistic encryption. J. Comput. Syst. Sci. **28**(2), 270–299 (1984). Massachusetts Institute of Technology, Cambridge
5. Fellows, M., Koblitz, N.: Combinatorial cryptosystems galore! In: Finite Fields: Theory, Applications, and Algorithms. Contemporary Mathematics, vol. 168, pp. 51–61. AMS (1994)
6. Hoffstein, J., Pipher, J., Silverman, J.H.: NTRU: a ring-based public key cryptosystem. In: Buhler, J.P. (ed.) ANTS 1998. LNCS, vol. 1423, pp. 267–288. Springer, Heidelberg (1998)
7. Brakerski, Z., Gentry, C., Vaikuntanathan, V.: Fully homomorphic encryption without bootstrapping. In: Innovations in Theoretical Computer Science Conference, pp. 309–325 (2012)

8. Gentry, C., Halevi, S., Smart, N.P.: Homomorphic evaluation of the AES circuit. In: Canetti, R., Safavi-Naini, R. (eds.) CRYPTO 2012. LNCS, vol. 7417, pp. 850–867. Springer, Heidelberg (2012)
9. Smart, N.P., Vercauteren, F.: Fully homomorphic SIMD operations. Des. Codes Crypt. **71**, 57–81 (2012)
10. Halevi, S., Shoup, V.: The HElib library (2015). https://github.com/shaih/HElib
11. Grigoriev, D., Ponomarenko, I.: Homomorphic public-key cryptosystems over groups and rings. Quad. di Math. **13**, 305–325 (2004)
12. Ireland, K., Rosen, M.: A Classical Introduction to Modern Number Theory, 2nd edn. Springer, New York (2000)
13. Richman, F.: http://math.fau.edu/richman/jacobi.htm
14. Shoup, V.: NTL: A library for doing number theory (2001)

Increasing the Robustness of the Montgomery kP-Algorithm Against SCA by Modifying Its Initialization

Estuardo Alpirez Bock[✉], Zoya Dyka, and Peter Langendoerfer

IHP, Im Technologiepark 25, Frankfurt (Oder), Germany
{alpirez,dyka,langendoerfer}@ihp-microelectronics.com
http://www.ihp-microelectronics.com

Abstract. The Montgomery kP-algorithm using Lopez-Dahab projective coordinates is a well-known method for performing the scalar multiplication in elliptic curve crypto-systems (ECC). It is considered resistant against simple power analysis (SPA) since each key bit is processed by the same type, amount and sequence of operations, independently of the key bit's value. Nevertheless, its initialization phase affects this algorithm's robustness against side channel analysis (SCA) attacks. We describe how the first iteration of the kP processing loop reveals information about the key bit being processed, i.e. bit k_{l-2}. We explain how the value of this bit can be extracted with SPA and how the power profile of its processing can reveal details about the implementation of the algorithm. We propose a modification of the algorithm's initialization phase and of the processing of bit k_{l-2}, in order to hinder the extraction of its value using SPA. Our proposed modifications increase the algorithm's robustness against SCA and even reduce the time needed for the initialization phase and for processing k_{l-2}. Compared to the original design, our new implementation needs only 0.12 % additional area, while its energy consumption is almost the same, i.e. we improved the security of the design at no cost.

Keywords: Elliptic curve cryptography · Montgomery kP-algorithm · Power analysis

1 Introduction

Side channel analysis (SCA) attacks have been a popular research topic in the last years. Parameters like power consumption, electromagnetic radiation and execution time of a cryptographic implementation can be analysed for identifying implementation details and based on this, extracting the private key. The Montgomery kP-algorithm using Lopez-Dahab projective coordinates [1] is an efficient method for performing the scalar multiplication kP in elliptic curve crypto-systems (ECC). This algorithm is a bitwise processing of the l-bit long scalar $k = k_{l-1}, k_{l-2}, \ldots, k_1, k_0$; which is the private key used for performing decryption in ECC. It is considered resistant against simple power analysis (SPA). Nevertheless its first loop iteration (performed for processing the key bit k_{l-2}) reveals

© Springer International Publishing AG 2016
I. Bica and R. Reyhanitabar (Eds.): SECITC 2016, LNCS 10006, pp. 167–178, 2016.
DOI: 10.1007/978-3-319-47238-6_12

information about the value of the key bit being processed. This key bit can be extracted with SPA. Besides this, the power profile of the processing of k_{l-2} can be used for understanding implementation details of the kP-algorithm and thus for the preparation of further attacks.

In this paper we describe how the initialization phase of the Montgomery kP-algorithm affects the algorithm's resistance against SCA attacks. We use simulated power traces (PTs) to show how the power profile of the processing of k_{l-2} differs from the power profiles of the processing of all other key bits. Moreover, we demonstrate that this power profile differs significantly for the cases $k_{l-2} = 1$ and $k_{l-2} = 0$. This leads to an easy extraction of bit k_{l-2} using SPA and exposes details of the implementation of the algorithm, which can be useful for the preparation of further attacks. As a countermeasure against this vulnerability, we propose to process key bit k_{l-2} outside of the algorithm's main loop, with a different operation flow. We show that with this modification, the power profiles of the processings of $k_{l-2} = 1$ and $k_{l-2} = 0$ look similar to each other and similar to the processing of all remaining bits of the key, i.e. the value of the key bit k_{l-2} cannot be extracted using SPA. The initialization phase of the algorithm is shortened, as well as the processing of k_{l-2}. The execution time of a kP-operation using our modified design was reduced by 11 clock cycles. Our modifications did not imply an increase on the energy consumption needed for the calculation of kP, which remains by 2.09 μJ, and our implementation's chip area was increased by only 0.12 %.

The rest of this paper is structured as follows. In Sect. 2 we describe the Montgomery kP-algorithm using Lopez-Dahab projective coordinates and discuss its resistance against SCA. Section 3 explains how the processing of k_{l-2} reveals information about the key bit being processed, as well as information regarding the implementation details. In Sect. 4 we present our modifications of the Montgomery kP-algorithm regarding its initialization phase and the processing of k_{l-2}. Section 5 shows results regarding the power profiles, area and energy consumption of our implementation of the original kP-algorithm and our modified version.

2   Montgomery kP-Algorithm

The Montgomery kP-algorithm using Lopez-Dahab projective coordinates was introduced in 1999 [1]. The work presented in [2] shows a possible way of implementing this algorithm (see Algorithm 1). Only the value of the x-coordinate of point P is used. No division operations and no operations with the y-coordinates of the EC points need to be performed in the main loop. This reduces the execution time and energy consumption of the calculation of kP. Due to this fact, the algorithm is often implemented for energy constrained devices such as wireless sensor nodes.

The Montgomery kP-algorithm is a bitwise processing of the scalar k. The scalar k is the private key used for performing decryption in ECC. Each bit of k, except its most significant bit (MSB), is processed with the same type, amount

Algorithm 1. Montgomery algorithm for the kP-operation using projective coordinates

Input: $k = (k_{l-1}, ..., k_1, k_0)_2$ with $k_{l-1} = 1, P = (x, y) \in E(GF(2^m))$.
Output: $kP = (x_1, y_1)$.
 1: $X_1 \leftarrow x, Z_1 \leftarrow 1, X_2 \leftarrow x^4 + b, Z_2 \leftarrow x^2$.
 2: **for** i from $l - 2$ downto 0 **do**
 3:   **if** $k_i = 1$ **then**
 4:     $T \leftarrow Z_1, Z_1 \leftarrow (X_1 Z_2 + X_2 Z_1)^2, X_1 \leftarrow x Z_1 + X_1 X_2 T Z_2,$
 5:     $T \leftarrow X_2, X_2 \leftarrow X_2^4 + b Z_2^4, Z_2 \leftarrow T^2 Z_2^2$.
 6:   **else**
 7:     $T \leftarrow Z_2, Z_2 \leftarrow (X_2 Z_1 + X_1 Z_2)^2, X_2 \leftarrow x Z_2 + X_1 X_2 T Z_1,$
 8:     $T \leftarrow X_1, X_1 \leftarrow X_1^4 + b Z_1^4, Z_1 \leftarrow T^2 Z_1^2$.
 9:   **end if**
10: **end for**
11: $x_1 \leftarrow X_1 / Z_1$.
12: $y_1 \leftarrow y + (x + x_1)[X_1 + x Z_1)(X_2 + x Z_2) + (x^2 + y)(Z_1 Z_2)]/(x Z_1 Z_2)$.
13: **return** $((x_1, y_1))$.

and sequence of operations, independently of the key bit's value. Due to this fact, the Montgomery kP-algorithm is in the literature referred to as resistant against some SCA attacks, such as SPA and simple electromagnetic analysis [3]. The algorithm consist of three parts. The first part is the initialization phase (see line 1 in Algorithm 1). During this phase, the conversion of affine EC point coordinates to Lopez-Dahab projective coordinates takes place and the MSB of the scalar k, the key bit $k_{l-1} = 1$, is processed. The second part corresponds to the processing of all remaining bits of the scalar k, i.e. bits $k_{l-2}, k_{l-3}, \ldots, k_1, k_0$ (see lines 2 to 10 in Algorithm 1). This is the main loop of the algorithm. Depending on the value of the key bit k_i the operations in lines 4 and 5 or the operations in lines 7 and 8 are executed. Both possible loop iterations, i.e. in case $k_i = 1$ and in case $k_i = 0$, are executed in exactly the same way. In both cases 6 multiplications[1], 5 squarings, 3 additions and 6 register write operations are performed. The two loops only differ in the interchangeable use of the registers as input and output parameters. The third part of Algorithm 1 corresponds to the conversion of the multiplication result $kP = (X, Z)$ back to affine coordinates (see lines 11 and 12).

2.1 Initialization Phase as Loop Iteration

In [4] the initialization phase of Algorithm 1 is simplified. Only the values given in (1) are assigned to the registers and no calculations are performed in this phase.

$$X_1 \leftarrow 1, Z_1 \leftarrow 0, X_2 \leftarrow x, Z_2 \leftarrow 1. \tag{1}$$

---

[1] For example if the product $X_1 X_2 T Z_2$ in line 4 is calculated as $X_1 X_2 T Z_2 = (X_1 Z_2) \cdot (X_2 T)$, this calculation corresponds to only one multiplication since the products $X_1 \cdot Z_2$ and $X_2 \cdot T$ are already calculated.

Then, the first iteration of the main loop is executed according to Algorithm 1, but for the MSB $k_{l-1} = 1$. Thus, the initialization phase in Algorithm 1 is performed as a regular loop. After processing key bit k_{l-1}, the registers have the following values, which are the same as those shown in line 1 of Algorithm 1:

$$X_1 \leftarrow x, Z_1 \leftarrow 1, X_2 \leftarrow x^4 + b, Z_2 \leftarrow x^2. \tag{2}$$

The purpose of this modification was to avoid the design of any additional modules, eventually needed for the calculations performed during the initialization phase of the algorithm. Recent publications such as [5,6] also implement the initialization phase of the Montgomery kP-algorithm in this way, i.e. as a regular loop with special inputs.

2.2 Implementation of the Montgomery kP-Algorithm and SCA

A lot of research has been done on efficient implementations of the Montgomery kP-algorithm. A possible way of achieving efficiency is through the parallel execution of the operations in the algorithm. [5,7,8] presented efficient implementations of the Montgomery kP-algorithm based on architectures that consist of one multiplier only. In these implementations the arithmetic and register write operations are performed in parallel to the multiplications during the executions of the main loop. In this case, the execution time of one loop iteration is defined by the time needed for performing all 6 multiplications in the loop. This is the minimum execution time for one iteration of the loop.

The focus of many research publications is only on the efficiency of the algorithm's implementation, while resistance against SCA is not considered (for example [5–7]). Other papers discuss only the resistance of the Montgomery kP-algorithm against SCA attacks, for example [9]. The resistance against timing, simple power analysis and simple electromagnetic analysis attacks is claimed based on the fact that the algorithm performs the same type, sequence and number of operations on every iteration, independent of the key bit value [3]. Implementations resistant to SPA attacks can still be attacked using differential power analysis (DPA). The randomization of the key k or of the EC projective coordinates, as well as blinding of the EC point P [10] are well known countermeasures against DPA attacks.

In the following section, we show that the value of k_{l-2} can be extracted through SPA if the Montgomery kP-algorithm is implemented using Lopez-Dahab projective coordinates and if no special countermeasures have been implemented. In Sect. 4 we show how we modified Algorithm 1 to avoid the easy extraction of key bit k_{l-2} through SPA.

3 Vulnerabilities Due to the Initialization Phase

In line 1 of Algorithm 1 the registers X_1, Z_1, X_2 and Z_2 are initialized. The registers are used with these initial values as inputs for the first iteration of the algorithm's main loop, i.e. for the processing of key bit k_{l-2}. Register Z_1 is initialized with the value 1. This means that for the processing of k_{l-2}, all operations performed with register Z_1 are operations performed with an operand with value 1:

if $k_{l-2} = 1$

$$T \leftarrow 1, Z_1 \leftarrow (X_1 Z_2 + X_2 \cdot 1)^2, X_1 \leftarrow xZ_1 + (X_1 Z_2)(X_2 \cdot 1),$$
$$T \leftarrow X_2, X_2 \leftarrow (X_2^2)^2 + b(Z_2^2)^2, Z_2 \leftarrow T^2 Z_2^2. \tag{3}$$

if $k_{l-2} = 0$

$$T \leftarrow Z_2, Z_2 \leftarrow (X_2 \cdot 1 + X_1 Z_2)^2, X_2 \leftarrow xZ_2 + (X_1 T)(X_2 \cdot 1),$$
$$T \leftarrow X_1, X_1 \leftarrow (X_1^2)^2 + b(1^2)^2, Z_1 \leftarrow T^2 \cdot 1^2. \tag{4}$$

This fact has the following consequences regarding the processing of k_{l-2}:

- Any multiplication performed with $Z_1 = 1$ as operand[2] will result in the value of the other operand.
- Any squaring operation performed with $Z_1 = 1$ as input will result in 1.
- The power consumption of such operations is significantly low in comparison to the power consumed by operations performed using operands with values higher than 1.

Thus, the power profile of the processing of k_{l-2} differs significantly from the power profile of the processing of all other key bits. Moreover, the power profiles in the cases $k_{l-2} = 1$ and $k_{l-2} = 0$ differ significantly from each other. Thus, the value of k_{l-2} can be extracted through SPA.

3.1 Easy Extraction of the Key Bit k_{l-2}

In the first loop iteration of Algorithm 1, a different amount of operations using register $Z_1 = 1$ as operand are performed depending on the value of k_{l-2} (compare (3) and (4)). If $k_{l-2} = 1$, register T is overwritten with $Z_1 = 1$ and only one multiplication uses $Z_1 = 1$ as operand. If $k_{l-2} = 0$, two squarings and three multiplications are performed using $Z_1 = 1$ as operand. This means that the power profile of the processing of k_{l-2} is different in case $k_{l-2} = 1$ and in case $k_{l-2} = 0$. In case $k_{l-2} = 1$ the corresponding power profile should have one dip, which corresponds to the multiplication $X_2 \cdot Z_1 = X_2 \cdot 1$. In case $k_{l-2} = 0$, the corresponding power profile should have three of such dips, corresponding to $X_2 \cdot Z_1 = X_2 \cdot 1; b \cdot Z_1^4 = b \cdot 1$, and $T^2 \cdot Z_1^2 = T^2 \cdot 1$. In this context, the value of k_{l-2} can be easily identified.

Figure 1 shows simulated PTs of an execution of the kP-operation with our implementation of the Montgomery kP-algorithm [8] using the IHP 130 nm technology [11]. Each trace is divided into slots, whereby one slot corresponds to the processing of one key bit k_i. Each simulation was made using a different

---

[2] Here, 1 is the integer value.

key.[3] The trace in Fig. 1(a) was simulated using key $k1$, whereby the value of the key bit $k1_{l-2} = 1$. The trace in Fig. 1(b) was simulated using key $k2$, whereby the value of key bit $k2_{l-2} = 0$. Our simulation results were obtained using the Synopsis PrimeTime suite [12].

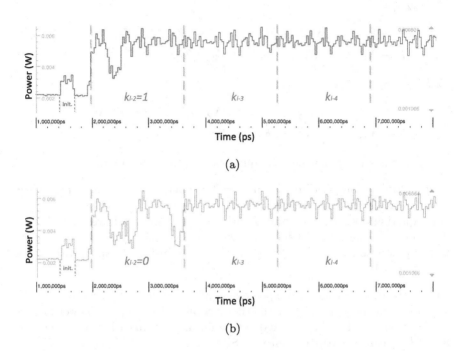

(a)

(b)

Fig. 1. Two PTs simulated using our implementation of the Montgomery kP-algorithm according to Algorithm 1. The trace in (a) was simulated for the point multiplication $k1 \cdot P$ with $k1_{l-2} = 1$. Only one dip can be seen during the processing of k_{l-2} in this trace. The trace in (b) was simulated for the point multiplication $k2 \cdot P$ with $k2_{l-2} = 0$. Three dips can be seen during the processing of k_{l-2} in this trace.

Figure 1(a) shows only one dip in the slot corresponding to the processing of k_{l-2}. Figure 1(b) shows three dips in the slot corresponding to the processing of k_{l-2}. Thus, it can be easily concluded that $k_{l-2} = 1$ has been processed in the first slot of the curve in Fig. 1(a). The same way it is easily observable that $k_{l-2} = 0$ has been processed in the first slot of the curve in Fig. 1(b). This means that the key bit k_{l-2} can be extracted through SPA.

3.2 Vulnerabilities to Other Attacks

In Sect. 3.1 we demonstrated that the key bit k_{l-2} can be extracted with SPA. The extraction through SPA can be done for only one bit of the key, but the

---

[3] $k1 = cd\ ea65f6dd\ 7a75b8b5\ 133a70d1\ f27a4d95\ 06ecfb6a\ 50ea526e\ b3d426ed$
$k2 = 93\ 919255fd\ 4359f4c2\ b67dea45\ 6ef70a54\ 5a9c44d4\ 6f7f409f\ 96cb52cc.$

power profile of the processing of k_{l-2} can be helpful for the preparation of other physical attacks.

For a successful extraction of the complete key, the attacker needs to know which operands are processed in operations within a certain clock cycle, i.e. he needs knowledge about the implementation details of the algorithm's main loop. If the kP operation is implemented according to Algorithm 1, the power profile of the processing of k_{l-2} is helpful to understand the implementation details. This power profile reveals details about the implemented operation execution sequence and the time needed for processing one key bit, i.e. for performing one loop iteration. This information is very useful for preparing, for example, DPA attacks [13], template attacks [14] or fault analysis attacks. For the processing of k_{l-2}, the attacker knows exactly which data is being processed, i.e. he knows the input values for this loop iteration (see line 1 of Algorithm 1) and can easily extract the key bit value being processed (see Sect. 3.1). Since he knows as well *how* this data is being processed, the processing of k_{l-2} can be used as a reference for creating templates for other attacks.

If the initialization phase of the Montgomery kP-algorithm is implemented according to [4], the implementation becomes even more vulnerable to other power analysis, template or fault analysis attacks. The attacker knows the value of the key bit and the input data that has been processed not only in the first loop iteration, i.e. $k_{l-1} = 1$, but also in the second loop iteration, i.e. k_{l-2}. The attacker has the processing of two bits as a reference for creating templates.

4   Countermeasure for Protecting the Key Bit k_{l-2}

To avoid the extraction of key bit k_{l-2} through SPA and to hinder the use of the processing of k_{l-2} for preparing other attacks, we suggest to process the key bit k_{l-2} outside of the main loop of Algorithm 1 using a simplified sequence of operations. Key bit k_{l-2} can be processed with a simplified operation sequence since each operation performed with an operand with value 1, i.e. each operation performed with register Z_1, can be skipped.

The initialization phase of Algorithm 1 can be simplified as well. The initialization for register $Z_1 \leftarrow 1$ (see line 1 of Algorithm 1) can be skipped since no operations will be performed using this value as an operand. This reduces the time and energy consumption needed for processing the key bits k_{l-1} and k_{l-2}.

By skipping all operations performed with operand 1 in both cases, $k_{l-2} = 1$ and $k_{l-2} = 0$, the value of k_{l-2} can also be easily extracted through SPA, because of the different number of operations performed in each case. In case $k_{l-2} = 1$, one register write operation and one multiplication can be skipped, while if $k_{l-2} = 0$, two squarings and three multiplications can be skipped. Thus, the execution time and power profiles of the processing of $k_{l-2} = 1$ and $k_{l-2} = 0$ differ significantly. To prevent the SPA in this case, the same operation flows should be performed independently of the value of k_{l-2}. Thus in case $k_{l-2} = 0$, in which two squarings and three multiplications can be skipped, both squarings and two of these multiplications should be replaced by dummy operations (all operands $\neq 1$), whose results can be ignored. In case $k_{l-2} = 1$, one dummy register write operation should be performed. The details of our modification are discussed in the rest of this section.

4.1   Shortened Initialization Phase

Since no operations using register $Z_1 = 1$ as input will be executed during the processing of k_{l-2}, the initialization of register Z_1 can be skipped. This makes the initialization phase of the algorithm shorter, consisting of only the following operations:

$$X_1 \leftarrow x, X_2 \leftarrow x^4 + b, Z_2 \leftarrow x^2. \tag{5}$$

4.2   New Sequence for Processing of Key Bit k_{l-2}

Algorithm 2 shows our modified version of Algorithm 1. The initialization phase and the processing of k_{l-2} are simplified. The operation flow for k_{l-2} (see lines 2–8) differs from the operation flow in the main loop (see lines 9–17).

Algorithm 2. Modified Montgomery algorithm for the kP-operation

---

Input: $k = (k_{l-1}, ..., k_1, k_0)_2$ with $k_{l-1} = 1, P = (x, y) \in E(GF(2^m))$.
Output: $kP = (x_1, y_1)$.
1: $X_1 \leftarrow x, X_2 \leftarrow x^4 + b, Z_2 \leftarrow x^2$.
2: **if** $k_{l-2} = 1$ **then**
3:    $T \leftarrow Z_2, Z_1 \leftarrow (X_1 Z_2 + X_2)^2, X_1 \leftarrow X_1 Z_2 X_2 + Z_1 x,$
4:    $T \leftarrow X_2, U \leftarrow b Z_2^4, X_2 \leftarrow X_2^4 + U, U \leftarrow T Z_2, Z_2 \leftarrow U^2$.
5: **else**
6:    $T \leftarrow Z_2, Z_2 \leftarrow (X_1 Z_2 + X_2)^2, X_2 \leftarrow X_1 X_2 T + Z_2 x,$
7:    $T \leftarrow X_1, U \leftarrow b X_2^4, X_1 \leftarrow X_1^4 + b, U \leftarrow T X_2, Z_1 \leftarrow T^2$.
8: **end if**
9: **for** i from $l - 3$ downto 0 **do**
10:    **if** $k_i = 1$ **then**
11:        $T \leftarrow Z_1, Z_1 \leftarrow (X_1 Z_2 + X_2 Z_1)^2, X_1 \leftarrow x Z_1 + X_1 X_2 T Z_2,$
12:        $T \leftarrow X_2, X_2 \leftarrow X_2^4 + b Z_2^4, Z_2 \leftarrow T^2 Z_2^2$.
13:    **else**
14:        $T \leftarrow Z_2, Z_2 \leftarrow (X_2 Z_1 + X_1 Z_2)^2, X_2 \leftarrow x Z_2 + X_1 X_2 T Z_1,$
15:        $T \leftarrow X_1, X_1 \leftarrow X_1^4 + b Z_1^4, Z_1 \leftarrow T^2 Z_1^2$.
16:    **end if**
17: **end for**
18: $x_1 \leftarrow X_1 / Z_1$.
19: $y_1 \leftarrow y + (x + x_1)[X_1 + x Z_1)(X_2 + x Z_2) + (x^2 + y)(Z_1 Z_2)]/(x Z_1 Z_2)$.
20: **return** $((x_1, y_1))$.

The processing of key bit k_{l-2} consists of 5 multiplications, 5 squarings, 3 additions and 8 register write operations, independently of the value of k_{l-2}. Two dummy multiplications and two dummy squarings are performed for the case

$k_{l-2} = 0$ (see line 8, operations $U \leftarrow bX_2^4$ and $U \leftarrow TX_2$). In case $k_{l-2} = 1$, one dummy register write operation is necessary (see line 4 the operation $T \leftarrow Z_2$). No operations are performed with an operand with integer value 1.

5   Results

With the goal of evaluating our proposed modification of the Montgomery kP-algorithm, we implemented the kP-operation according to Algorithms 1 and 2 and synthesized both using the IHP 130 nm technology. The main difference between both designs is the processing of the key bits k_{l-1} and k_{l-2}.

Figures 2(a) and (b) show simulated PTs of the kP-operation executed with our implementation of the Montgomery kP-algorithm according to Algorithm 1. Figures 2(c) and (d) show simulated PTs of the kP-operation executed with our implementation of the Montgomery kP-algorithm according to Algorithm 2. The traces in Figs. 2(a) and (c) were simulated using key $k1$, whereby $k1_{l-2} = 1$. The traces in Figs. 2(b) and (d) were simulated using key $k2$, whereby $k2_{l-2} = 0$. The power profiles of the slots corresponding to key bit k_{l-2} in Figs. 2(c) and (d) look similar and show no dips in contrast to the power profiles of the first slots in Figs. 2(a) and (b).

Table 1 shows a comparison of both implementations. We compare the execution times and energy consumption of both implementations with special focus on the execution times and energy consumption demanded for the initialization phase of the algorithm and the processing of k_{l-2}.

Table 1. Comparison of our implementation of Algorithm 1 with our implementation of Algorithm 2.

ECC implementation		Algorithm 1	Algorithm 2
Initialization Phase	Clock cycles	7	5
	Energy	0.63 nJ	0.46 nJ
Processing of k_{l-2}	Clock cycles	54	45
	Energy $k_{l-2} = 1$	8.60 nJ	7.45 nJ
	$k_{l-2} = 0$	7.60 nJ	7.45 nJ
Extraction of k_{l-2} through SPA		Yes	No
Revealed implementation details		Yes	No
kP	Clock cycles	12915	12904
	Energy	2.10 μJ	2.09 μJ
	Area	0.274503 mm^2	0.274843 mm^2

The time and energy consumption needed for processing the key bits k_{l-1} and k_{l-2} has been reduced in our implementation of Algorithm 2. Thus, the complete implementation of the Montgomery kP-algorithm according to Algorithm 2

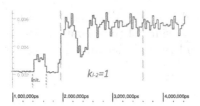

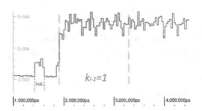

(a) $k1 \cdot P$ according to Algorithm 1   (c) $k1 \cdot P$ according to Algorithm 2

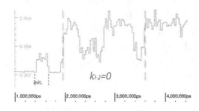

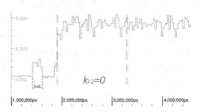

(b) $k2 \cdot P$ according to Algorithm 1   (d) $k2 \cdot P$ according to Algorithm 2

Fig. 2. PTs simulated using our implementations of the Montgomery kP-algorithm according to Algorithm 1 (see PTs (a) and (b)) and to Algorithm 2 (see PTs (c) and (d)). The traces in (a) and (c) correspond to the simulations made for key $k1$ with $k1_{l-2} = 1$. The traces in (b) and (d) correspond to the simulations made for key $k2$ with $k2_{l-2} = 0$. The power profiles of the processing of k_{l-2} look similar for the two traces simulated using the implementation of Algorithm 2.

consumes slightly less energy for the complete calculation of kP. Moreover, protection for the key bit value of k_{l-2} against SPA has been reached through Algorithm 2. Since key bits k_{l-1} and k_{l-2} are processed in a different way as the rest of the bits of k, our implementation of the Montgomery kP-algorithm does not give the opportunity to learn/understand implementation details of the main loop of the kP calculation. Thus, it no longer helps preparing other PA or fault analysis attacks. The modifications made for Algorithm 2 only demanded an increase in the chip area of 0.12 % in comparison to our implementation of Algorithm 1.

6   Conclusions

The Montgomery kP-algorithm using Lopez-Dahab projective coordinates is considered to be an SPA resistant method for performing the kP-operation. We showed using simulated PTs that the power profile of the processing of k_{l-2} differs significantly in the cases $k_{l-2} = 1$ and $k_{l-2} = 0$. This leads to an easy extraction of the value of k_{l-2} with SPA and reveals information about the analysed implementation of the algorithm. We proposed a modification of the algorithm's initialization phase and of the processing of bit k_{l-2} as a counter-measure (see Algorithm 2). We showed that our modifications of the algorithm provide protection of the key bit k_{l-2} against SPA.

In comparison to the original implementation, the execution time of the kP-operation has been slightly reduced by 11 clock cycles with our modification of the Montgomery kP-algorithm. Our modifications did not demand an increase on our implementation's energy consumption needed for the calculation of kP, which remained by 2.09 μJ and only demanded a very small increase of the implementation's chip area by 0.12 %. Thus, we achieved to increase the robustness of our implementation against selected SCA attacks without any additional costs.

Acknowledgements. The research leading to these results has received funding from the European Commissions Horizon 2020 under grant agreement from project myAirCoach No. 643607.

References

1. López, J., Dahab, R.: Fast multiplication on elliptic curves over $GF(2^m)$ without precomputation. In: Koç, Ç.K., Paar, C. (eds.) CHES 1999. LNCS, vol. 1717, pp. 316–327. Springer, Heidelberg (1999)
2. Hankerson, D., Lopez Hernandez, J., Menezes, A.: Software implementation of elliptic curve cryptography over binary fields. In: Koç, Ç.K., Paar, C. (eds.) CHES 2000. LNCS, vol. 1965, pp. 1–24. Springer, Heidelberg (2000). doi:10.1007/3-540-44499-8_1
3. Joye, M., Yen, S.-M.: The montgomery powering ladder. In: Kaliski, B.S., Koç, K., Paar, C. (eds.) CHES 2002. LNCS, vol. 2523, pp. 291–302. Springer, Heidelberg (2002). doi:10.1007/3-540-36400-5_22
4. Mahdizadeh, H., Masoumi, M.: Novel architecture for efficient FPGA implementation of elliptic curve cryptographic processor over $GF(2^{163})$. IEEE Trans. Very Large Scale Integr. (VLSI) Syst. **21**(12), 2330–2333 (2013)
5. Liu, S., Ju, L., Cai, X., Jia, Z., Zhang, Z.: High performance FPGA implementation of elliptic curve cryptography over binary fields. In: 13th International Conference on Trust, Security and Privacy in Computing and Communications (TrustCom), pp. 148–155. IEEE (2014)
6. Li, L., Li, S.: High-performance pipelined architecture of elliptic curve scalar multiplication over $GF(2^m)$. IEEE Trans. Very Large Scale Integr. (VLSI) Syst. **PP**(99), 1–10 (2015)
7. Ansari, B., Hasan, A.: High-performance architecture of elliptic curve scalar multiplication. IEEE Trans. Comput. **57**(11), 1443–1453 (2008)
8. Alpirez Bock, E.: SCA resistent implementation of the montgomery kP-algorithm. Master thesis, BTU Cottbus-Senftenberg (2015)
9. Fan, J., Verbauwhede, I.: An update survey on secure ECC implementations: attacks, countermeasures and cost, cryptography and security. In: Naccache, D. (ed.) From Theory to Applications, pp. 265–282. Springer, Heidelberg (2012)
10. Coron, J.-S.: Resistance against differential power analysis for elliptic curve cryptosystems. In: Koç, Ç.K., Paar, C. (eds.) CHES 1999. LNCS, vol. 1717, pp. 292–302. Springer, Heidelberg (1999). doi:10.1007/3-540-48059-5_25

11. IHP. http://www.ihp-microelectronics.com/en/start.html
12. Synopsis, *PrimeTime*. http://www.synopsys.com/Tools/Implementation/SignOff/Pages/PrimeTime.aspx
13. Clavier, C., Feix, B., Gagnerot, G., Roussellet, M., Verneuil, V.: Horizontal correlation analysis on exponentiation. In: Soriano, M., Qing, S., López, J. (eds.) ICICS 2010. LNCS, vol. 6476, pp. 46–61. Springer, Heidelberg (1999). doi:10.1007/978-3-642-17650-0_5
14. Chari, S., Rao, J.R., Rohatgi, P.: Template attacks. In: Kaliski, B.S., Koç, K., Paar, C. (eds.) CHES 2002. LNCS, vol. 2523, pp. 13–28. Springer, Heidelberg (2002). doi:10.1007/3-540-36400-5_3

Security Technologies for ITC

When Pythons Bite

Alecsandru Pătraşcu$^{(\boxtimes)}$ and Ştefan Popa

Intel Corporation, Bucharest, Romania
alecsandru.patrascu@gmail.com, popa.stefan@gmail.com

Abstract. Python is a common used programming language in many environments, such as datacenter software, embedded programming or regular desktop computers, due to its dynamic and interpreted nature. Furthermore it is easy to write applications and test them because no recompilation is needed. At the heart of everything lies the Python interpreter which is responsible with converting input scripts into an platform-independent representation, called bytecode, and then executing them in a contained environment.

In this paper an in depth security analysis of the CPython interpreter is made. Also, a proof of concept general attack targeting the bytecode generation engine is presented and detailed. To emphasize the importance of the findings it also takes into consideration a study case on the OpenStack framework, that is widely used today in various Cloud deployments and as a software basis for many datacenters. It is chosen because it is implemented entirely in Python, rather easy to understand its internals and how to deploy it in real environments. The point made is that using our technique, or something similar, a malicious user can affect the good function of the framework, which translates into possible access gain over all the users data and applications that are stored in a Cloud environment.

Keywords: Python interpreter · CPython · Bytecode dissassembly · Bytecode infection

1 Introduction

Python is one of the most used programming languages out there today. It is a general purpose and uses a high-level programming approach. It is designed in such a manner to emphasize source code readability and to permit programmers to express their ideas using fewer lines of code than it would be otherwise necessary in languages such as C or C++. Another advantage that Python brings to table is that it is easier to debug any problems that can appear in the development and usage phase.

Because it can use various programming paradigms, such as imperative, object oriented or functional, it gained a lot of traction over time and it is now used in many projects, both small and big, such as the Django framework [1], and even as a basis for Cloud Computing deployments, under the form of OpenStack framework [2].

© Springer International Publishing AG 2016
I. Bica and R. Reyhanitabar (Eds.): SECITC 2016, LNCS 10006, pp. 181–192, 2016.
DOI: 10.1007/978-3-319-47238-6_13

Being a scripting language at its core, an interpreter is needed to transform the source files (script files) into instructions that then get executed on a real processor. The canonical implementation is the CPython interpreter [3], which is a free and open-source software that benefits from a community based model of development [4].

Another thing that makes Python such a popular language is the way the interpreter manages internally the scripts. Internally, all the scripts are converted into an platform-independent intermediate representation, called bytecode. This is specific to a major version of CPython and currently we have just two implementations - bytecode for the CPython 2 or 3 family of interpreters.

In this paper is presented a top level organization of the CPython interpreter, the way it manages Python source code and how it manages to compile and execute the scripts. The security involving script execution is then approached and it is detailed the way the interpreter manages existing pre-compiled scripts and the points that makes our findings possible to use in real cases.

The structure is as follows. In Sect. 2 is presented an overview of other research that also tried to pursue this thread, emphasizing their approach and what we did different to improve it. In Sect. 3 is detailed the way CPython is working and what it internally does to execute the input scripts. In Sect. 4 it is listed the internal Python bytecode structure and how it is executed by the interpreter. Section 5 presents the proposed model used for infection of both single and multiple Python bytecode files. In Sect. 6 it is presented a study case on OpenStack and a proof-of-concept attack that target such a deployment in real case scenarios and in Sect. 7 we conclude the paper.

2   Related Work

The idea of infecting Python script files was previously studied in several white-papers or Internet blogs such as [5], but from our knowledge up to this point, there is no public mention of these approaches in the security bulletins. As we will see later, the steps needed to do it have a fair complexity to successfully gain access to a remote deployment, it works in absolute stealth mode, therefore it is very likely that such findings be in use today as 0-day infections.

One of the first documented weak points of the interpreter was in [6]. In it, the authors presents a bug existing in the Python interpreter that can theoretically permit exploiting the virtual processor in favor of an malicious user. Recent versions of the CPython try to fix it, but not completely, and in our approach we still managed to use this vulnerability, even in the latest version of the interpreter - 2.7.11.

The main problems that rise from this security perspective is given by the fact that Python can use, for speed purposes, a compiled script that exists on the computer disk, without having any mechanism to prove its origin or validity. In [7] we can see that the author tries to trigger an alarm regarding this issue and mention the fact that the interpreter runs the bytecode without additional check upon its origin or correctness. This idea represented the point of start for this paper.

An interesting piece of work is detailed in [8], which presents in detail how the interpreter starts and loads all the standard libraries. This information was used and improved in our work at the point of the initial remote infection of a remote system.

A proof-of-concept vulnerability exploit is presented in [9] and [10]. Nevertheless, their approach is limited and they do not have a real case scenario to support their findings. In this work we start the implementation following a similar path, we analyze the most interesting parts, add a more complex work flow on top of it and present an improved version, together with the possibility to infect all the bytecode files found inside a local and remote machine.

3   The CPython Interpreter

The main Python interpreter, called CPython, is the default and most widely used implementation of this programming language. It is written entirely in C and it contains an internal compiler to transform input scripts into bytecode and an interpreter to execute it at run-time. A top view representation can be seen in Fig. 1.

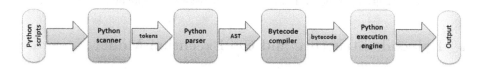

Fig. 1. CPython interpreter top level architecture

CPython features four main components, as follows. The first one, the *Python scanner* is responsible with reading the input scripts as a string stream and converting it into tokens, that are passed to the *Python parser*. The parser will create a tree internal representation of the input data, under the form of an Abstract Syntax Tree (AST). The AST is then fed to the *Bytecode compiler*, which in term converts the tree structure and its components into a stream of bytes, in an formalized structure [11]. The bytecode is then executed by the *Python execution engine*, which is in essence a virtual machine execution engine that features an internal garbage collection mechanism and various memory management modules.

An example of a simple Python input script and the corespondent bytecode can be seen in Fig. 2 and was obtained using the "dis" Python module [12].

In order to execute faster, the CPython interpreter has a feature that permits it to store the bytecode representation in a file on the computer disk. If the Python scanner detects that an input script has been already compiled into bytecode, it will directly load it and send it to the Python execution engine, bypassing the parser and the compiler. A graphical representation is depicted in Fig. 3.

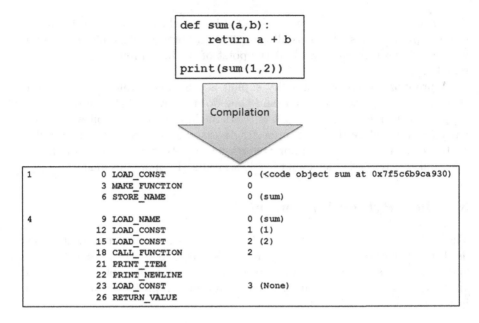

Fig. 2. Python input script and bytecode corespondent

4   Bytecode Structure and the Execution Model

But why does CPython use a bytecode? The answer to this question is rather complex, but to make it simpler, the bytecode is portable, even though machine code is much faster. Creating and interpreting bytecode is a common used technique used by many other interpreters, such as Java [13] or PHP [14] among many others. Having this separate representation makes it easier to write complex interpreters based on it, other than the canonical ones. Furthermore, another advantage of it on modern CPU architectures is that the bytecode is stored in linear fashion in computer memory, thus being cache friendly.

A question may rise at this point - what other interpreters are doing to keep their bytecode safe? As mentioned above, Java uses bytecode packed in a .jar file, which is in essence a ZIP archive. The way they are implementing security at this level is to have every jar file signed with a trusted certificate and therefore every time the interpreter needs to access the bytecode will have to check the signature. On the other hand, the PHP interpreter has a feature called OPcache [15] which stores precompiled script bytecode in the memory and nothing on the computer disk.

The CPython bytecode execution engine can be described as a simple stack machine, meaning that the abstract bytecode instructions (opcodes) are using a stack for pushing and popping instructions, expressions, values and states. It features dedicated opcodes to access variables, that are used under different

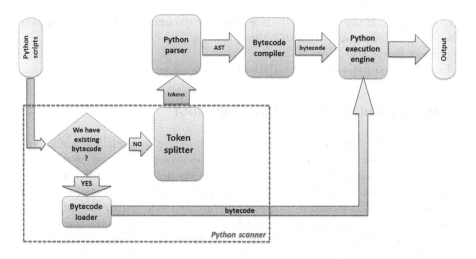

Fig. 3. Python scanner check for existing bytecode

circumstances and they look in different places. They can be split in four different families of opcodes:

- *_FAST opcodes are used to access a function local variable and are used inside a function scope. Example: LOAD_FAST, STORE_FAST
- *_DEREF opcodes are used to access variables that are used in closures. Example: LOAD_DEREF, STORE_DEREF, DELETE_DEREF
- *_GLOBAL opcodes are used for variables that are known to be global for the running script. Example: LOAD_GLOBAL, STORE_GLOBAL
- *_NAME opcodes are used for variables that are stored in Python modules or classes. Example: LOAD_NAME, STORE_NAME, DELETE_NAME, IMPORT_NAME.

The bytecode also has dedicated instructions for other things, like iterators, list creation or various standard types such as lists, numbers or strings. The generated bytecode is stored to disk, for convenience, in various formats. We can use .pyc, .pyd, .pyo, .pyw or .pyz files. But all these encapsulation have on thing in common: they do not verify the internal bytecode or its origin. They feature just a simple mechanism to detect if a script (.py file) has change, in order to re-compile the scripts and create new bytecode.

At a simple level, a .pyc file is a binary file that contains four different things:

- A magic number. This has 4 bytes in length; the first two bytes store a binary representation of the CPython interpreter needed to unserialize the stored bytecode and the last two bytes are fixed and contain the values 0x0D and 0x0A.
- A modification timestamp. This field represents the Unix modification timestamp of the source script that generated the .pyc file. This is used

to determine if the stored bytecode must be re-compiled, by comparing the script's file timestamp with the stored value.

– The pyc script size
– The serialized bytecode that CPython interpreter generated.

5   Implementation of a Pyc Backdoor

Regarding security, the Python bytecode is not secure by itself. Even if it does not allow the execution of random machine operations, it can be used to generate hand-based instruction sequence that can crash the interpreter or lead to arbitrary code execution. CPython is not implemented to be a general purpose interpreter, but it is designed to execute bytecode generated by the interpreter itself, which is guaranteed to run according to the language specification and not do other unexpected things behind the scene.

In this section we present a proof-of-concept (POC) attack under the form of Python bytecode based backdoor. Furthermore, the design of it makes it persistent and resistant to recompilation of the original script files. We present in detail the internal mechanism and the infection method.

A quick recap, we want to exploit the fact that the CPython interpreter uses a bytecode representation of every .py file its executing, in a file having the same name, but with a .pyc extension; when you run a script file, the equivalent pyc file is search in the same directory and if the timestamps match, it is executed directly.

Our POC presents itself as a self infecting payload and once a bytecode file is infected, it will automatically search for all pyc files in the current directory and infect them also. If the user modifies the source script file, the pyc will be re-generated and soon will get re-infected, as other malicious bytecode files than remain unmodified will make sure of this. Furthermore, to respect the pyc specification, every time we infect a bytecode file, we make sure that the timestamp that signs the file remains intact and we copy the original pyc size over to the new pyc file.

In order to make the code self-reproduce, a different approach must be taken. Every time a pyc is executed, it will create a list of other pyc files that exist in the same directory, and read their internal structure and scans for a dedicated marker. If the file was infected before, it is skipped, otherwise the malicious payload is copied. For the malicious payload you can use anything that can compile to a Python bytecode.

As previously stated, in order for our payload to work, it must be stored in Python bytecode format and guarded with a dedicated infection marker. For this we have chosen the magic number 0xCAFEBABE, the same magic number used by the Java interpreter, and it will be stored in a variable called marker. The generated bytecode in this case will be as follows:

```
LOAD_CONST 0xCAFEBABE
STORE_NAME marker
```

The pseudo-code for the infection mechanism can be see in the *infect_pycs* listing.

```
infect_pycs(payload)
{
    f = list_pyc_files
    for every file in f
        open file and read content
        locate the start marker 0xCAFEBABE
        if marker is found
            skip file
        else
            save timestamp
            append payload to file
            update timestamp
            save file to disk
        end
    end
}
```

A question might pop at this point - what about the pyc size? For sure, if the payload contains a lot of malicious code, infecting every .pyc file in a system will consume a significant amount of space. For modern computers this can be easily forgotten, but what about the embedded devices that have rather limited storage capabilities? To solve this issue we can reduce the payload size by using the Python capabilities to compress data offered by the zip module. An additional decompressing instruction is needed to inflate at runtime the desired payload and restore its bytecode form. By doing this we get up to 70 % reduction of payload size.

With all this information so far, a graphical representation of the modified pyc file can be seen in Fig. 4.

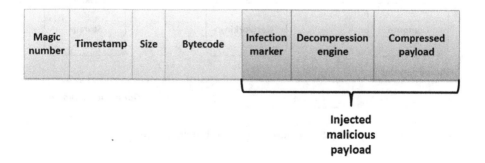

Fig. 4. Infected Pyc file

Another point worth mentioning is the fact that the user can update all the Python script files or delete all the pyc files and thus triggering an entire re-compilation. This can be done if the users suspect that the bytecode on the disk has different internal structure than the one that is generated from the script. However this risk is minimal, as most of the users do not even get notified by the antivirus software for this malicious action.

6   Study Case on OpenStack

6.1   OpenStack Overview

In this section we apply the mechanism presented in the previous section to a real case deployment scenario using OpenStack [2].

OpenStack is a widely used Cloud Computing framework that is written entirely in Python. It is a set of software tools for building and managing platforms for public and private Clouds which lets users easily deploy virtual machines and any other virtual instances that handle different tasks.

From a top level perspective, it features four main components, that can be seen in Fig. 5.

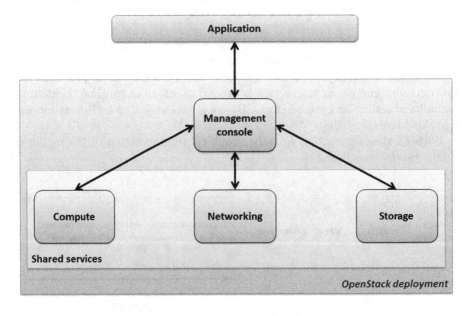

Fig. 5. OpenStack top level architecture

A software application that runs on top of OpenStack has access to its *Management console*, installed on a **master node**, from which it can start virtual environments under the form of virtual machines and/or containers. The console has a connection to the rest of the OpenStack modules and even if it does not do anything important besides acting as a front-end for the framework, it is important to mention it at this point because it acts as a centralized management unit and every administrative action, such as setting network parameters or updating the software in the Cloud deployment, is done through it.

The rest of the modules are split in three directions, based on their role in the software ecosystem. The *Compute* module is responsible with virtual instances management and monitoring them, the *Storage* module is responsible with storing virtual instances templates and other things that the running applications need, like input files. Finally, the *Networking* module assures that communication is always kept alive between all the running modules from the deployment.

OpenStack is maintained and deployed by many companies, such as Mirantis and RedHat. In this paper the focus is on one of the biggest contributor and developer of this framework - Mirantis [16]. Their approach make the entire framework easy to deploy and upgrade, with very little user intervention. This is good from administrator and user point of view, but lacks the possibility to fine tune the security details. For example, one particularity is that they deployment uses dedicated hardware which have only "root" access to their installed operating system. This means that every software application running inside it will have unrestricted access to any parts of the deployment, with full administrative privileges. This is also true for the Python interpreter, that is in discussion here.

6.2   Initial Infection

The goal in such a deployment is to infect the master node and through it to infect the rest of the deployment. In order to achieve this, an attacker can create payload with two purposes - one that keeps a connection alive with an external Command and Control server and another that scans the entire infrastructure and propagates to all the Python libraries. We discuss each of them individually in the next paragraphs.

Before detailing the first functionality, it is necessary to know several details behind an OpenStack deployment. First of all, the network connections are split based on the roles of each service. Therefore a typical deployment has a minimum of three separate network connections; the configured address is not important, as the payload can scan all the available interfaces, make a list of all of them and then attempt connection to each of the involved servers.

The second part to keep in mind is that the services are running into full administrative mode, under the user "root". Even more, for many providers, it is the only user configured to run on the host operating system, a Linux distribution in our case.

Another important detail is that the master node must have direct access to all machines that host the services. This is done by using the "ssh" application, configured with certificates for authentication. In this mode, the connection to a remote machine for the administrator or master node is simple as giving the command "ssh root@remote_ip".

Regarding the location on disk of all targeted libraries, it is not necessary to scan the entire disk to find them. Being based on Python, the target libraries are stored in a fixed location - */usr/lib/python2.7*. Walking the entire tree structure in order to find .pyc files is trivial in this case, as the Python environment offers out-of-the-box all the needed methods to do it.

After a malicious pyc is loaded into the master node, it will start by checking if already infected the files on it. It is enough to check if a magic number is found in the structure of a bytecode file. If the system was not infected before, we can apply an algorithm, as listed in the function *initial_infection*. The parameter *command_payload* represents the bytecode needed to connect to an external server, and *infect_payload* represents the code needed to recursively infect a single host, following a guideline presented in the *infect_pycs* listing.

```
initial_infection(command_payload, infect_payload)
{
    connect to an external C&C server
    report to the C&C server that acces is established
    f = list_pyc_files('/usr/lib/python2.7')
    infected_before = false
    for every pyc in f
        open pyc and read content
        locate the marker for this module
        if marker is found
            skip pyc
        else
            infected_before = true
            inject into pyc the infect_payload
        end
    end
    if infected_before
        report to the C&C server that infection was previously done
    else
        scan network interfaces
        for every interface
            save the network address and mask
            scan each of the hosts
            for every alive host
                connect through ssh
                push the infect_payload into a single remote file
            end
        end
        report to the C&C server that infection is done
    end
}
```

The attack scenario can be seen in Fig. 6. The C&C server is located outside the OpenStack deployment and the initial infected pyc, together with the two modules are located at the master. Following the red lines, we can see how the

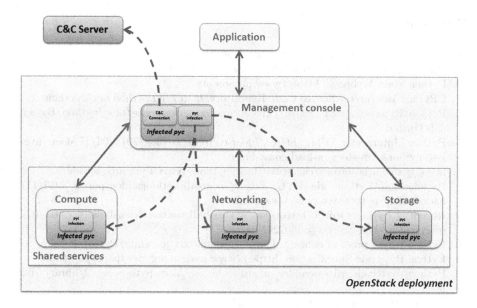

Fig. 6. Infected OpenStack deployment

malicious payload is sent to all the servers in the infrastructure. Once the infected file is ran, it will trigger the infection of all pyc files located on that host.

7   Conclusions and Future Work

In this paper a new approach was presented, that can be used for gaining unrestricted access to a workstation that is running the Python interpreter by modifying the bytecode used by it. The way the interpreter loads and uses external pre-compiled scripts represents the point of origin for the findings; also a simple code that detail the way the malicious script can be structured was presented.

To apply the findings on a larger scale implementation, a real case scenario is presented by applying our approach over an OpenStack deployment, that has the particularity of being widely used in production and being entirely written in the Python programming language. The top level architecture of this framework, together with some details regarding the way it is used in production was detailed and the previous simple code was extended to a full representation that can be used in malicious attacks.

As future work we intend to further investigate other security issues that exist in the Python interpreter and that can lead to other exploits. Of course, the notification of the Python developer community is a high priority, as this matter of insecure script loading and execution is vital to the well function of many applications and frameworks based on Python.

References

1. Django Framework. https://www.djangoproject.com/
2. OpenStack Cloud Framework. http://www.openstack.org
3. Python Main Webpage. http://www.python.org
4. CPython Interpreter Source Code Repository. http://hg.python.org/cpython
5. Python Bytecode trust. https://utcc.utoronto.ca/cks/space/blog/python/BytecodeIsTrusted
6. Python Interpreter VM. https://doar-e.github.io/blog/2014/04/17/deep-dive-into-pythons-vm-story-of-load_const-bug/
7. https://utcc.utoronto.ca/cks/space/blog/python/WhyCPythonBytecode
8. Backdooring Python via PYC. http://secureallthethings.blogspot.ro/2015/11/backdooring-python-via-pyc-pi-wa-si_9.html
9. Reversing Python Object. https://www.virusbulletin.com/virusbulletin/2011/07/reversing-python-objects#id3072912
10. Python trojan proof of concept. https://github.com/jgeralnik/Pytroj
11. Python Bytecode Specification. https://www.python.org/dev/peps/pep-0339/
12. Python Bytecode disassembler module. https://docs.python.org/2/library/dis.html
13. Java Interpreter. https://www.java.com/en/
14. PHP Interpreter. http://php.net/
15. PHP OPcache. http://php.net/manual/en/book.opcache.php
16. Mirantis OpenStack. https://www.mirantis.com/

Secure Virtual Machine for Real Time Forensic Tools on Commodity Workstations

Dan Luţaş[1,2(✉)], Adrian Coleşa[2], Sándor Lukács[1,2], and Andrei Luţaş[1,2]

[1] Bitdefender, Cluj-Napoca, Romania
{dlutas,slukacs,alutas}@bitdefender.com
[2] Technical University of Cluj-Napoca, Cluj-Napoca, Romania
adrian.colesa@cs.utcluj.ro

Abstract. Forensic analysis of volatile memory is a crucial part in the Incident Response process. Traditionally, it requires acquiring and transferring a memory dump from the affected workstation over to the analyst's system, where it is analyzed using established forensic tools such as Volatility or Rekall. Hardware-based virtualization support of modern x86 CPUs was previously used on endpoints to acquire volatile memory in a way that can't be interfered by malware, but which doesn't support reusing exiting forensic tools to perform live analysis. We introduce a system that leverages a small, security-oriented hypervisor (HV) to run the original endpoint's OS inside a virtual machine (VM), alongside another VM dedicated to live forensic analysis using existing forensic tools. The HV enforces isolation between the analyzed OS and the forensic VM, while allowing reliable remote connection to the forensic VM through a dedicated physical network card.

Keywords: Live analysis · Volatile memory forensics · Hypervisor · Memory acquisition · Virtualization · Endpoint · Workstation

1 Introduction

The cyber-threats landscape has changed a lot in recent years as we entered the era of APT attacks [1]. With these kinds of threats it is important for the organization to rapidly detect an attack and take appropriate measures to limit the damage, making the Incident Response (IR) process a critical part of an organization's information security program. The initial foothold into an organization is usually obtained by exploiting vulnerabilities in commonly used software on employees workstations (usually termed as *endpoints*). To limit the extent of the attack, *fast response* by an IR team is crucial, but the IR team needs accurate and relevant information from the affected endpoint in order to perform its analysis. An important phase of IR is the forensic analysis of volatile memory of the affected systems. This can be done either statically or dynamically.

In the case of the *static analysis*, the first step is to get a copy of the contents of the volatile memory via different means: software-based [4,6,10,27],

© Springer International Publishing AG 2016
I. Bica and R. Reyhanitabar (Eds.): SECITC 2016, LNCS 10006, pp. 193–208, 2016.
DOI: 10.1007/978-3-319-47238-6_14

hardware-based [19,36], virtualization-based [35,42,48] or even by leveraging a more privileged mode of CPU operation (SMM as used in [41,47]). Then the image is transmitted to a separate system and analyzed *offline* using memory forensic frameworks such as Volatility [15] and Rekall [11]. Offline forensics may provide both accurate and relevant information for an IR team if the volatile memory image was properly acquired [46], but does not enable fast response.

Dynamic analysis enables fast response by performing *remote live forensic analysis* directly on the compromised workstation. For example, GRR [26] framework uses Rekall to perform volatile memory analysis and requires the installation of an agent on each enterprise endpoint. One of the agent's roles is to provide the forensic tools access to the system's physical memory (usually with a custom OS driver). This suffers from the problem of running the agent at the same privilege level with the malware/rootkit inside the OS: the agent can be subverted or disabled, rendering the IR process ineffective. Dynamic analysis performed in virtualized environments, i.e. *Virtual Machine Introspection* (VMI), examines the physical memory of a virtual machine (VM). Access to the physical memory of the analyzed VM is facilitated by the hypervisor (HV), with the forensic tools running either inside the HV or in another VM dedicated to forensic activities [29,40]. Using a HV to isolate the analyzed environment from the analysis environment reduces the risk of forensic tools being compromised.

In our opinion, a gap exists between the analysis of volatile memory performed on endpoints and dynamic analysis performed in hosted (virtualized) environments. This gap is created because the implementation requirements for live analysis on endpoints are different from the requirements on dedicated servers supporting multiple VMs. On one hand, infrastructure HVs such as Xen [20], KVM [32] or VMWare ESXi [16] are too general and heavy in terms of disk and memory footprint. Using them on endpoints would require HDD repartitioning and reinstalling the OS in a VM created on top of those HVs. The user experience would be degraded since infrastructure HVs typically provide emulated devices (storage, audio, network and video) for the virtualized OS. On the other hand, security oriented HVs dedicated to endpoints [24,49] are limited because typically do not support running multiple VMs concurrently, being focused on providing one or more security properties (such as trusted-path [23,38], protect the kernel of the OS [43] or an application against a malicious OS [22,25,28,31]).

We addresses this gap by exploring the use of live analysis of volatile memory on the endpoint and providing isolation of forensic tools from the analyzed environment by the use of a small, bare-metal hypervisor capable of running two VMs in parallel. In this paper we present the design and implementation of a system that provide incident responders remote access a compromised endpoint, perform live volatile memory analysis using established forensic tools and frameworks (Volatility, Rekall) and acquire and store a copy of the volatile memory offsite for further investigation. Our main contributions are the following:

- We propose transparently running the endpoint's original OS unmodified in a VM, above a small, security oriented hypervisor called MiniSecHV (Sect. 4), alongside another small forensic VM, whose main role is to support live memory forensics of the original OS.
- We show the necessary components needed for our forensic VM's OS in order to support remote network access and have a small disk and memory footprint, while being able to run complex software such as the Python [17] interpreter in order to support the existing forensic tools (Sect. 5).
- We detail the design of our forensic tools integration middleware (Sect. 6), which enables the execution of established memory forensics tools (Volatility, Rekall) on the forensic VM's OS and provides access for those tools on the physical memory space of the original OS.

2   Design Goals

Our security solution aims endpoint systems, enabling fast IR and attack containment. From this perspective our design goals were the following:

- *Ease of installation*: our system should be easy to install on top of an existing OS, without repartitioning the HDD or reinstalling the original OS.
- *Secure remote access*: it should be possible for an IR team to remotely access any endpoint on which it needs to perform analysis, in a secure way.
- *Live analysis*: the IR analyst should be able to observe the running state of the endpoint and perform analysis on it volatile memory, without interrupting the endpoint user's work.
- *Use of established forensic tools*: an IR analyst should be able to use the same tools and frameworks that are already being used in offline memory forensics and which she is already accustomed to, during live analysis.
- *Sound capture of the volatile memory*: an IR analyst should be able to obtain a capture of the analyzed system's volatile memory that respects the principles of sound memory acquisition [46]: correctness, integrity and atomicity.
- *Resilience against attacks originating from within the analyzed environment*: since the forensic tools run on the analyzed (and potentially compromised) endpoint, we have to ensure that they are isolated from any malicious action originating from the analyzed environment. The endpoint should not be able to deny remote access to the forensic VM.

Figure 1 shows the main components of our system. The original OS running on the endpoint is placed inside the analyzed VM. MiniSecHV supports parallel execution of both forensic and analyzed VMs. An incident responder connects to the forensic VM over a secure SSH connection and uses the forensic tools running inside the forensic OS to perform live memory analysis of the original OS. MiniSecHV enforces isolation between the two VMs.

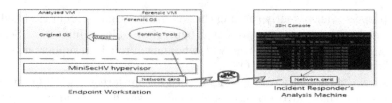

Fig. 1. High level view of the system

3   Threat Model

In our model the attacker could completely compromise the analyzed VM, getting administrator access and code execution capabilities within the analyzed VM's OS. She can further try to compromise MiniSecHV or the forensic VM, so we need to protect them. We assume the attacker has no physical access to the user's system. We assume the endpoint platform has hardware virtualization support with second level address translation support (e.g. Intel EPT) and DMA protection (e.g. Intel VT-d). For remote attestation of the hypervisor's and forensic VM integrity we also re-quire the platform to support Intel Trusted Execution Technology (Intel TXT). The TCB in our model is composed of the platform hardware, firmware, hypervisor and forensic VM.

4   MiniSecHV: Minimal Security-Oriented Hypervisor

Our system uses a small, security-oriented, bare-metal hypervisor to enforce isolation between the analyzed VM and the forensic VM. This isolation is achieved by leveraging the hardware virtualization extensions (VT-x, VT-d, EPT) present in modern Intel CPUs. MiniSecHV builds and controls the second level addresses translation tables (EPT on Intel CPUs) for each VM and ensures that the analyzed VM cannot access physical pages belonging to the forensic VM or the hypervisor. One of our design goals is to enable live memory analysis: MiniSecHV supports concurrent execution of the analyzed and forensic VMs, utilizing a scheduler policy that takes into account multiple attributes, such as the interrupts received on a virtual CPU, C1 halting states of virtual CPUs and timer expirations. Another design goal was the ease of installation on an already existing OS of an endpoint, without needing to reinstall or modify the OS in any way. MiniSecHV meets this goal by starting at boot time before the original OS and running the later inside the analyzed VM. Modern endpoints utilize UEFI-compatible firmware to boot and use any of more possible UEFI loaders stored inside a small dedicated FAT32 partition to load the needed OS. This enables the ease of installation of our hypervisor: the MiniSecHV's binary entry point is an UEFI-compatible loader that extracts from its own image the hypervisor itself. That image is installed on the FAT32 UEFI partition alongside the original OS loader but being marked as the default loader. Once loaded, the hypervisor creates the analyzed VM and executes the original OS inside it. We do not support loading on legacy (non-UEFI) platforms. To support remote attestation MiniSecHV launches first as a MLE [18], utilizing Intel TXT extensions, and establishes a secure environment for the hypervisor to load and create the analyzed and forensic VMs.

MiniSecHV controls the platform interrupts and delivers them to the corresponding VM for handling. It exposes to each VM virtual devices critical for interrupt handling (LAPIC, IO-APIC), while the corresponding platform devices remain under the hypervisor's control. To minimize impact on the user experience, the analyzed VM has direct access to any device not deemed critical for the security of the hypervisor or the forensic VM. Protection against DMA attacks [21,44] originating from within the analyzed VM is enforced with the Intel VT-d technology, which MiniSecHV uses to contain physical devices assigned to the analyzed VM in an I/O domain that excludes DMA transfers to physical memory occupied by the hypervisor or the forensic VM. Details about the way MiniSecHV partitions the system resources between the hypervisor, the analyzed VM and the forensic VM are given in Annex A.

5   Building a Minimal OS for the Forensic VM

The forensic VM has access to the minimum needed number of virtual devices emulated by the MiniSecHV (the LAPIC, I/O APIC, a timer device) and to a physical network card for communication. This limited operating environment means that the OS running in the forensic VM needs to be flexible and configurable. Also, the total size of the OS, including the forensic tools and middleware, has to be small (in the order of tens of MB) such that the physical memory footprint of the forensic VM to be used efficiently. For these reasons, we choose Linux as our forensic VM OS, since it is widely used in embedded systems that have similar restrictions of operation with our operating environment.

The Linux kernel is highly configurable and can be custom built to remove unnecessary hardware support modules and various subsystems. In our build, we removed the majority of kernel subsystems (e.g. USB, ATA, SCSI) and kept only the network and file subsystems (EXT2/3 and NFS). We also removed the vast majority of default modules (such as drivers for mouse/keyboard IO, graphics and multimedia cards) and included only drivers needed for the network cards (for remote communication) and the TPM device (for remote integrity attestation). Support for these devices has been compiled directly into the custom built kernel. The forensic VM in our model does not have access to the physical storage devices of the platform: both the memory acquisition and the live analysis are performed over the network. Since we don't need to store any permanent data, the file system (FS) in the forensic VM uses a virtual disk, backed by the VM's physical memory, greatly reducing the access speed compared to accessing a physical disk. The FS contains the small BusyBox [2] environment, the Dropbear SSH server [3] (for remote access), the Trousers [14] package for managing the TPM chip and the Open Attestation client [9]. We obtain a self-contained compressed binary image, bzImage, of approximately 13.3 MB in size.

This binary comprises the entire OS that will run in the forensic VM and is embedded inside MiniSecHV's binary image.

6 Forensic Tools Integration Middleware

To perform live analysis on the physical memory of the analyzed VM from within the forensic VM we had to solve three problems. Firstly, *access* the physical memory of the analyzed VM from within the forensic VM in a safe and efficient (fast) way. Secondly, enumerate/classify the physical memory ranges of the analyzed VM in order to identify those ranges that are backed up by device memory, in order to ex-clude them from analysis (since randomly accessing device memory can cause unpredictable behavior). Thirdly, transparently interface the forensic analysis tools with the physical address space of the analyzed VM, considering that they normally work on *static* memory images. The solutions to these problems resulted in a number of mechanisms that we generically called *forensic tools integration middleware*. Communication between the forensic VM and MiniSecHV is implemented using *hypercalls*. The forensic VM uses hypercalls when it needs services from the hypervisor. A hypercall transfers execution into MiniSecHV, which performs the needed work on behalf of the calling VM.

6.1 Providing Access to the Physical Memory of the Analyzed VM

The forensic tools running in the forensic VM need to have read access to the actual physical memory of the analyzed VM. Translating a virtual address obtained from the analyzed VM to a physical address using the translation tables of the OS inside it (first level address translation) will result in a *Guest Physical Address* (GPA) that will be subject to a second level address translation using EPT tables setup by the MiniSecHV for the VM. The resulting address is called a *Host Physical Address* (HPA) and is the address actually used by the CPU to address the platform's physical memory. MiniSecHV controls the memory translations from GPA space to HPA space of the analyzed and forensic VMs by building and managing the EPT tables for each VM. We can thus request the hypervisor to map the whole physical space (HPA space) assigned to the analyzed VM inside the forensic VM. This is done by manipulating the EPT tables of the forensic VM to translate a contiguous area of its memory (i.e. a range of its GPAs) to the physical memory allocated to the analyzed VM (i.e. its associated range of HPAs). Figure 2 illustrates the mappings from GPA space to HPA space of the analyzed and forensic VM through MiniSecHV's EPT tables. The HPA space contains ranges backed up by DRAM memory, ranges which map memory of devices (graphics card or network controller memory) and ranges reserved for configuration mechanisms of PCI devices. Based on the HPA space and the device assignment policy (Sect. 4), MiniSecHV constructs the EPT translation tables for the analyzed VM and the forensic VM. The forensic VM informs the MiniSecHV of the GPA range that it intends to use to access the analyzed VM's memory and the hypervisor modifies its EPT tables accordingly.

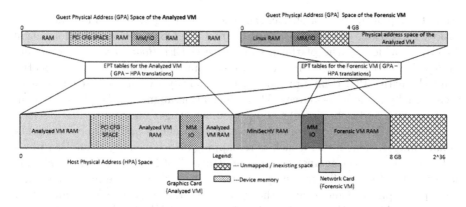

Fig. 2. EPT-based mapping of the physical address space of the analyzed VM inside the forensic VM address space

Consequently, the updated EPT tables of the forensic VM allow access to the entire HPA space of the endpoint, excepting the physical memory reserved for the hypervisor (*MiniSecHV RAM* in Fig. 2).

We mapped the physical address space of the analyzed VM inside the GPA space of the forensic VM above 4 GB, to let enough lower GPA space available for the network drivers in the forensic VM to map the network card buffers. Our strategy for accessing the analyzed VM's physical memory from the forensic VM is efficient in terms of both access time and memory requirements. By mapping the whole physical space of the analyzed VM inside the forensic VM we avoid costly exists into the hypervisor to require assistance in translating analyzed VM's GPAs to HPAs [34]. The memory requirements for the page tables of the forensic VM's OS and the EPT in the MiniSecHV are low: considering an endpoint with 8 GB of RAM, with 6 GB assigned to the analyzed VM and 2 GB assigned to the forensic VM we need 24 MB for all the page tables, if using 4 level translations in both the first level (in the OS of the forensic VM) and EPT.

6.2 Enumerating the Physical Memory Ranges of the Analyzed VM

Figure 2 shows the different types of memory ranges that comprise the physical address space of an endpoint. It is necessary to properly identify, for each range, the size and the type of the range to correctly acquire the volatile memory. Ranges not backed by physical RAM need to appear in the resulting memory image at the correct offset and filled with 0 for the forensic tools to function properly. Many of the software methods used for acquiring the physical memory content rely on information about the physical memory map obtained from the OS itself [4,6,10] and hardware virtualization based acquisition methods [48,50] use OS APIs to identify memory ranges types. But any acquisition method that relies on information obtained from the OS can be subverted [45].

In our system, MiniSecHV does not depend on information from the analyzed VM, since it directly controls the platform and the peripherals and maintains an accurate map of the type of physical address space ranges, at any moment of execution. First, the MiniSecHV is loaded *before* the OS and relies on information directly provided by the platform's firmware (UEFI *BootServices's GetMemoryMap* API) to construct the initial physical memory map. Next, MiniSecHV scans the entire PCI configuration space to identify PCI devices together with their initially assigned resources. This information augments the physical memory map with additional insight about memory ranges mapped to PCI devices. The analyzed VM directly controls most of the devices and can perform additional configuration on them, such as remapping device memory to another physical range. To protect against remapping attacks [38] MiniSecHV *intercepts* any access to the PCI configuration space and ensures that device memory cannot overlap the physical memory of the hypervisor, the forensic VM or any other PCI device. MiniSecHV maintains for the analyzed VM the list of its assigned physical memory ranges and types, the list of device mapped memory and the list of the physical memory ranges assigned to emulated devices (LAPIC, HPET times and so on). None of these lists is under the analyzed VMs control so there is no risk of malicious code altering information regarding physical space and hiding artifacts from the forensic analysis process.

When the forensic VM asks MiniSecHV to map the analyzed VM's physical address space, the HV consults the lists above and constructs additional EPTs. For ranges that are not backed by actual physical RAM, EPT translations lead to a HPA page containing zeros. For ranges that are backed by actual physical RAM, the EPT translations lead to the actual HPA ranges of the analyzed VM.

6.3   Enabling Forensic Tools Access to Memory of the Analyzed VM

The LibVMI [39] library offers a common API for VMI tools to access the physical memory of VMs running on Xen and KVM hypervisors. It provides a Volatility plugin, which allows Volatility to access the target system's address space. We extended LibVMI to support MiniSecHV, enabling the use of the Volatility and Rekall frameworks within our system. We provide a new LibVMI module that interfaces with MiniSecHV. Functions of this module enter the hypervisor through hypercalls and implement the logic required for LibVMI's functionality.

LibVMI allows one to develop his own VMI or forensic tools as standalone C programs that link against LibVMI library and use its interface for accessing the physical memory of a VM. However, the VMI programmer needs to be careful regarding C memory management and pointer arithmetic. Forensic analysis frameworks such as Volatility and Rekall are written in Python, which offers automatic memory management and lets the analyst focus on the actual VMI logic and corresponding data structures. However, Python programs need the Python interpreter to run. A newly installed-from-scratch Python 2.7.1 on a Debian Squeeze x64 OS, capable of running both Volatility and Rekall, takes 239 MB disk space. Including the Python interpreter into the forensic VM would result in an unacceptable increase of MiniSecHV size. In addition, any update to the interpreter or to the forensic frameworks or adding a new forensic/VMI script, would result in the modification of the forensic OS image, the MiniSecHV

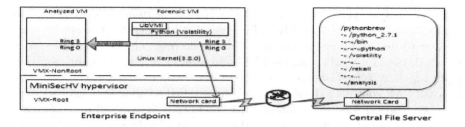

Fig. 3. Loading and running forensic analysis tools from a remote, dedicated file server

binary and its redeployment across the entire enterprise endpoints, negating the initial advantage of rapid development offered by Python.

To mitigate these problems we propose the following solution: installing the Python interpreter and the forensic frameworks on a central server, in a directory that is remotely accessible by using standard network protocols (e.g. NFS – *Network File System*) and mounting this remote directory inside the forensic VM that runs on each enterprise endpoint. This has the advantage of using a centralized workflow, with the forensic tools being stored in a single place, easy to update and add a new plugin, and eliminates the need to redeploy MiniSecHV on each endpoint following an update. Figure 3 shows an endpoint running the MiniSecHV hypervisor, with the original OS virtualized inside the analyzed VM.

The forensic analysis tools and the Python interpreter reside remotely in a directory located on a Central File Server (CFS). This directory is mounted inside the forensic VM and Volatility is run inside the forensic VM from the mounted directory. Memory snapshots are saved remotely, in a sub-directory of the CFS. At the first run the executable content of the Python interpreter is transferred from the CFS to the forensic VM's RAM FS. On subsequent runs, the interpreter is loaded from the RAM FS, which has caching capabilities, so a new network transfer of the entire interpreter and corresponding libraries would not occur. Beside live analysis using established forensic tools, another design goal of our system was to allow an IR analyst to perform acquisition of the volatile memory of the analyzed VM and store it offline for future investigations. Live analysis allows the responder to quickly determine if an infection occurred but a sound volatile memory capture can be required to perform additional in-depth forensics or to be used as legal evidence. To obtain a *sound* memory image, the IR analyst can *pause* the execution of the analyzed VM and perform memory acquisition of the analyzed VM using tools within the forensic VM.

7 Evaluation

We evaluate our system from two perspectives. First, from static forensic analysis perspective, we show that acquiring the volatile memory of the analyzed VM results in a sound memory image and then compare our memory acquisition time with times reported by other closely related research. Second, from the live forensics analysis perspective, we compare the list of running processes inside the analyzed VM with that of Rekall's integrated live memory forensic system.

Our testing environment consists of the following. The endpoint platform, on which the MiniSecHV, analyzed VM and forensic VM are running, is a Dell Optiplex 9020 (Intel Core i7-4770 at 3.40 GHz, 8 GB DDR3 RAM). Beside the onboard LAN controller (Intel I217-LM) we installed an additional network card (Intel Gigabit CT Desktop Adapter) with Intel I217-LM assigned to the forensic VM and the Intel Gigabit Adapter to the analyzed VM. The Central File Server was installed in a VMWare Workstation VM on a Dell Latitude E5500 (Intel Core i7-3720QM at 2.6 GHz, 12 GB DDR3 RAM, Windows 8.1). The CFS's OS was Debian Squeeze 2.6.32-5.amd64. We assigned 2 GB of RAM to CFS VM and two logical CPUs. In the CFS we further installed Python 2.7 and LibVMI 0.11, Volatility 2.4 and Rekall 1.4.1. Access to the forensic VM was done via SSH from the Dell Latitude workstation.

7.1 Sound Memory Acquisition for Static Forensics

The *correctness* principle of the memory capture is achieved because all the infor-mation about the memory map of the analyzed VM is obtained, by Lib-VMI running in the forensic VM, directly from MiniSecHV and cannot be altered in any way by malware running inside the analyzed VM. *Atomicity* is enforced because the analyzed VM doesn't run (its virtual CPUs are unscheduled from execution by MiniSecHV) during the time the memory acquisition takes place. The forensic VM requests the hypervisor to *pause* the analyzed VM, performs the acquisition and then tells the hypervisor to resume the analyzed VM. *Integrity* is achieved by the design of the system: no new code is inserted into the ana-lyzed VM when we need to acquire its volatile memory. All acquisition steps are performed *outside* the analyzed VM by the forensic VM, with MiniSecHV's assistance. No new processes are created and no changes done on the analyzed VM during acquisition. Unlike other methods [35, 42, 48, 50] MiniSecHV is loaded before the analyzed OS, preserving the integrity of the captured memory.

To perform the memory acquisition of the analyzed VM we used *dump_memory* tool present in the LibVMI suite. The tool sequentially reads each page of the analyzed VM and writes its content in a remote file on the CFS server. The 8 GB RAM memory of the test endpoint were split in 6 GB assigned to the analyzed VM and 2 GB assigned to the hypervisor and the forensic VM. The acquired memory image was successfully opened and interpreted by the testing forensic tools. Table 1 shows acquisition times reported by other meth-ods. While the size of the capture and the transport medium differ between test environments, we feel that our 325 s needed for 6 GB is a reasonable time, con-sidering that the atomic acquisition would typically take place *after* the incident responder performs a live analysis and decides that an in-depth investigation is required.

Table 1. Time required for acquiring physical memory by different hypervisor-based tools

	BodySnatcher	HyperSleuth	Vis	MiniSecHV
Medium	Serial cable	Network	HDD	Network
Mem. size	128 MB	3 GB	2 GB	6 GB
Time	45 min	180 min	105.86 s	325 s

7.2 Live Forensics

To evaluate the performance of our system when performing live memory forensics we measured the execution time required to obtain the list of the running processes inside the analyzed VM. We used Rekall in this test because it supports *live analysis*. Different from our solution, it runs the forensic plugins and the acquisition module *inside* the compromised OS, but it offers a strong baseline to compare our solution against, in terms of performance evaluation. Obtaining the list of the running processes is representative, since it implies parsing multiple sources of information in the raw memory image that contain pointers to data structures of running processes: this stresses our forensic middleware and our method that reads the analyzed VM physical memory from the forensic VM.

On our testing machine, we first installed Windows 7 x64 as the original OS, then Python 2.7 and Rekall 1.4.1. Then we generated the kernel's JSON profile need for Rekall [12]. Table 2 presents the comparative performance between different configurations we used to run (5 times) the Rekall's pslist plugin on the test machine. First, we established a baseline by running Rekall in live mode, without our solution and listing the running processes from the Rekall's console (Table 2, T1). The next tests were performed with our system installed. From MiniSecHV we assigned 6 GB to the original Windows 7 OS (in the analyzed VM) and 2 GB to MiniSecHV and the forensic VM. Then we ran Rekall in live mode from within the analyzed VM (Table 2, T2). This test measures the performance impact introduced by MiniSecHV due to interrupt virtualization. The average impact is negligible (10 ms). In the third test (Table 2, T3) we copied at runtime the Python interpreter from the CFS to the RAM FS inside the forensic VM, which took 19.40 s. Then, we ran Rekall from within the forensic VM. The performance impact in this scenario, compared to the baseline, is around 3.4 % mostly due to the speed differences in the Python interpreter used on Windows versus the one we used on Linux and to MiniSecHV actively performing scheduling of the two guests. In our last test (Table 2, T4) we ran Rekall inside the forensic VM from the mounted CFS share. Here we observed a 23 % increase of the time needed to list the running processes of the analyzed VM, acceptable, in our opinion, in most real-life scenarios.

Table 2. Comparative performance between different configurations used to run the Rekall framework to list running processes (*pslist* plugin) on a Windows 7 x64 OS

	Operating system/configuration	Avg (sec)
T1	W7x64SP1 without MiniSecHV hypervisor	2.6
T2	W7x64SP1 with MiniSecHV hypervisor, single guest	2.61
T3	Linux 3.8.0 with Python locally copied	2.69
T4	Linux 3.8.0 with Python ran over the mounted network share	3.2

8   Related Work

Researchers have previously studied methods for acquiring a volatile memory capture from a compromised endpoint using hardware based virtualization [35, 42,48,50] and leverage the isolation from the compromised OS provided by a custom baremetal hypervisor. Like our solution, VIS and Vail use EPT page tables to control the OS's access to the physical address space of the platform. Because they load *after* the compromise has taken place they rely on possibly altered crucial information regarding the physical memory ranges and types and do not respect the principle of maintaining sound memory integrity of the analyzed OS. We designed our system to load *before* the OS and by using Intel TXT we obtain unaltered physical memory maps, maintain them until shutdown. Also, these virtualization based memory acquisition solutions do not support a *second* dedicated forensic VM in which established forensic analysis frameworks can be used to perform *live* forensic analysis.

Reducing the incident response times by actively monitoring the system's activity and detecting malicious actions has been the focus of several commercially available products [5,8,13]. These products use agents running inside the compromised OS and are susceptible to attacks from malware running at the same privilege level with the agent. Frameworks such as Google Rapid Response (GRR [26,37]) or Mozilla InvestiGator (MIG [7]) provide comprehensive monitoring and data aggregation about security incidents on endpoints but they also use agents designed to run inside the monitored OS. We feel that our solution could be integrated inside these frameworks to eliminate the dependency of in-guest agents and provide a more secure forensic analysis environment.

Another research area involves the use of forensic analysis tools inside virtualized environments to enhance the memory introspection of VMs [29,30,33]. For example the DRAKVUF [33] system utilizes LibVMI and Rekall to detect malicious activity occurring inside a VM running on top of Xen. While sharing many things in common with our research, we note that they are not directly applicable on an endpoint, due to their reliance on an infrastructure hypervisor, which cannot be easily installed over an existing OS.

9   Conclusions and Future Work

Our system enhances the IR process by allowing an IR analyst to perform live memory forensics on enterprise endpoints using established forensic tools. A small, security-oriented hypervisor, capable of concurrently running two VMs, places the original endpoint's OS in a VM and enforces isolation between the VM and the forensic tools running in the forensic VM. The analysis is performed remotely: an analyst connects over SSH to the forensic VM and the compromised OS cannot deny the connection. We require the endpoint to have two network cards: one assigned to the forensic VM for external communication and the other to the analyzed VM. We plan to address this by emulating, from the hypervisor, a network adapter for the analyzed VM. We intend to explore integrating our system into existing IR frameworks (GRR, MIG) in a future work.

A   Annex 1

See Annex Table 3.

Table 3. Details about the way MiniSecHV partitions the system memory and devices between the hypervisor, the analyzed VM and the forensic VM

Endpoint hardware component	MiniSecHV	Analyzed VM	Forensic VM
CPU	In control of the logical (platform) CPUs. Exposes virtual CPUs to VMs	Virtual CPUs, one for each corresponding logical CPU	One virtual CPU
Physical memory	A range of contiguous physical memory assigned to the hypervisor	All physical memory, excluding the range assigned to the hypervisor	A range of physical memory assigned to the forensic VM
TPM (Trusted Platform Module)	MLE controlled during Intel TXT launch	No access	Direct access (for remote attestation)
KVM,&storage	No access	Direct access	No access
Interrupt controllers (8259,LAPIC, IO-APIC)	Direct access	Virtual devices, emulated by MiniSecHV	Virtual devices, emulated by MiniSecHV
Timers (HPET, PIT, RTC, LAPIC timer)	Direct access	Virtual devices, emulated by MiniSecHV	Virtual devices, emulated by MiniSecHV
Network cards	No access	Direct access to all except one reserved to the forensic VM	Direct access to the one reserved to the forensic VM

References

1. Data Breach Investigations Report (DBIR). http://www.verizonenterprise.com/DBIR/2015/
2. BusyBox. http://www.busybox.net/about.html

3. Dropbear SSH. https://matt.ucc.asn.au/dropbear/dropbear.html
4. FTK Imager version 3.2.0 – AccessData. http://accessdata.com/product-download/digital-forensics/ftk-imager-version-3.2.0
5. Immunity Inc: Knowing You're Secure. http://www.immunityinc.com/products/eljefe/
6. Memoryze – FireEye. https://www.fireeye.com/services/freeware/memoryze.html
7. MIG: Mozilla InvestiGator. http://mig.mozilla.org/
8. Next-Generation Endpoint Protection – CrowdStrike Falcon Host. http://www.crowdstrike.com/products/falcon-host/
9. OpenAttestation - OpenStack. https://wiki.openstack.org/wiki/OpenAttestation
10. Products – MoonSols. http://www.moonsols.com/products/
11. Rekall Memory Forensic Framework. http://www.rekall-forensic.com/index.html
12. Rekall Memory Forensic Framework. http://www.rekall-forensic.com/faq.html
13. RSA ECAT – Advanced Endpoint Threat Detection – EMC. http://www.emc.com/security/rsa-ecat.htm
14. TrouSerS - The open-source TCG Software Stack - FAQ. http://trousers.sourceforge.net/faq.html#1.1
15. The Volatility Foundation - Open Source Memory Forensics. http://www.volatilityfoundation.org/
16. vSphere ESXi Bare-Metal Hypervisor — United States. https://www.vmware.com/products/esxi-and-esx/overview
17. Welcome to Python.org. https://www.python.org/
18. Intel Trusted Execution Technology Software Development Guide, July 2015. http://www.intel.com/content/dam/www/public/us/en/documents/guides/intel-txt-software-development-guide.pdf
19. Balogh, S.: Memory acquisition by using network card. J. Cyber Secur. Mobil. **3**(1), 65–76 (2014)
20. Barham, P., Dragovic, B., Fraser, K., Hand, S., Harris, T., Ho, A., Neugebauer, R., Pratt, I., Warfield, A.: Xen and the art of virtualization. In: Proceedings of the Nineteenth ACM Symposium on Operating Systems Principles, SOSP 2003, pp. 164–177. ACM, New York (2003)
21. Breuk, R., Spruyt, A.: Integrating DMA attacks in exploitation frameworks pp. 2011–2012 (2012). https://homepages.staff.os3.nl/~delaat/rp/2011-2012/p14/report.pdf. Accessed 14 Jan 2014
22. Chen, X., Garfinkel, T., Lewis, E.C., Subrahmanyam, P., Waldspurger, C.A., Boneh, D., Dwoskin, J., Ports, D.R.: Overshadow: a virtualization-based approach to retrofitting protection in commodity operating systems. In: Proceedings of the 13th International Conference on Architectural Support for Programming Languages and Operating Systems, ASPLOS XIII, pp. 2–13. ACM, New York (2008)
23. Cheng, Y., Ding, X.: Virtualization based password protection against malware in untrusted operating systems. In: Katzenbeisser, S., Weippl, E., Camp, L.J., Volkamer, M., Reiter, M., Zhang, X. (eds.) Trust 2012. LNCS, vol. 7344, pp. 201–218. Springer, Heidelberg (2012)
24. Cheng, Y., Ding, X.: Guardian: hypervisor as security foothold for personal computers. In: Huth, M., Asokan, N., Čapkun, S., Flechais, I., Coles-Kemp, L. (eds.) TRUST 2013. LNCS, vol. 7904, pp. 19–36. Springer, Heidelberg (2013)
25. Cheng, Y., Ding, X., Deng, R.H.: AppShield: protecting applications against untrusted operating system. Technical report, School of Information Systems, Singapore Management University, November 2013
26. Cohen, M., Bilby, D., Caronni, G.: Distributed forensics and incident response in the enterprise. Digit. Invest. **8**, S101–S110 (2011)

27. Cohen, M.: WinPMEM (2012). https://volatility.googlecode.com/svn-history/r2091/branches/scudette/tools/windows/winpmem/README

28. Dewan, P., Durham, D., Khosravi, H., Long, M., Nagabhushan, G.: A hypervisor-based system for protecting software runtime memory and persistent storage. In: Proceedings of the 2008 Spring Simulation Multiconference, pp. 828–835. Society for Computer Simulation International (2008)

29. Dolan-Gavitt, B., Payne, B., Lee, W.: Leveraging forensic tools for virtual machine introspection (2011). https://smartech.gatech.edu/handle/1853/38424

30. Hizver, J., Chiueh, T.C.: Real-time deep virtual machine introspection and its applications. In: Proceedings of the 10th ACM SIGPLAN/SIGOPS International Conference on Virtual Execution Environments, VEE 2014, pp. 3–14. ACM, New York (2014)

31. Hofmann, O.S., Kim, S., Dunn, A.M., Lee, M.Z., Witchel, E.: InkTag: secure applications on an untrusted operating system. In: Proceedings of the Eighteenth International Conference on Architectural Support for Programming Languages and Operating Systems, pp. 265–278. ACM (2013)

32. Kivity, A., Kamay, Y., Laor, D., Lublin, U., Liguori, A.: KVM: the Linux virtual machine monitor, pp. 225–230, July 2007. http://www.kernel.org/doc/ols/2007/ols2007v1-pages-225-230.pdf

33. Lengyel, T.K., Maresca, S., Payne, B.D., Webster, G.D., Vogl, S., Kiayias, A.: Scalability, fidelity and stealth in the DRAKVUF dynamic malware analysis system. In: Proceedings of the 30th Annual Computer Security Applications Conference, pp. 386–395. ACM (2014)

34. Luţaş, A., Lukács, S., Coleşa, A., Luţaş, D.: Proposed processor extensions for significant speedup of hypervisor memory introspection. In: Conti, M., Schunter, M., Askoxylakis, I. (eds.) TRUST 2015. LNCS, vol. 9229, pp. 249–267. Springer, Heidelberg (2015)

35. Martignoni, L., Fattori, A., Paleari, R., Cavallaro, L.: Live and trustworthy forensic analysis of commodity production systems. In: Jha, S., Sommer, R., Kreibich, C. (eds.) RAID 2010. LNCS, vol. 6307, pp. 297–316. Springer, Heidelberg (2010)

36. Martin, A.: FireWire memory dump of a windows XP computer: a forensic approach. Black Hat DC, pp. 1–13 (2007). http://www.friendsglobal.com/papers/FireWire%20Memory%20Dump%20of%20Windows%20XP.pdf

37. Moser, A., Cohen, M.I.: Hunting in the enterprise: forensic triage and incident response. Digit. Invest. 10(2), 89–98 (2013)

38. Newsome, J., McCune, J.M., Zhou, Z., Gligor, V.D.: Building verifiable trusted path on commodity x86 computers. In: 2012 IEEE Symposium on Security and Privacy, SP 2012, pp. 616–630. IEEE, May 2012

39. Payne, B.D.: Simplifying virtual machine introspection using LibVMI. Sandia report (2012). http://prod.sandia.gov/techlib/access-control.cgi/2012/127818.pdf

40. Payne, B.D., De Carbone, M.D.P., Lee, W.: Secure and flexible monitoring of virtual machines. In: Twenty-Third Annual Computer Security Applications Conference, ACSAC 2007, pp. 385–397. IEEE (2007)

41. Reina, A., Fattori, A., Pagani, F., Cavallaro, L., Bruschi, D.: When hardware meets software: a bulletproof solution to forensic memory acquisition. In: Proceedings of the 28th Annual Computer Security Applications Conference, pp. 79–88. ACM (2012)

42. Schatz, B.: BodySnatcher: towards reliable volatile memory acquisition by software. Digit. Invest. 4, 126–134 (2007)

43. Seshadri, A., Luk, M., Qu, N., Perrig, A.: SecVisor: a tiny hypervisor to provide lifetime kernel code integrity for commodity OSes. ACM SIGOPS Oper. Syst. Rev. **41**(6), 335–350 (2007)
44. Stewin, P., Bystrov, I.: Understanding DMA malware. In: Flegel, U., Markatos, E., Robertson, W. (eds.) DIMVA 2012. LNCS, vol. 7591, pp. 21–41. Springer, Heidelberg (2013)
45. Stüttgen, J., Cohen, M.: Anti-forensic resilient memory acquisition. Digit. Invest. **10**, S105–S115 (2013)
46. Vömel, S., Freiling, F.C.: Correctness, atomicity, and integrity: defining criteria for forensically-sound memory acquisition. Digit. Invest. **9**(2), 125–137 (2012)
47. Wang, J., Stavrou, A., Ghosh, A.: HyperCheck: a hardware-assisted integrity monitor. In: Jha, S., Sommer, R., Kreibich, C. (eds.) RAID 2010. LNCS, vol. 6307, pp. 158–177. Springer, Heidelberg (2010)
48. Yu, M., Lin, Q., Li, B., Qi, Z., Guan, H.: Vis: virtualization enhanced live acquisition for native system. In: Proceedings of the Second Asia-Pacific Workshop on Systems, p. 13. ACM (2011)
49. Zaharia, M., Katti, S., Grier, C., Paxson, V., Shenker, S., Stoica, I., Song, D.: Hypervisors as a foothold for personal computer security: an agenda for the research community. Technical report, UCB/EECS-2012-12, EECS Department, University of California, Berkeley (2012)
50. Zhong, X., Xiang, C., Yu, M., Qi, Z., Guan, H.: A virtualization based monitoring system for mini-intrusive live forensics. Int. J. Parallel Program. **43**(3), 455–471 (2015)

Pushing the Optimization Limits
of Ring Oscillator-Based
True Random Number Generators

Andrei Marghescu[1,2]($\boxtimes$) and Paul Svasta[1]

[1] "Politehnica" University of Bucharest, CETTI, Splaiul Independentei, nr. 313,
Sector 6, 060042 Bucharest, Romania
{andrei.marghescu,paul.svasta}@cetti.ro
[2] Advanced Technology Institute, Str. Dinu Vintila nr. 10,
Sector 2, 021102 Bucharest, Romania
ati@dcti.ro

Abstract. True Random Numbers are widely used in different security areas, like Public Key Cryptography, Symmetric Encryption Algorithms, security protocols (key exchange, nonce generator), etc., because of their defining unpredictability. True Random Number Generators (TRNG) are formally composed of three main components: a Noise Generator, which is based on a physical nondeterministic phenomenon (like cosmic radiations or the jitter of an oscillator), a Randomness Extractor and a Randomness Tester. Ring Oscillators (RO) are commonly chosen for this generators because of their simplicity in FPGA implementation. A RO consists of an odd number of inverters representing basically a clock signal of whose frequency depends mainly on the number of inverters. This paper describes a novel optimization technique (aiming the speed and resource consumption) for the implementation of TRNG based on Ring Oscillators and some good conclusive results.

Keywords: FPGA · CPLD · TRNG · Security · Randomness

1 Introduction

Random Number Generators are widely spread in engineering, being used in various applications like cryptography, artificial intelligence, simulations, gaming, etc. These generators split into two categories: Pseudo Random Number Generators (PRNG), which are reproducible, being based on a mathematical function and True Random Number Generators (TRNG), which are non-predictable, being based on physical nondeterministic phenomenon. The PRNGs are mostly used in stream cipher algorithms (to generate the same cryptographic key by 2 parties, at the same time).

True Random Numbers represent a very sensible part of a cryptographic system. They are mainly used in generating either symmetric (for algorithms like One Time Pad) or asymmetric (when generating a public/private key, a good

© Springer International Publishing AG 2016
I. Bica and R. Reyhanitabar (Eds.): SECITC 2016, LNCS 10006, pp. 209–224, 2016.
DOI: 10.1007/978-3-319-47238-6_15

generator is needed to output a random sequence that is further tested according to some requirements) encryption keys. These generators are also used in key-exchange protocols like Diffie-Hellmann [9] or "challenge-response" schemes.

This paper is structured as follows: the second chapter describes the True Random Number Generator concept and its components while the third chapter will present the Ring Oscillator along with two noise acquisition techniques. The forth chapter presents the steps needed for a personalized solution of a True Random Number Generator that is based on Ring Oscillators to be optimal. The fifth chapter will present the statistical testing results of the proposed TRNG running in different setups, demonstrating that the generator is stable. Finally, the last chapter will present some conclusions.

Since True Random Numbers requires a dedicated hardware resource, the challenge is to develop a small-sized and cost-efficient generator. This paper describes how to create a good TRNG while using FPGA (or CPLD) resources at minimum.

2   True Random Number Generators

Generating True Random Numbers implies the interconnection of three main components, as described in Fig. 1.

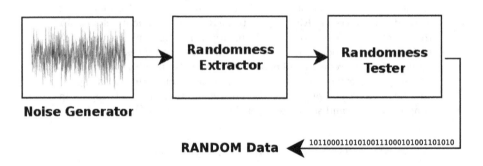

Fig. 1. True random number generator scheme.

The first component (the Noise Generator) is basically the one responsible for the generation process, outputting Random Data based on some unpredictable and non-deterministic phenomenon. The Randomness Extractor is responsible for uniform distribution of the data acquired from the Noise Generator and the last component, the Randomness Tester, is responsible for testing the random sequences according to a battery of statistical tests.

2.1   Noise Generators

Noise Generators are basically the pillars of a True Random Number Generator. They consists mainly of a hardware structure with unpredictable properties. The unpredictability comes from a physical process like cosmic radiations, hardware imperfections, the reaction of a specific component while exposed to certain external factors, etc.

2.2 Randomness Extractors

Usually, the output (0 or 1) of a Noise Generator tends towards 50 %, defining a Gaussian Distribution. The Randomness Extractor is used to prevent the eventual deviations, by trying to uniformly distribute the output bits as much as possible.

The most usual and simple Randomness Extractor is Von Neumann which works with pairs of two bits, dropping the pairs where there are two identical bits and outputting the first bit of the others. Von Neumann's Randomness Extractor's output table can be seen in Table 1.

Table 1. Von Neumann randomness extractor output

Input1	Input2	Output
0	0	DROP
0	1	0
1	0	1
1	1	DROP

The main idea behind the Randomness Extractor is that if we play a heads or tails game with a biased coin and if we toss the coin twice, the probability that the first result is head and the second is tail and the probability that the first result is tail and the second is head tends to equality.

2.3 Randomness Testers

Randomness Tests are used to find correlations of some sort over a bunch of random data. Their aim is to apply a battery of statistical algorithms and problems and trying to find out in which way the next outputted bit (or sequence) can be predicted [6, 7].

The most known Statistical Tests were developed by the United States of America's National Institute of Standards and Technology [10] treating the following:

Frequency - This test is based on the counting of "1" and "0" bits.
Block Frequency - This test analyzes the frequencies of blocks of data, having the same algorithm as the first one.
Cumulative sums - This test calculates the sums of partial sequences within the tested ones;
Runs - This test tries to identify sequences of bits that occur multiple times among the tested ones, calculating the number of occurred runs;

Longest Run - This test uses the data from the previous one and calculates the length of the longest run;

Rank - This test calculates the rank of disjoint matrices that could be computed with the input sequence;

FFT - This test calculates and interprets the Fast Fourier Transform peak heights;

NonOverlappingTemplates - This test comes with a set of predefined patterns, calculating their occurrences.

OverlappingTemplate - This test works the same as the previous one but it uses different search engines.

Universal - This test is trying to apply compression algorithms over the sequence, knowing that a True Random Sequence cannot be efficiently compressed.

Aproximate Entropy - This test compares the frequencies of n bit blocks and the $n + 1$ bit blocks.

Serials - This test searches for fixed length patterns and counting their apparitions among the data;

LinearComplexity - Any random data can be regenerated using a custom LFSR (Linear Feedback Shift Register). This test calculates the length of such LFSR that could generate the tested sequence.

3   Rig Oscillators as Noise Generators

Using an odd number of inverters (*"NOT"* gates) that are interconnected like in Fig. 2 provides a digital clock signal (alternating the logical states 0 and 1). The signal frequency is directly dependent on the number of inverters as well as their position inside the FPGA logic (the distance between them influences the timing).

Due to fabric and/or technology imperfections, a phenomenon called *jitter* occur, resulting in a slightly different clock period (Fig. 3).

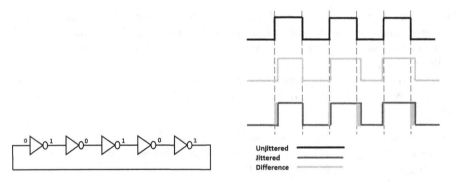

Fig. 2. Ring oscillator.   **Fig. 3.** Jittery oscillator.

The jitter, which is very small in terms of period, has a Gaussian Distribution and could be very hard to enhance and emphasize through measurements.

A lot of different setups are used in order to exploit the imperfections of the ring oscillators [4] some by using schemes consisting of a large number of them (emphasizing a randomness acquisition technique called De-synchronization Technique) and others by using a jittery oscillators in which the jitter is measured (using the randomness acquisition technique called Jitter Counting Technique).

Some other setups are using the scheme in a slightly different way in a generator named TERO [2,3], which is mainly based on both de-synchronization and counting as measurement, also providing a reliable TRNG.

3.1 Jitter Counting Technique

The first approach in the Randomness Acquisition Techniques is based on the jitter measurement. This technique implies a very fast counter, that is usually implemented in FPGA logic. Since the jitter is not a reproducible phenomenon and its behavior is fully random, it can be used as a good and reliable Noise Source. Figure 4 emphasizes the jitter of an analog Trigger Schmitt Inverter-based Oscillator.

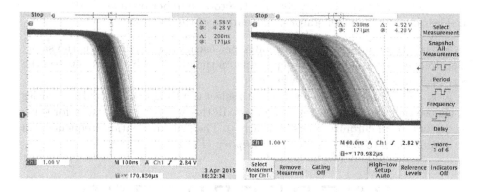

Fig. 4. Highlighted jitter from a trigger-schmitt oscillator [4]

It can be clearly observed from Fig. 4 that the jitter has a Gaussian Distribution. The Jitter Counting Technique highlights the jitter presence and works as follow (Fig. 5):

1. The Ring Oscillator is running freely (having no input source), outputting a clock signal;
2. A very fast counter starts counting while the RO signal is 1, emphasizing the period differences between clock periods. The counter resets itself when the RO outputs 0;
3. This technique usually uses the Least Significant Bit (LSB) of the counter's output.

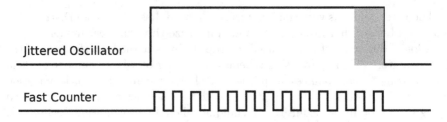

Fig. 5. Jitter counting technique

3.2   De-synchronization Technique

This technique uses a large number of different frequencies free running Ring Oscillators, which are connected to a XOR gate (Fig. 6). The scheme works using the following properties:

1. Each Ring Oscillator freely oscillates (does not require an input clock signal) at the frequency of F_i;
2. The XOR logical gate is powered by a clock signal running at the frequency of F_{sample};
3. $F_i \neq F_{sample}, \forall\, i \in (1, n)$, where n = the total number of RO's used;
4. The output of the Generator is the output of the XOR gate.

Even if the number of inverter gates per each Ring Oscillators is the same, their frequencies usually differ, depending on the physical distances between the corresponding logic gates that were used.

It is a good practice, when it comes to select the Ring Oscillators Frequencies to choose them as relative prime numbers. In this way, the probability for some oscillators to synchronize tends to nearly 0. The synchronization frequency can be approximate to *Least Common Multiplier* (Fi).

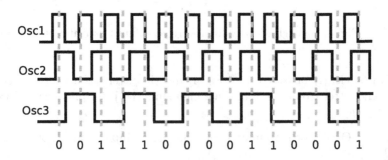

Fig. 6. De-synchronization technique

4   Proposed Solution

4.1   Related Work

Sunar et al. [1] proposed and demonstrated that a generator consisting of a large number of Ring Oscillators (114 for that paper) is provably secure. Their scheme works as presented in Fig. 7.

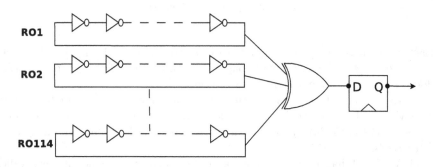

Fig. 7. Sunar's et al. TRNG scheme [1] and adapted for the ZYBO Zynq development board by Marghescu et al. in [5].

Sunar's scheme has the advantage of being secure and mathematically provable while having the disadvantage of using a lot of hardware (FPGA or CPLD) resources.

Marghescu et al. adapted Sunar's solution in [5] for a custom hardware that was used for this paper as well, using a slight different setup, obtaining positive results. This adaptation is one of the pillars of the proposed TRNG presented in this paper, being the speed "booster" of the scheme.

4.2   Chosen Hardware

The chosen hardware for this research is the Zybo Zynq-7000 System on Chip Development Board [11] that is based on an ARM Cortex A9 which powers a FPGA. The FPGA is essential for our project because it will store the TRNG, while the ARM side will manage the Randomness Testing and the communication protocol with the user (Fig. 8).

In other words, this hardware provides the capabilities of both generating and statistical testing of True Random Numbers.

4.3   Description of the Solution

Firstly, the first scheme, that is presented in Fig. 9, uses free running Ring Oscillators and works as follows:

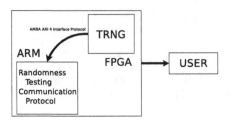

Fig. 8. Zynq TRNG schematic.

- Each RO consists of a prime number of inverter gates and a latch. The latch is present within the circuit to bypass the optimization of the compiler which doesn't recognize such schemes as valid ones;
- Each RO is connected to a Von Neumann Randomness (VN) Extractor Block;
- The VN block is connected to a clock signal as input (in our case the clock of the FPGA = 150 MHz) which tells it when to sample the free running Ring Oscillators;
- Each VN block has a *data_valid* signal, telling a controller when it has a valid bit to offer;
- The controller passes to each individual RO + VN joint, acquiring and storing the corresponding valid bit only when the *data_valid* signal of the VN block is 1;
- After passing to all RO + VN joints, the controller calculates the modulo 2 sum of the bits, outputting the resulting one, that is to be considered the True Random one.

By introducing the VN blocks within the scheme, we can assure that sequences collected from each RO are uniformly distributed and by combining them altogether we can compute a complex generator.

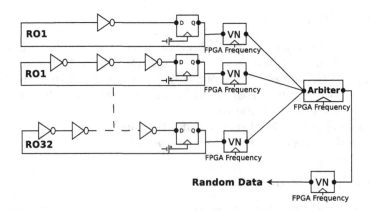

Fig. 9. Proposed TRNG scheme.

Sunar's scheme has two big advantages (the stability and its security) but it uses a lot of FPGA resources. Therefore, the authors tried to use its principle and combine it with the first generator. As a result, the second scheme, presented in Fig. 10, works mainly the same as the first one, but it splits the output of each Ring Oscillator in two. The first "half" of the signal is connected to the VN block (just as in the first one) powering the mechanism presented above.

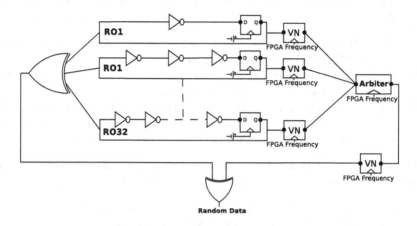

Fig. 10. Optimized TRNG scheme.

The second "half" is connected to a parallel scheme which uses the principle used by Sunar [1] and Marghescu et al. in [5]. Therefore, the second part of the generator is based on a free running XOR gate which combines the signals from all Ring Oscillators, outputting one bit. The output of the generator consists of the modulo 2 sum of the outputs of the two component parts.

This second "half" provides a very fast generation rate approximated at $CLK_{FPGA}/32$ (while working with 32 bit buffers), although, if it is taken alone, it doesn't offer a good generator itself (because the number of ROs is quite small).

Since it is well known that if a random sequence is XORed with any other, the result will still be random, the merging of the first half (greater speed, reduced complexity and statistical properties) with the second one (low speed and good statistical properties) provides a high speed True Random Number Generator with good statistical properties.

The Statistical Test Results of this two schemes are presented in Table 2.

For the proposed generator, the first 32 prime numbers were chosen for the number of inverter gates for each Ring Oscillator. The number 32 was presumed to be high enough for the first test and it led to positive results and since one of the goals of this paper is to optimize the generator by reducing the number of ROs, this number was chosen to be the starting point of the analysis.

The further optimization implies reducing the number of RO (by 2 for each step, dropping the biggest ROs each time) and testing the solution if it still provides good data.

5 Results

After the implementation of the presented schemes, the testing platform consists of the following:

- The TRNG IP from the FPGA, which runs at 150 MHz frequency, is communicating with the ARM side via AXI4 protocol;
- The ARM standalone application receives the random data from the FPGA and tests it using the NIST Statistical Test Suite;
- After the data is statistically validated, it is transmitted to the user using the UART at 115200 baud rate (this baud rate was chosen just for demonstrating the concept, the generator's output being much higher);

The proposed TRNG was the subject of the NIST Statistical Test Suit, and the results are presented in the next Tables, including the following:

1. A table that presents the results of the two generators described in the previous subsection (with and without speed acceleration);
2. The results of other 15 different TRNG setups (containing 32 RO, 30 RO, ..., 4 RO), that aim to optimize the resource consumption of the FPGA;

Each table presents on each row the statistical test that was applied to the random data, the P-value (described by NIST STS documentation [10]), the number of passed tests within the total amount of them (for instance 98/100) and the result (also described by the NIST STS documentation [10]).

As we can see from the presented tables, we can conclude that, from a statistical testing point of view, the generator which consumes the less hardware resources (4 Ring Oscillators), is suitable for using in TRNG applications (Tables 3, 4, 5, 6, 7, 8, 9, 10).

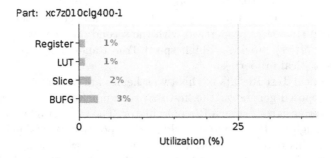

Fig. 11. Resource consumption of the 4osc implementation.

Table 2. NIST STS results for the TRNG with and without speed acceleration at a 150 MHz FPGA frequency

No	Statistical test	Without acceleration			With acceleration		
		P-value	Proportion	Result	P-value	Proportion	Result
1	Frequency	0.935716	97/100	Pass	0.946308	100/100	Pass
2	Block frequency	0.719747	100/100	Pass	0.534146	99/100	Pass
3	Cumulative sums	0.304126	98/100	Pass	0.514124	100/100	Pass
4	Runs	0.017912	100/100	Pass	0.262249	96/100	Pass
5	Longest run	0.275709	99/100	Pass	0.249284	97/100	Pass
6	Rank	0.494392	100/100	Pass	0.719747	98/100	Pass
7	FFT	0.419021	100/100	Pass	0.657933	100/100	Pass
8	NonOverlappingTemplates	0.035174	99/100	Pass	0.595549	98/100	Pass
9	OverlappingTemplate	0.987896	99/100	Pass	0.055361	96/100	Pass
10	Universal	0.213309	98/100	Pass	0.181557	98/100	Pass
11	Aproximate entropy	0.851383	98/100	Pass	0.994250	99/100	Pass
12	RandomExcursions	0.706149	60/60	Pass	0.327854	70/70	Pass
13	RandomExcursionsVariants	0.772760	60/60	Pass	0.169178	70/70	Pass
14	Serials	0.401199	99/100	Pass	0.867692	98/100	Pass
15	LinearComplexity	0.249284	100/100	Pass	0.474986	98/100	Pass

Table 3. 32osc and 30osc NIST STS results

No	Statistical test	32osc			30osc		
		P-value	Proportion	Result	P-value	Proportion	Result
1	Frequency	0.514124	100/100	Pass	0.514124	100/100	Pass
2	Block frequency	0.030806	97/100	Pass	0.419021	100/100	Pass
3	Cumulative sums	0.816537	100/100	Pass	0.996335	100/100	Pass
4	Runs	0.006196	100/100	Pass	0.350485	99/100	Pass
5	Longest run	0.350485	100/100	Pass	0.964295	100/100	Pass
6	Rank	0.494392	98/100	Pass	0.595549	97/100	Pass
7	FFT	0.494392	100/100	Pass	0.066882	96/100	Pass
8	NonOverlappingTemplates	0.455937	100/100	Pass	0.071177	99/100	Pass
9	OverlappingTemplate	0.401199	99/100	Pass	0.637119	100/100	Pass
10	Universal	0.678686	99/100	Pass	0.637119	100/100	Pass
11	Aproximate entropy	0.236810	99/100	Pass	0.616305	100/100	Pass
12	RandomExcursions	0.08217	60/60	Pass	0.976060	65/66	Pass
13	RandomExcursionsVariants	0.350485	60/60	Pass	0.739918	63/66	Pass
14	Serials	0.935716	99/100	Pass	0.946308	100/100	Pass
15	LinearComplexity	0.534146	100/100	Pass	0.419021	100/100	Pass

Figure 11 presents the FPGA resource consumption of the generator which uses 4 Ring Oscillators (with 1, 3, 5 and 7 inverters). Taking this in account and correlated with the statistical testing results from the Tables above, we can state that this generator is optimum and that 4 oscillators are sufficient for the proposed construction.

Table 4. 28osc and 26osc NIST STS results

No	Statistical test	28osc			26osc		
		P-value	Proportion	Result	P-value	Proportion	Result
1	Frequency	0.494392	98/100	Pass	0.779188	98/100	Pass
2	Block frequency	0.574903	99/100	Pass	0.145326	100/100	Pass
3	Cumulative sums	0.699313	98/100	Pass	0.401199	99/100	Pass
4	Runs	0.202268	97/100	Pass	0.739918	99/100	Pass
5	Longest run	0.759756	97/100	Pass	0.719747	100/100	Pass
6	Rank	0.145326	100/100	Pass	0.595549	97/100	Pass
7	FFT	0.304126	98/100	Pass	0.935716	100/100	Pass
8	NonOverlappingTemplates	0.048716	97/100	Pass	0.678686	99/100	Pass
9	OverlappingTemplate	0.834308	99/100	Pass	0.455937	97/100	Pass
10	Universal	0.574903	99/100	Pass	0.637119	100/100	Pass
11	Aproximate entropy	0.080519	99/100	Pass	0.678686	99/100	Pass
12	RandomExcursions	0.723129	60/61	Pass	0.407091	61/62	Pass
13	RandomExcursionsVariants	0.186566	60/61	Pass	0.534146	61/62	Pass
14	Serials	0.366918	100/100	Pass	0.236810	99/100	Pass
15	LinearComplexity	0.739918	99/100	Pass	0.554420	99/100	Pass

Table 5. 24osc and 22osc NIST STS results

No	Statistical test	24osc			22osc		
		P-value	Proportion	Result	P-value	Proportion	Result
1	Frequency	0.534146	98/100	Pass	0.739918	99/100	Pass
2	Block frequency	0.955835	99/100	Pass	0.455937	98/100	Pass
3	Cumulative sums	0.955835	99/100	Pass	0.455937	98/100	Pass
4	Runs	0.978072	98/100	Pass	0.275709	100/100	Pass
5	Longest run	0.275709	98/100	Pass	0.616305	100/100	Pass
6	Rank	0.616305	100/100	Pass	0.319084	99/100	Pass
7	FFT	0.897763	100/100	Pass	0.867692	98/100	Pass
8	NonOverlappingTemplates	0.319084	100/100	Pass	0.455937	98/100	Pass
9	OverlappingTemplate	0.779188	100/100	Pass	0.851383	100/100	Pass
10	Universal	0.474986	100/100	Pass	0.236810	98/100	Pass
11	Aproximate entropy	0.946308	99/100	Pass	0.657933	100/100	Pass
12	RandomExcursions	0.619772	63/63	Pass	0.551026	63/63	Pass
13	RandomExcursionsVariants	0.551026	62/63	Pass	0.070445	63/63	Pass
14	Serials	0.637119	98/100	Pass	0.366918	98/100	Pass
15	LinearComplexity	0.171867	97/100	Pass	0.383827	98/100	Pass

Table 6. 20osc and 18osc NIST STS results

No	Statistical test	20osc			18osc		
		P-value	Proportion	Result	P-value	Proportion	Result
1	Frequency	0.897763	99/100	Pass	0.637119	99/100	Pass
2	Block frequency	0.816537	97/100	Pass	0.017912	100/100	Pass
3	Cumulative sums	0.678686	100/100	Pass	0.437274	99/100	Pass
4	Runs	0.739918	99/100	Pass	0.030806	97/100	Pass
5	Longest run	0.055361	99100	Pass	0.678686	100/100	Pass
6	Rank	0.437274	99/100	Pass	0.224821	99/100	Pass
7	FFT	0.419021	99/100	Pass	0.334538	99/100	Pass
8	NonOverlappingTemplates	0.419021	99/100	Pass	0.350485	99/100	Pass
9	OverlappingTemplate	0.514124	99/100	Pass	0.437274	98/100	Pass
10	Universal	0.678686	98/100	Pass	0.657933	99/100	Pass
11	Aproximate entropy	0.554420	100/100	Pass	0.739918	99/100	Pass
12	RandomExcursions	0.534146	67/68	Pass	0.162606	66/66	Pass
13	RandomExcursionsVariants	0.637119	67/68	Pass	0.350485	66/66	Pass
14	Serials	0.304126	100100	Pass	0.798139	98/100	Pass
15	LinearComplexity	0.554420	97/100	Pass	0.834308	99/100	Pass

Table 7. 16osc and 14osc NIST STS results

No	Statistical test	16osc			14osc		
		P-value	Proportion	Result	P-value	Proportion	Result
1	Frequency	0.419021	100/100	Pass	0.834308	99/100	Pass
2	Block frequency	0.637119	98/100	Pass	0.129620	100/100	Pass
3	Cumulative sums	0.699313	100/100	Pass	0.153763	99/100	Pass
4	Runs	0.289667	100/100	Pass	0.102526	100/100	Pass
5	Longest run	0.334538	97100	Pass	0.202268	100/100	Pass
6	Rank	0.699313	100/100	Pass	0.978072	100/100	Pass
7	FFT	0.851383	98/100	Pass	0.955835	99/100	Pass
8	NonOverlappingTemplates	0.366918	98/100	Pass	0.514124	99/100	Pass
9	OverlappingTemplate	0.213309	98/100	Pass	0.474986	99/100	Pass
10	Universal	0.851383	99/100	Pass	0.455937	99/100	Pass
11	Aproximate entropy	0.236810	100/100	Pass	0.455937	99/100	Pass
12	RandomExcursions	0.033552	74/75	Pass	0.671779	60/60	Pass
13	RandomExcursionsVariants	0.411329	75/75	Pass	0.213309	60/60	Pass
14	Serials	0.657933	100/100	Pass	0.699313	100/100	Pass
15	LinearComplexity	0.719747	98/100	Pass	0.122325	100/100	Pass

Table 8. 12osc and 10osc NIST STS results

No	Statistical test	12osc			10osc		
		P-value	Proportion	Result	P-value	Proportion	Result
1	Frequency	0.096578	99/100	Pass	0.383827	99/100	Pass
2	Block frequency	0.971699	98/100	Pass	0.275709	99/100	Pass
3	Cumulative sums	0.071177	99/100	Pass	0.262249	99/100	Pass
4	Runs	0.090936	98/100	Pass	0.678686	99/100	Pass
5	Longest run	0.366918	98/100	Pass	0.851383	99/100	Pass
6	Rank	0.595549	100/100	Pass	0.719747	98/100	Pass
7	FFT	0.191687	100/100	Pass	0.851383	97/100	Pass
8	NonOverlappingTemplates	0.115387	100/100	Pass	0.129620	99/100	Pass
9	OverlappingTemplate	0.202268	99/100	Pass	0.000757	97/100	Pass
10	Universal	0.401199	99/100	Pass	0.262249	100/100	Pass
11	Aproximate entropy	0.401199	99/100	Pass	0.678686	99/100	Pass
12	RandomExcursions	0.474986	56/57	Pass	0.819544	64/65	Pass
13	RandomExcursionsVariants	0.554420	57/57	Pass	0.287306	65/65	Pass
14	Serials	0.816537	100/100	Pass	0.366918	99/100	Pass
15	LinearComplexity	0.003712	99/100	Pass	0.401199	100/100	Pass

Table 9. 8osc and 6osc NIST STS results

No	Statistical test	8osc			6osc		
		P-value	Proportion	Result	P-value	Proportion	Result
1	Frequency	0.419021	99/100	Pass	0.401199	100/100	Pass
2	Block frequency	0.181557	99/100	Pass	0.275709	100/100	Pass
3	Cumulative sums	0.883171	99/100	Pass	0.191687	100/100	Pass
4	Runs	0.816537	98/100	Pass	0.798139	99/100	Pass
5	Longest run	0.035174	98/100	Pass	0.071177	98/100	Pass
6	Rank	0.637119	98/100	Pass	0.334538	100/100	Pass
7	FFT	0.637119	99/100	Pass	0.964295	99/100	Pass
8	NonOverlappingTemplates	0.719747	100/100	Pass	0.816537	97/100	Pass
9	OverlappingTemplate	0.883171	100/100	Pass	0.096578	97/100	Pass
10	Universal	0.779188	99/100	Pass	0.051942	99/100	Pass
11	Aproximate entropy	0.595549	98/100	Pass	0.834308	97/100	Pass
12	RandomExcursions	0.759756	59/59	Pass	0.452799	61/61	Pass
13	RandomExcursionsVariants	0.595549	58/59	Pass	0.078086	61/61	Pass
14	Serials	0.013569	99/100	Pass	0.437274	100/100	Pass
15	LinearComplexity	0.759756	100/100	Pass	0.055361	99/100	Pass

Table 10. 4osc NIST STS results

No	Statistical test	4osc		
		P-value	Proportion	Result
1	Frequency	0.834308	99/100	Pass
2	Block frequency	0.616305	99/100	Pass
3	Cumulative sums	0.739918	100/100	Pass
4	Runs	0.037566	100/100	Pass
5	Longest run	0.996335	99/100	Pass
6	Rank	0.897763	100/100	Pass
7	FFT	0.066882	98/100	Pass
8	NonOverlappingTemplates	0.129620	100/100	Pass
9	OverlappingTemplate	0.137282	100/100	Pass
10	Universal	0.236810	99/100	Pass
11	Aproximate entropy	0.798139	100/100	Pass
12	RandomExcursions	0.468595	60/60	Pass
13	RandomExcursionsVariants	0.378138	59/60	Pass
14	Serials	0.851383	99/100	Pass
15	LinearComplexity	0.071177	99/100	Pass

6   Conclusions

This paper described the concept of True Random Number Generators and the steps needed to be made in order to create one. Moreover it presented a personalized TRNG, based on Ring Oscillators, and the optimization techniques used for reducing the number of ROs and therefore the FPGA resources that were allocated for the generator.

The optimizations aimed not only the resource consumption but the speed of the generator as well, obtaining a high speed True Random Number Generator with good statistical properties.

In the final part, this paper presented some conclusive results which demonstrate that the proposed TRNG is suitable for using in sensible applications and/or environments (cryptographic usage).

Acknowledgments. This work was supported by the Romanian National Authority for Scientific Research (CNCSUEFISCDI) under the project PN-II-PT-PCCA-2013-4-1651.

References

1. Sunar, B., Martin, W.J., Stinson, D.R.: A provably secure true random number generator with built-in tolerance to active attacks. IEEE Trans. Comput. **56**(1), 109–119 (2007)
2. Varchola, M., Drutarovsky, M.: New high entropy element for FPGA based true random number generators. In: Mangard, S., Standaert, F.-X. (eds.) CHES 2010. LNCS, vol. 6225, pp. 351–365. Springer, Heidelberg (2010). doi:10.1007/978-3-642-15031-9_24

3. Haddad, P., Fischer, V., Bernard, F., Nicolai, J.: A physical approach for stochastic modeling of TERO-based TRNG. In: Güneysu, T., Handschuh, H. (eds.) CHES 2015. LNCS, vol. 9293, pp. 357–372. Springer, Heidelberg (2015). doi:10.1007/978-3-662-48324-4_18

4. Marghescu, A., Svasta, P., Simion, E.: Randomness extraction techniques for jittery oscillators. In: 38th International Spring Seminar on Electronics Technology (ISSE), pp. 161–166 (2015)

5. Marghescu, A., Teeleanu, G., Maimut, D., Neaca, T., Svasta, P.: Adapting a ring oscillator-based true random number generator for Zynq system on chip embedded platform. In: 20th International Symposium for Design and Technology in Electronic Packaging (SIITME), pp. 197–202 (2014)

6. Simion, E.: The relevance of statistical tests in cryptography. IEEE Secur. Priv. **13**(1), 66–70 (2015)

7. Oprina, A., Popescu, A.S.E., Simion, G., Simion, G.: Walsh-Hadamard randomness test and new methods of test results integration. Bull. Transilv. Univ. Braov **2**, 51 (2009)

8. Drumea, A., Dobre, R.: Clicks counting methods for a scope knob. Hidraulica **4**, 79 (2013)

9. Diffie-Hellmann Key Exchange Protocol. https://tools.ietf.org/html/rfc2631

10. National Institute of Standards and Technology. http://csrc.nist.gov/groups/ST/toolkit/rng/documentation_software.html

11. http://www.xilinx.com/products/boards-and-kits/1-4azfte.html

TOR - Didactic Pluggable Transport

Ioana-Cristina Panait[2]([✉]), Cristian Pop[2], Alexandru Sirbu[2], Adelina Vidovici[2], and Emil Simion[1]

[1] Faculty of Applied Sciences, University Politehnica of Bucharest,
Bucharest, Romania
`esimion@upb.ro, esimion@fmi.unibuc.ro`
[2] Faculty of Automatic Control and Computers,
University Politehnica of Bucharest, Bucharest, Romania
`{ioana.panait,cristian.pop,alexandru.sirbu,adelina.vidovici}@cti.pub.ro`

Abstract. Considering that access to information is one of the most important aspects of modern society, the actions of certain governments or internet providers to control or, even worse, deny access for their citizens/users to selected data sources has lead to the implementation of new communication protocols. TOR is such a protocol, in which the path between the original source and destination is randomly generated using a network of globally connected routers and, by doing so, the client is not identified as actually accessing the resource. However, if the ISP knows that the first hop is part of TOR or if it can identify the contents of the exchanged packages as being TOR packages, by using advanced detection algorithms, it can still perform it's denial policies. These types of detection are circumvented by the usage of bridges (TOR routers which aren't publicly known) and pluggable transports (content changing protocols, in order to pass through as innocent-looking traffic). The development of a didactic pluggable transport in a simulated TOR network is the main purpose of this paper, in order to investigate the current state of the art of TOR development and analysis.

Keywords: TOR · Pluggable transport · ExperimenTOR · Obfsproxy

1 Introduction

This paper starts by presenting the motivation to develop a didactic pluggable transport and, also, some aspects of the TOR, such as its history, protocol, known vulnerabilities and some improvements, then inspects the current state of the art in terms of pluggable transports for TOR, followed by the main contribution of the article in our own implementation of a pluggable protocol over the simulated TOR network and finishing with the results of running TOR with the implemented protocol.

Many of the previous solutions based themselves on transforming the traffic between the source and the first hop have increased the amount of data sent by adding the overhead of masking the content, our proposed solution performs

© Springer International Publishing AG 2016
I. Bica and R. Reyhanitabar (Eds.): SECITC 2016, LNCS 10006, pp. 225–239, 2016.
DOI: 10.1007/978-3-319-47238-6_16

changes on the actual content in order to pass it as uncorrelated bytes which cannot be used in order to obtain information from the sent packets.

Thus, we decided to perform an inversion of the bit values in each of the content bytes of each packet, rendering the content unreadable without performing another inversion on the whole content. Knowing that both the sender and the first hop know of the usage of this pluggable transport, the data can be exchanged between them without a deep packet inspection determining that the traffic is part of the TOR network.

The main result of our work is the fact that the communication between the client and the TOR network, inside the isolated environment, works with our implemented pluggable transport, as well as with the original communication protocol and with only using bridges (without pluggable transport).

The results show us that, by using a bridge (the same first hop for all requests), the performance is slightly worse than the one when using the directory service to generate routes, as by changing the first hop we can get a better route and get better performances. Further comparing the results from the bridge tests, with and without pluggable transports, we see that using the pluggable transport comes with a small increase in duration, accounting for the coding and decoding of the content.

2   Motivation

In a world in which global communication is considered as one of the modern building blocks of modern civilization, the Internet, which appeared in the early 1990s, has been a major influence in the way information is exchanged between point A and B, allowing the interconnection of computers from all around the world. However, as with anything man made, malicious uses of this can produce data leaks, causing major problems to all the parties involved, even without their knowledge.

Thus, the protection of data transmission is one of the major concerns when talking about information exchange and, because of this, many protocols have been invented and implemented in order to allow the secure transfer of information from any sources. Many of these are at an application level, meaning that the data is encrypted at the source and decrypted at the destination. The data flow, however, is usually the same and a man in the middle attack, with sufficient knowledge, can disrupt the transmission and track the sender and receiver and, given sufficient time, can try and break the protocol of their transfer or at least can trace the pattern of communication and can cause harm to one of the entities involved by attacking the other.

This vulnerability of data transmission, that the communication can be traced back to the source and destination, is also important when talking about security. This is where the TOR protocol tries to come with a solution, in which the exchange between the two is anonymous, using a global infrastructure of servers. The route used by the sender is chosen at the beginning of the transfer and is changed at regular intervals, in order to not permit the analysis of traffic, and also almost no servers know their role and the route before or after them besides their neighbors (only the exit node knows that the next destination is the original destination the sender wanted to contact), allowing for the actual sender to be forgotten when the data arrives at its final receiver.

However, many internet service providers try (or are obliged by the law) to not allow the use of TOR. The most basic way in which this is done is by black-listing the public IPs of known TOR servers, but this is countered by the usage of bridge relay servers, which aren't listed anywhere and which allow connection to the network. A more intrusive way is to do deep packet inspection, in which the actual data is inspected and, from known patterns, it can be determined that it uses TOR and, thus, can deny the sending of the packet. For this issue, pluggable transports have been introduced to TOR, in which the traffic between the client and bridge is transformed into innocent-looking traffic instead of the normal TOR flow, tricking the DPI into allowing the packages.

3 TOR

3.1 Protocol

TOR is the second generation of Onion Routing and the name of an Internet network that allow people to communicate anonymously. Onion Routing is a distributed overlay network designed to anonymise applications like web browsing, instant messaging or secure shell, TCP-based applications by encryption in the application layer of a communication protocol stack. Clients choose a path through this network by building a circuit made of nodes. Each node/onion router knows only its predecessor and its successor [2].

To hide the identity over the Internet, TOR uses a group of volunteer-operated servers/relays which are employed by its users by connecting through a series of virtual tunnels. TOR encrypts the information several times and sends it through the circuit. The IP address of the destination is also encrypted. Each relay decrypts only a layer of encryption to reveal the necessary information about the next node in the circuit as we can see in Fig. 1.

The TOR network can be used to transport TCP streams anonymously. The network is composed of a set of nodes that act as relays for a number of communication streams, from different users. Each TOR node tries to ensure that the correspondence between incoming data streams and outgoing data streams is obscured from the attacker. Therefore the attacker cannot be sure about which of the originating user streams corresponds to an observed output of the network.

Each onion router maintains a long-term identity key and a short-term onion key. The identity key is used to sign TLS certificates, to sign the onion router's descriptor (a summary of its keys, address, bandwidth, exit policy, and so on), and (by directory servers) to sign directories. The onion key is used to decrypt requests from users to set up a circuit and negotiate ephemeral keys. The TLS protocol also establishes a short-term link key when communicating between onion routers. Short-term keys are rotated periodically and independently, to limit the impact of key compromise.

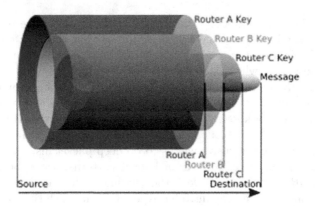

Fig. 1. Onion routing (Picture from Security Stack Exchange http://security.stackex change.com/questions/76438/about-onion-packet-and-onion-routing).

Onion routers communicate with one another, and with users' of onion proxys, via TLS connections with ephemeral keys. Using TLS conceals the data on the connection with perfect forward secrecy, and prevents an attacker from modifying data on the wire or impersonating an onion router.

The TOR architecture is similar to conventional circuit switched networks. The connection establishment has been carefully crafted to preserve anonymity, by not allowing observers to cryptographically link or trace the route that the connection is using. The initiator of the stream creates a circuit by first connecting to a randomly selected TOR node, negotiating secret keys and establishes a secure channel with it. The key establishment uses self-signed ephemeral Diffie-Hellman key exchange and standard Transport Layer Security (TLS) is further used to protect the connections between nodes and provide forward secrecy.

All communications are then tunneled through this circuit, and the initiator can connect to further TOR nodes, exchange keys and protect the communication through multiple layers of encryption. Each layer is decoded by a TOR node and the data is forwarded to the next Onion router using standard route labeling techniques.

Finally, after a number of TOR nodes are relaying the circuit (by default three), the initiator can ask the last TOR node on the path to connect to a particular TCP port at a remote IP address or domain name. Application layer data, such as HTTP requests or SSH sessions, can then be passed along the circuit as usual (Fig. 2).

TCP streams traveling through TOR are divided and packaged into cells. Each cell is 512 bytes long, but to cut down on latency it can contain a shorter useful payload. This is particularly important for supporting interactive protocols, such as SSH, that send very small keystroke messages through the network. TOR does not perform any explicit mixing. Cells are stored in separate buffers for each stream, and are output in a round-robin fashion, going round the

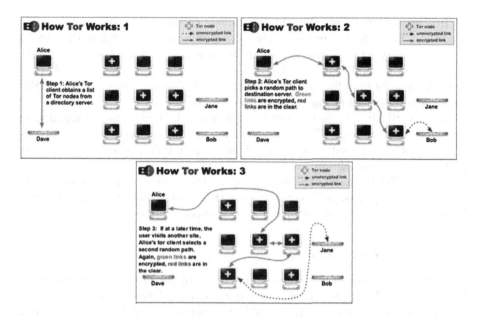

Fig. 2. TOR protocol (Picture from TOR Project Overview https://www.torproject.org/about/overview.html.en#thesolution).

connection buffers. This ensures that all connections are relayed fairly, and is a common strategy for providing best effort service.

Importantly, when a connection buffer is empty, it is skipped, and a cell from the next non-empty connection buffer is sent as expected. Since one of the objectives of TOR is to provide low latency communications, cells are not explicitly delayed, reordered, batched or dropped, beyond the simple-minded strategy described above.

TOR has some provisions for fairness, rate limiting and to avoid traffic congestion at particular nodes. Firstly, TOR implements a so-called token bucket strategy to make sure that long-term traffic volumes are kept below a specified limit set by each TOR node operator. Since the current deployment model relies on volunteer operators, this was considered important.

This approach would not prevent spikes of traffic from being sent, and propagating through a connection. These spikes of data would, of course, be subject to the maximum bandwidth of each node, and could saturate the network connection of some TOR nodes.

To avoid such congestion, a second mechanism is implemented. Each stream has two windows associated with it, the first describes how many cells are to be received by the initiator, while the other describes how many are allowed to be sent out to the network. If too many cells are in transit through the network and have not already been accepted by the final destination the TOR node stops accepting any further cells until the congestion is eased.

It is important to note that this mechanism ensures that the sender does not send more than the receiver is ready to accept, thereby overfilling the buffers at intermediary TOR nodes. It also makes sure that each connection can only have a certain number of cells in the network without acknowledgment, thus preventing hosts from flooding the network. TOR does not, however, artificially limit the rate of cells flowing in any other way [4].

Each TOR circuit can be used to relay many TCP streams, all originating from the same initiator. This is a useful feature to support protocols such as HTTP, that might need many connections, even to different network nodes, as part of a single transaction.

Unused TOR circuits are short-lived replacements are set up every few minutes. This involves picking a new route through the TOR network, performing the key exchanges and setting up the encrypted tunnels [3].

3.2   Known Vulnerabilities

Client can obtain all TOR routers information. In the process of circuit establishment, each TOR client fetches all onion routers information from Directory Server, which gives an adversary the ability to obtain a total TOR network view. With the complete network view it is possible for the adversary to perform DDOS attack or low-cost traffic attack on TOR network.

TOR does not use any batching strategy. To decrease the latency of communication, TOR does not consider any batching strategy in node design. Instead cells from different circuits are sent out in a round robin fashion. When a circuit has no cells available, it is skipped and the next circuit with cells waiting to be delivered is handled. This means that the load on the TOR node affects the latency of all connection circuits switched through this node. An extra connection can result in higher latency of all other connections routed through the same TOR node. So by producing specific traffic, and measuring the latency of all TOR nodes, the adversary can identify all relay nodes of target circuit.

TOR does not check TOR node information. Within TOR's routing model, each TOR node advertises its information such as uptime, IP address, bandwidth and so on in Directory Server. Directory Server does not perform any checking on the information. OP chooses a relay node to establish the circuit according to the information registered in Directory Server. It is possible for the adversary to perform low-resource routing attack with this weakness because an adversary can use the weakness to advertise very high bandwidth, very long uptime and unrestricted exit policies.

The information is reported by TOR node voluntarily. When the TOR node exits TOR network, it is possible for the node not to report its withdraw. In such case both Directory server and other TOR nodes would not know the situation. It causes the OP failure when relaying cells along the circuit passing through the node or trying to establish the circuit with the node [1].

3.3 Improving Performance

It can be seen that, despite previous research proposals, scalability problems are still lurking in the future of TOR. P2P proposals can not be adopted because their lookup process reveals circuit information, and they are susceptible to attacks where the adversary controls a large fraction of the network by introducing bogus nodes (using a botnet, for example).

PIR-Private Information Retrieval approaches look promising, but they still need further investigation. PIR-TOR, for example, requires node reuse in its CPIR (Single-server computational PIR schemes) instantiation, lowering the security of TOR, while in its IT-PIR (Information-theoretic PIR schemes) instantiation, requires multiple guards for each user to act as PIR servers [6].

This creates tension with recent considerations to reduce the number of guards to improve anonymity. Providing incentives for users to run as routers can have a positive impact on scalability and congestion. Incentive-based proposals suffer from shortcomings that need to be addressed.

One promising direction is an approach based on proof-of-bandwidth like tor-coin, where routers are rewarded with digital coins based on how much bandwidth they use relaying anonymous traffic. One challenge for a proof-of-bandwidth protocol is performing secure bandwidth measurements to ensure all network participants can easily verify that routers indeed spend what they claim to spend [7].

Furthermore, while there have been several transport layer proposals that aim to reduce congestion in TOR, it is still unclear what transport design provides the required trade-off between anonymity and performance for TOR. There is a need to experimentally compare the different transports under realistic user, network and traffic models that can emulate the real TOR network. Once a transport design is identified, a deployment plan must be carefully crafted in order to gradually and smoothly upgrade the network without denying service to its users [5].

4 Pluggable Transports

In order to restrain the Internet access when using TOR, some countries or ISPs use different techniques for detecting unwanted Internet traffic flows by protocol. If the ISP is filtering connections to TOR relays, there is a solution for overpassing this issue by using bridge relays (or bridges). These are also TOR relays, but they are not listed in TOR directory and there is no complete public list for them. Besides filtering connections, ISPs can also analyze the traffic by using DPI (Deep Packet Inspection), so the censor will be able to recognize and filter TOR traffic based on some samples. A solution for this problem is given by the use of pluggable transports.

Pluggable transports can transform the data passing between the client and the bridge so that it looks like "normal/expected traffic". This way, the censors cannot detect and filter TOR traffic as long as they cannot decide if a TOR connection is in use.

However, we cannot state that pluggable transports are undetectable. Given enough time for research into how these methods manipulate traffic, one can find means to detect when certain pluggable transports are used. This way, some transports become deprecated over time and they need to be replaced by more improved ones.

As state of the art, there are several pluggable transports already deployed and also there are several in progress to be deployed or developed. Obfsproxy is a framework used for implementing new pluggable transports and it is written in Python. It is an application independent from TOR which has a client and a server that support numerous pluggable transports protocols. The obfsproxy client is placed between TOR client and the censor and the obfsproxy server is placed between the censor and TOR bridge, as we can see in Fig. 3. Some of the pluggable transports supported are obfs2 and obfs3 (protocol obfuscation layer for TCP protocols). Flashproxy brings another overview of skipping censors' system and allow access to TOR [9]. It is a proxy that runs in a web browser and checks for clients that request access, then it transmits data between those clients and the TOR relay. The technologies used in implementing Flashproxy are JavaScript and WebSocket, and the objective of this project is to outrun the censors' ability to recognize the bridge's IP address, by creating many temporary bridge IP addresses.

Fig. 3. Obfsproxy

Another deployed transport is Format-Transforming Encryption (FTE) [8] which modifies TOR traffic to streams that match a user-specified regular expression. FTE is a novel cryptographic primitive, which differs from a traditional one by the introduction of a new input as a set descriptor. In the traditional form, the cryptographic primitive has a key and message as input and outputs a simple ciphertext based on them. FTE has a key, a message and a format as input and outputs a ciphertext in the format set described. This way, censored traffic can pass as legitimate traffic, because of its resemblance with normal traffic, like HTTP for instance.

Another pluggable transport which is part of Obfsproxy framework previously describer is ScrambleSuit [10]. The exchanged traffic between the TOR client and the TOR bridge is encrypted, authenticated and disguised. From a technical point of view, this protocol protects against active probing attacks and can generate unique flow signature by altering the inter-arrival time and the packet length distribution. As an observation, ScrambleSuit can transport many other protocols besides TOR, like VPN, SSH etc.

Meek is a transport used to relay traffic through a third-party server like a CDN, which is hard to block by the censor. The method is called "domain fronting", which means that different domain names are used for different communication layers. The request of the meek-client has the domain that appears on the "outside" of the request, and a different domain that appears on the "inside" of the request, and cannot be seen by the censor. The CDN does see the inside domain and forwards the packet accordingly to a meek-server from a TOR bridge. The meek-server will process the data and send it to TOR.

Obfs4 is a transport which resembles ScrambleSuit, but has a different public key obfuscation technique and a protocol for one-way authentication. The project is written in Go and it is faster than ScrambleSuit.

Obfsclient is a pluggable transport proxy, which is written in C++ and implements the client side of obfs2, obfs3, ScrambleSuit.

SkypeMorph currently has an undeployed status and it is designed to cover TOR traffic flows by using a widely known protocol over the Internet. The target protocol investigated is Skype video call [11].

These are just a few of all the pluggable transports, implemented or in progress so far, and they can be found on the official page of TOR project [12]. The objective is to have as many designs as possible in order to better avoid capturing the TOR traffic by deep packet inspection.

5   Architecture and Implementation

As TOR is a fully functional protocol, already running over the Internet, the addition of a new pluggable transport requires, therefore, its development to be done in an isolated environment, in order to not add new routers with functionality which may negatively influence the activity of clients which already use the service.

5.1   Development Environment - ExperimenTOR

Thus, in order to start our implementation we needed to create an environment in which to run our development and testing process. The environment needed to actually run TOR code and not simulate the packages sent between the entities (as the pluggable transport needs to actually send and receive packages over the network), to be easy to start, modify and analyze (in order to be able to perform multiple tests on possible different networks) and to be reliable (elements must not break during usage).

These requirements meant that the best option would be to use an already existing tool. The TOR project presents two options in this matter: the Shadow simulator (which has an implemented extension for TOR) and the experimen-TOR simulator, presented as an testbed for TOR development. As the second one is solely oriented on TOR simulation, we decided to utilize it as our environment.

However, as experimenTOR is an old tool and its released version dated back from 2011, we encountered several problems during its setup and configuration, presented below as well as our solutions for each one of them:

- the solution came as a bundle of two virtual machines, one containing the ModelNet simulated network and one containing the actual running code; the latter was installed on an Ubuntu 11.04 machine, which finished it's support life and this meant that we needed to change it's rpm sources in order to use the archived latest versions
- in order to work, TOR routers require signed certificates, to identify themselves in the network to the other entities; as the virtual machines were from 2011, the allocated certificates were expired and, thus, when running TOR, the routers would stop working, requiring correct certificates; our solution was rather hackish, but worked in the environment - we turned the clock back for the virtual machine in 2011, re-activating the allocated certificates
- the TOR code provided was at version 0.2.3.0, largely outdated from the latest version of 0.2.7.6; it also didn't have support for bridges or pluggable transports, meaning that we needed to update to a newer version in order to be able to do our intended work over the network
- version 0.2.7.6 of TOR requires the minimum version 1.01h for OpenSSL; the latest version in the rpm sources was 0.99o, meaning that we needed to install OpenSSL from sources which usually has a degree of danger and may cause incompatibilities with already generated elements without any further issues
- the configuration files for TOR routers and clients changed from the format present in the tool in 2011, so we needed to bring them up to date
- manually install obfsproxy, as it wasn't already provided

By doing the previous changes, we managed to create a working environment with 10 routers, with the latest versions for all the needed tools (TOR and obfsproxy), in which to do our research.

5.2   Obfsproxy

The simplest way to implement a new pluggable transport was to use the obfsproxy. The framework comes with a list of already implemented pluggable transports as presented beforehand, but can also permit the implementation of new ones easily. The framework takes care of the full pluggable transport API implementation and network communication, leaving to developers only the implementation of the content changing algorithm.

In order to utilize pluggable transports, the TOR clients and servers need to be configured to use obfsproxy. The client needs to be informed that it needs to use bridges (thus, it will choose the first hop from the list of provided bridges in the configuration file) and, further, to use the named transport (in our case, reverse) which is provided by obfsproxy. The managed parameter sent to obfsproxy states that the connection between client and proxy is fully managed by the TOR client. The server is configured in order to run as a bridge relay, listening for content changed with the named transport (the same one used as the client, reverse), again by using obfsproxy in a managed state.

```
Client configuration
UseBridges 1
ClientTransportPlugin reverse exec obfsproxy managed
Bridge reverse 127.0.0.1:39201

Server configuration
BridgeRelay 1
ServerTransportPlugin reverse exec obfsproxy managed
ServerTransportListenAddr reverse 127.0.0.1:39201
```

5.3   Proposed Solution Pluggable Transport Algorithm

As almost all of the previous solutions based themselves on transforming the traffic between the source and the first hop, increasing the amount of data sent by adding the overhead of masking the content, our proposed solution goes a different path, by performing changes on the actual content in order to pass it as uncorrelated bytes which cannot be used (without other changes) in order to obtain information from the sent packets.

In order to perform a proof of concept of this concept, we decided to implement the simplest of changes, in order to allow the masking of content. Thus, we decided to perform an inversion of the bit values in each of the content bytes of each packet, rendering the content unreadable without performing another inversion on the whole content. Knowing that both the sender and the first hop know of the usage of this pluggable transport, the data can be exchanged between them without a deep packet inspection determining that the traffic is part of the TOR network.

This proposed solution comes with the following benefits:

- no overhead over the original content, as each of the bytes of the original content gets changed to another byte of data
- easy and fast operation in order to encode/decode the content, without a big impact on the transmission speed
- the simple change drastically changes the semantics of the content, allowing it to pass through filters which only check the content

However, as the change is simple, it can also be added to the deep packet inspection solutions in order to detect traffic which uses this change. In this case, the time needed to inspect one packet will increase at least twofold, as the original packet needs to be inspected first, then the packet needs to be transformed and the checked again, a time increase that isn't feasible when inspecting packages on the go without impacting the client performance. This can also be increased if a more complex algorithm is used on the content, as this inversion is just a proof of concept that such a pluggable transport can be implemented.

The implementation of this algorithm as part of the obfsproxy came as an extension to the BaseTransport protocol. As the algorithm is symmetric (the client and server do the same operation), the difference between the server and client functions is strictly concerning the flow of data. Thus, the client will receive the data from downstream, change it and send it upstream and the server receives the data from upstream, changes it again to get the original data and then sends it downstream, in order to be actually used. The added class is the following:

```
class ReverseTransport(BaseTransport):
    """

    Implements the reverse protocol. A protocol that reverses bytes
    and then proxies data.
    """

    def __init__(self):
        """

        If you override __init__, you ought to call the super method too.
        """
        super(ReverseTransport, self).__init__()
    def receivedDownstream(self, data):
        """

        Got data from downstream; reverse and relay them upstream.
        """

        buffered = data.read()
        reverse=''
        for i in range(0,len(buffered)):
                reverse+=chr(~ord(buffered[i]) & 0xFF)
        self.circuit.upstream.write(reverse)
    def receivedUpstream(self, data):
        """

        Got data from upstream; reverse and relay them downstream.
        """

        buffered = data.read()
        reverse=''
        for i in range(0,len(buffered)):
                reverse+=chr(~ord(buffered[i]) & 0xFF)
        self.circuit.downstream.write(reverse)


class ReverseClient(ReverseTransport):
    """

    ReverseClient is a client for the 'reverse' protocol.
    Since this protocol is so simple, the client and the server
    are identical and both just trivially subclass ReverseTransport.
    """


class ReverseServer(ReverseTransport):
    """

    ReverseServer is a server for the 'reverse' protocol.
    Since this protocol is so simple, the client and the server
    are identical and both just trivially subclass ReverseTransport.
    """
```

As obfsproxy is written in python, reversing the bits of a byte needed to also be implemented in the same language. By doing $chr(\sim ord(byte)\&0xFF)$, this functionality is achieved (the $\sim$ operator inverts the bits of an integer number). The usage of the extra $\&0xFF$ was mandatory, as the $\sim$ operator returns a signed number and chr needs a value between 0 and 255 in order to work.

6 Results

The main result of our work is the fact that the communication between the client and the TOR network, inside the isolated environment, works with our implemented pluggable transport, as well as with the original communication protocol and with only using bridges (without pluggable transport).

Having the possibility of running the client with any of these communication protocols, we decided to run a test in order to determine the possible performance differences of the three. Thus, we booted up the network with 10 routers with the following flags:

- Router 1 - Exit Fast HSDir Running Stable V2Dir Valid
- Router 2 - Fast Running V2Dir Valid
- Router 3 - Exit Fast Running V2Dir Valid
- Router 4 - Fast Guard HSDir Running Stable Valid
- Router 5 - Fast Guard HSDir Running Stable V2Dir Valid
- Router 6 - Fast Running Stable V2Dir Valid
- Router 7 - Fast Guard HSDir Running Stable Valid
- Router 8 - Fast Running Valid
- Router 9 - Fast HSDir Running Stable Valid

The first five nodes were also directory services and the bridge service ran on router 6 (for the two tests requiring bridges). After the network started, consensus was reached and all routers were connected, the client connects to the network using one of the three connection possibilities and, then, the connection is used to download files from a webserver. By varying the sizes of the files, the performances for each of the connection method can be obtained. For each file size, we performed 10 tests and the given value is the mean value of all.

The results show us that, by using a bridge (the same first hop for all requests), the performance is slightly worse than the one when using the directory service to generate routes, as by changing the first hop we can get a better route and get better performances.

Further comparing the results from the bridge tests, with and without pluggable transports, we see that using the pluggable transport comes with a small increase in duration, accounting for the coding and decoding of the content. The difference, however, is small when compared to the first test, showing that, by having an overhead of around 10–15 %, we can achieve a better bypassing of deep packet inspectors (Table 1).

Table 1. Results

	100 kb	200 kb	300 kb	500 kb	5 mb
Directory connection	0.05 s	0.06 s	0.07 s	0.1 s	1.3 s
Bridge (no pluggable transport)	0.05 s	0.07 s	0.07 s	0.1 s	1.4 s
Bridge with reverse transport	0.05 s	0.07 s	0.08 s	0.12 s	1.47 s

7 Conclusion

The introduction of new elements in TOR, such as bridges and pluggable transports, has permitted more and more users to bypass security measures and access information denied to them until now, due to the inspection systems put into places by governments and ISPs.

The development of such a pluggable transport requires the existence of an isolated environment, in order not to interfere with the actual usage of the TOR network. The existing tools for such an environment are outdated, but with some changes, it can be brought up to date in order to implement the most recent version of TOR and obfsproxy, in order to properly simulate real-life conditions. By using obfsproxy, the addition of a new pluggable transport is facilitated, as the developer is left to implement data and decoding, leaving the framework to do the actual communication.

The results of our tests show that using these censorship circumventing methods adds a slight overhead over the traditional way of using the TOR network. However, the overhead is more than manageable as these methods are used when access is more important than speed. In the future, we wish to implement a more complex algorithm for data coding and decoding (as the one we chose here was for the sake of having a proof of concept of using the environment) and to run tests on different type of networks, not only with the default one.

Acknowledgments. This work partially supported by the Romanian National Authority for Scientific Research (CNCSUEFISCDI) under the project PN-II-PT-PCCA-2013-4-1651.

References

1. Xin, L., Neng, W.: Design improvement for TOR against low-cost traffic attack and low-resource routing attack privacy enhancing technologies. In: International Conference on Communications and Mobile Computing (2009)
2. Dingledine, R., Mathewson, N., Syverson, P.: TOR: the second-generation onion router. Information Security Research Group (2014)
3. Murdoch, S.J., Danezis, G.: Low-cost traffic analysis of TOR. In: IEEE Symposium on Security and Privacy (2005)
4. Murdoch, S.J.: Covert channel vulnerabilities in anonymity systems. Technical report (2007)

5. AlSabah, M., Goldberg, I.: Performance and security improvements for TOR: a survey. In: International Association for Cryptologic Research (2015)
6. Mittal, P., Olumofin, F.: PIR-TOR: scalable anonymous communication using private information retrieval. USENIX Security (2014)
7. Ghosh, M., Richardson, M.: A TorPath to TorCoin: proof-of-bandwidth altcoins for compensating relays. USENIX Security (2011)
8. Dyer, K.P, Coull, S.E., Ristenpart, T., Shrimpton, T.: Protocol misidentification made easy with format-transforming encryption. In: Proceedings of the 2013 ACM SIGSAC Conference on Computer & Communications Security, pp. 61–72. ACM (2013)
9. Fifield, D., Hardison, N., Ellithorpe, J., Stark, E., Boneh, D., Dingledine, R., Porras, P.: Evading censorship with browser-based proxies. In: Fischer-Hübner, S., Wright, M. (eds.) PETS 2012. LNCS, vol. 7384, pp. 239–258. Springer, Heidelberg (2012)
10. Winter, P., Pulls, T., Fuss, J.: ScrambleSuit: a polymorphic network protocol to circumvent censorship. In: Proceedings of the 12th ACM Workshop on Workshop on Privacy in the Electronic Society, pp. 213–224. ACM (2013)
11. Mohajeri Moghaddam, M., Li, B., Derakhshani, M., Goldberg, I.S.: protocol obfuscation for TOR bridges. In: Proceedings of the 2012 ACM Conference on Computer and Communications Security, pp. 97–108. ACM (2012)
12. TOR Project - Pluggable Transports. https://www.torproject.org/docs/pluggable-transports.html.en

Preparation of SCA Attacks: Successfully Decapsulating BGA Packages

Christian Wittke[(✉)], Zoya Dyka, Oliver Skibitzki, and Peter Langendoerfer

IHP, Im Technologiepark 25, Frankfurt (Oder), Germany
{wittke,dyka,skibitzki,langendoerfer}@ihp-microelectronics.com

Abstract. In this paper we explain detailed how we successfully decapsulated a state of the art FPGA realized in a 45 nm technology and packaged in a BGA housing. For running SCA attacks it is important that the IC is still fully functional after decapsulation. The challenge here is the BGA package since the acid used to remove the plastic can easily destroy the substrate that is under the die. We achieved a success rate of 100 %. The effect of the decapsulation for measuring EM traces is that the traces show an about 30 % higher amplitude.

Keywords: Decapsulation · FPGA · Ball-Grid-Array (BGA) · Package · EMA · Side Channel Analysis (SCA)

1 Introduction

Some types of physical attacks e.g. optical inspection, fault injections, etc. require the device under attack (DUA) to be decapsulated. But also more common attacks such as analysis of electromagnetic traces are benefiting from decapsulations since the amplitude of the measured signal is higher and by that allows simpler analysis. Ball-Grid-Array (BGA) packages are not really new but not as common as Quad-Flat-Packages (QFP). BGA packages are considered to be more challenging for an attacker when it comes to decapsulation. We report on how we opened BGA packaged FPGA already placed on a PCB with a success rate of 100 %. We did a thorough but low cost preparation that consumed only one additional device to detect where the die is in the package, how thick the package is and how the plastic reacts on different types of acid. In order to prove that the decapsulation was successful i.e. that we could access the bare die and that the die was still working properly, we present EM traces of an elliptic curve kP operation recorded before and after the decapsulation. These traces show that after decapsulation the amplitude of the measured EM traces is about 30 % higher.

The rest of this paper is structured as follows. Section 2 summarizes typical packages and their structure. In Sect. 3 the preparation for decapsulation is given and Sect. 4 presents the decapsulation process and the impact for EM measurements. The paper finishes with short conclusions.

© Springer International Publishing AG 2016
I. Bica and R. Reyhanitabar (Eds.): SECITC 2016, LNCS 10006, pp. 240–247, 2016.
DOI: 10.1007/978-3-319-47238-6_17

2   Packages

Integrated circuits (ICs) usually come in a package. The packages are standardized, e.g. by JEDEC Solid State Technology Association which is an organization for the standardization of semiconductors, including packages [1].

The package protects the die against damage and environmental influences. Furthermore the package bridges the different geometric connections from the die to the circuit board. An additional advantage is the better handling in terms of placement for component placement systems.

(a) QFP with pins on all sides

(b) BGA package with 484 solder balls (pins) on the back side

Fig. 1. Two different package types with their pins

(a) QFP leadframe

(b) BGA substrate

Fig. 2. (a) Leadframe as bridge in a QFP. The pads of the die are connected by bond wires. (b) Partially exposed substrate of a BGA package sample after etching attempts.

Common package types are e.g. the Quad-Flat-Package and the Ball-Grid-Array package. Both are surface mounted devices. The QFP has a rectangular form and pins on all four sides. An example QFP is shown in Fig. 1a. The connection from the pads of the die to the pins is realized by bond wires from the pads to the lead frame (see Fig. 2a). Instead of pins on the sides the BGA package has balls of solder in a grid on the bottom. One benefit of BGAs is a higher density of pins, including a smaller pitch. Figure 1b shows the under surface of a BGA with the grid of solder balls. The connections from the pads of the die to the pins of the package is realized through a substrate in the package (Fig. 2b).

For running semi-invasive attacks or to improve measurements of EM radiation, the package of the attacked IC needs to be opened but the device has to be fully functional. We decided to open the BGA package of the Spartan-6 FPGA on the PCB. But we used a single FPGA to prepare the decapsulation.

3   Preparation

As preparation for opening the BGA package we decided to x-ray the Spartan-6 FPGA and also made a cross-section before decapsulation to learn about the dimensions of the die (see Fig. 3a) and the thickness of the package over the die (see Fig. 3b).

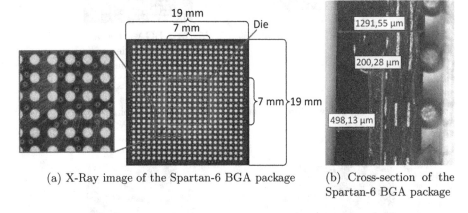

(a) X-Ray image of the Spartan-6 BGA package

(b) Cross-section of the Spartan-6 BGA package

Fig. 3. X-ray image and cross-section of the Spartan-6 package

For chemical opening of the package we examined various acids at room temperature for 24 h at the center of the sample packages. We tested hydrofluoric acid (HF 50 %), hydrochloric acid (HCl 37 %), sulfuric acid (H_2SO_4 95–97%) and nitric acid (HNO_3 65 % and 85–100%). Afterwards HCl (37 %), HF (50 %), H_2SO_4 (95–97%) and HNO_3 (65 % and 85–100%) were heated at 50 °C, 75 °C to 100 °C (or boiling temperature) and put at the center of sample packages again. In this second experiment we exposed the packages to the acids for 5 min and 2 h respectively.

The best etching results were achieved with nitric acid ($\geq$90 %) [2] heated close to its boiling point of 84 °C. But this highly depends on the compound of the package, i.e. for different packages other acids may give better results. So we recommend to run similar tests on packages to be opened before trying to open the real target device.

4   Decapsulation of Spartan-6 in a BGA Package

4.1   Preparation

The DUA is a Xilinx Spartan-6 FPGA. The board with the Spartan-6 was designed at IHP [3] based on the Fault Extension Board of the TU Graz. The board is shown in Fig. 4. The FPGA is placed on the front side of the board (see Fig. 4a) and most components are placed on the backside (see Fig. 4b). This improves measurements and ensures that all EM-probes can reach any measurement points on the FPGA board, without harming the probe. The board has several GPIOs to control and communicate with the FPGA, e. g. start an elliptic curve cryptography (ECC) computation, trigger the oscilloscope and provide input data. The FPGA is clocked with 4 MHz and has 1.2 V core and 3.3 V GPIO voltage.

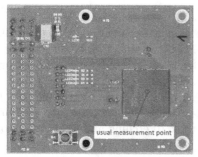

(a) Front side of the FPGA board with usual measurement point over the die

(b) Back side of the FPGA board

Fig. 4. Front and back side of the Spartan-6 Board

We decided to open the BGA package on the PCB. Therefore a good protection of the PCB and its components is needed. Otherwise the nitric acid could harm electrical components and the solder mask coating of the PCB. That would make the FPGA board inoperable.

To protect the PCB and its components against nitric acid we used adhesive aluminum foil similar to [4]. To prevent perforating the foil, we covered the whole back side of the board with a piece of polystyrene (see Fig. 5a) before covering the PCB with the aluminum foil. This shall prevent the acid passing through a hole in the foil. Furthermore, we have protected the cutout with multiple overlapping layers of aluminum foil to avoid that the acid dissolves the glue (see Fig. 5b). The cutout was made at the end and the size was determined by the x-ray image of the chip.

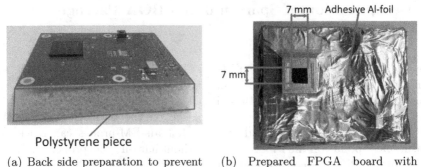

(a) Back side preparation to prevent GPIO pins from piercing the foil

(b) Prepared FPGA board with cutout over the die

Fig. 5. Preparation of the Spartan-6 Boards for the decapsulation

4.2 Decapsulation

We prepared two FPGA boards for the decapsulation and opened the two BGA packages in parallel. The heated nitric acid ($\geq 90\%$) was dripped on the package for a minute and after that time the surface was cleaned with acetone spray. The cleaning with acetone spray removes remainings of the nitric acid and the package material. At the beginning the etch rate was low. We assume that the smooth surface is the reason behind this fact since the etch rate increased after the first etching steps. The decapsulation took 10 etching and cleaning periods.

Fig. 6. Opened BGA package after cleaning with acetone spray

Figure 6 shows the opened BGA package. Nearly the whole die is visible. Only in the bottom corners some material of the package is left. We tried to remove

(a) Die from first FPGA board with still package material behind the bond wires (black material)

(b) Die from second FPGA board with underetching behind the die and bond wires (brighter material and deeper focus)

Fig. 7. Microscope images of the dies and bond wires after decapsulation

these remainings with several additional etch and clean cycles. The result of these attempts can be seen in Fig. 7. There is still some material of the package behind the bond wires in Fig. 7a and a slight underetching of the die in Fig. 7b (marked with circle respectively). The optical inspection of both decapsulated FPGAs did not reveal any damage of the bond wires.

Next the aluminum foil was removed carefully. Intentionally the foil was left on the package and was cut with a scalpel to prevent the adhesive foil from damaging the bond wires while removing. Also the foil is some kind of shielding for EM measurements, which ensures that the EM radiation really stems from the die.

Figure 8 shows the whole board with the decapsulated FPGA and the remaining foil. The functionality of the boards was successfully tested with our ECC design.

Fig. 8. FPGA on the board after decapsulating it

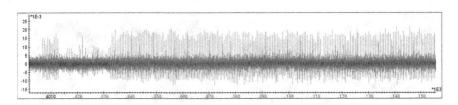

Fig. 9. EMT measured on top of a non decapsulated FPGA

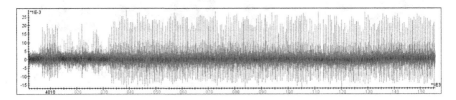

Fig. 10. EMT measured on top of a decapsulated FPGA

4.3 EM Measurements

In order to determine the influence of the decapsulation on measured EM traces we measured the EM radiation over a non- and a decapsulated FPGA on our boards. The whole measurement setup (including probe, oscilloscope, power supply), ECC design, its input values and the position over the die were kept constant for fair comparison. Only the altitude of the probe over the die differs. We used the MFA-R-75 EM probe from Langer [5] to measure the traces. The probe was positioned at exactly the same position for both measurements using a high precision x-y-z table. The measured electromagnetic traces (EMT) are shown in Figs. 9 and 10.

The amplitude of EMT measured on top of the decapsulated FPGA (see Fig. 10) is approximately 30 % higher than the amplitude of EMT measured on the non decapsulated FPGA (see Fig. 9). This is due to the smaller distance of approximately 500 μm (see Fig. 3b) between the probe and die and the missing package material in the measurement of the decapsulated FPGA.

5 Conclusion

In this paper we have shown that decapsulation of BGA packages even though more challenging than the one of QFP packages is doable if prepared thoroughly. If the information about the package is not available, we propose to x-ray the device and to cut/break it in order to learn about the actual placement of the die in the package as preparation. We did this as a first step. The second step was to run a series of experiments with different acids at different temperatures to learn how fast the plastic reacts to the acids. We consumed only one device for experiments and successfully opened two devices on boards which is a success rate of 100 %.

In addition we recorded EM trace of an elliptic curve point kP multiplication to show that the die and the PCB were still fully functional and that decapsulation improves the quality of the measured EM traces, i.e. the amplitude of the traces, by 30 %.

Acknowledgments. The work presented in this paper has been partially funded by the "Ministry of Sciences, Research and Cultural Affairs (MWFK)" from resources of the European Social Fund (ESF) and of the state Brandenburg.

We thank Dipl.-Stom. Nikolai Kljagin for x-raying of the FPGA in his dental clinic.

References

1. JEDEC - Global Standards for the Microelectronics Industry. www.jedec.org
2. Acros Organics - Data Sheet Nitric Acid Fuming, 85–100 %. http://www.acros.com/Ecommerce/msds.aspx?PrdNr=27062&Country=EN&Language=en
3. IHP - Innovations for High Performance Microelectronics. http://www.ihp-microelectronics.com/en/start.html
4. Loubet Moundi, P.: Cost effective techniques for chip delayering and in-situ depackaging. In: COSADE 2013 Short Talks Session. https://www.cosade.org/cosade13/presentations/session5b_a.pdf
5. LANGER EMV-Technik GmbH: MFA02 micro probe set. http://www.langer-emv.com/produkte/stoeraussendung/nahfeldsonden/set-mfa02/

Comparative Analysis of Security Operations Centre Architectures; Proposals and Architectural Considerations for Frameworks and Operating Models

Sabina Georgiana Radu[✉]

Computer Science Department, Military Technical Academy, Bucharest, Romania
sabina.georgiana.radu@gmail.com

Abstract. Few initiatives tried to define an architectural framework for an Information Security Operations Centre (SOC) at this point. As it is a topic that encompasses the three dimensions of technology, processes and people, the documentation and resources available are usually treating only one or two of these three dimensions. This article tries to treat the Security Operations Centre in the complexity that it demands, looking at all the stated three dimensions and trying to propose a few architectural considerations regarding frameworks and operating models that can be used when building a variably sized SOC, with its applicability throughout organisations in different fields of interest.

Keywords: Security operation centre · Incident handling · Operational security · Security architecture and design · Information security services

1   Introduction

The paper is focused on analysing a relevant characteristics of SOC models and tries to propose a few guidelines for architecting this type of security organisation. A summary of relevant existing work is naturally necessary for analysis, so in the first part of the paper, a short review of the evolution and key milestones of SOC development is made, and following a summarised classification of various types of SOCs, seen from different perspectives.

Further, based on reviewed literature and current models, a few proposals and architectural considerations are described in trying to classify decisions based on size and complexity. Also, proposals for further research are demanded, as the vastness of the topic asks for further work, in the attempt to get more practical and granular results.

1.1   Key Factors in the Evolution of CERTs

Since the first creation of the CERT Coordination Centre (CERT/CC) in 1988, when the first internet worm triggered an immediate need for incident and emergency handling capabilities among governmental agencies, computer emergency

© Springer International Publishing AG 2016
I. Bica and R. Reyhanitabar (Eds.): SECITC 2016, LNCS 10006, pp. 248–260, 2016.
DOI: 10.1007/978-3-319-47238-6_18

and defence teams have been organised throughout other national defence institutions and state organisations [1]. After the need for standalone network defence teams arose, the natural demand for interconnecting these teams and their intelligence came into high-light and materialised into the creation of the Forum of Incident Response and Security Teams (FIRST) in October 1989 as the first network of interconnected CSRITs, focused on exchanging intelligence about security incidents and coordination of response activities.

Subsequently, many more working groups throughout the world started their own projects of developing research networks starting with Europe (CERT-NL, DFN-CERT, TERENA) and together with initiatives in the Asia Pacific region (AusCERT, APSIRC), Latin America (APSIRT, CAIS) and more, between late 1990 and early 2000. Many of these initiatives followed the model of the defence organisation; focused on providing incident response capabilities, coordinate information exchange, education and awareness initiatives. Their number has grown exponentially since 1990, reaching a number of 188 registered CSIRTs by 2003 [1].

Certainly, an emerging trend and an appetite for information sharing led to a tremendous amount of new ideas, development models, in an effort to grow maturity in an organic manner. It would be inadequate to say that just silo developments were created, but the heterogeneity of environments, the constant change in demands, and the explosion of the threat landscape were the premises for developing CSIRTs lacking an integrated structure, framework, with common methodologies and mechanisms.

Integration initiatives followed, from an architectural standpoint, processes and procedures creation, standards development, and technology alignment. Different definitions and differentiations between terms like Computer Security Incident Response Team (CSIRT), Computer Incident Response Team (CIRT), Security Incident Response Team (SIRT), Security Emergency Response Team (SERT), and finally SOC set the stage for even more variables instead of heading to an integrated view. It is not the scope of this article trying to compare different SOC definitions; neither does building a new one. What actually serves for the purpose of this research is defining a clear picture of the role, responsibility and boundaries of a SOC.

1.2 De-facto Standards for Organisational Models and Structures

The first and perhaps the most comprehensive publication on CSIRT organisational models, frameworks and structures is the Organisational Models for Computer Security Incident Response Teams (CSIRTs) from Carnegie Mellon University [2]. This serves as a starting point when defining SOC constituency (previously defined in [3]), responsibilities and boundaries. Models are briefly described in the table below.

Another important aspect that will have a big influence on the SOC architecture, from the perspective of the ownership of the systems, data, and configuration and management rights is the authority the CSIRT exercises on its constituency [2]. Having full authority, the operational team can perform any

Security team	No group or section of the organisation has been given the formal responsibility for all incident handling activities. No CSIRT has been established. Available personnel, usually system, network or security administrators handle security events on an ad hoc basis as part of their overall responsibilities
Internal distributed CSIRT	In this model, the organisation utilises existing staff to provide a virtual distributed CSIRT, which is formally chartered to deal with incident response activities. The distributed team members can perform CSIRT du-ties in addition to their regular responsibilities or could be assigned to CSIRT work on a full-time basis
Internal centralised CSIRT	Fully staffed, dedicated CSIRT provides the incident handling services for an organisation. In many cases team members spend 100 percent of their time working for the CSIRT. The team is centrally located in the organisation and is responsible for all incident handling activities across the constituency or enterprise
Internal combined distributed and centralised CSIRT	A combination of the distributed CSIRT and the centralised CSIRT. It maximises the utilisation of existing staff in strategic locations throughout the organisation with the centrally located coordinating capabilities
Coordinating CSIRT	The CSIRT coordinates and facilitates the handling of incidents across a variety of external or internal organisations, which could include other CSIRTs. It can be a coordinating entity for individual subsidiaries of a corporation, branches of a military organisation, etc.

action necessary to improve the organisation's security posture, without waiting for approval from higher-level management. This widens the scope of the SOC architecture, bringing more complexity of the topology, but allows for faster response in incident situations. The second scenario is having shared authority, where the security team works with its constituency in deciding actions that should be taken and changes that should be made. They can of course have an influence on the outcome of the decision, making recommendations for possible solutions, but they are not the final decision maker. Finally, the scenario where the CSIRT has no authority and cannot take any actions of its own, being fully dependent upon the management of the organisation for any decision or change that should be made. The security team only acts as an advisor, and the systems of the constituency will be external to the SOC boundaries.

Going further, using organisational models, constituency size and authority, [4] proposes five SOC templates which serve as a basis for further defining tiering SOC functions and the necessary level of granularity. The table below summarises the five models.

Having this five-level structure based mostly on constituency size, functions of SOC are starting to differentiate from a decentralised security team doing ad-hoc monitoring activities to a highly organised hierarchy of coordinating and subordinate entities. Based on these templates, [4] defines a hierarchy of functional roles that can be applied within SOCs of variable sizes, increasing granularity with dimension.

Virtual SOC	This can be an internal distributed SOC with its constituency smaller than 1,000 users/IPs, with no proactive/reactive authority, serving a small to medium sized business
Small SOC	This is an internal centralised SOC serving for an organisation with 10,000 users/IPs, having shared authority and a relevant influence in decisions regarding preventative or responsive actions
Large SOC	An internal distributed SOC, but with elements from a distributed SOC, serving for a large enterprise or large government agency, or a constituency of 50,000 users/IPs. This SOC has full authority on reactive measures and shared for proactive
Tiered SOC	This is a blend between functions from internal centralised SOC, internal distributed SOC and coordinating SOC. It can support up to 500,000 users/IPs and its authority varies, as it can operate through subordinate SOCs. This model can constitute from multiple distinct SOCs, coordinated by a central entity
National SOC	The national SOC is almost always a coordinating SOC. Its constituency can be up to 50,000,000 users/IPs, serving entire national governments or nations

Actually, it has always been size the main aspect that stood as the basis of architectural decisions and models, because size brings complexity, heterogeneity, the need for granularity and for integration. Also, size will generate the need for standardisation and for well-defined processes.

1.3   Typical SOC Architecture

Within a SOC, there are a few components that can be separated from a functionality standpoint, in order to build an architecture around functional layers.

– Generation Layer: This is where events are recorded using various devices in the infrastructure: network devices, security devices, servers, storage, and applications. These devices send logs in real time as soon as events on the network occur.

- Acquisition Layer: This is the layer responsible for transporting and receiving events from the generation layer in raw format. A first round of filtering and prioritisation is made, but not close to deep manipulation and filtering of events.
- Data Manipulation Layer: The central component of the SOC from a technological standpoint; here, a SIEM, Log Management, or other analysis tools should re-side. All the event normalisation, correlation, analysis and filtering is made at this layer. The core mechanisms should be able to transform raw data into relevant intelligence, reduce its volume and present it in a human readable format.
- Output/Presentation Layer: This is the point where automated tools and mechanisms are interfacing with the human component. It is important to understand that analysts are the heart of the SOC? They bring value through their awareness of the situation, judgment, subjectivity and experience, and they are not replaceable by any automated tool.
- Policies/Procedures: Here are the defined organisation's policies, procedures, standards, best practices and guidelines. They constantly interact with the data manipulation layer and the presentation layer to exchange information.

2   Architectural Considerations of SOC Frameworks

Having put together some of the most relevant aspects to be considered when developing a security operations centre and based on the current work that has been written until now, in the following sections a few proposals are made, regarding some architectural considerations that should be taken into account when building, design-ing, or scaling a SOC. Of course, like in any IT or technology related solution, the magic poison doesn't exist, there is no "one size fits all" or a general accepted solution for any environment. The best approach is to try to consider some relevant variables, look at previous experience and lessons learned, and position the ready to build SOC on a scale, in order to find its perfect fit, its hybrid between simplicity and complexity, between size and agility, between strength and flexibility (Fig. 1).

The considerations and scenarios involve technical, organisational and human component aspects and generally avoid closed answers or conclusions, as every organisation should find its own fit that is best suitable for their business requirements, technical constraints, and specifics of the organisation.

2.1   Consideration 1: Start Lean or Think Big?

Every organisation has a method of approach when thinking about dimensioning and scaling. Some like to start lean, start from simple and move to complex as demand starts to arise. Others like to "think big", think in advance of all the facets of the situation first, in order to have the complete landscape, and then decide to let go of the aspects that are not in the interest or scope of the organisation.

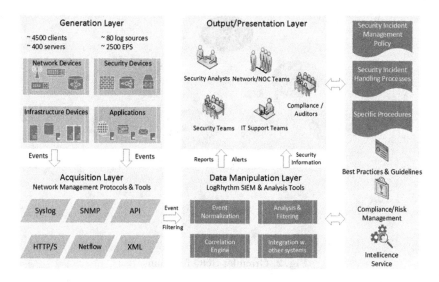

Fig. 1. Typical SOC high-level architecture

When applying these two ways of thinking to building a SOC, the main aspect to take into consideration is the granularity of the functions. Positioning the organisation into one of the five categories is a good starting point, but it is a heuristic categorisation. In the real world, few SOCs fall exactly into one category or another, and the in majority of cases, a SOC would have most components close to one of the templates, but also components from other templates. A small SOC may have the need to do scanning or vulnerability analysis, which are functions specific for larger SOCs. Or the other way around, a large SOC might not want or need (or not have the budget for) Tier 3 analysis or forensics. Tailoring SOC functions by their specific needs is a crucial task for the its later efficiency.

Figure 2 presents a hierarchical structure of SOC functions. The two strategies that could be applied are top-down or bottom-up. When choosing top-down, we are start-ing from simple to complex. Incident handling and system admin are for sure separated from the start, for any small sized SOC. Further, the organisation must decide: do they need to have two tiers of incident handling and analysis? (Tier 1 being real-time monitoring and Tier 2+ as in-depth analysis); do they need to separate devices administration to engineering/development? Further granularity can be achieved by dividing Tier 2+ into more tiers - in-depth incident analysis, Tier 3+, forensic analysis, etc. - or adding more proactive functions like vulnerability analysis, scanning, penetration testing etc. This process stops when the organisation reaches the right structure for its security demands.

The second strategy, bottom-up is starting from the most complex picture (e.g. large SOC or bigger) and deciding which are the functions that do not demand for full time capabilities, and starting to merge them on the basis on

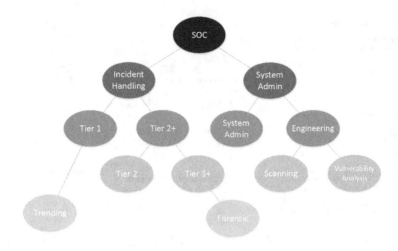

Fig. 2. Granular SOC functions

the forecasted needs. In the end, a given organisation does not have to fit in a single category, layer or template; the most important is for it to find the appropriate structure for their needs.

2.2 Consideration 2: Trust the Analysts or Automate?

A subject of debate in most security organisations is finding the perfect compromise between the amount of automation they use from the acquired technology/tools and the need for the human component. Almost none resides on either of the two extremes of the axis, but the desire would be to find their spot somewhere in between. The better the SIEM and analysis tools are configured, the less amount of work will be put on the analysts. At this point, the decision should be whether to invest in admin and engineering resources for fine-tuning, SIEM configuration and automation or to improve incident handling and analyst capabilities. This decision has many variables:

- The technology and security devices used. Are they open source or commercial? Linux based analysis tools can offer a wide variety of features, but they need skilled engineers for configuration and fine-tuning and they lack the vendor sup-port provided by commercial solutions. On the other hand, commercial (COTS) solutions can be easier to install and configure, but might not have the tuning capabilities that Linux based platforms offer.
- Even COTS tools have their cornerstones. Choosing a vendor like Arcsight or Splunk, a significant investment in engineers' knowledge and capabilities must be made, as it is widely known that they are not solutions to function out-of-the-box. A big investment in tuning and configuration must be made, and the results are visible in terms of complexity, flexibility and features that the solutions can offer. On the other hand, choosing easy to use, easy to configure, mostly GUI oriented tools will show its limitations at some point.

– The availability of skilled admins. Not rarely, companies using niche technologies loose their key personnel and find themselves lacking the capabilities to continue their critical business. It is not in the scope of this article to discuss about human resources career development paths, or employee satisfaction programmes, but to weight the opportunity and possibilities to find skilled resources and to avoid the situation of "single points of failure" in terms of people, meaning irreplaceable personnel. When choosing solutions that demand skilled expertise, any organisation should consider the availability of finding, or possibly replacing, key employees.

"Nothing can substitute the analyst" [4] - is a fact and a fundamental truth that should always be considered. Any raw or filtered data provided by security tools, alarms or reports does not have value if they are not analysed by the human component. Analysts bring value through their capacity to filter information based on skills, experience, trends and can make subjective, situational based decisions.

2.3   Consideration 3: Have an Affinity for Proactive or Reactive?

Defence-In-Depth is the principle guiding security experts since the rise in complexity in the information security industry. Defence measures had always been exponentially more complex than the offence strategies, as attacking a system means finding a single weakness while protecting it supposes the covering of all vulnerabilities. This is the philosophy under which all defence strategies operate. But every organisation will focus their efforts more or less in one of these two directions: proactive or reactive measures.

Initially, SOCs or CSIRTs were focused on responding to incidents rather than trying to prevent them, but as soon as security strategies started to grow in complexity and scope, and information sharing between hierarchies of SOCs began to increase, proactive services like situation analysis and trending became more and more relevant functions of security organisations. Like all architectural facets and decisions a SOC must take into consideration, it's all about finding the best compromise that suites its purpose: finding the hybrid between offering proactive services - like vulnerability analysis, penetration testing, trending and situational awareness - and the traditional reactive services - like monitoring, incident handling and responding, patching and remediation.

Depending on the organisation's affinity for being predominantly proactive or reactive, each will start its security strategy from one of the two extremities of the axis - beginning or end of the attack - in a reach for heading to a "middle" position (Fig. 3).

Hence, taking security measures from one side or the other will consequently drive their efforts of defence into investing in different security solutions that fall more or less into the areas of prevention, detection and remediation. Of course, none of these measures are drawn with a single colour; virtually all security solutions and tools on the market try to cover as many areas, and widen their scope as much as possible. A good example is the evolution of the Intrusion Detection

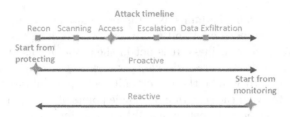

Fig. 3. Timeline of attack and defence strategies

System, which lately be-came the Intrusion Prevention System, or the traditional firewall that nowadays we call Next Generation Firewall which covers functions from traditional rule-based blocking device to behavioural analysis, in-depth application-layer inspection, and newer technologies like Data Loss Prevention or Security Analytics (Fig. 4).

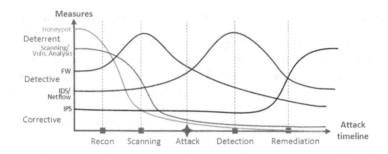

Fig. 4. Security measures vs. Attack timeline

2.4 Consideration 4: Find the Best Mix of Ownership and Authority

One of the most important decisions that a SOC must take from the first stages of the design is the boundary where its authority begins and ends. Depending on the ownership of the constituency, their security policies and their overall organisation's specifics, the SOC's authority will reside somewhere on a scale from full, shared or no authority. This further drives many architectural consid- erations, as security devices can be external or internal to the SOC monitoring infrastructure, they can be included or not as generation sources of events for the SIEM and analysis tools or they can or cannot be a point where the security team can make configuration changes when trying to respond to an attack. The sample architecture in Fig. 5 shows a typical SOC infrastructure monitoring its constituency's infrastructure. This picture is meant to highlight that there are three types of devices in the security infrastructure from the SOC's standpoint:

– devices owned by SOC, residing either at the SOC's premises or at the constituency's premises, participating in the monitoring process - highlighted in orange;
– devices owned by the constituency, that participate in the monitoring process - highlighted in green;
– devices owned by the constituency, that do not participate and are not included in the security infrastructure;
– a forth type will be a mix of orange and green, meaning the SOC and constituency will have shared authority on the specific devices.

A few principles guide the positioning and the authority applied on different types of devices. First of all, the SOC will never have full authority on devices critical for the infrastructure availability. These will be in the administration of the constituency. Any device that is inline will generally be in green: routers, switches, firewalls, web application firewalls in the DMZ, IPSs, endpoint security solutions like antivirus, etc. The SOC does not want to be involved in IT Support and admin activities in the constituency's infrastructure, and thus should only reside on monitoring capabilities from these selected devices.

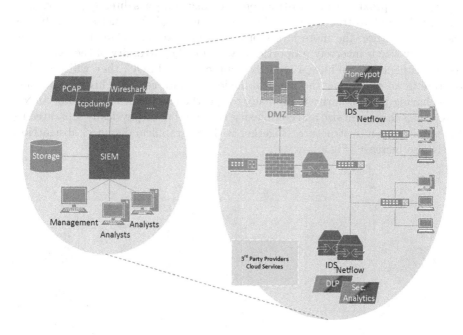

Fig. 5. SOC monitoring infrastructure (Color figure online)

Regarding the devices highlighted in orange located at the constituency's premises, these will generally be based on reactive mechanisms, only with monitoring and alert-ing capabilities, and no prevention functions. A SOC can place at the constituency's premises: IDSs (note that inline IPSs are in green, out-of-band IDSs can be in orange), Netflow collectors, both for the internal network or for the DMZ, or a honey-pot located near the web servers. Also, many devices can have shared authority, like a network data loss prevention solution, or security analytics.

Finally, it's the decision of the organisation how authority will be given to the SOC, a decision that must weight the level of trust they can provide and the urgency of response needed in case of an attack. A SOC that has full authority can more rapidly respond to an attack by making configuration changes, or blocking traffic paths. This of course will have a high impact on business operations, and no one wants to be responsible for the potential situation in which business is interrupted because of false positives.

2.5   Consideration 5: Choose the Best Compromise Between Proximity and Abstraction Level

An interesting, through self-explanatory architectural consideration that is observed by looking at various SOCs and their constituencies is the relationship between size, proximity and abstraction level. Size is always directly proportional with the level of abstraction needed in the monitoring infrastructure. The bigger the infrastructure, the more layers of abstraction we have. On the other side, we can say size is inversely proportional with for the proximity of the SOC with its constituency. If we have a security team or virtual SOC, they will probably operate in an office near the physical devices or data centre. This is important when having just a security team ready to act when an incident is arising. As the SOC starts to grow in size and complexity, they tend to be physically separated to the monitoring infrastructure. Together with geographical distance, abstraction levels also increase (Fig. 6).

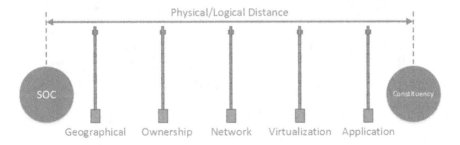

Fig. 6. Physical/logical distance and abstraction levels

After taking into consideration geographical distance, the next 'layer' or 'barrier' that separates the SOC from its constituency would be the ownership. If the owner-ship is the same, the SOC can have more authority and more flexibility on the infra-structure that they are monitoring. If we are talking about

MSSP, or a SOC monitor-ing the infrastructure of another organisation, they will have limited room to apply security measures, respond quickly to an incident, etc. Further, as complexity starts to grow, more abstraction levels arise, and one would be the specifics of the network that is monitored. If it is a cloud infrastructure, the virtualisation layer will impose great limitations (technical and legal) and is a crucial barrier to consider when trying to monitor a cloud environment. Here, logical network segregation issues, multi-tenancy, and integration aspects in virtualised environment will certainly impose some technical constraints. The last layer of separation, or logical barrier between the SOC and the object of their monitoring activities will be the application layer. The majority of the monitoring and analytics tools will work at layer 3 or 4 on the OSI stack, while applications at layer 7. Usually, layer 3–4 devices are somehow limited in understanding layer 7. Further more, layer 7 is much more time consuming to analyse. That is the reason why dedicated application-aware, deep packet inspection and application-centric security devices are starting to replace traditional network or TCP session monitoring.

3 Conclusions

Due to the vastness of this domain, such a concise writing can only summarise a few concerns that demand further research. What this article wished to achieve is offering the rushed designer a few glimpses into a SOCs anatomy; when looking from the inside or from the outside, she must understand a considerable amount of variables and scenarios. A complex system must be seen with all its facets and from different perspectives, with all its components, interactions, and interdependencies. The same applies to SOCs.

Proposing a "one size fits all" model is way long outdated and never has been a solution in the technology-oriented world. A certain amount of abstraction is needed, as we are discussing general guidelines, but concepts like real-time/in-depth analysis, incident handling/resolution, vulnerability assessment and scanning and many others can have slightly different flavours from one organisation to another. It is ultimately the designer's decision how she chooses to define them. Documentation can only provide direction guidance, not set the destination.

In security organisations, like in all technology environments, size will always bring complexity and heterogeneity. Virtually all systems architectures, regardless of their field, scope, and applicability have at the very basis of their foundation this fundamental consideration: size. Together with size, the number of pieces of the puzzle grows, hence the need for integration. The number of flavours, vendors and systems grows, hence the need for standardisation. The diversity of the environment demands centralisation and visibility. Interaction with other entities is further needed, thus compliance related considerations appear. From their first appearance (CERT/CC) in 1988, CSIRTs, like all complex systems, evolved in an organic manner, and will continue to have a natural evolution, a kind of Darwinism of IT driven systems and environments. Proposals for future work in this field can start with drafting a set of SOC standards and best practices frameworks for organisations. Also, interactions between SOCs can be simplified if proper standardisation is in place. In the attempt to blue-print a set of SOC standards, flexibility and granularity will have to match all environments, small to large, without adding un-useful complexity.

Compliance and regulations are important issues that will arise as usability of security services starts to grow. As data privacy constraints are becoming more and more strict, especially in the European Union, but also in the US, all services providers manipulating customer data will have to comply with laws and regulations. Ideally, special models of architecture for MSSP will be differentiated from traditional organisational SOCs, because different ownership brings many compliance, but also technical issues.

References

1. Killcrece, G., Kossakowski, K.-P., Ruefle, R., Zajicek, M.: State of the Practice of Computer Security Incident Response Teams (2003)
2. Killcrece, G., Kossakowski, K.-P., Ruegle, R., Zajicek, M.: Organizational Models for Computer Security Incident Response Teams (2003)
3. West-Brown, M.J., Stikvoort, D., Kossakowski, K.-P., Killcrece, G., Ruefle, R., Zajicekm, M.: Handbook for Computer Security Incident Response Teams (CSIRTs) (2003)
4. Zimmerman, C.: Ten Strategies of a World-Class Cybersecurity Operations Centre (2014)

Secure Transaction Authentication Protocol

Pardis Pourghomi[1]([⊠]), Muhammad Qasim Saeed[2], and Pierre E. Abi-Char[1]

[1] College of Engineering and Technology,
The American University of the Middle East, P.O. Box: 220, Dasman 15453, Kuwait
{pardis.pourghomi,pierre.abichar}@aum.edu.kw
[2] Information Security Group, Royal Holloway University of London, Egham, UK
muhammad.saeed.2010@live.rhul.ac.uk

Abstract. A protocol for NFC mobile authentication and transaction is proposed by W. Chen et al. This protocol is used for micropayments, where the Mobile Network Operator pays for its customers. The main advantage of this protocol is its compatibility with the existing GSM network. This paper analyses this protocol from security point of view; as this protocol is used for monetary transactions, it should be as secure as possible. This paper highlights a few security related issues in this protocol. The most serious of all is the authentication of a false Point of Sale terminal by simply replaying the old message. The user interaction with the system also needs improvement. At the end of this paper, we have addressed all the vulnerabilities and proposed an improved version of the existing protocol that caters for such weaknesses. We also added an additional layer of security by 'PIN' authentication in Chen's Protocol.

Keywords: Near field communication · Mobile transaction · Secure protocol

1 Introduction

This paper takes a close look at the authentication and transaction protocol proposed by W. Chen et al. [1]. This protocol is used for payment through mobile device using existing Global System for Mobile Communications (GSM) infrastructure. The protocol first authenticates the mobile device to the Mobile Network Operator (MNO), and after successful authentication, monetary transaction is being performed by the MNO. The mobile device is equipped with the Near Field Communication (NFC) technology. The overall scenario is a user who purchases some goods from a shop and pays through his mobile device. The transaction is being performed through the MNO. The link of the MNO to the banking sector is through the Billing Centre of the MNO. The three major entities in this protocol are the user with mobile device, registered shop with NFC Point-of-Sale (POS) terminal and the MNO. Since this protocol involves monetary transaction, it must be secure against known attacks to maximum possible extent.

© Springer International Publishing AG 2016
I. Bica and R. Reyhanitabar (Eds.): SECITC 2016, LNCS 10006, pp. 261–273, 2016.
DOI: 10.1007/978-3-319-47238-6_19

This paper looks at this protocol from various angles. We have discovered that the protocol has a few vulnerabilities that may be exploited in future. The details of such vulnerabilities are described in Sect. 6.

Apart from discovering the vulnerabilities in the existing protocol, our main contribution is an improved version of this protocol. We have successfully countered the vulnerabilities by proposing a more efficient solution. We have also revised the user interaction with the system making it more user-friendly.

This paper is organized as follows. The first part introduces the NFC technology and its application in the field of m-commerce. After this, the GSM authentication process is explained followed by the Chen's authentication and transaction protocol. It is followed by its vulnerabilities and weaknesses. In the last part, a modified version of the protocol is proposed with the detailed analysis.

2   Near Field Communication

NFC is a short-range wireless technology compatible with contactless smart cards (ISO/IEC 14443) and Radio-Frequency Identification (RFID). NFC communicates on the 13.56 MHz frequency band at a distance of less than 4 cm. It uses magnetic field induction for communication and powering the chip [2].

This technology is now available on the cell phones. Considering the exponential growth in the mobile technology, the use of NFC technology is also on the sharp rise. A wide variety of applications is possible using the technology because of the different operation modes supporting both communication from device to device (peer-to-peer mode), communication between a device and a passive tag (read/write mode) and an emulation mode where the mobile device can act like a contactless smart card [3]. Since this technology has a very short range of operation, it is considered to be hard to eavesdrop. This makes NFC suitable for monetary transaction.

3   Mobile Commerce

Mobile Commerce, also known as m-Commerce, is the ability to conduct commerce using a mobile device, such as a mobile phone, a Personal Digital Assistant (PDA), a smartphone, or other emerging mobile equipment such as dashtop mobile devices. This usually, but not at all times, involve the network carrier. The use of m-commerce has seen rapid growth in the recent years, with several different services like Short Message Service (SMS), Wireless Application Protocol (WAP), Unstructured Supplementary Service Data (USSD) and K-Java on GSM network and NFC. The concept of m-commerce is not matured yet in terms of new technology and modes. Zhang has compared the differences between online payment services and mobile payments. He concluded that the main problem of the m-commerce is the insufficient choice of payment methods [4]. Alpár et al [5] introduced Tap2 technology where the users need only their NFC-enabled mobile devices and credentials implemented on their smart cards.

They proposed the use of NFC technology in the online banking solution based on EMV Chip Authentication Program (EMV-CAP) [6].

The NFC technology over mobile devices has given a new direction to m-commerce. W. Chen et al. proposed an authentication and transaction protocol that utilizes the existing GSM network [1]. In this protocol, the user buys some services and the payment to the shop is made through the MNO of the user. It is mostly suitable for such customers that do not have their bank account; yet people need to be pay bills, receive money from abroad, transfer it between each other, and access microcredit. Since 2010, Orange, a French based telecom company, has launched a project 'Orange Money' in Africa where only 3 to 7 percent of most countries' population have bank accounts. The project is very successful and has tripled its customer base in the past one year [7].

4 GSM Authentication

When a Mobile Station (MS) signs into the network, the Mobile Network Operator (MNO) first authenticates the MS. Authentication verifies the identity and validity of the SIM card and ensures that the subscriber has authorized access to the network. The Authentication Centre (AuC) of the MNO is a responsible to authenticate each SIM card that attempts to connect to the GSM core network through Mobile Switching Centre (MSC). The AuC stores two encryption algorithms A3 and A8, as well as a list of all subscribers' identity along with corresponding secret key K_i. This key is also stored in the SIM. The AuC first generates a random number known as R. This R is used to generate two numbers, signed response S and K_c as shown in Fig. 1, where $S = E_{K_i}(R)$ using A3 algorithm and $K_c = E_{K_i}(R)$ using A8 algorithm. The triplet (R, S, K_c) is known as authentication triplet generated by AuC. AuC sends this triplet to MSC. On receiving a triplet from AuC, MSC sends R (first part of the triplet) to the MS. SIM computes the response S from R, as K_i is already stored in the SIM. MS transmits S to MSC. If this S matches the S in the triplet (which it should in case of a valid SIM), then the mobile is authenticated. K_c is used for communication encryption between the mobile station and the MNO.

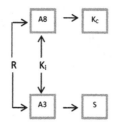

Fig. 1. Generation of K_c and S from R

The following table lists the abbreviations used to describe security properties of the protocols.

AuC	Authentication Centre
HLR	Home Location Register
IMSI	Internet Mobile Subscriber Identity
K_i	SIM specific key. Stored at a secure location in SIM and at AuC
K_c	$E_{k_i}(R)$ using A8 algorithm
K_{c_1}	H(Kc). Used for MAC calculation
K_{c2}	H(K_{c_1}). Encryption key
K_{c_3}	H(K_{c2}). MAC key
K_1	Encryption key generated by shop
K_2	MAC key generated by shop
K_p	Shared key between PG and shop POS terminal
MCC	Mobile Country Code
MNC	Mobile Network Code
MNO	Mobile Network Operator
MSC	Mobile Switching Centre
NFC	Near Field Communication
R	Random Number (128 bits)
R_s	Random number generated by SIM (128 bits)
PI	Payment Information
PF	Payment Flag. It indicates the direction of money flow
PG	Payment Gateway. Part of MNO
POS	Point of Sale. Part of shop
S	Signed Response SRES. $S = S = E_{k_i}(R)$ using A3 algorithm (32 bits)
TC	Transaction counter
TEM	Transaction Execution Message
TI	Transaction Information
TRM	Transaction Request Message
TMSI	Temporary Mobile Subscriber Identity
TP	Total Price
TS_U	User's Time Stamp
TS_B	Billing Centre Time Stamp
VLR	Visitor Location Register

5   Security Model

We need to explain the security model for the purpose of defining the security requirements in the authentication protocol.

- The protocol is compromised when an illegitimate message is accepted as a legitimate message by the receiving entity.

- Separate encryption keys are used for data confidentiality and for data integrity.
- No other than the required information is revealed to a participating entity.
- The communication over NFC is encrypted for data confidentiality.

6   Chen's Protocol

This protocol is used for monetary transaction through MNO. Three basic entities involved are the MNO, shop POS terminal registered with the corresponding MNO and the user who has an NFC enabled mobile device operating with the same MNO. The user buys some items from the shop and pays through his mobile device. He places his mobile device on the shop POS terminal, the mutual authentication occurs between the mobile device and the MNO. The MNO billing centre makes the payment against the specific user after successful authentication. This protocol is subdivided into three parts; Price checking, Triple Authentication and Transaction execution. The detail of the execution of this protocol is available at [1].

6.1   Analysis of the Existing Protocol

Mutual authentication between the Mobile device and the MNO is performed from step 10 to 13. Payment Gateway (PG), a part of MNO, receives authentication triplet (R, S, K_c) from MSC. PG initializes a challenge response mutual authentication protocol by sending $R, MAC_{K_c}(R)$ to the mobile device through the shop POS terminal in step 10. Once user SIM receives $R, MAC_{K_c}(R)$, it first computes K_c from R and K_i (already stored in the SIM), as mentioned in Sect. 4. SIM generates MAC on the received R and compares with the received MAC. Correct matching verifies the correctness of R and authentication of shop PG and the MNO. In step 13, the SIM transmits response of the challenge as $E_{S_1}(R)$, where $S_1 = H(S)$.

6.2   False POS Terminal Attack

A legitimate $R, MAC_{K_c}(R)$ pair always remains valid irrespective of SIM location, time or any other variable for a specific SIM. This pair is transmitted in step 10 of the protocol. This message can be eavesdropped by an attacker or if the shopkeeper is dishonest, he can keep the record of such pairs of its target customers. If such pair is replayed by a false POS terminal to the same mobile device to which it was transmitted earlier, the MAC will be valid resulting in successful authentication of the false POS terminal. Although False POS terminal attack gets detected during the transaction execution part of this protocol, an exploit may develop in future based on this vulnerability.

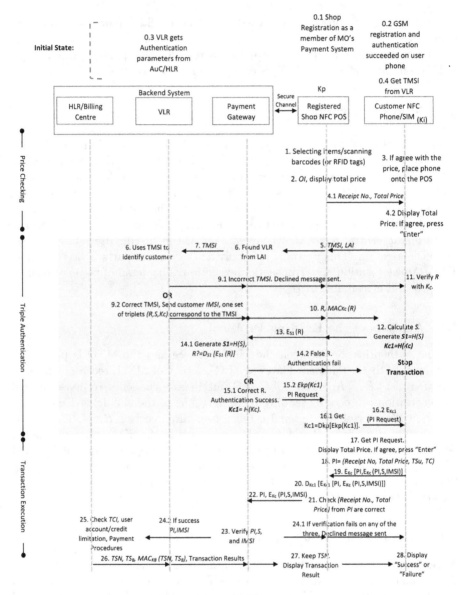

Fig. 2. GSM authentication and transaction (Chen's protocol [1])

6.3   Challenge Response Pairing

During the mutual authentication phase of the protocol, no freshness is added by the mobile device to compute the response. Therefore, a specific R, $MAC_{K_c}(R)$ message to a SIM in step 10 will always result in the same response in step 13. In this way, various challenge-response pairs can be generated for a particular SIM (Fig. 2).

6.4   Weak Key Authentication

R is encrypted by key S_1 while computing the response in step 13, where $S_1 = H(S)$. S is a 32-bit number so the entropy of key S_1 is only 2^{32}. $S1$ is computed by the PG and the mobile device to get a shared secret; whereas K_c is already available on both sides as a shared secret. This results in additional computational overhead.

6.5   User Interaction

A user is required to press 'Enter' after step 4.1 if he agrees to the total price. Mutual authentication process gets initiated by this action. The user is required to press 'enter' again if he agrees to the price at the end of the authentication process (step 17). As the authentication process takes a negligible amount of time, the user has to interact twice for the same information being displayed and with the same action. This may result in user annoyance. Moreover, the transaction is not protected by a PIN verification so a user may feel less secure.

6.6   Unexplained Terminologies

There are a few unexplained terminologies in the existing protocol. In step 26, HLR/Billing centre sends a message to shop POS terminal and the user for the confirmation of billing deduction. This information contains $TSN, TS_B, MAC_{K_B} (TSN, TS_B)$, and *Transaction Result*. The authors have not explained MAC key K_B and TS_B. Moreover, a different message (TSN, $E_{K_c} \{TSN\}$) for step 26 is suggested in [1], section IV, Scenario 2, para 3.

6.7   Extra Computations

In step 19, the user encrypts PI, S, $IMSI$ with K_c and appends the Payment Information PI to it. The user encrypts the entire message with K_{c1}, whereas only the PI needs encryption.

7   Modification in the Existing Protocol

We assume that the communication is secure between various subsystems of the MNO. The shop POS terminal, registered with one or more MNO, shares an MNO specific secret key K_p with the corresponding MNO. This key is issued once a shop is registered with the MNO. The bank details of the shopkeeper is also registered with the MNO for monetary transactions. The communication between the shop POS terminal and the mobile device is wireless using NFC technology. The mobile device has a valid SIM.

Steps 1–3. All the purchased items are scanned and the list with total price is displayed to the user. If the user agrees to the price, he places his mobile device at the NFC enabled place for the payment.

Step 4. As soon as the user places his mobile device, NFC link between the mobile device and the shop POS terminal is established. The shop POS terminal sends an ID Request message to the mobile device.

Steps 5–6. The mobile device sends TMSI, LAI as its ID. On receipt of the information from the mobile device, the shop POS terminal determines the user's mobile network. The network code is available in LAI in the form of Mobile Country Code (MCC) and Mobile Network Code (MNC). An MNC is used in combination with MCC (also known as a 'MCC/MNC tuple') to uniquely identify a mobile phone operator/carrier [6].

Steps 7–8. The shop POS terminal sends TMSI, LAI to respective MNO for customer authentication.

Steps 9.1–9.2. In case of incorrect TMSI, a declined message is sent. Else, MSC sends one set of authentication triplet (R, S, K_c) and corresponding IMSI to payment gateway PG.

Step 10. PG sends R to mobile device through shop POS terminal.

Step 11. SIM computes K_c from R as explained in Sect. 4. SIM generates a random number R_s and concatenates with R, encrypts with key K_c and sends it to PG through shop POS terminal.

Step 12. The PG checks the validity of the SIM (or mobile device). The PG receives $E_{K_c}(R\|R_s)$ from the mobile device. The PG decrypts the message by K_c, the key it already has in authentication triplet. The PG compares R in the authentication triplet with the R in the response. In case they do not match, a 'Stop' message is sent to the mobile device and the protocol execution is stopped. If both Rs are same, then the mobile is authenticated for a valid SIM. In this case, the PG swaps R and R_s, encrypts with K_c and sends it to mobile device.

Steps 13–14. This step authenticates the PG (or MNO). The mobile device receives the response $E_{K_c}(R_s\|R)$ and decrypts it with the key K_c already computed in Step 11. The mobile device compares both R and R_s. If both are same, then the PG is authenticated and a 'successful authentication' message is sent to PG.

Step 15. Key Generation Phase. K_p is a shared secret between PG and the shop POS terminal. K_c is the shared secret between PG and the customer's mobile device (computed in step 11). K_c is used for encrypting communication between both entities. PG and mobile device compute one-way hash function of K_c to generate K_{c1}, the key for MAC calculation. There is no shared secret between the POS terminal and the mobile device till this stage. PG computes K_{c2} from K_{c1} using one-way hash function and sends it to shop POS terminal by encrypting it with K_p. Mobile device can compute K_{c2} as it already has K_{c1}. K_{c2} is the encryption key between PG, shop POS terminal and the customer's mobile device. All three entities compute one-way hash function of K_{c2} to generate K_{c3}, the key for MAC computation (Fig. 4).

Steps 16–18. The shop POS terminal sends Payment Information (PI) request to the mobile device along with the Payment Flag, Total Price and the Receipt Number encrypted with K_{c2}. Payment Flag is a one bit flag which determines the direction of money flow. If clear, the money is transferred from MNO to the

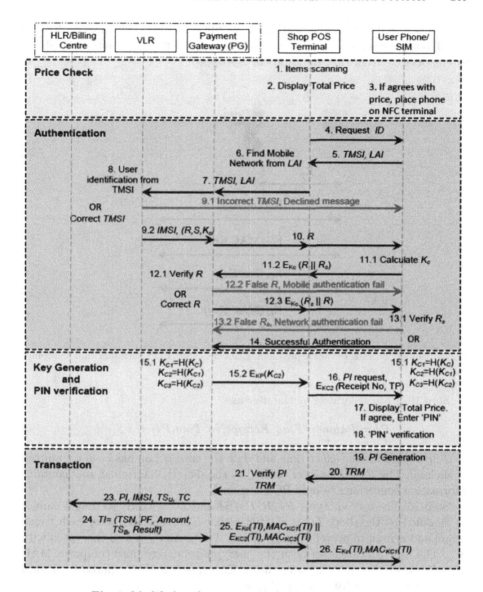

Fig. 3. Modified authentication and transaction protocol

shopkeeper, otherwise in opposite direction which corresponds to return of goods to the shopkeeper by the user. The user's mobile device decrypts the information and displays to the user. If he agrees, he enters the PIN. The PIN is an additional layer of security and adds trust between the user and the shopkeeper. A PIN binds a user with his mobile device, so the shopkeeper is to believe that the user is the legitimate owner of the mobile device. Moreover, the user feels more secure as no one else can use his mobile device for transaction without his consent (Fig. 3).

PIN is stored in a secure location in the SIM. The SIM compares both PINs and if both are same, the user is authenticated as the legitimate user of the mobile device. Otherwise, the protocol is stopped.

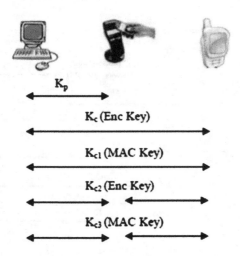

Fig. 4. Shared secrets between payment gateway, shop POS terminal and customer mobile

Step 19. PI is generated by the user as:

$$PI = PaymentFlag, ReceiptNo, TotalPrice, TS_U$$

TS_U represents the exact time and date the transaction has been committed by the user. The PI will be later verified by the shop POS terminal, so it contains information concerning to only POS terminal.

Step 20. The user encrypts $PI, R, TMSI$ and TC with K_c so that it cannot be modified by the shop. TC is a counter that is incremented after each transaction and is used to prevent replay attack. The same PI is also encrypted with K_{c_2}. The user concatenates both the encrypted messages and computes MAC with K_{c_1} over the entire message using Encrypt-then-MAC approach to form Transaction Request Message (TRM) as:

$$TRM = [E_{K_{c_2}}(PI)||E_{K_c}(PI, R, TMSI, TC)], MAC_{K_{c_1}}$$

Steps 21–22. The POS terminal can decrypt only the first part of the message encrypted with by K_{c2} to check the correctness of PI. POS terminal does not need to verify the MAC (and it cannot do so), as it already knows the main contents of PI. Shop POS terminal also verifies the TS_U to be in a defined time window. If PI is correct, the POS terminal relays the entire message to the PG.

Steps 23–24. First of all, the PG checks the integrity of the message by verifying the MAC with K_{c_1}. If the MAC is invalid, the transaction execution is stopped. In case of valid MAC, the PG decrypts the message as it has both the keys, K_c and K_{c_2}. It compares the PI information in both parts of the message. If both PIs are same, the PG compares the $TMSI$ and the R with the information it received in Step 7 and step 9.2 respectively. The correct match confirms that the user is the same who was authenticated. PG checks for the IMSI against received R from step 9.2. PG sends the PI, $IMSI$, TS_U and TC to the Billing Centre.

The Billing Centre checks for the user's account limitations against the $IMSI$ provided. It also verifies the TC and TS_U. In case of successful verification, the Billing Centre executes the transaction and generates Transaction Information (TI) (as shown below) and sends it to PG.

$$TI = TSN, PaymentFlag, Amount, TSB, Result$$

Steps 25–26. The PG encrypts TI with K_c and K_{c_2}, and computes MAC with K_{c_1} and K_{c_3} to form a Transaction Execution Message (TEM) as:

$$TEM = E_{K_c}(TI), MAC_{K_{c_1}}(TI) \| E_{K_{c2}}(TI), MAC_{K_{c3}}(TI)$$

Both MACs are computed using encrypt-then-MAC approach and the entire message is transmitted to the shop POS terminal. The Shop POS terminal checks for the validity of the second half of the TEM, and if found valid, sends the first half of the TEM to the user. The customer's mobile device checks the integrity of the message, decrypts the TI and checks for the transaction result. It also computes the time difference between TS_U and TS_B. If this difference is greater than a specified limit, it warns the user to verify the transaction through some other means.

7.1   Protocol Analysis

No False POS Terminal Attack: During the mutual authentication of PG and the user, the PG has to encrypt the user's random number R_s with K_c. Similarly, there is no possibility for challenge-response pairing as every challenge gets a different response even from the same SIM.

The keys used for encryption and MAC calculation ($K_c, K_{c_1}, K_{c_2}, K_{c_3}$) are 64 bit keys, so the problem of weak keys in the existing protocol is resolved. This key length cannot be increased because of the limitation of the GSM specification, where K_c is 64 bit key.

The user interaction has been improved to a single interaction, rather than twice, with the system. The user feels more secure as the transaction is protected by 'PIN' verification. There are chances that a user withdraws his mobile device from NFC terminal as a psychological move to enter 'PIN'. This will break NFC link, but as the PIN is stored in the SIM, it does not require NFC link for verification. Once the user PIN has been verified by the SIM, the user places his mobile device back on the NFC terminal and the protocol resume from the same point.

There are chances that a dishonest user withdraws his mobile device in order to enter the PIN, and then places back another mobile device for transaction. To counter this threat, R and $TMSI$ are transmitted by the mobile device in Transaction Request Message (TRM). This ensures that the mobile device does not change.

Separate keys are used for encryption and MAC calculation making the protocol more secure. Encrypt-then MAC is an approach where the ciphertext is generated by encrypting the plaintext and then appending a MAC of the encrypted plaintext. This approach is cryptographically more secure than other approaches [8]. Apart from cryptographic advantage, the MAC can be verified without even performing decryption. So if the MAC is invalid for a message, the message is discarded without decryption. This results in computational efficiency.

K_p is the long term secret so it is used only once.

An IMSI is a unique identification associated with all GSM and UMTS network mobile phone users. It is sent as rarely as possible, to avoid it being identified and tracked. In our proposed protocol IMSI in never transmitted by the mobile device.

TC is a counter that increments after each successful transaction. The record of the TC is kept by both SIM and the Billing Centre. Shop POS terminal does not need to know the TC. In our proposed protocol, the TC is not exposed to POS terminal, in contrast to the Chen's protocol where TC was a part of PI and was exposed to the POS terminal.

No computation of S by the mobile device.

8   Conclusion

In this paper, a security analysis is carried out of an existing protocol that is used for monetary transactions using GSM network. It is discovered that the existing protocol is vulnerable to false POS terminal authentication attack, weak keys and inconvenient user interaction. We proposed an improved version of this protocol that caters for the weaknesses of the existing protocol. We provide freshness in the authentication part by introducing randomness by the mobile device. The entropy of the encryption keys are increased to 64 bits from 32 bits. We have added another security layer by introducing 'PIN' authentication. This binds a user with his mobile device making the system more secure and user friendly.

References

1. Chen, W., Hancke, G.P., Mayes, K.E., Lien, Y., Chiu, J.H.: NFC mobile transactions and authentication based on GSM network. In: 2nd International Workshop on Near Field Communication, pp. 83–89. IEEE press (2010)
2. Mulliner, C.: Vulnerability analysis and attacks on NFC-enabled mobile phones. In: International Conference on Availability, Reliability and Security, pp. 695–700. IEEE press (2009)

3. Saeed, M.Q., Walter, C.D.: A record composition/decomposition attack on the NDEF signature record type definition. In: 6th International Conference for Internet Technology and Secured Transactions, pp. 283–287. IEEE press (2011)

4. Zhang, Q.: Mobile payment in mobile e-commerce. In: 7th World Congress on Intelligent Control and Automation, pp. 6650–6654. IEEE press (2008)

5. Alpár, G., Batina, L., Verdult, R.: Using NFC phones for proving credentials. In: Schmitt, J.B. (ed.) MMB & DFT 201. LNCS, vol. 7201, pp. 317–330. Springer, Heidelberg (2012)

6. Murdoch, S.J., Drimer, S., Anderson, R., Bond, M.: Chip and PIN is broken. In: IEEE Symposium on Security and Privacy, pp. 433–446. IEEE press (2010)

7. Kamau, M.: Orange money triples its customer numbers in Africa. http://www.standardmedia.co.ke/?id=2000047310&catid_=14&a=1.&articleID=2000047310

8. Bellare, M., Namprempre, C.: Authenticated encryption: relations among notions and analysis of the generic composition paradigm. In: Okamoto, T. (ed.) ASIACRYPT 2000. LNCS, vol. 1976, pp. 531–545. Springer, Heidelberg (2000). doi:10.1007/3-540-44448-3_41

Proposed Scheme for Data Confidentiality and Access Control in Cloud Computing

Ana-Maria Ghimeş$^{(\boxtimes)}$ and Victor Valeriu Patriciu

Military Technical Academy, Doctoral School, Bucharest, Romania
ghimes.ana@gmail.com

Abstract. Nowadays, cloud computing is the main core of IT development. Due to its security issues and lack of security mechanisms, users are delaying the fast adoption of this technology. The privacy of data is usually limited by access policies for resources provided by cloud vendors, but nobody can confirm that only authorized entities have access to them. The present paper provides a practical solution to important security issues encountered in the cloud: privacy, confidentiality and access control. For preventing unauthorized access, the data is encrypted using Key-Aggregate Algorithm before being uploaded to the cloud. Commutative encryption is used for Key Management. There are also third party services that handle keeping the keys safe and controlling the access policies.

Keywords: Cloud computing · Encryption · Key-Aggregate · Policy management · Access control

1 Introduction

The term Cloud has been used for a long time as a metaphor on the Internet. This concept has been evolving over the years and has become the central core of IT development. Cloud computing is a kind of Internet-based computing that provides shared processing resources and data to computers and other services on demand [1]. The majority of cloud computing infrastructures are represented by tested and trusted services that are delivered from different servers which support a great variety of technologies for virtualization. Cloud services are accessible wherever an Internet connection is available. Cloud computing is not only about the services it offers, but also about the hardware and software providing those services.

According to NIST, the essential characteristics that define cloud computing are [2]:

- On-demand self-service
- Broad network access
- Resource pooling
- Rapid elasticity
- Measured service

© Springer International Publishing AG 2016
I. Bica and R. Reyhanitabar (Eds.): SECITC 2016, LNCS 10006, pp. 274–285, 2016.
DOI: 10.1007/978-3-319-47238-6_20

There are six principles of cloud computing that one must take into consideration when using it [3]:

- The Enablement Principle (think of cloud computing more as a strategic helper than as an outsourcing platform)
- The Cost/Benefit Risk Principle
- The Capability Principle
- The Accountability Principle
- The Trust Principle (when using this kind of platform, you must trust all the services and processes that are offered by cloud computing)

According to these principles, the main idea of cloud computing is for the user to pay only for what he is using, depending on business requirements. You can choose from three approaches regarding the type of services that you need: Infrastructure as a Service (IaaS), Software as a Service (SaaS) and Platform as a Service (PaaS). Also, some vendors can offer different environments for the cloud: private cloud, community cloud, public cloud, hybrid cloud.

When using cloud computing, you are exposing your data to different security problems and risks. The privacy of data represents an important security issue for most of the organizations [4]. Before migrating applications to the cloud, the data owner must clearly identify objects, services and processes with whom his applications will interact in order to ensure the security level required for his data. There are some security services that must exist in all cloud computing environments:

- Ensuring the privacy of the data
- Keeping the integrity of the data
- Guaranteeing availability
- Secure access to data
- Rules and obligations
- Auditing services

Confidentiality of data must be at the core of data protection. In cloud computing, it is important for this security feature to be offered and used because of the cloud computing vulnerabilities like unauthorized access or data leaks. Most of the vulnerabilities are determined by remote data storage, undefined borders for the network, third party services offered by untrusted vendors, multi-tenant infrastructure and unlimited sharing.

Moreover, in cloud computing, there are always new technologies being integrated which can generate more vulnerabilities as far as the implementation and design are concerned. When you want to introduce new security methods, you must take the following factors into consideration: data security vs data usability and the scalability of the system.

The safest security method to ensure confidentiality of the data is encryption. The data will be encrypted before it is stored, processed and sent to cloud servers. Then, the key management problem must be solved. There are some issues that may appear when the data is encrypted. How will the decryption keys be efficiently distributed to the authorized users, how will changes and permission granting be taken into consideration, how will operations be performed over the data.

2   Encryption Algorithms in Cloud Computing

In the last decades, the study of elliptic curves has become the central subject of many security related research papers. Elliptic curves based cryptography (ECC) has been intensively used in public-key protocols, like digital signatures and key management. The benefits of using elliptic curves in cryptography are the smaller dimensions of keys and more efficient schemes that are preserving the same security level (e.g. RSA) [5].

The most known usages of elliptic curves are in Bitcoin, Transport Layer Security (TLS) and Austrian e-ID [5].

The field of PairingBased Cryptography has experienced an excellent growth in the last few years. The main idea is the construction of a mapping between two cryptographic groups which permit the creation of a new scheme based on the reduction of a problem from a group to an easier and different problem in another group.

A mapping represents a function which receives as inputs two points on an elliptic curve and returns an element from an abelian multiplicative group.

2.1   Key-Aggregate Encryption

Key-Aggregate Cryptosystem is an encryption scheme with aggregate keys and is developed using five polynomial-time algorithms.

The data owner is establishing the public parameter in the Setup phase using a random bilinear group G, a generator for this group $g \in G$ and a random variable, $\alpha \in_R \mathbb{Z}_p$. Every ciphertext class is represented by an integer from $\{1, 2, ...,n\}$ set, where n is the number of ciphertexts. Using the public parameter, the data owner will generate the public-master pair of keys using the KeyGen method (pk-public key, msk -master secret key).

Each message will be encrypted using the Encrypt method which receives as parameters the public key pk and the index for ciphertext i from $\{1,2,...,n\}$. The algorithm encrypts the message and produces a ciphertext that only a user with a set of specific attributes can decrypt. Then, the owner of the data will be using the master key and the set of indices of permitted messages to access for generating the aggregate key for decryption). Any user who has the decryption key will decrypt any ciphertext contained in the classes for which the aggregate key was generated [6].

2.2   Attribute-Based Encryption

There are two main ABE schemes: Key-Policy ABE (KP-ABE) and Ciphertext-Policy ABE (CP-ABE). ABE Encryption, based on attributes, is a generalization of the identity-based encryption scheme which attributes sets embedded at a cryptographic primitives level. The ABE schemes are public keys schemes of type one to many. The encryption method is available to be executed by many users, but the decryption method will be accessible only for the users with certain attributes. In this scenario, the decryption will be possible only if a set of attributes from the user key will match the attributes from the ciphertext. The main drawback of these schemes is considered to be the usage of unique Trust Authority. This third party is generating a vulnerable and critical point at the system level, because it has access to all available decryption keys.

The KP-ABE schemes offer a better and more flexible data access control. Ciphertexts are marked with a set of attributes and the private keys are mapped to access structures which control what ciphertext a user can decrypt. The data can be encrypted with public keys generated inside the scheme or alternatively, optimized hybrid schemes can be used. The KP-ABE scheme is based on Linear Secret Sharing Schemes. There are four algorithms used: the Setup algorithm run by TA (which will generate the public key PK and a master key MK held by TA), the Encryption algorithm run by the data owner (will receive as inputs: the message M, the public key PK and a set of attributes), the Key Generation algorithm run by TA (will receive as inputs: an access structure T and the master secret key MK and will return a secret key SK), the Decryption algorithm ran by the user of the data (will receive as inputs: the secret key SK and the encrypted text with the attributes set A, will return the initial message M only if the attributes set A will satisfy the access structure T from secret key SK). A limitation of this type of system is that the owner of data cannot choose who will decrypt his data, he can only establish the set of attributes on which TA will generate the access structure and he must trust the TA [7].

The CP-ABE schemes are similar to the KP-ABE schemes with the difference that data associations are made between two components Private Key, Ciphertext and Access Policy, Attributes Set. In CP-ABE, every ciphertext has an access policy and every private key has an associated set of attributes [7]. The decryption of an encrypted message can be made only if the associated set of attributes with the private key will satisfy the access policy associated with the ciphertext. The access policy is enciphered at the ciphertext level and it will permit the decryption only for the private keys that contain the necessary attributes. The major difference is that the owner of the data will establish the access structure to the encrypted data. The TA will authorize users at key generation time.

2.3   Homomorphic Encryption

Homomorphic systems are used for performing different operations over encrypted data without knowing the secret key, the owner of data being the only one who is holding the secret key. When the result of any operations is decrypted, this is similar to the result of the operations computed over plaintext data. An entity should be able to send an encrypted message to another and also to receive results based on operations performed on encrypted data. The results should also be encrypted and the server would not have access to the decryption keys and data. The server knows only the processing algorithm. The main idea is that any operation, algorithm or program can be reduced to basic operations such as addition or multiplication on bits. Moreover, data is encrypted before being sent to the cloud and the encryption scheme should be of a homomorphic type. Every homomorphic scheme is based on a so-called difficult problem. There is, nevertheless, a certain issues regarding this type of encryption; is it efficient for cloud computing? The efficiency should be analyzed by verifying the necessary time required to implement the encryption/decryption algorithms and the necessary computational resources for both the client and the server.

This mechanism is used for hiding information and the fully-homomorphic schemes are based on an accumulation of random "noise" which will make text illegible after encryption. The main problem in this type of schemes is the growth of noise information once the operations are performed over encrypted text. Moreover, this noise should be kept in a limited range. A solution to these issues is to use a refreshing technique (bootstrapping) which will diminish the quantity of noise and readmission it in the mathematical range which will allow consistent mathematic operations and decryptions.

2.4 Traditional Encryption Algorithms

For ensuring data privacy, traditional cryptographic techniques based on symmetric algorithms (e.g. AES, Blowfish, 3DES) or asymmetric algorithms (e.g. RSA, El Gamal, ECC) can be used. The most used schemes are based on the AES algorithm for protecting data and RSA algorithm for safely delivering it. The data is encrypted on the client side using AES algorithm and is sent to the cloud for storage. For keeping the integrity of data, digital signature based on RSA algorithm is used [8]. The main advantage in using this hybrid scheme is that data is not available at the server level.

3   Access Control Mechanisms

3.1 Policy Management as a Service (PMaaS)

A central management system of access policies for the cloud resources improves the quality of security services, offering a better vision of overall security criteria that would apply to the organization's services.

This type of management is based on the concept of centralizing all the security requirements that could apply to all the resources stored in different cloud systems/data-centers. The components of this service have different roles like cloud user, policy management service, cloud service provider (CSP), the requester. The components of the service are: policy editor (behaves as a Policy Administration Point and offers a single interface to manage all the access policies and also, allows for registering of cloud users and makes recommendations based on resources stored in the cloud), policy server (behaves as a Policy Information Point and is responsible for the interactions between the policy editor and the cloud vendor and also for translating natural language into machine language; it is also responsible for granting access to resources) [9].

A Policy Management Service acts as KDC (Key Distribution Center) for key management. It also has the role of trusted authority, because it will keep the decryption key for documents and will control access to resources.

3.2   Attribute Based Encryption and Key Distribution Center

The scheme proposed by G. Lenin et al. [10] for securing data storage and decentralized access control is to use the encryption/decryption RSA algorithm with a 2048-bit key. The keys will be stored in four different locations. If the user wants to access the documents he must have the four sets of keys (from four locations) to obtain the secret key for encryption/decryption. When the client wants to upload a document, he must make a request to the key manager for the public key, which will be generated regarding the associated policies. The policies are different for each document, so the public keys will be different too. For every public key, there will be only one access policy. Then, the client will generate a private key using his security credentials. After obtaining the secret key, the document will be encrypted and sent to the cloud server.

When the client wants to download documents, he must first authenticate and then he will ask the KDC for the public key. Then, the authenticated client can decrypt the documents using public and private keys. User credentials are stored on the client side and, during the download, the cloud server will authenticate the user to see if it is a valid one.

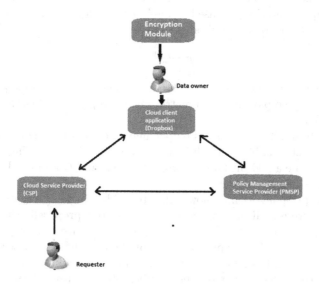

Fig. 1. Main components of the proposed scheme

4   Proposed Solution

We propose a framework based on some of the presented solutions in the previous sections which have the potential of giving good results for a cloud platform with the minimum amount of resources.

The main components can be observed in Fig. 1. They include an encryption component installed on the client side, a cloud client application which will access the cloud service provider environment (CSP) and a policy management service provider (PMSP).

4.1   Encryption Module

The encryption component is developed using Key Aggregate Algorithm as mentioned in 2.1. For implementing this algorithm, the PBC (Pairing-Based Cryptography) Library and the GMP library (GNU Multiple Precision Arithmetic Library) were used. The API was developed in C++ and was integrated into a cloud client application as a DLL (Dynamic Link Library). The purpose of using KAC was to encrypt as many documents as we can without increasing the key dimension. The algorithm allows the user to encrypt a message using a public key system and brings a new concept to identify the ciphertext called class (the encrypted texts are categorized in different classes). The owner of the data holds the master secret key called master-key, which is used for generating the aggregate keys for different classes. The aggregate key is as compact as a key for a single class, but it has the power of many keys (e.g. with an aggregate key you can decrypt a set of ciphertexts that belong to the subset of classes) [6].

In our implementation, we used Type-A pairings for a number of ciphertexts until 2^{16}, which are constructed on the curve:

$$y^2 = x^3 + x \tag{1}$$

over the field F_q for some prime ($q = 3 \bmod 4$). The order r is some prime factor of $q + 1$. This type o pairing is symmetric since groups $G1$ and $G2$ are the group of points $E(F_q)$.

In PBC library, Type-A curves (supersingular) offers the highest eficiency of all the types of curves. In our module, we use a generator for pairing parameters. We choose p to be a 160-bit Solinas prime number, and G and G_T be two cyclic bilinear groups of prime order p.

This encryption algorithm allows Alice to send a single aggregate key to Bob through a secure e-mail or using a service (as in our proposed scheme). Then, using this key, Bob can decrypt the documents from Alice's cloud provider (e.g. Dropbox). The sizes of the ciphertext, the public key, the master secret key and the aggregate key in KAC algorithm are constant. The public system parameter has linear growth depending on the number of ciphertext classes and it can be stored in a non-confidential store in the cloud. Figure 2 presents how KAC algorithm is implemented in our solution.

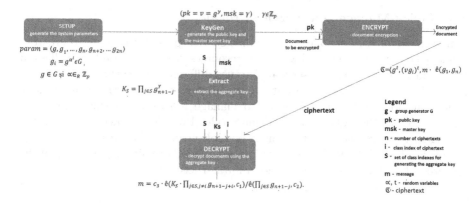

Fig. 2. Key-Aggregate cryptosystem

In our tests, we observed that the master secret key has a constant size of 20 bytes. Also, the size of the aggregate key is constant and it has 128 bytes, as well as the ciphertext size.

For the client cloud application, we implemented a Dropbox Client using the REST API offered by Dropbox. The application was implemented using C# and the Nemiro library

4.2 Key Management

For passing the aggregate key, we suggest encrypting the key using commutative encryption. We have taken into consideration the following scenario: Alice, who is the owner of the data, wishes to share her files stored on Dropbox (cloud) with Bob. Alice encrypts her files before uploading them to Dropbox. Then, she extracts the aggregate key that she wants to pass to Bob. After this phase, she must encrypt the aggregate key using different layers of commutative encryption. After the key is encrypted, it is stored in PMS (Policy Management Service). In the first phase, Alice encrypts the aggregate key using commutative encryption and transmits the encrypted key to CSP (Cloud Service Provider). The CSP will add another encryption layer and it returns the encrypted key to Alice. Then, Alice removes her encrypted layer and the encrypted key is safely stored in the PMSP. After beeing stored in the PMSP, the encrypted key is ready to be distributed to any requester for whom access was granted.

The documents are shared under the access policies which are defined by the owner of the data. If for Bob access was granted, he will download the documents from the CSP to decrypt the data, Bob needs the aggregate key from the PMSP. After receiving the encrypted key, Bob will add a new layer of encryption to the key and will send the key to CSP. CSP will remove its layer from the encrypted key and it will send the encrypted key to Bob. Bob will decrypt the key and can have the plain aggregate key to decrypt his documents.

4.3   Policy Management Service Provider

Management of access policies through a service provider intends to create a single access point to control access to resources stored on cloud regardless of the cloud vendor. When a user wants to use different applications and services for storing and analyzing the data from different vendors (financial services, education, etc.), it would be easier to manage it through a single interface. The purpose of the Policy Management Service Provider is to centralize all the management tasks and also, to identify possible errors and inconsistencies found in policies. Using this type of service, a user can define a single policy for all the resources distributed on different cloud infrastructures.

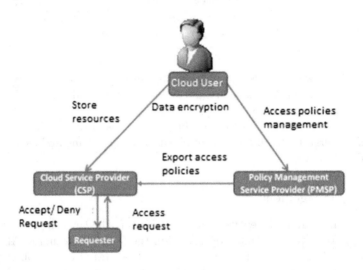

Fig. 3. Workflow using PMSP

The main components of PMSP were defined in 3.1. The purpose of using a service to manage the access policies is to create a single access point through which a user can control the access to resources stored in the cloud, regarding the cloud vendor. Every cloud environment offers its own solution for controlling access and a custom authorization mechanism which, most of the time, do not address every security requirement that a user needs. Usually, the clients use different control mechanisms for every cloud vendor for securing their data and control access to it. When this kind of mechanisms are used, a large overhead is added, because these services are difficult to manage when trying to accomplish even certain vital features. This service should allow on-boarding of all cloud vendors, discovery of all user resources from every cloud vendor and defining the custom access policies (Fig. 3).

To develop this type of service, we use the XACML ("eXtensible Access Control Markup Language") standard to define the access policies. This standard defines a declarative language for implementing access control policies and a processing model which describes how the requests will be evaluated under the policies' rules. XACML implements a system based on attributes (Attribute Based Access Control), where the attributes associated with a user, an action or a resource represent entries in decision-making mechanism: if a user would have permission to a resource or not.

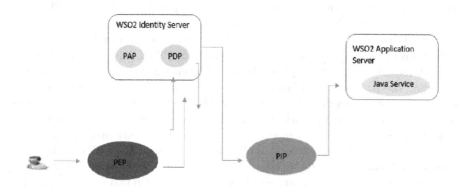

Fig. 4. Policy management service provider workflow

In our proposed solution, we generate the access policies for resources using Java and AXIOMATIC libraries. For implementing these services, we use WSO2 Identity Server and WSO2 Application Server. In Fig. 4, the workflow in PMSP using the elements mentioned above is explained. The request of a user is sent using PEP (Policy Enforcement Point). The policy is written using PAP (Policy Administration Point) from the Identity Server and published in PDP (Policy Decision Point). When the request was received by the Entitlement Engine, this will take the username from the web service through PIP (Policy Information Point). In the Identity Server, the user can establish policy information points (PIP) for extracting informations about authorization. After establishing these points, access policies will be defined through the Identity Server (policy name, rules etc). For example, if Alice wants to give Bob the right to read some documents for a certain information.

4.4 Performance End Efficiency of the Proposed Scheme

The Key-Aggregate Cryptosystem represents an efficient way to preserve data privacy in cloud computing. In our tests, we have noticed that it is sufficient to use Type-A pairing for a maximum number of 65536 classes and for this approach, the compression factor F is equal to n-number of cipher texts. The system parameters require approximately 2.6 megabytes. While encryption can be done in a constant amount of time, the decryption has linear growth depending on the set of cipher texts decryptable by the granted aggregate key ($|S| < n$). Decryption can be done in $O(|S|)$ group multiplications with 2 pairing operations [6]. For a larger number of ciphertexts, Cheng et al. [6] it is recommended to deploy this scheme using Type-D pairing, which requires 170-bits for the representation of an element in G. For a better performance, we precompute $\hat{e}(g_1, g_2)$ since it is exponentiated many times across different encryptions. Since cloud computing, doesnt allow to use a single authorization mechanism or a single management tool, we proposed to use a third party provider which will control access to resources and will offer a single access point to manage and use the same access policies in multiple CSPs. One limitation of using this type of services is the fact that authorization mechanisms are bound to service providers (each CSP has its own mechanisms). Also, the configurations of these applications cannot be easily modified to address all the users security requirements. Developing this type of services may encounter some issues regarding the access control language. Another limitation may be the fact that some cloud service vendors do not use XACML language for specific access policies and may lead to policy conflicts. The advantage of using this service is also the time spent learning interfaces and how management tools work in one single application. A user will learn only one application and not all the CSPs applications interfaces and workflows and will share his resources more efficiently and securely. In our scheme, the implementation of this services required two machines, one for the server and one for the client. The tests consisted in launching multiple threads, each representing a resource from different CSPs. The purpose of our tests was to stress the policy management system with concurrent requests. Also, we use PMSP as a KDC (Key Distribution Center), but the aggregate-keys are generated only by the owner of the data who holds the master-secret key. We assume that between CSPs and PMSP there are no trust relationships. For the key to be transmitted securely between parties, we use commutative encryption, but other security mechanism can also be used which are more efficient and are not adding overhead in the scheme.

5   Conclusion

We presented a secure scheme for storing documents in the cloud and for restricting access to documents based on access control policies. From data security challenge standpoint, there are three types of data in the cloud: data that is just stored by cloud services, stored user data and also transition data between client and cloud services. There is no complete and efficient faultless solution to protect all data. Encrypting data is an element of cost, especially for large amounts of data. It is recommended that we encrypt only important data. The key element in these processes is the choice of encryption algorithms. The main characteristics taken into consideration for choosing KAC algorithm were: complexity, resources and feasibility. In the proposed solution, key management, sending the keys in a safe way and access policies management represent important components in creating a secure application. The complexity of the scheme consists of creating an efficient policy management service provider which adds another security layer over the encrypted data.

References

1. Cloud Computing. https://en.wikipedia.org/wiki/Cloud_computing
2. Mell, P., Grance, T.: The NIST Definition of Cloud Computing. Special Publication 800–145, September 2011
3. ISACA Issues Six Principles for Effective Cloud Computing. ISACA (2012). http://www.isaca.org/About-ISACA/Press-room/News-Releases/2012/Pages/ISACA-IssuesSix-Principles-for-Effective-Cloud-Computing.aspx
4. Aich, A., Sen, A.: Study on cloud security risk and remedy. Int. J. Grid Distrib. Comput. **8**, 155–156 (2015)
5. Box, J.W., et al.: Elliptic Curve Cryptography in Practice, Eprint IACR (2013). http://eprint.iacr.org/
6. Chu, C.-K., Chow, S.S.M., Tzeng, W.-G., Zhou, J., Deng, R.H.: Key-Aggregate cryptosystem for scalable data sharing in cloud storage. IEEE Trans. Parallel Distrib. Syst. **25**(2), 468–477 (2013)
7. Bobba, R., Khurana, H., Prabhakaran, M.: AttributeSets: a practically motivated enhancement to attribute-based encryption, computer security. In: 14th European Symposium on Research in Computer Security, ESORICS 2009, vol. 5789, pp. 587–604 (2009)
8. RSA Data Protection Manager for cloud. http://india.emc.com/collateral/white-papers/h11748-rsa-data-protectionmanager-afore-cloudlink-seucre-vsa.pdf
9. Maui, H.I.: Policy management as a service: an approach to manage policy heterogeneity in cloud computing environment. In: 2012 45th Hawaii International Conference on System Science (HICSS), pp. 5500–5508. IEEE, 4–7 January 2012
10. Lenin, G., Vanitha, B., Vijayalakshm, C.K.: Secure data storage using decentralized access. Int. J. Innov. Res. Comput. **3** (2015)

Author Index

Printed in the United States
By Bookmasters